House of Commons
Foreign Affairs Committee

The Decision to go to War in Iraq

Ninth Report of Session 2002-03

Volume III

Oral Evidence and Appendix

Ordered by The House of Commons
to be printed 3 July 2003

HC 813-III
Published on 1 October 2003
by authority of the House of Commons
London: The Stationery Office Limited
£20.50

The Foreign Affairs Committee

The Foreign Affairs Committee is appointed by the House of Commons to examine the expenditure, administration, and policy of the Office of the Foreign and Commonwealth Office and its associated public bodies.

Current membership

Rt Hon Donald Anderson MP (Labour, Swansea East) (Chairman)
David Chidgey MP (Liberal Democrat, Eastleigh)
Fabian Hamilton MP (Labour, Leeds North East)
Eric Illsley MP (Labour, Barnsley Central)
Andrew Mackinlay MP (Labour, Thurrock)
John Maples MP (Conservative, Stratford-on-Avon)
Bill Olner MP (Labour, Nuneaton)
Richard Ottaway (Conservative, Croydon South)
Greg Pope MP (Labour, Hyndburn)
Rt Hon Sir John Stanley MP (Conservative, Tonbridge and Malling)
Gisela Stuart MP (Labour, Birmingham Edgbaston)

The following ember was also a member of the committee during the parliament.

Sir Patrick Cormack MP (Conservative, Staffordshire South)

Powers

The Committee is one of the departmental select committees, the powers of which are set out in House of Commons Standing Orders, principally in SO No 152. These are available on the Internet via www.parliament.uk.

Publications

The Reports and evidence of the Committee are published by The Stationery Office by Order of the House. All publications of the Committee (including press notices) are on the Internet at www.parliament.uk/parliamentary_committees/foreign_affairs_committee.cfm. A list of Reports of the Committee in the present Parliament is in the inside front cover of this volume.

Committee staff

The current staff of the Committee are Steve Priestley (Clerk), Geoffrey Farrar (Second Clerk), Elizabeth Sellwood (Committee Specialist), Jane Appleton (Committee Assistant), Sheryl Bertasius (Secretary) and Andrew Boyd (Senior Office Clerk).

Contacts

All correspondence should be addressed to the Clerks of the Foreign Affairs Committee, Committee Office, House of Commons, London SW1A 0AA. The telephone numbers for general enquiries are 020 7219 6106/6105/6394; the Committee's email address is foraffcom@parliament.uk.

Witnesses

List of written evidence

Oral evidence

Taken before the Foreign Affairs Committee

on Tuesday 17 June 2003

Members present:

Donald Anderson, in the Chair

Mr David Chidgey
Mr Fabian Hamilton
Mr Eric Illsley
Andrew Mackinlay
Mr John Maples

Mr Bill Olner
Mr Greg Pope
Sir John Stanley
Ms Gisela Stuart

Witness: **Mr Robin Cook,** a Member of the House, examined.

Q1 Chairman: Mr Cook, may I on behalf of the Committee welcome you to start off our inquiry into the Decision to go to War in Iraq. You had a pretty unequalled position from your background in seeing the evidence. I understand that the opening statement which you have given to the Committee of course is now part of the proceedings and is available in any event; but perhaps you could give a brief synopsis of the main points that you make.

Mr Cook: I shall be very brief, Chairman. Can I just say what a pleasure it is to be appearing before this Committee no longer as Foreign Secretary, a much easier position.

Q2 Chairman: With one bound he was free!

Mr Cook: The full paper has been circulated to the Committee. I set out in that paper the cluster of five questions which I think it would be helpful for the Committee to address. Firstly, why is there such a difference between the claims made before the war and the reality established after the war? Much of that is not going to change with any more period of time. We have found no chemical production plants. We have found no facilities for a nuclear weapon programme. We have found no weapons within 45 minutes of artillery positions. Those are not going to change however much more time is now given. Secondly, did the Government come to doubt these claims before the war? It is very well known that the State Department came to have doubts in February. Did they share those doubts with us? It is interesting that those key claims in the September dossier were not actually repeated in the March debate. Had the Government itself come to lose confidence in them? If so, should it not have corrected the record before the House voted? Thirdly, could biological or chemical agents have fallen into the hands of terrorists since the war? One of the points that was made very strongly, particularly in the March 18 debate, was the danger that such material would pass to terrorist organisations? If they existed in Iraq at the time of the war, they have existed for the past two months unguarded and unsecured, which is very alarming. Is there any clarity that that material has now not passed into the hands of terrorists? Fourthly, why do

we not allow the UN Weapon Inspectors back into Iraq? I find it difficult to avoid the conclusion the reason we do not is because they would confirm Saddam did not have an immediate threatening capability. Lastly, does the absence of weapons of mass destruction undermine the legal basis of the war? The opinion of the Attorney General is entirely on the justification for war being the need to carry out the disarmament of Saddam Hussein. If he can find no weapons to disarm does that legal opinion still have basis? Finally can I just say, Chairman, reading the record it is striking that the Foreign Office and Mr Straw were more cautious in the statements that they made in the run-up to the war. I understand that your inquiry is looking at the Foreign Office in the context of the Government as a whole but, in fairness to the Foreign Office, I hope it will be acknowledged that they did exercise care in what they said.

Q3 Chairman: Concise as you promised. Two questions arise: firstly, the quality of the original intelligence; and, secondly, the use made of that intelligence by the Government of the September 24 dossier and thereafter? From what must be a privileged position in the Cabinet, what conclusion do you now draw generally on the quality of the intelligence material which came from the agencies?

Mr Cook: I had no access on a privileged basis to secret material after I had ceased to be Foreign Secretary. I saw the published dossiers and I took part in the Cabinet discussions on them, and I also had a briefing from the SIS[1] in the way that all members of the Cabinet had in the closing stages. If I could just say something about the intelligence available to us up until the time when I left Office in the 2001 General Election. At that time we were fairly confident that Saddam did not have a nuclear weapons capability, did not have a long-range missile capability and indeed, at one point in the late 1990s, we were willing to consider closing those files and moving from inspection on to monitoring and verification. We never actually got to the point of reaching agreement on that, but we were fairly confident they had been

---

[1] Secret Intelligence Service.

closed down; which is one of the reasons why I was surprised to see allegations of a nuclear programme resurfacing. It was very difficult to achieve any precision about the chemical and biological portfolios because they were much more easy to hide and to disperse. Nevertheless, we did make a number of moves in the late 1990s to try and make programmes. For instance, we did negotiate a new text at the Security Council in which the removal of sanctions would be dependent upon progress towards disarmament, not on the completion of disarmament. I was a bit startled that the general tendency of Western policy up until 2001 was sharply thrown into reverse thereafter.

Q4 Chairman: Come back to the intelligence, given the disclaimer you have made that you were aware of the intelligence which was going to Government?
Mr Cook: I did not see secret material after I ceased to be Foreign Secretary.

Q5 Chairman: But you were briefed?
Mr Cook: Yes, I was briefed.

Q6 Chairman: Was there any difference between the briefing which you received and that which appeared in the dossier to give credence, or not, to the allegation that the evidence was hyped, sexed up, exaggerated for political purposes?
Mr Cook: I have always been very careful in how I have expressed myself and have become practised in evading questions from broadcasters seeking to draw me further than I wish to go. I actually have no doubt about the good faith of the Prime Minister and others engaged in this exercise. If anything, I think perhaps the problem was the burning sincerity and conviction of those who were involved in the exercise. Intelligence, one should understand, comes in an enormous broad range. It is a bit like alphabet soup—you get all the letters of the alphabet. You can study it carefully to try and come up with a coherent statement. I fear on this occasion what happened was that those bits of the alphabet that supported the case were selected. That is not deceit, it is not invention, it is not coming up with intelligence that did not exist, but it was not presenting the whole picture. I fear the fundamental problem is that instead of using intelligence as evidence on which to base the conclusion of a policy, we used intelligence as the basis on which we could justify a policy on which we had already settled.

Q7 Chairman: So the burning conviction led to a distortion of the evidence?
Mr Cook: I think it would probably be fair to say there was a selection of evidence to support the conclusion, rather than a conclusion that arose from a full consideration of the evidence.

Q8 Sir John Stanley: Mr Cook, from what you have said, would the Committee be right to conclude that as Leader of the House you did not have access to Joint Intelligence Committee papers?

Mr Cook: No, and I would not have expected to necessarily. That circulation is very tight. On ceasing to be Foreign Secretary you sign off your clearance under the Official Secrets Act. That is perfectly proper. I have no objection to that. I would say that all of us in the Cabinet had briefing in groups and, in my case, individually with SIS. I heard nothing in their briefing that was inconsistent with the statement I made in my resignation speech that Iraq probably does not have weapons of mass destruction in the normally understood sense of that term, and that is plainly now the case.

Q9 Sir John Stanley: I was going to refer to that particular statement you made in your resignation speech which clearly was very much at variance with what the Government was saying publicly in the assessment which was produced in September and then what became known later as the "dodgy dossier". Can you tell the Committee at what point you came to have serious anxieties as to the accuracies of the intelligence material that was being put into the public domain in those two documents?
Mr Cook: My anxiety about the drift to military confrontation goes back a very long way to the spring of 2002. I assumed during that summer period it may be that intelligence had appeared since I had left of which I had not been aware; but I must say I was disappointed at the quality of intelligence laid out in the September dossier. If you read the September dossier very carefully there is a striking absence of any recent and alarming and confirmed intelligence. The great majority of the paper is derivative. That is, it starts out from what we know we had in 1991, what we know he has disposed of since 1991 and, therefore, there is a leap of assumption that the balance is therefore still around. It is also a highly suggestible document, in that there are a lot of boxes there telling you how you go about producing a nuclear weapon, or what sarin does; but there is no evidence actually that he did have that capacity to produce a nuclear weapon, nor indeed a capacity to produce sarin. Stripped down, there was very little in that document that actually represented intelligence of a new, alarming, urgent and compelling threat. I remember in the Cabinet discussion saying at the time I was disappointed just how derivative the document actually was.

Q10 Sir John Stanley: Could I just ask you about the second document, the one known as the "dodgy dossier" entitled *Iraq—its infrastructure of concealment, deception and intimidation*. I want to ask you this in the context of your previous appointment as Foreign Secretary. One of the questions that we have put to the Foreign Office is to ask them, in connection with the second document, at what dates were drafts of the second document put to Ministers in the Foreign Office. The answer we have now received from the Foreign Secretary is that no Ministers were consulted in the preparation for the document. How do you react, as a former Foreign Secretary, to the production of this document, laid before Parliament, subject to major national, international and parliamentary attention and one that would not have been at any point put to Foreign Office Ministers?

Mr Cook: I remember these questions being put to me when I was Leader of the House. One of the considerations that impelled me towards resignation was the impossibility of answering these questions at the time, and I am not sure I am in any better position to answer them now. The dossier plainly was a glorious, spectacular own goal. I personally do not think there is anything wrong whatsoever in re-printing an academic study of Saddam Hussein's security apparatus, but it ought to have been labelled as precisely that and taken from an academic study. Certainly we should not have tampered with the language in it. I think the most outrageous error, and one that is impossible to defend, was the decision to remove the words "opposition groups" and replace them with the phrase "terrorist organisations", which was not in the original academic study. What I find interesting about that document is that actually it does not add an iota to the case that Saddam Hussein had weapons of mass destruction. In all three parts of the entire document there is nothing whatsoever to suggest that he does have a capacity for weapons of mass destruction. I do find it extraordinary that after the September claims nothing subsequently happened either to advance those claims, in the sense of taking them forward, or to defend them, or even to repeat them; which does beg the question of whether the authors of the September dossier themselves had come to doubt it before they printed the second one.

Q11 Sir John Stanley: Finally, one of the additional papers we have received is one from a WMD expert of Cambridge University, Dr Glen Rangwala, which made a very interesting, detailed textual analysis of the second dossier, the so-called dodgy dossier. He has said to the Committee that of the 19 pages of this document, 11 of the pages, 6–16, were directly copied without acknowledgement of three different sources that are on the internet. I would like to ask you, if you had been Foreign Secretary at the time I wonder how you would have reacted to the Government, of which you were a member, publishing what purported to be directly from intelligence sources a document, the great body of which was apparently made up from plagiarised sources on the internet?

Mr Cook: As I remember, the foreword actually said "from intelligence sources, among others". The answer to your question is that I would be livid. Frankly, I have no reasons to suspect that the present Foreign Secretary was not equally livid.

Q12 Mr Illsley: Just following on from Sir John Stanley's point, one of the key issues before us is the fact that no Minister saw that dodgy dossier. I would like to ask you some background questions to help the Committee in relation to the Joint Intelligence Process. Obviously these relate to a time when you were Foreign Secretary. I would like to ask whether you as Foreign Secretary did see all the JIC[2] Reports?

---

[2] Joint Intelligence Committee.

Mr Cook: It would be a very large question to say I saw them all. I am familiar that if I answer yes to that question somebody will produce a document that somehow missed me. All such reports were, as a matter of routine, sent to my Private Office who would, in turn, draw my attention to all of those they felt it was important for me to see or be relevant to the current policy issues. I do not think there is any difficulty for the Foreign Office, as it were, being plugged into that circulation. I would also add the point that, during the time I was Foreign Secretary, we did take care to make sure that the Chairman of JIC was actually a serving member of the Foreign Office staff, which made sure that we were firmly linked into it; and also perhaps gave the Chairman a departmental strength on which he could draw and make sure that he could maintain the independence of the Committee.

Q13 Mr Illsley: What you have just said links in to my next couple of questions. Were you able to contribute to the process? Were your comments taken on board by the JIC if you questioned anything in the report?

Mr Cook: I would never have dreamt of trying to influence their assessment of the Report, which was a technical matter for them on which they draw from a much, much larger volume of intelligence than I would see. Remember that the advantage of the JIC assessment is that you are perhaps seeing 1% of the total volume of intelligence that went into that assessment—and probably much less than 1% in terms of total paperwork. However sometimes, yes, we would ask the JIC to carry out an assessment if it would be helpful to policy formulation. There were occasions when I would not necessarily share the assessment they came to. For all I know, quite properly, my Private Office would have fed that back.

Q14 Mr Illsley: It would be fair to assume that the same principle would have occurred after you left the Foreign Office? It would have been the assessment which Ministers would have seen rather than the raw intelligence?

Mr Cook: No, you receive both. If the intelligence community and the Private Office believe there are specific items of intelligence that it would be worthwhile your seeing and important for you to see it can be passed to you. Sometimes that can be extremely helpful; also because JIC assessments often do come with a summary of intelligence.

Q15 Mr Illsley: Are those reports and assessments provided to special advisers in the Foreign Office or in Number Ten? Do special advisers to Ministers have the opportunity or an input into those assessments

Mr Cook: Not an input but they would see it. They do have security clearance and, indeed, could not do the job if they did not. I repeat the point I made earlier—the point of that assessment, of course, is in order to inform policy and to enable you to draw up a policy that is more soundly based. I fear that in Iraq we got into a reverse process, in which the intelligence was not being used to inform and shape policy, but to support policy that had already been settled.

Q16 Mr Illsley: How would your comments on any intelligence assessment or intelligence report have been accepted? Were the JIC obliged to take account of any comments you made? I think you just mentioned you would not have attempted to try to alter the actual intelligence report. If you are seriously questioning an assessment how would the JIC respond to that? Would they take that on board?

Mr Cook: At the end of the day decisions on policy were a matter for me as Foreign Secretary, the Prime Minister and the Government as a whole. If I chose to take the view that I felt this assessment was unsound that was entirely my prerogative. I was under no pressure to act upon their assessment. It was a rare occasion when you ended up in that kind of black and white situation, to put it in those terms. A JIC assessment is rather more like an academic research paper than a speech in the House of Commons. In other words, it canvasses all the evidence; it may well contain contrary pieces of evidence; it does not necessarily point to one clear conclusion at the end. It is often very helpful to have the whole package, even if it does not necessarily lead you to one clear conclusion. I notice that one of my Special Advisers at the time has since written of his frustration in reading JIC documents, in that he was not quite clear what we were supposed to do at the end of it because it often would have contradictory information.

Q17 Mr Illsley: Finally, was there any role played by Number Ten in intelligence? I heard you say that the Chairman of JIC was within the Foreign Office, and was within your chain of command presumably. Did Number Ten have a role in this? If it did, did Alastair Campbell have a role in intelligence reports during the time you were Foreign Secretary?

Mr Cook: First of all, could I say I have a high regard for the individual who is currently the chair of JIC, who I know to be a first-class intelligence officer. The point I made I would not want to be seen in any way as an *ad hominem* point, but I think there is a structural point there which I think is worth reflecting upon. Number Ten of course would receive all the reports I saw and, indeed, may well themselves also request particular assessments; but they would not themselves have any influence on what the assessment was. Certainly I would not imagine that Alastair Campbell would have any input to an assessment, although he may well have had access to the assessment.

Q18 Mr Maples: Mr Cook, what I am interested in is when it is decided to use intelligence in a public document, as happened in this case, and the roles which various people play. If we go back to 1998 when the Foreign Office and the Ministry of Defence did publish a short paper which was sent to all Members of Parliament over the signature of one of your Ministers of State at that time about Iraq, there was a three-page note attached to that about Iraq's weapons of mass destruction and that is clearly based on intelligence. I wonder how that went from the point of being a JIC assessment, looked at by you and

the Prime Ministers, into being a published document? Who had input into that? Who drafted it? Whose hands did it go through?

Mr Cook: I would have to be quite frank and say that, after five years, I would need to refresh my memory and go through the papers before I could hope to give you an authoritative reply to that. 1998 was a time when the inspectors were being removed from Iraq and when we had a substantial confrontation over the operation of inspectors. If I am blunt, there was at the time a lot of frustration, particularly in Washington, with the repeated political controversy when Saddam had refused to allow inspectors to go into one building or another. There was also a sense that we could successfully contain Saddam without inspectors by making sure we maintained a tight cage of sanctions around him. That was effectively the policy the West then adopted. Actually, from what we have learned in Iraq since we went in, containment worked even better than we had hoped at the time.

Q19 Mr Maples: Coming back to production of the published document, I understand how the process works if things are not going to be published, and intelligence is simply informing policy. Can you remember whether that document was prepared in the Foreign Office or in Number Ten

Mr Cook: Sadly, as I say, after five years I have no recollection at the back of my mind. I can certainly ask to see papers and see what I can find out.

Q20 Mr Maples: It is possible that in the production of a document which is going to be published like that maybe somebody on Number Ten staff, government information service people, would have had a hand in how that was presented?

Mr Cook: Quite possibly. Can you remind me which Minister signed it?

Mr Maples: Derek Fatchett. This was Desert Fox, I think. 10 November 1998.

Chairman: Perhaps, Mr Cook, on that you could refresh your memory and give a supplementary note to the Committee[3].

Andrew Mackinlay: As a matter of procedure, when I come in with my questions I want to take Mr Cook through that. I would ask that Mr Cook could have a copy in front of him. It is not to pre-empt you from going away and having a look at it, but there are some things which would be helpful if he could have a copy in front of him.

Q21 Mr Maples: This was, as you say, when the inspectors were being denied access. I think they went back and they were thrown out. I forget the exact sequence of events, but there were two or three instalments of it. The document which was then published on Foreign Office writing paper did say, for instance, "Iraq's declarations to the UN on its WMD programmes have been deliberately false . . . He has under-reported his materials and weapons at every stage, and used an increasingly sophisticated concealment and deception system". "31,000 [tonnes of] CW munitions and 4,000 tonnes of precursor

[3] Ev 11–12

chemicals . . . still have to be properly accounted for". It goes on building a reasonably substantial case, known as conclusions, saying that "Some CW agents and munitions remain hidden. The Iraqi chemical industry could produce mustard gas almost immediately, and limited amounts of nerve gas within months . . . Saddam almost certainly retains BW production equipment, stocks of agents and weapons. In any case, Iraq has the expertise and equipment to regenerate an offensive BW capability within weeks. If Iraq's nuclear programme had not been halted by the Gulf conflict, Saddam might have had a nuclear weapon by 1993. If Iraq could procure the necessary machinery and materials abroad, it could build a crude air-delivered nuclear device in about five years. Iraq could design a viable nuclear weapon now". What we were told in the assessment that came out in September last year obviously was much more elaborate than that but basically the same case. That document was presumably produced with your full knowledge and endorsement. I just wonder if the intelligence you thought you were seeing in the run-up to Desert Fox—for which we did authorise military action and Iraq was bombed by American and UK planes as a result of this—presumably at that time the Government was confident that this intelligence was correct and this WMD capability or threat existed and you shared that confidence?

Mr Cook: We were certainly quite clear that we had not come to the bottom of the chemical and the biological portfolios—the different portfolios that UNSCOM[4,] as it then was, was pursuing. Indeed it was the case that Saddam was extremely obstructionist in trying to enable us to get to the bottom of it. You mention a number of phases. There was a crisis early in the year round about February when we drew back from military action following a visit by Kofi Annan which resulted in an agreement. That agreement was to provide for wider access for the UNSCOM inspectors and it was constantly frustrated by Saddam over the next six months. That is what brought us to Desert Fox. We had managed to avoid military action at the previous time. Frankly, I do not think either the British or American governments had any alternative but to proceed to military action in the autumn of that year, given that we had entered into an agreement that we would not act if Saddam honoured his side of the bargain, and he did not. Having said that, I would just point out that, with the extreme difference of quantity and quality of military that was taken then and the action that followed in March and April of this year, we did not attempt to invade Iraq or to take over Iraq. Indeed, the bombing campaign itself was aimed very strictly at what we thought might be part of any weapons programme. Can I repeat what I said earlier. Whilst at the time, and it is perfectly fairly set out here, we had anxieties about his chemical and biological weapons capability, we did not believe he had a nuclear weapons programme; nor did he have a satisfactory long-range missiles programme. I cheerfully say, frankly I am rather surprised we have not discovered some biological toxins or some chemical agents.

Indeed, in my resignation speech I said they probably are there. The position actually has turned out to be even less threatening than I anticipated at the time I resigned.

Q22 Mr Maples: You apparently thought at the end of 1998 with Desert Fox that the intelligence we held on WMD justified military action, admittedly more limited than has been taken more recently but, nevertheless, the bombing of another person's country. Yet here we are four years later and you feel either the situation has changed or the intelligence does not any longer justify the same action?

Mr Cook: The case being made four years later was a very different case. I was not arguing in 1998, none of us were, that Saddam represented an urgent and compelling threat that required preemptive action, which is what was taken in 2003. We carried out a limited number of bombing runs in order to destroy what we believed was the remaining chemical and biological capacity; but we did not attempt to invade the country.

Q23 Mr Chidgey: In your earlier statements and in some of the follow-ups you have made it very clear that intelligence assessment is an imperfect art. I recall you making a comment that it was rather like alphabet soup and the right letters had been chosen to form the desired word, if I can put it that way. What I want to suggest with you is whether it is not normally the case that in any intelligence assessment there can be two or three explanations of what has been going on and what the raw intelligence is showing. In that scenario it is often the case that there is a best case scenario, a worst case scenario and there are bits in the middle. What I want to ask is whether in this particular scenario, where the Government chose to present information to the House justifying their policy, there was a process where the most supportive case was chosen to back that, and the other options were not recognised or accounted for?

Mr Cook: Intelligence is not a perfect science. I expressed the difficulties slightly differently from the way you did, in that often when you are told a piece of information you are left with very real doubts over why you are being told that information. Are you being told it to mislead you? Are you being told it by somebody who actually wants to be paid but may not actually turn out to be reliable; or is not somebody— as I think was the case with some of the Iraqi exiles pursuing their own political agenda—who wants you to hear what suits them? All these questions and motivation form very great difficulty over making your assessment of intelligence. I hope I have made it clear throughout all of this I do not criticise the intelligence services whom I think have tried very hard to do their best in extremely difficult circumstances. In fairness to the intelligence community one should recognise that Iraq was an appallingly difficult intelligence target to break. We had very little access to human intelligence on the ground and no hope whatsoever of putting in Western agents.

---

[4] United Nations Special Commission.

Q24 Mr Chidgey: Did the intelligence services actually present to Government different options of what might be happening on the basis of intelligence they were getting?

Mr Cook: The point of a JIC assessment is to lead up to a conclusion, and the conclusion will express on the balance of evidence what their view is; but the assessment will usually include the balance of evidence which may point in different directions to the conclusion. As I said earlier, the intelligence community do not see themselves there to lobby you to a particular point of view. Their papers much more reflect an academic approach to gathering the evidence and trying to make an intelligence appraisal of that evidence, rather than arguing for a specific course of action.

Q25 Mr Chidgey: Can I then turn to the chemical and biological programme which you have already said was the area, as far as you were concerned, where there were questions. In a previous stage of our reporting on weapons of mass destruction, we were advised by one key witness that a thousand litres of anthrax or less would be almost impossible to discover in a place like Iraq. I would like you in a moment to ask me whether that was the intelligence services' view as well. Presumably that information would have been passed to Government. The real key to this for me is, if it is impossible to discover a thousand litres or less of anthrax, which clearly has a potential to do incredible damage to many people, would the advice have been that if it was impossible to remove the threat of a chemical or biological weapon the only sensible policy to pursue would be to remove the organisation that would use that threat? At what stage was an assessment made that the only safe way to go forward in terms of our interest would be pursue a policy regime change rather than suppression or destruction of chemical weapons that were so difficult to find?

Mr Cook: I think you reflect more of the United States' debate than the British debate. For the period that I was Foreign Secretary we did not have anxiety that anthrax, to which you refer, was on the verge of being turned into a weaponised capability. As I said earlier, we were frustrated by the fact, as you rightly say, that these things are difficult to find, easy to conceal and, therefore, we were not able to make the progress that we had hoped up until 1998. On the other hand, after 1998 we did not have any compelling, urgent reason to believe that containment was not working in the sense of keeping Saddam in his cage. I would also make the point that biological agents such as anthrax are extremely toxic and a menace to anybody near them, but they were not weaponised then, and if not weaponised cannot be used for military purpose. We are fortunate in that it is not particularly easy to weaponise biological agents because weapons do tend either to explode or incinerate, which tends to have the effect of destroying the biological agent that they are carrying. This is fortunate for humanity because it is actually quite easy to get hold of biological agents; it is fortunate it is not particularly easy to turn them into weapons. I never actually saw any intelligence to

suggest that Saddam had successfully weaponised that material. The one other point I would make is that, whilst it is certainly true that 10,000 litres is a small volume and not terribly easy to find if you are searching for it, we now actually have under interrogation all the senior figures from the Iraqi weapons programme. It makes it particularly odd, if these exist, that we have not been led to them. Their existence must be known to scores if not hundreds of people who were involved in the transport, storage and protection of such material. It is curious that none of them have come forward, since the reward would be immense. They could have their own ranch in Texas if they were to lead us to such a thing at the present time. That does also leave the very real anxiety, if they have not come forward to us and if these things exist, have they come forward to a terrorist organisation? If priceless works of art can be smuggled out of Iraq could 10,000 litres of anthrax?

Q26 Mr Chidgey: Just to slightly change the focus, in your view just to make this absolutely clear for the record, was the case for military action against Iraq more compelling in December 1998 than it was in March 2003? Was the intelligence on Iraq more compelling in 1998 than it was in 2002–03?

Mr Cook: It was adequate for the action that was carried out, but it was a very limited action. Nobody, either in Washington or in London, was imagining that we should pursue this to an invasion and regime change. The bombing campaign, despite the pyrotechnics on television, was actually relatively limited. To be truthful, the military action in 1998 suited the then agenda of the West, which was to move to a system of trying to contain Saddam, rather than go through the repeated frustration of having the inspectors on the ground being blocked. One thing that was much better in 2003 than in 1998 was that the terms on which UNMOVIC[5] went back in were much better than UNSCOM. Indeed, Hans Blix's reports make it plain that they did get better cooperation, process and access than we were receiving in 1998.

Q27 Ms Stuart: So far I get a sense the main charge is that the Government was not very Cartesian in its approach to policy development, which is a very British approach I am told. Just because something remains true for a number of years does not make it untrue. If something was correct in, say, 2001 unless there is evidence to undermine that assessment there is still every reason to believe it is still true in 2003. I particularly ask this because I make reference to an article which I believe you wrote in *The Telegraph* on 20 February 2001 where it says, "UN measures remain in place because of Saddam's determination to retain and rebuild his weapons of mass destruction and threaten the region. His use of chemical weapons against his own people and his neighbours make him unique amongst modern dictators". I am wondering has anything happened within that period which would lead you to believe that either the assessment or the evidence itself was no longer viable?

---

[5] United Nations Monitoring, Verification and Inspection Commission.

Mr Cook: I was alerted to this article by Mr Straw in debate the other week and I did take the precaution of refreshing my memory. I am delighted to see in that article I said, "Too many commentators overlook the fact that Britain's robust approach has contained the threat that Saddam poses. Since the UN imposed a policy of containment Iraq has not used chemical weapons against the Kurds in Northern Iraq, or against Iran, and it has not invaded its neighbours. UN efforts and our vigilance have ensured that Saddam does not have a long-range missile capacity. He has had to dismantle his programme, and we actually carried out some destruction of facilities. As a result there is no current high risk of his being able to attack us". That was the view I came to in 2001. It would seem to me, with everything we have learnt since we went in in 2003, that was right.

Q28 Ms Stuart: What I am really trying to get at is do we have a structural weakness in the use of the way intelligence information is used? As I understand it, in the light of Kosovo and Bosnia, there was a review of how intelligence information is used. As you yourself said, it is always an alphabet soup but the letters are actually there; it is question of how you assess them. There was a clear sense, even two years ago, that there were chemical weapons there and he is retaining them. Has something structural happened which would give you reason to reassess that evidence?
Mr Cook: No, the conclusion I came to in that article, and repeatedly throughout my period as Foreign Secretary, was that we could contain the threat of Saddam Hussein by the policy of containment. Indeed, we did do so. The onus is on those who argued that containment should be abandoned and replaced with a policy of invasion and regime change to justify that, not on me.

Q29 Ms Stuart: I come back to that review on the use of intelligence. Is there a structural problem in the way we use and assess that intelligence, or is it just the conclusions we have drawn? I therefore come back to my opening point, that we could be accused of not having been Cartesian in the way we arrive at the conclusion.
Mr Cook: I think the charge is graver than we have lacked a proper philosophic method. We went to war. 5,000–7,000 civilians were killed. Some British troops were killed. To go to war you need to have a real compelling justification for breaking that taboo which war should necessarily represent and to embark upon wholesale military action. It is not a matter of simply sitting around debating whether we had a Cartesian approach to intelligence reports. It is a question of whether you really did have compelling, convincing evidence posing, as the Prime Minister expressed it, a current and serious threat. It is plain from what we now know he did not pose a current and serious threat. It is therefore a grievous error of policy to have gone to war on the assumption he was.

Q30 Mr Hamilton: Mr Cook, on 3 September last year the Prime Minister announced that the Government's assessment of Iraq's weapons of mass destruction capabilities would be published. The Foreign and Commonwealth Office led the drafting of Parts 2 and 3 of the final dossier and began this work in spring 2002. I want to move on to the September dossier, and this is obviously after the time you ceased to be Foreign Secretary and became Leader of the House of Commons. Can I ask you whether you saw the Cabinet Office assessments staff paper on weapons of mass destruction in March 2002, which it was eventually decided not to publish?
Mr Cook: No.

Q31 Mr Hamilton: What papers did you see that related to the dossier finally published in September 2002?
Mr Cook: I saw the dossier. As I said earlier, I did not have access, and would not have expected to have access, to secret material after I ceased to be Foreign Secretary. Frankly, I was rather taken aback by how thin the dossier was. If you strip out the boxes of facts which are not facts related to Iraq, and if you strip out the historic material you are actually not left with very much there. I notice that on three or four occasions, when referring to an existing capability, it says that Iraq has retained the scientists who worked on the programmes. I am not quite sure what Iraq could have done other than allow them to continue, other than possibly assassinate them. There is not much there that represents evidence that there is a new and compelling threat. Although I did not see the March document, I suspect that is possibly why the March document was not published.

Q32 Mr Hamilton: Were there any other documents submitted to the Cabinet which you would have been able to see as a member of the Cabinet before the September dossier was finally presented to you?
Mr Cook: Not that I can recall. I would have thought it would be unwise to circulate documents that were not intended for publication; because by the time they had been through everybody's office and department they might as well be published.

Q33 Mr Hamilton: That is interesting. Can I ask you whether you recall how much of the intelligence that was used in the September dossier was there as a result of the intelligence sharing between the United Kingdom and other countries?
Mr Cook: I cannot speak at first hand because I was not involved in the process, but I would be astonished if it was not immense. The United States and the United Kingdom have a unique intelligence relationship which has probably never existed in any period of history, in which on our side we have full transparency and we strive to secure full transparency on their side. Therefore, it is often difficult when you look at intelligence assessments to spot which raw data was originally gathered by the United Kingdom and which was originally gathered by the United States. As a rough rule of thumb, and it is very rough, we tend to be rather better at gathering human intelligence; and, although we have an excellent GCHQ station, the Americans are even more formidable in technological ways of gathering

intelligence. That said, neither of us really had much human intelligence inside Iraq. The Americans were drawing heavily on exiles who were inside America.

Q34 Mr Hamilton: You referred earlier in your opening statement to the fact that much of the evidence presented in the run-up to the war was evidence that supported a policy that had been decided, if I am not misinterpreting that. Can I ask you, in your view do you think the September dossier was an accurate reflection of intelligence available, or was it simply one more example of trying to confirm a policy which had already been decided?
Mr Cook: First of all, as I have said, I would not make the allegation that anything in the document was invented. I think in some ways that is a blind alley. I think the debate has run far too impetuously down the argument—were matters invented; were they sexed up? The plain fact is a lot of the intelligence in the September dossier has turned out in practice to be wrong. I think it is important that we fasten on how wrong it was, why it was wrong, and were there other parts of intelligence around which might have suggested more caution? That I cannot answer because I did not have access to the material; but from all I know from previous experience, it would be surprising if in a large intelligence haul there were not bits of intelligence that cast doubt on the other parts of it. I noticed that the September dossier had a number of very large claims, which I detail in my statement, which were actually not subsequently repeated, which does prompt me to wonder if somebody somewhere spotted that they were not entirely reliable.

Q35 Mr Hamilton: Do you think there was a deliberate attempt to exaggerate the threat posed by Iraq to the United Kingdom?
Mr Cook: "Exaggerate" is a loaded term. I think those who produced the dossier did not imagine they were exaggerating it, because they were convinced that Saddam and Iraq posed an urgent and compelling threat of a kind that would require military action. One should not forget the political context in which that is produced, which was one in which there was deep scepticism within Parliament and much more marked scepticism among the public.

Q36 Mr Olner: Could I bring you back to Operation Desert Fox. I am still struggling to understand now in your mind that it was okay to do that operation, to bomb, and obviously thousands of civilians got killed in Operation Desert Fox. That was without a United Nations resolution and without international support, and it was right to do that but not the original Gulf War?
Mr Cook: I am not sure I would say "okay". With great reluctance and a heavy heart we undertook the military action because we had arrived at a situation in which the agreement entered into in February had been broken. That was, of course, an agreement with the Secretary General of the United Nations. Throughout all this process we had a solid degree of support within the United Nations for what we were doing. To remind you again, Operation Desert Fox

was strictly a bombing campaign of a rather limited character. I would be sceptical whether thousands actually were killed on the ground, but it is very difficult to tell given the capacity of Saddam to produce figures of his own. We did not have direct access on the ground at the time. It was quite deliberately undertaken by us in the knowledge this would mean that the inspections regime would come to an end and would have to be replaced by a policy of containment. It was that policy of containment I think which was very successful. I have seen nothing to suggest it was right to replace that policy of containment with a major arms invasion of the territory of another state.

Q37 Mr Olner: Coming back to the dodgy dossier, you did say earlier to a question you did think that the February dossier was a mistake?
Mr Cook: Yes. I do not think anybody does not now.

Q38 Mr Olner: At the time did you think it was a mistake; did you say so; and did others say so?
Mr Cook: As I recall it the dodgy dossier was not discussed in Cabinet, and I took part in every Cabinet discussion over four months on Iraq and it was almost weekly. I do not recall us discussing this. I do remember hearing it from the radio when I was in the north-west at the time and being pretty appalled by what I heard. It was not a command paper, of course. It was not issued as a White Paper and, therefore, probably did not have the departmental clearance of the kind that would have been appropriate. Hence the fact that you are now advised that the Foreign Secretary and Ministers of the Foreign Office did not hear it.

Q39 Mr Olner: How many members of the Cabinet shared your horror wherever they heard it?
Mr Cook: It would be a mere guess, but I should imagine pretty well everybody recognised that this was a significant own goal. In terms of the broad picture, no, members of the Cabinet did not express anxiety about the drift to military action. I would regularly comment on it. Clare [Short] would sometimes join in those discussions. I would quite often join the discussions. Other than that I do not recall anybody consistently questioning the drift to military action.

Q40 Mr Pope: I am just interested as to how you arrived at a different conclusion from that of the Joint Intelligence Committee. In the dossier of 24 September JIC concluded that there had been a step change in Iraq's missile programme and they were in the early stages of developing a missile with a range of over 1,000 kilometres. In your resignation statement to the House on 17 March you concluded that: "Iraq probably has no weapons of mass destruction in the commonly understood sense of the term—namely a credible device capable of being delivered against a strategic city target". Perhaps you could share with the Committee how you came to such a widely different conclusion?

Mr Cook: I am not sure it is so widely different. If you read the September dossier with a sceptical eye you will find that it does not actually produce evidence that there is a weaponised capability for a weapon of mass destruction capable of long-range delivery. As I say, I did have the briefing with SIS before I came to the point of resignation. I took the precaution before today of checking the notes I made at the time and I was rather relieved to see that the note I made at the end of the discussion was almost word for word what I said in my resignation speech.

Q41 Mr Pope: I think there is a difference here between a capability which Iraq had or has and one which is developing. I do not think the charge against Iraq was that it had a weapon capable of doing this but that it was developing one. I think the danger here or the difficulty is that the JIC concluded that Iraq was developing a weapon which was capable of reaching our sovereign bases in Cyprus. That seems to me an extraordinarily serious concern for our intelligence services to raise with Ministers, that a hostile nation is developing a system capable of reaching one of our most sensitive bases in Cyprus; and it is therefore reasonable for the Government to take action against that hostile nation. Yet you concluded something completely different after meeting with the SIS.
Mr Cook: I can only offer the view that it does appear what I concluded appears to be more consistent with the facts on the ground.

Q42 Mr Pope: You would accept that absence of evidence is not in itself evidence of absence?
Mr Cook: No, but the absence of evidence is a bloody thin ground on which to build a war.

Q43 Mr Pope: Do you think Ministers misled the House intentionally or otherwise?
Mr Cook: I think it is quite clear that some of the facts put to the House, both in the September dossier and some of the speeches to the House, cannot be reconciled with the facts as we know them on the ground. That does not mean to say that the Ministers at the time did not genuinely believe what they were saying, even if they have turned out since to have been in error. I think what is important is that Ministers do not compound that original error by denying the fact that it was wrong at the time.

Q44 Andrew Mackinlay: Mr Cook, what I do not understand is what was the case for military action? Why was it less compelling in 2003 as compared with 1998?
Mr Cook: We did not invade in 1998.

Q45 Andrew Mackinlay: No, but there was military action. We are agreed there is a difference in the nature of the war.
Mr Cook: A very, very substantial difference.

Q46 Andrew Mackinlay: But if you are on the receiving end of a bomb it spoils the rest of your day, does it not?

Mr Cook: Unquestionably that is true and we, therefore, sought to minimise the civilian targets that were identified in that campaign. What we sought to do in 1998 was to destroy what we knew or believed we knew of the capacity for Saddam to develop chemical and biological weaponry, and thereafter we changed our whole gear in terms of policy. The basic thing which happened in 1998 was we moved from inspection on the ground to containment by sanctions and they worked.

Q47 Andrew Mackinlay: How do you know containment was working? What is the proof that containment was working?
Mr Cook: During the time I was there as Foreign Secretary I saw no evidence to suggest that containment was not succeeding. All we have learnt since we went into Iraq is actually it worked rather better than we had hoped.

Q48 Andrew Mackinlay: The Fatchett document[6,] who was your Minister of State, indicates throughout the continuing theme and vein that this continued concealment, the skill in concealment both in chemical and biological, could soon mean a capacity of missiles. I think 650 kilometres is quite long-range and a substantial threat to the peace of the region. Also that there was clearly the capacity to pursue, if not to frustrate, the threat of nuclear weapons?
Mr Cook: As I have said, as I recall the evidence of the time we were not actually concerned about Saddam's missile programme. Indeed part of the process of negotiation in 1998 before the end of inspections was to close down the missile and the nuclear portfolios. That was not an area of live concern at the time. Yes, he did conceal. Yes, he did give inspectors the run-around. Indeed, it was precisely because of that we ended up with a stand-off in February which then produced an agreement that he would cooperate better which he failed to honour.

Q49 Andrew Mackinlay: Which he abrogated?
Mr Cook: Yes, he failed to keep it. "Honour" is probably not the right word to use in any sentence that includes Saddam Hussein. He did not keep to that agreement, and that is what resulted in the bombing campaign of 1998.

Q50 Andrew Mackinlay: What I do not understand, he then over succeeding years continued to abrogate agreements. He abrogated agreements really in the past 12 months. I think you have reported to the House of Commons when you were Leader of the House, he was playing cat and mouse with the weapons inspector. He never complied with the armistice terms and subsequent resolutions which required him to give unimpeded access?
Mr Cook: That is perfectly true, he never did and that goes back to 1991. That never explained, which is one of the questions I kept asking in the months up until March 2003, why having lived in that situation for a decade, and during that time successfully containing

---

[6] Paper deposited in the House of Commons Library, 10th November 1998, Dep 98/1236.

any threat from Saddam Hussein, suddenly in the spring of 2003 it was urgent and compelling that we launched a major invasion.

Q51 Andrew Mackinlay: You have never produced any evidence to show that containment was working?
Mr Cook: I think that the evidence is already there on the ground in the absence of any evidence that he either had chemical or biological weapons, or long-range missiles, or a nuclear weapon, or weapons capable of being fired 45 minutes, or a rebuilt chemical factory, none of which have been found. That, to me, does suggest that containment was working quite well.

Q52 Andrew Mackinlay: I think you criticise, both in your resignation speech this morning, some of the documentation, the "spin" (not your word) in the period leading up to the war.
Mr Cook: I have never used the word "spin".

Q53 Andrew Mackinlay: You criticise the nature of the things which were put in the public domain and into Parliament persuading us to go to war?
Mr Cook: They have turned out plainly to be wrong and, to that extent, Parliament did not receive, and indeed perhaps Ministers did not, advice on which they could base a sensible decision.

Q54 Andrew Mackinlay: The Fatchett memorandum of 1998, you would have signed that off in red pen, would you not, because I remember from the Sierra Leone inquiry it was made quite clear that you as Foreign Secretary would have signed off documents such as this. Would you have signed off that document which was presented to Parliament?
Mr Cook: I could not offhand respond. I would need to check that.

Q55 Andrew Mackinlay: Would you?
Mr Cook: Possibly[7]. I can check it. I had complete confidence in Derek Fatchett and I would not necessarily see everything that Derek would sign off.

Q56 Andrew Mackinlay: No, but apart from the dodgy document, which we are all agreed was crass, stupid and deceived no-one from day one, and we just fell about laughing, but putting that aside, why should the voracity of the Fatchett document, which I think we will find has your imperator on it, be any less valid than subsequent information which was put to Parliament and the public?
Mr Cook: I find the dodgy dossier an immense red herring. There is nothing whatsoever in the supposed dodgy dossier which is actually about a weapons capability, which I find in its own way quite interesting. Secondly, I would need to study this paper first. At first glance I think the great bulk of what I see here was well in the public domain and was not necessarily drafted by intelligent services, but I can look that up.

[7] Ev 11–12

Q57 Andrew Mackinlay: None of us, apart from yourself, have been privy to being in Cabinet, how are decisions taken? Can you give us a fly on the wall? Does the Cabinet go through the rubrics and ritual of consultation? There must have been a critical day when the chips were down when either you or your colleagues could have said, "Dear Prime Minister, we're not persuaded", or whatever. How does it work? There is, as you know, lots of suspicion that Cabinet government does not exist today?
Mr Cook: I think on the question of Iraq you could not have hoped for fuller opportunities to discuss in Cabinet the matter. We discussed it in Cabinet more than any other issues, probably more than the other issues added together in the six months between September 2002 and March 2003. It was a very unusual Cabinet meeting in which we did not discuss Iraq certainly from the turn of the year onwards. The Prime Minister commendably left it open to any member to express any view that they wished to on the subject. It did resolve quite often into a standard procedure in which, perfectly properly, the Foreign Secretary and the Defence Secretary would start the discussion. I would then express intelligent points of dissent and questioning. Clare Short might well express points from the humanitarian front, but there was no great debate in the sense of people disagreeing with the Prime Minister's perspective. I would entirely concur that on this occasion it would be perfectly reasonable for the Prime Minister to conclude that the sense of the Cabinet was with him because, apart from myself and occasionally Clare, nobody disagreed with that.

Q58 Andrew Mackinlay: Was there a particular date where conclusion would have been reached when he would have said words to the effect, "I sense the mood of the Cabinet shared my view about the threat and the way to resolve this matter". He might not use those terms, but rather than reportage and discussion, was there a point when—
Mr Cook: For most of the time, although you could replay the discussion in terms of where do we stand in the event of military action taking place, it was plain I stood in one corner and the majority of the Cabinet stood in the other, but actually that was not for much of the time what was under discussion. What was under discussion was the particular state of the diplomatic process at that moment, and on that there was a broad degree of agreement. I was entirely with the rest of the Cabinet that we should try and secure a second resolution. Those conclusions you are looking for were more of the interim character, "Yes, we're agreed we should try and proceed and secure the United Nations approval", rather than, "Well, let's go to war".

Q59 Andrew Mackinlay: Can I ask a last question, a machinery government question. The impression one has got is that over successive months, particularly under this one, and after you left in particular, there was a drift from the Foreign Office and the Foreign Secretary (and I do not mean this to disparage the present holder) is really the Deputy Foreign Secretary. The portfolio of the Foreign Secretary is *de* *facto* with the Prime Minister, that things have shifted to Number Ten. Clearly there have been occasions, even when you had the stewardship of this, where shots were being called from Number Ten. I want to put to you that here the Foreign Office would have a slightly different read on the situation to that of Number Ten. Is that your feeling or observation?

Mr Cook: You mean in terms of the last few months.

Q60 Andrew Mackinlay: Yes. It is a general issue that we are concerned about the future decision-making of government in these critical areas, and precisely in relation to the conflict in Iraq.

Mr Cook: The Foreign Office, by its very nature, is responsible for conducting international relations around the globe, not just in Washington. Undoubtedly many of those diplomats and career Foreign Office civil servants who work in these other fronts would have shared my concern about the consequence of us being involved in unilateral action with Americans. I address a number of those in the last paragraph of my paper, the extent to which it has set us at odds with our major partners within the European Union; the extent to which it has undermined the authority of the United Nations; the extent to which it has undermined our own status with the Third World countries who were universally against the war; and also, in terms of the narrow focus where the specific immediate question of terrorism is the most relevant, the breakup of that global coalition against world terrorism which came into being after the attack on the Twin Towers. Those are very heavy prices to pay in international relations. I hope the Committee at some future date may be able to look at the overall impact on Britain's standing as a result of our participation in the war.

Andrew Mackinlay: Chairman, before the former Foreign Secretary does conclude, can we give him an opportunity to put anything else?

Q61 Chairman: Are there any matter which has not been covered which you think should be? You have the opportunity to do that now?

Mr Cook: I put in a fairly full paper to the Committee and would encourage it to address the range of those questions there[8]. If I can just highlight one of those. I am deeply perplexed as to why we persist in denying access to the UNMOVIC inspectors. It seems to me if we want to establish any capability on the part of Saddam which the rest of the world can respect we do need to have the UN inspectors there to validate it. I can understand the Americans are probably not going to admit it because they have a long-standing hostility under the administration at the United Nations, but there is presumably no reason, and it is a perfectly fair question I would have thought to put to the Foreign Secretary, why we could not admit the UN inspectors to that sector of Iraq that we ourselves control.

Q62 Ms Stuart: I am just trying to draw conclusions which take us forward. Is it in your assessment that the problem is we all operate under 20:20 hindsight which is a great privilege, or is it wrong evidence in which case we must look at the quality of our intelligence services, or missing evidence in which case we need to look at the evidence gathered by our intelligence services?

Mr Cook: I think I would equip myself with 20:20 hindsight. I did resign before and not after the war. On the question you pose, I am not sure it quite matches the gravity of the situation. War should always be a last resort. Before you go to war you need to be convinced that this is a matter of dire necessity. I do not see what is funny about that. It must be the case that war should only be a matter of dire necessity. It is not as if what we have discovered since the war was over should have come as a surprise to us. Hans Blix himself at the time pointed to the failure of Western intelligence to provide any leaps to weapons on the ground. The rest of the world, famously, was not convinced by the case and did not agree on the case for war. I, therefore, think those who took the decision for war have the obligation to justify it in terms of producing that compelling evidence it said was there.

Chairman: Mr Cook, a very helpful platform on which the Committee will build. Thank you very much.

_____

[8] Ninth Report from the Foreign Affairs Committee, Session 2002–03, *The Decision to go to War in Iraq*, HC 813-II, Ev 1.

Supplementary memorandum from the Rt Hon Robin Cook MP

Letter from the Rt Hon Robin Cook MP to the Clerk of the Committee, 3 July 2003

At the hearing of the Foreign Affairs Committee I undertook to come back to the Committee concerning the letter of 10 November 1998 signed by Derek Fatchett and Doug Henderson.

I have now had an opportunity to consult the files and I am grateful to the FOG Records and Historical Department for their help. We have not found any evidence that the letter was shown to me for approval. That said, having now had time to read the letter I find it unexceptional. All the material in it was already in the public domain and the covering note makes no attempt to claim that it was from intelligence sources.

I also took the opportunity to refresh my memory from the files on the confrontation with Iraq in 1998. I would stress the following point in response to any attempt to draw parallels with the present situation.

Throughout 1998 we were confronted with determined efforts by Iraq to end any inspections, culminating in their announcement of 31 October that they would permit no further site inspections. The Security Council unanimously denounced the Iraqi ban in inspections as a "flagrant violation". The threat of military action forced Iraq to rescind that decision on 14 November, but by December UNSCOM reported that it was unable to secure the co-operation they needed to carry out inspections. This was in contrast to the situation this year when UNMOVIC reported that It was receiving co-operation at least on the process of inspections, and when Hans Blix informed the Security Council he could conclude the remaining disarmament tasks in months. Had we received the same cooperation in 1998, there would have been no bombing campaign.

I hope this is helpful to the Committee and I look forward to their Report.

Rt Hon Robin Cook MP

3 July 2003

Witness: **Clare Short,** a Member of the House, examined.

Q63 Chairman: Can I say first, my apologies for the short delay in starting. There is a lot of ground to cover and we hope that you will be able to help the Committee in our inquiry on the decision to go to war in Iraq. You have been quite trenchant in your criticism since, I notice, for example, the conclusion of your article to the *New Statesman* on 9 June where you say in terms, "My conclusion is that our Prime Minister deceived us". Do you still labour under that sense of deception?

Clare Short: I am afraid I do very sadly and I think it is a series of half-truths, exaggerations and reassurances that were not the case to get us into conflict by the spring and I think that commitment had been made by the previous summer. I think nothing else explains the failure to allow Blix to complete his process and the way in which certainly I personally was deceived and I think the country was deceived about what the French decision was, the claim that the French said, "No second Resolution of any kind", when it is absolutely clear now that President Chirac said, Blix must be given enough time to complete his inspection process, but if disarmament is not achieved through the Blix process, then the matter will have to come back to the Security Council, and then war would be inevitable.

Q64 Chairman: I am sure colleagues will take up some of those other points, but you mentioned that the decision had been made in the summer. That is the decision between the Prime Minister and the President on going to war?

Clare Short: Yes. The reason I say that is that three extremely senior people in the Whitehall system, whom I will not name, said that to me very clearly and specifically, that the target date was mid-February and later extended to March because of a difficulty with the Turks and so on and to give our Prime Minister a little more time, but at that time we were being assured, and I personally was being assured by the Prime Minister, that we were committed to a second Resolution.

Q65 Chairman: So you think that come what may, following that decision in the summer, war would inevitably have followed?

Clare Short: I think short of Saddam Hussein coming out with his hands up or going to Saudi Arabia or something, they were committed to war. The question is and everyone must ask themselves this question, why, when Blix got 64 ballistic missiles, some say, 70 dismantled—that was a considerable amount of disarmament—and yet his process was truncated. So he was succeeding, yet he was not given the time he asked for, and the question is why? Now, we were told that you have to threaten war in order to avoid war and I accepted that. That is how we got Resolution 1441. Therefore, you have to deploy some troops to threaten war and then we are told that the troops cannot sit in the desert because they have been deployed and we have to go to conflict, and the Blix process was truncated. Why were we all working to a target date which did not permit enough time for the Blix process to be completed?

Q66 Chairman: Well, I am not totally following you. Let's say, for example, after 1441, which gives "a final opportunity", after which there would have been "serious consequences", if Saddam Hussein had recognised that this was indeed the final opportunity, the troops were massing at his frontier, if he had then published a dossier on 8 December which was followed and he had co-operated with Blix, do you think the coalition would still have gone to war?

Clare Short: When 1441 was passed, because of course that was a resolution that was put together in the normal way that takes place in New York with a long process of negotiation and amendment so you get buy-in and you build consensus and indeed get unanimity, we and others assured the Security Council, because there was some dispute and the French wanted to make sure that the matter would have to come back to the Security Council, if there was to be an authorisation of military action, and verbal assurances were given that the matter would have to come back to the Security Council, and then Blix achieved considerable disarmament and made it clear himself that he needed more time. After all, it was not until November that it was passed and you have to get the weapons inspectors into Iraq and get them there with all their equipment, and there was the question of sharing intelligence. I was seeing our intelligence agencies at that time and they were

saying that the scientists' records and laboratory equipment and so on were hidden and being hidden across the country and they knew where it was, and I was arguing with them, "Why don't we give the information to Blix then and facilitate Blix going to the houses where things are hidden?", so there was not very much time between 1441 being passed, Blix getting in, getting started and getting going. If you remember, he complained that he was not getting much help with intelligence information and then the UK was more helpful. Then he was making progress in achieving a destruction of ballistic missiles and he made it clear that he needed more time and then suddenly the Resolution or the draft saying that 1441 had not been fulfilled was tabled and the whole process was brought to an end. We were misled about the French position and everything was blamed on the French, but I happened to talk to Kofi Annan on the telephone around that time about the situation in the Congo and he said, that it was absolutely clear that the majority of the Security Council thought that Blix needs more time. Now, this is a very serious matter and I understand how serious a matter it is, but I am afraid, I am very sorry that this is my conclusion.
Chairman: We hear that.

Q67 Mr Hamilton: Clare, to what extent were you aware of the threat posed by Iraq prior to the events of 11 September 2001?
Clare Short: I have been very troubled by sanctions and the suffering of the people of Iraq for a very long time and certainly since I took office in the Government in 1997, and we have attempted to improve the humanitarian programmes and the effectiveness of UN actions and to get some relief in the way in which sanctions worked, so I have been absolutely clear that the situation was unsatisfactory. I do not believe it could have just been left and I did not believe in containment both because Saddam Hussein was defying the UN, but also because the people of Iraq were suffering so badly.

Q68 Mr Hamilton: Did you believe that there was a threat to British interests posed by Iraq prior to 11 September 2001?
Clare Short: No, I did not believe that. I believed that the people of Iraq were suffering badly and that Saddam Hussein was in defiance of the UN over the question of working to try to achieve chemical and biological weapons. I believed and I still believe that he did try nuclear, but the previous inspection regime dismantled that, so I still do not think he was an imminent threat. I think that is where one of the exaggerations came, but I think he was, and I believe still, that he was committed to having laboratories and scientists and doing work and trying to develop chemical and biological weapons, and we know that he had ballistic missiles of a range beyond that permitted in the Security Council Resolution. My view was that the problem needed attending to, but that there was not an imminent threat and, therefore, we should do it right. The new urgency which came into the US was because of September

11, and this false suggestion that there was any link to al-Qaeda is another of the falsities to try to get an urgency for that, so I think the right way would have been to say, "We are going to attend to this and we are going to attend to the Middle East". The Road Map had already been negotiated, so we should have started off with publishing that and started implementation and showing a commitment to move to justice in the Middle East and then we should have turned to Iraq, trying to keep the support of Arab governments, and we should have tried for disarmament and we could have even had the UN authorised military action to support the inspectors, it seems to me. We should have tried indicting Saddam Hussein and we should have lifted sanctions. If you take the Kosovo parallel, and I was one who believed that we should have acted on Milosevic earlier with all the ethnic cleansing from Bosnia and so on, but it was absolutely right to act when the Kosovars being pushed out of their country. And this was reversed and then the military action stopped, but Milosevic was indicted and other action was taken and we got him to The Hague without a full-scale invasion of Serbia. I hope that is not too long an answer, but the point is that I am very aware of it. My deepest concern was the suffering of the people of Iraq and the anger that was causing in the Middle East and I think it should have been attended to, but we had time to attend to it right. Let me make it clear that from the beginning of this crisis, and indeed before, I have always thought that we had to be willing to use military force to back up the authority of the UN, so I was not saying, "No military force at all at any price", but I was saying that we should avoid it if at all possible and that is the teaching on the just wall and you have to make sure that there is no other way, and we should have tried that. I thought for a long time in this crisis that the UK was playing the role of trying to restrain the US and trying to examine all other means, and I now think that we were not and that we pre-committed.

Q69 Mr Hamilton: Well, that leads me to a second question. Throughout 2002 there was a renewed focus on Iraq being discussed in the media. How often was it discussed in the Cabinet and how far do you think that the renewed focus on Iraq was being pressed by Washington?
Clare Short: Well, I am certain it was being pressed by Washington, and I presume you will get the clerks to go back over the media story because it kept breaking into our media and we kept getting an echo of the arguments in Washington from our Prime Minister and our Foreign Secretary. To discuss Iraq. Occasionally pre-Cabinet you are asked if you want to raise anything, not every week, some weeks, interestingly, and I asked to raise certain situations in Africa departmentally and then personally Iraq in September time and the Prime Minister at that time said that he did not want it raised in the Cabinet and he would see me personally. I saw him when I was in Mozambique. We went to Mozambique before we went to the World Conference on Sustainable Development in Johannesburg and that dates it in

my mind. The Prime Minister came back from that trip and, if you remember, in one of his press conferences that he did from his constituency, if you check the press reports, he was quite belligerent, and he had been to the US just before that. In the *Guardian* instant book, which I do not know if any of you have seen, which was clearly written, the part in the run-up to the war, with collaboration from the Prime Minister's entourage, close entourage, because it was only the close entourage which were really part of this or part of the detailed day-to-day, week-to-week activity, it says very clearly that by September 9 they were both committed to military action, if you just examine the record in the book.

Q70 Mr Hamilton: So you think that by September 9 war became inevitable and that was the date?
Clare Short: I think the Prime Minister had said to President Bush, "We will be with you", and he had not laid down the conditions that were needed to bring Britain's influence to bear to temper the position of the US and to try and keep the unity of the international community and the Security Council. I think he had committed us and he did not say, "We will be with you on a series of conditions", trying to operate through the UN and so on. Then I think that is why he lost weight, that he had given commitments in Washington and there was a feeling in Britain, in the Cabinet, in Parliament, in the Party and the country that caused him to give assurances on the second Resolution and the two were rather contradictory and it conflated over truncating the Blix process and then the big fig-leaf became, "Blame France" and misleading us about France's position to get through that crisis of contradictory policies.

Q71 Mr Hamilton: Finally, if I can just add this, what did you believe were the real reasons for the war in Iraq?
Clare Short: I think if you read, and I have since, some of the publications of the Republican, neo-conservatives, Wolfowitz, Rumsfeld, Vice President Cheney and some of the others, they were writing from 1997 on, or that is the earliest material I have read, and there was some sensitivity about this, that there had been a failure to complete the first Gulf War and leave Saddam Hussein in Iraq and that action had to be taken. Now, I understand that, it was an evil regime and it was in defiance of the UN, but they were very committed to it. Then if you read the Bob Woodward book, *Bush at War*, I think it is called, that was written with full White House co-operation and it is about the run-up to Afghanistan, and you have got Rumsfeld arguing straight after September 11 that we have to go for Iraq and, as we all know, there was no link to al-Qaeda. Yes, it was an unresolved crisis, but they were not politically committed. In the *Guardian* book, you have got President Bush saying, and he is saying this in September 2002 that a year ago I was discussing with my officials the possibility of dealing with Saddam Hussein by tightened sanctions and more containment, but now everything has changed and it has to be war.

Q72 Mr Chidgey: Can I take you back to some of the opening remarks that you made, particularly in connection with the step change in policy within the Cabinet of moving to war. I want to look at the intelligence perspective of this and the influence that had on you and the Cabinet in coming to that conclusion. I think everyone would agree that intelligence is an inexact art, let alone a science. Can you tell us what intelligence assessments were made of what was happening inside the Saddam regime? Were you presented with a range of options, best-case, worst-case scenarios, explanations of what was happening in Iraq, or did it just come to you as a focused, "This is what is happening, this is the way forward and this is what we should be doing"?
Clare Short: Well, the first thing you should know is that the Defence and Overseas Policy Committee never met. There was never a paper. There was never an analysis of options and there was never an analysis on paper before any Cabinet committee or any meeting and it was all done only verbally. That is quite a collapse of normal British procedures for decision-making and I think some of the poor quality goes with the collapse in the proper decision-making processes, I really do, and I think that these are extremely serious matters for our government system. I think if there had been papers and analysis, we probably would have got—

Q73 Mr Chidgey: Well, if I can lead you on, and I think actually you have answered the question, but I will just ask it: do you feel the Government's policies on Iraq in the period leading up to the war were soundly based on good intelligence?
Clare Short: Well, let me just say a word about intelligence because most members of the Cabinet do not see the raw intelligence, the day-to-day bits that come through, the reports from individuals or telephone taps.

Q74 Mr Chidgey: But you did see it?
Clare Short: I did see it all for months because I saw it over Africa, Nepal, Pakistan and so on and, therefore, I normally dealt with that kind of material. Of course the raw intelligence is just droplets of information and I think someone once said that it is like cornflakes. It is bits and pieces and it did not say anything devastatingly clear. It indicates that scientists from the regime say yes, experiments are going on, and that type of thing, and then the Joint Intelligence Committee every so often pulls it together and makes an assessment. Could I say to the Committee that I think you should press to see the material. The reason for secrecy is to protect sources in Iraq. The whole situation in Iraq has changed and I think most of the material you could now safely see in terms of there is no one who would be threatened by your seeing it given all the changes. I did ask, and this is relevant, Defence Intelligence for an assessment because I knew they must be making an assessment in terms of the threat to our troops, the chemical suits and what kind of drugs they had to take and so on, and obviously my responsibility was thinking about the people of Iraq, so if there was a risk of chemical and biological

weapons being used so that our troops had to be protected, what about Iraqi civilians? So I was asking for the best possible assessment that defence intelligence could make, and all the other stuff was coming from SIS, of that risk. A paper was prepared, saying, and I am speaking from memory of course, that there is a risk, and it was thought not to be very high, but it was definitely there, which I thought was a very serious matter. Then I had a number of individual briefings from SIS which the Prime Minister authorised partly because I was so troubled by the whole process and he was trying to keep me inside the tent at that stage. The view that was taken by the person that briefed me after Blix started his inspection was that the scientists, their work and whatever they had was being hidden and the risks of use were less. That is my summary.

Q75 Mr Chidgey: That is very helpful. If I can stick on that point, one of the issues which certainly troubles me from the evidence we have taken over a long period of time on this issue is the difficulty of actually locating and finding stocks of chemical weapons, particularly anthrax, of less than 1,000 litres, impossible to find. I have been wanting to try to find out whether the Government was actually briefed on this particular issue of how difficult it was to find these weapons and, therefore, it was clearly very difficult to remove the threat and whether then the policy formulation process moved on so that the only way to remove the threat is in fact to remove the perpetrator of the action and, therefore, the regime. Was that part of the step change or not?
Clare Short: No, it was not like that. The first proper open discussion was in October some time when members of the Cabinet just gave their opinions about the whole situation in the Middle East. After that, most weeks there was a discussion and indeed I often instigated it, but it was what I call "guided discussion". It was, "So what's the latest?" and by then there was a compliant atmosphere in the Cabinet and it was clearer and clearer where things were going and there was a kind of loyalty, so it was arranged at one point that small groupings of the Cabinet would go for briefings with the Chair of the Joint Intelligence Committee, and we went in groups of two or three. I think for most members of the Committee, but you would have to check with them, they did not see even the Joint Intelligence Committee assessments, all of them.

Q76 Mr Chidgey: So you were never advised from the intelligence reports that it was impossible for them to give you an assessment which told you that the Government could successfully remove or could not successfully remove the threat from chemical and biological weapons through the inspections process?
Clare Short: There was never a discussion in Cabinet at that kind of level of detail.

Q77 Mr Illsley: You have just covered some of the issues that I want to raise actually, but I will try and press you a little bit more on this. In particular, you have just told us that you saw Joint Intelligence

Committee reports, the raw intelligence material and the assessments because you asked for them, particularly in relation to Africa.
Clare Short: Well, I had a relationship with that material and I saw it regularly. I made a point of seeing everything on Iraq.

Q78 Mr Illsley: So you actually saw the assessments. You have also said there that you were putting in comments along the lines of, "Why aren't they putting this to Blix to tell him where to go?", so was anybody taking any notice of that? Were your comments accepted?
Clare Short: Well, this is why I reached this sad judgment that I reached. I also saw the Prime Minister personally quite frequently and this question of when Blix asked for more help, if you remember, and again I am speaking from memory, but I am sure this is a matter of record in the media at that time, Blix asked for more help with the intelligence, and the UK said, yes, we would give him more intelligence, and I know I had a personal briefing from SIS at that time. They told me that the UK had got better intelligence than the US because of our links into Iraq and that there were brave Iraqi scientists and so on who were giving us information and we knew about books, records and equipment being moved to people's houses. I tell you this because it is an important exchange. I said to them—in that case, let's give Blix the information. Let's give him the helicopters or whatever he needs. Let's get that house raided. Let's go there, let's find it", and I had that conversation with the Prime Minister also, and he said, "Yes, yes", but it did not happen, did it?

Q79 Mr Illsley: Do you think they were stopped from giving that information to Blix?
Clare Short: I think it is a matter of record that Blix said, but again I am speaking from memory, that in one of his reporting sessions to the Security Council he had started to have more co-operation from the UK, but still not from the US. Again I am speaking from memory, but he has said more recently that it all led nowhere and they chased it and there was nothing there when they got there.

Q80 Mr Illsley: The quality of intelligence was not good enough when Blix acted on it, when he had been given it. You just mentioned earlier that Cabinet members were allowed to go in twos and threes to joint briefings from the intelligence staff.
Clare Short: That is from the Chair of the Joint Intelligence Committee who is a former member of the security service and then he takes on a different role when he assesses the raw intelligence in order to make reports.

Q81 Mr Illsley: Just before, you said that the PM authorised you to see this intelligence, so was the Prime Minister or Ten Downing Street controlling exactly what members of the Cabinet could see or could be briefed on?
Clare Short: Earlier on, after September/October, I asked to see SIS, which I often did over Africa or different situations in the world, so I knew them

quite well and I often asked to see them. So I asked to see whoever the expert was for a briefing on Iraq, and they came back and said the answer was no, because Number Ten says no, and I made a fuss and it had to go to the Prime Minister individually and then I did see them. Then I saw them throughout, myself, when I asked, as well as seeing the material, but I think there are a lot of ministers who do not deal with intelligence material because they are in domestic departments or whatever and would not be in that relationship, and I presume they did not see it, and Defence and Overseas Policy, where normally the senior figures in the Cabinet come together, was not meeting, never met, never had any papers before it, so there was this one occasion when it was suggested by the Prime Minister at Cabinet that Cabinet members should be given a briefing by the Chair of the Joint Intelligence Committee and that happened, so people went in twos and threes and had an hour or so and he gave his assessment of where things were.

Q82 Mr Illsley: In that sort of control of access by Number Ten, but of you in particular because you knew the system and the individuals, do you think that was coming from the Prime Minister himself or from his advisers?
Clare Short: Unquestionably coming from the Prime Minister himself and when I pressed Sir David Manning, he made it clear that he had to ask the Prime Minister to get me permission to see the security services over Iraq in the same way when I saw them normally over other situations in the world.

Q83 Sir John Stanley: Were you suggesting to the Committee a moment ago that there was some deliberate policy by the US and the UK Government not to co-operate fully with Mr Blix's inspectors?
Clare Short: I think that they wanted to make an effort through the UN for the sake of international public opinion and probably United States' public opinion, so they wanted 1441 and, therefore, wanted the return of weapons inspectors. Well, you can remember the dissident voices, and I think Vice President Cheney said publicly that he did not want weapons inspectors, so there were different views in the Administration and you will know that the US Administration does have different views always and it is usually quite a fractured system, and particularly so through the state departments and the Pentagon through the early stages of this crisis. Certainly President Bush and our Prime Minister wanted 1441, wanted the weapons inspectors back in, but then I think in the US they were worried about getting entangled in the weapons inspection process and it taking longer than they would have liked, maybe trapping them into that way forward, and there was some of this briefing against Blix which again was in the media and I see he is talking about this publicly. So I think they wanted to try through the UN, but they did not want to get entangled in the UN and they wanted to be free to act, having tried the UN, when they wanted to act.

Q84 Sir John Stanley: So are you saying that there was a policy of only giving partial assistance to Mr Blix and thereby ensuring that perhaps weapons of mass destruction were not found as rapidly as might be the case, assuming they are still there, in order to keep the military option open?
Clare Short: Well, my understanding is, and I think Blix asked for more help publicly in one of his sessions at the Security Council, that the UK determined to give him more help and I think it is a matter of record him saying that the US were less helpful, but it is a fractured Administration. You cannot assume coherence in that decision like a conspiracy to make Blix fail. You have got different parts of the US Administration, some of them never wanting to go back to the Security Council and never wanting Blix in anyway, so who was controlling the decision not to give him full help on the intelligence, I do not know.

Q85 Sir John Stanley: You have made the, to my mind, extraordinary statement that the Defence and Overseas Policy Sub-Committee of the Cabinet never met on Iraq.
Clare Short: Never met.
Andrew Mackinlay: At all.

Q86 Sir John Stanley: That is exactly what Ms Short said.
Clare Short: It is a long time since it has met.

Q87 Sir John Stanley: Did you make a formal or informal request to the Prime Minister that that very, very important Cabinet sub-committee should meet?
Clare Short: No, I did not. The way I pursued matters was both by bringing everything up in Cabinet, reading all the intelligence, seeing and getting regular briefings from SIS and seeing the Prime Minister quite frequently myself individually. I was working absolutely on the assumption that the UK could see its role as being to use our relationship with the US to try and keep the US with the UN and with the international community if we could possibly do it, and I operated in the way that I have described, and I think now I was working on a false premise, but that is what I decided to do. This is happening actually in our government system, a breakdown of normal decision-making procedures and decision-making getting very individualised in Number Ten, and that is happening in general.

Q88 Sir John Stanley: You have made two references to areas where you thought the intelligence picture was exaggerated in the sense that the threat was exaggerated, and you referred to the issue of imminence and you referred also to links with al-Qaeda. Were there any other areas where you believed the intelligence position was exaggerated?
Clare Short: No. I think our intelligence service absolutely believed, as I do, that Saddam Hussein was going on with the science and going on with trying to get chemical and biological weapons. They were absolutely clear that he was a long way from

nuclear, that he did not have any capacity and it would take years, though he had tried it before. Their briefing and the conversations with them were like that, but I think it is this phrase "weapons of mass destruction", when that is used, people think of bombs full of chemical and biological weapons that are going to rain down out of the sky and drop on people or whatever. They did not think of scientists in laboratories doing experiments, and I think that is where the falsity lies. Yes, he was dedicated to having scientists doing the work to try and create chemical and biological capacity, but the suggestion made to the public was that it was all weaponised and could be used imminently and was a dangerous threat to us and other neighbouring countries, and I think there was talk of Cyprus being reachable and so on.

Q89 Sir John Stanley: So you are suggesting that it was the use of the intelligence material by members of the Government and politicians which was responsible for the exaggeration?
Clare Short: That is my suggestion, yes.

Q90 Chairman: Was there any complaint at the time when you met the JIC and the SIS people that their raw material was going to be misused by the Government?
Clare Short: They never said that to me, but we discussed the desirability of the second Resolution, which they thought highly desirable. My understanding of their judgment was that this should not be left, but that we should try and keep the world together. I have read the media, as have you, and my own reading of the analysis is that when there were no WMD found, and now so much information you get through off-the-record briefings to the press, it started to be suggested that maybe the intelligence was defective and that made the intelligence community so angry that they started to brief about the way in which their material had been exaggerated politically. That is my reading of it.

Q91 Mr Hamilton: Clare, can I move on to the September dossier which I think on 3 December the Prime Minister announced would be published with the Government's assessment of Iraq's weapons of mass destruction capability. Can I ask you whether you saw any related papers to that dossier before it was published in September?
Clare Short: Well, I just said that I saw the raw intelligence as it comes in, which is telephone reports and reports of conversations with individuals, and it does not say who they are, but it says, "a reliable source" or "a new source", but that kind of material all the time, and then the dossier, or I saw all the Joint Intelligence Committee reports and then the dossier which was threatened once, then held back and then it came again. I have to say that there were three dossiers, were there not, and they were all pretty shoddy pieces of work, even the human rights one. There is no doubt that even the human rights piece was very old material, a lot of it preceding the

first Gulf War, so I am afraid I was not surprised that it was not a kind of forensic, highly accurate document because I think that is the house style.

Q92 Mr Hamilton: Do you recall how much of the information which was included in the September dossier came through shared intelligence arrangements with other countries? Were you ever told?
Clare Short: No. My understanding is that we share with the US, but I have been informed that our intelligence is better. I understand that we share with France and theirs is good and that was uninterrupted right through the crisis, funnily enough, or that is my understanding, or France shares with us.

Q93 Mr Hamilton: That is interesting. I do not think I have heard that before. Can I ask you whether it was an accurate reflection of Iraq's threat at the time or was it, how shall I put it, exaggerated?
Clare Short: I have not reread it, so now this is quite a long time, but my sense is that lots of it was accurate and the exaggeration and the suggestion of immediate threat and the suggestion, which is not in the dossier, but was made in press briefings and maybe in the House of the potential link to al-Qaeda, that is where the falsity lay. Of course when you see the picture of what happened, the exaggeration of immediacy means you cannot do things properly and action has to be urgent.

Q94 Mr Hamilton: So you think there was a deliberate attempt to emphasise certain aspects of the intelligence to make the threat more credible, real and immediate?
Clare Short: To make it more immediate, more imminent, requiring urgent action, yes.

Q95 Mr Hamilton: Did you try and oppose that in any way in Cabinet? Did you try and challenge it?
Clare Short: I think I was seen as pretty awkward throughout. I raised the question of Iraq repeatedly in the Cabinet and kept questioning, but you cannot fire on all sides on all issues all the time. I was still dedicated to the second Resolution as the way of restraint and, therefore, I did not fight over the dossier.
Mr Hamilton: I cannot believe you would have been awkward, Clare.

Q96 Mr Maples: I wonder if we can just pursue this question of the dossier. What was, as far as you are aware, the process by which the September dossier, the weapons of mass destruction one, was produced? Did a draft come to the Cabinet? Were you involved in the raft of comments in the process of it being drafted since you were seeing the Chief of Staff?
Clare Short: No, a draft did not come and I did not comment on a draft. Again speaking from memory, there was talk of a dossier earlier, the publication of intelligence material, and then I think that went quiet for a bit and then it was brought back. Alastair Campbell and co. were involved, so I left it to them. That is not my speciality, that side of things.

Q97 Mr Maples: I was going to ask you about that because when you said that the Prime Minister's close entourage was involved, you were including the Head of Government Information Service in that category—
Clare Short: Well, Alastair Campbell individually, Jonathan Powell, Baroness Morgan, Sir David Manning, that close entourage.

Q98 Mr Maples: And what do you know of their involvement in producing this dossier? Do you think they were involved in that?
Clare Short: I do not know in any direct way. That was the team, they were the ones who moved together all the time. They attended the daily 'War Cabinet'. That was the in group, that was the group that was in charge of policy.

Q99 Mr Maples: Campbell, Manning, Morgan, and you mentioned somebody else.
Clare Short: Jonathan Powell.

Q100 Mr Maples: You also said in relation actually to all of the dossiers that you think they were a bit shoddy, but then you said that that did not surprise you because it was the house style.
Clare Short: Well, that is a bit harsh, is it not, but I think I mean it. I am really shocked by the way these decisions were made. This is of such profound importance to human life, to the record of our country that I think one has to go to a sort of higher level of commitment to truth and accuracy and proper decision-making, and we should do it all the time, but particularly in a question like this when you are going to war and when people lose their lives and the future of a country is at stake, but things were not decided properly. There were no records, no papers. Decisions were made in the Prime Minister's study all informal around this small in group of people and obviously Alastair Campbell is responsible for the presentation of government policy, and that soon becomes propaganda and there is a place for that. Once proper decisions have been made, then the Government should put forward what it is trying to do as well as it can and communicate to the public, but the two often conflate and they were conflated there.

Q101 Mr Maples: One of the allegations about this document is that into the foreword had been pulled two or three of the bits which might scare people more than others, one of which of course was the 45 minutes allegation. Are these the sort of things that you think that that inner group would decide on?
Clare Short: I do not know about the writing of the foreword, but in every government publication that I have been involved in when I have written a foreword, I do my own foreword, and that is the nature of it. With ministers who take personal responsibility for what they do, you would expect that to be very personal in a document of that kind.

Q102 Mr Maples: But you do not know if it happened?

Clare Short: No.

Q103 Mr Maples: Just on this 45 minutes allegation, in the formal briefings that you had and the SIS briefings that you had and the JIC stuff that you saw, was that a feature of that?
Clare Short: No, not ever. Do not forget, because of my focus, and I do not know what arrangements you have made to see material, but I do hope you press to see this defence intelligence assessment because of course they made an assessment about our troops and that is relevant to the Iraqi people's risk, so I was very, very fixated on what was the risk of the use of this material on unprotected Iraqi people, so I attended to all of that in some considerable detail and I never noticed the 45-minute threat. It was not—

Q104 Mr Maples: That was never a feature of the personal briefings to you?
Clare Short: No.

Q105 Mr Maples: And that this was something you really ought to worry about?
Clare Short: No, but it is there as a risk, and the risk of use is probably not high, but a danger, was kind of the tone of it.

Q106 Mr Maples: On the Defence and Overseas Policy Committee, other than on Iraq, does it meet regularly?
Clare Short: No. It has met. At the beginning, in 1997, my Department was not a member of it and we became a member of it and there were some early meetings. I can remember the Ministry of Defence giving, they always give those wonderful overhead projections, they are terribly good at that because they like all that equipment, those type of presentations, but we never had a presentation on military options or the military strategy, though I did personally, but there was never a presentation of that either and it has not met for years, I think.

Q107 Mr Maples: On the big other issues you were involved in, big humanitarian efforts in Africa and things like that, the DOP did not meet to consider those issues?
Clare Short: No, but the other crisie would have been Afghanistan, Kosovo.

Q108 Mr Maples: West Africa?
Clare Short: Sierra Leone had a special committee chaired by the Foreign Secretary which met a number of times, not Defence and Overseas Policy.

Q109 Mr Maples: So it did not meet on Afghanistan or Kosovo?
Clare Short: I do not think it did. Maybe, I cannot remember now, it is a long time since it met and I have only been to one or two meetings of it and they were only on, it may have been Kosovo, but I do not think they met on Afghanistan, but there was a ministerial committee on Afghanistan that started to

17 June 2003   Clare Short MP

meet after military action. Similarly, on Iraq, when the military action started, then we had the daily Cabinet and it took reports of what was going on.

Q110 Mr Maples: So what we are getting a picture of here is that the relevant Cabinet committee did not consider this in detail which is what one would have expected?
Clare Short: There was no paper or analysis of the risks, the dangers, the military options, the political and diplomatic options, the strategy for the UK, there was never that.

Q111 Mr Maples: But not just at that level, but full Cabinet level either?
Clare Short: No.

Q112 Mr Maples: And decisions were being taken by a very small group of people close to the Prime Minister, none of whom, apart from him, are elected?
Clare Short: Yes.

Q113 Mr Maples: So there were no ministers involved in that part of it?
Clare Short: That is right.

Q114 Chairman: Did you know about the role of the Foreign Secretary at this time?
Clare Short: Well, the Foreign Secretary would have a close relationship with the Prime Minister and the entourage, but I think the decisions were being made by the Prime Minister and the entourage and the Foreign Secretary was helpful. He went along with those decisions, but I think the decision-making was sucked out of the Foreign Office which I think is a great pity because there is enormous expertise about the Middle East in the Foreign Office and certainly the Foreign Office has the expertise to understand what is necessary to achieve the second Resolution.

Q115 Chairman: You are saying that the Foreign Secretary was helpful. Are you suggesting that he was ancillary and the decision was elsewhere?
Clare Short: I am suggesting that he was extremely loyal to the Prime Minister and his decisions.

Q116 Mr Olner: Can I ask you, Clare, whether you think that was the decision in 1998 when we actually had a military conflict with Iraq in Desert Fox? What was different then to what happened recently?
Clare Short: Well, of course it was more restrained. It was not full-scale war in1998. It was a much more limited military action which was taken.

Q117 Mr Olner: Somebody said yes to that military action.
Clare Short: Yes, indeed, but it was relatively short. I do not remember a lot of fuss about the decision-making about it. I think the limited action was agreed on and it was taken.

Q118 Mr Olner: Could I refresh your memory to the fact that the United Nations did not support that action, the international community did not support

that action and President Bush was not even elected then. I am just wondering why there was no fuss made by certain members of the Cabinet then to what is happening now. The only constant thing is Saddam Hussein.
Clare Short: I am sorry, but I think that is a rhetorical and inaccurate question. Limited military action was taken, and I am now speaking from very old memory, Kofi Annan was involved and went to Iraq to try and restrain that from escalating, and I know some of the neo-cons are critical of the actions he took at that time, but it was not a full-scale conflict of anything comparable to the conflict that has just taken place, and I do not think your comparison is accurate, and on the length of it, it was not long either and nothing like the same scale.

Q119 Mr Olner: There were an awful lot of civilians killed in that particular military action.
Clare Short: Were there? I would have to check the record. I do not think that is so.

Q120 Mr Olner: Could I bring you just quickly to the February dossier. You have made it crystal clear that if you were a literary critic, you would not be giving any of the dossiers any sort of—
Clare Short: No, it is not literary; it is attachment to accuracy.

Q121 Mr Olner: So the grammar was right?
Clare Short: Well, I have not checked the grammar. I could go back and do that, but I was not pretending to do the literary style.

Q122 Mr Olner: Could I just ask whether the February dossier in particular, these are not your words, but certainly in most people's words, now termed the 'dodgy' dossier, did any members of the Cabinet see that before its publication?
Clare Short: I do not think so. I certainly did not read it. This is a shameful piece of work. To think that in the run-up to a declaration of war when people's lives are at stake, to lift a PhD thesis off the Internet and distort it because you know that the young man concerned has complained that even the words of his PhD thesis were distorted?

Q123 Chairman: He will be appearing before us.
Clare Short: Is he? Okay. I think it is shocking. I just am shocked that our government system can come to this. I do not think we should permit this. Obviously what has happened in Iraq has happened, but let us learn the lessons in trying to help the people of Iraq rebuild their country, but I hope that some lessons will be learned about our government system and we will not make decisions like this again.

Q124 Ms Stuart: Your final sentence moved into a question I want to raise with you. After 1441, which was passed unanimously and countries like Syria did not have to vote yes, this was seen as a clear indication by the then international community as a desire to have a second Resolution, and I seem to recall that even after the final vote, the feeling was they would not get a final Resolution, so Jeremy Greenstock, in an article, said that this was a kind of failure of diplomacy because only 15 countries signed up. They knew in their own minds that they had not actually signed up to the same thing and we did not have a dialogue which made it quite clear where do we go after 1441. Do you think that all of that confusion in the mind of the international community added to a process where the policy essentially was decided and governments were just looking for evidence to support it?

Clare Short: No, I do not think there was any confusion in the mind of the international community. I think there were two different strategies. I think that the willingness to use force and the determination of the US to do so helped to get us 1441. That was a difference and I personally think that we needed to resolve the Iraq crisis, so I am with those who say that it was a good to bring it to a head, but that got us to 1441 and unanimity was remarkable, including Syria. Of course Syria was pressed by a lot of Arab countries, and being there as a rotating member it was representing the Arab world, to co-operate because the Arab world was very keen for the thing to be resolved by the international community without all-out war if at all possible, and I think most members of the Security Council really hoped that inspection and Blix would work. I think the US wanted to go to war in the spring and the UK, I now think, had pre-committed to that timetable. I thought then that we were trying to use our friendship with the US to hold the international community together and see post-1441, which was a great achievement, if we could move forward with full international co-operation, and 64 ballistic missiles were destroyed. That is no small thing. This is the delivery mechanism for the chemical and biological weapons, so I think we were getting a lot of success and then it was truncated, and that is the tragedy. We never found out whether Blix could have been more successful, and we could have looked at a sanctions lift, we could have looked at indicting Saddam Hussein, and I thought that was the route Britain was on, but now I think Britain was never on that route and that was the difference. We have to remember with Jeremy Greenstock, who is a very, very, very fine diplomat, he receives telegrams giving him instructions and that is the process with the UN, so even a guy of his seniority all the time, over every country in Africa and so on, instructions are issued from London, so where he says that we could not get agreement because one country would not agree, he has got instructions. You know, he has been appointed today to be the UK representative in Baghdad. I wonder whether he has volunteered for his penance. He was going into retirement. He is taking over from John Sawers.

Q125 Ms Stuart: I think you repeatedly said that the Prime Minister deceived you, the Cabinet and Parliament—deceived you deliberately or deceived you on the basis of wrong information?

Clare Short: I believe that the Prime Minister must have concluded that it was honourable and desirable to back the US in going for military action in Iraq and that it was, therefore, honourable for him to persuade us through the various ruses and devices he used to get us there, so I presume that he saw it as an honourable deception.

Q126 Mr Pope: Could I just go back to the answers you gave to the questions that John Maples put about the decision-making process in the run-up to the war and during the conflict. You were saying in answer to John that there was a small unelected coterie around the Prime Minister which comprised Sally Morgan, Jonathan Powell, David Manning and Alastair Campbell, and you also said the Defence and Overseas Policy Committee never met in this period. Is it not also the case that these things were discussed in Cabinet at the same time?

Clare Short: As I have said, the first discussion at Cabinet was in October time and thereafter it was discussed at most Cabinets and I often initiated that discussion, but there were no papers and it would be to ask the Foreign Secretary how he got on in the last visit to New York, or, to ask the Defence Secretary this, and then the Prime Minister would speak a number of times and I would usually say something and some others might say something, so it was not a thorough investigation of an options-type discussion, but kind of updates, "Where is everything?", and then often a, "Yes, I'm very hopeful we will get a second Resolution" type of assurance. It is that kind of guided discussion and update, not an analysis of options and a thorough kind of collective decision-making, but it is kind of giving consent, I suppose, by not objecting. The Prime Minister would ask the Foreign Secretary and others to update on what is going on and then he gives his own conclusion as to where things are.

Q127 Mr Pope: We seem to be getting conflicting messages really. You said in your resignation statement, "the Cabinet has become, in Bagehot's phrase, a dignified part of the Constitution", and it does not really seriously decide things. It clearly did discuss Iraq probably at every meeting between the beginning of this year and when you left the Cabinet. Would it be fair to say that it meets weekly and it cropped up at every meeting? The reason I ask is that we were told earlier on today by Robin when he was giving evidence, and I jotted it down because I thought it was interesting, "You could not have hoped for a fuller discussion in Cabinet. It was a rare meeting which did not discuss Iraq", so that seems to me different from what you said, that there was a collapse in the decision-making process.

Clare Short: Well, the collapse in the decision-making process, not having Defence and Overseas Policy Committee, not having any papers, not considering options, diplomatic and military options, I think is very, very poor and shoddy work and is a deterioration in the quality of British administration which is shocking and this deterioration has been taking place for some time. There were discussions in the Cabinet, I often instigated them, but I do not agree with whatever the words about "you could not have had more thorough discussion". It was the same kind of discussion we have at Prime Minister's Question Time in Parliament with people raising their concerns and the Prime Minister saying, "Yes, I think we will get a second Resolution", whatever the concern of that week was. It was not what I consider a thorough decision-making discussion and there was no kind of collective decision-making. I really mean what I said and it is not just in relation to Iraq, but it is more generally, on foundation hospitals, top-up fees. These things have not been discussed in a way that says, "What can we do to decentralise the Health Service?" or, "What can we do to get more money into higher education?" and so on, and then you get sort of at the last minute the appropriate Secretary of State saying what the position is and people toe the line. That was how it operates now and this is not what I think collective Cabinet decision-making should be like.

Q128 Mr Pope: I am just trying to get a feel of how this operates, so there is a brief discussion in Cabinet and presumably votes are not taken, but people are able to dissent or to put an alternative view and that would be listened to?

Clare Short: Well, people do not. Famously we did on the Dome at, I think, the first Cabinet and the dissent was completely ignored. People do not now. This is our political system. Yes, this is Iraq and yes, this our Party in power, but this is our political system, this is our country's decision-making system and it is not good enough. That is what I am saying to you and I think your Committee has to take this seriously for the sake of our country's good governance.

Q129 Mr Pope: Let's move on to what I think is perhaps the more serious allegation which you made. In the article that you wrote in the *New Statesman* in which you were saying that the Prime Minister deceived us, it seems to me that the most grave choice one could make against a Member of Parliament and especially against a minister is that they have misled the House of Commons. You appear to be concluding that the Prime Minister has misled us on at least two occasions, first, by exaggerating the threat posed by the weapons and, secondly, you were saying that he agreed with President Bush a timetable for war as early as 9 September of last year. First of all, can you confirm that those are the allegations because I think those are incredibly serious allegations to make against a minister? Secondly, you were telling us earlier on that you had access to pretty much all the bits of the intelligence data, so I was wondering if you could tell us how you tried to use that intelligence data to restrain what you must have seen at the time was the Prime Minister deceiving Parliament?

Clare Short: It is an incredibly serious thing to conclude that your Prime Minister has been misleading you and Parliament, so when the Prime Minister kept assuring me personally and saying to the House and Cabinet that he was going for a second Resolution, if you remember, he said quite often, that he was sure we will get one unless one fickle country might veto, but I believed in that

strategy and I believed in that role for the UK, so despite people saying to me that a date had been fixed, which very senior people did say, I still was going along with believing in the strategy. However, examining everything that happened and what happened to the Blix process and the views of all of the other countries involved and the people who work in the UN system, my conclusion is the sad conclusion that I have reached and it is even worse than that because I think that this way of making the decision led to the lack of proper preparation for afterwards and I think that a lot of the chaos, disorder and mess in Iraq flowed from not having made the decision properly and made the preparations properly. However, let me say because my former Department were getting clearer and clearer about Geneva Convention obligations—and at first, only the military would be there—our military took very seriously and started ordering food and preparing for their Geneva Convention obligations and did a lot better in Basra than US troops did in Baghdad, but this unit, which was set up in the Pentagon to govern Iraq after the conflict, was not properly prepared for its duties, so I think this way of making the decision on top of the allegations about misleading us all are a large part of the explanation of the very bad situation in Iraq now and that is what I am saying.

Q130 Mr Pope: Could I briefly ask you about the intent here. I can see what you are saying, but it seems to me that there is a different way of looking at this, that the Prime Minister genuinely believed that Iraq posed a threat, that he desperately wanted the second Resolution not just in terms of the wider international community, but in terms of domestic politics, and he must have been devastated when he failed to secure a second Resolution and it made life much more difficult for him and actually he has acted honourably in all of this. If he has misled the House of Commons or the public, it was not his intention.

Clare Short: You have to ask if you reach that conclusion, and I agree that is a possible conclusion, why Blix could not have more time. The only thing we were told on that was that we could not leave the troops in the desert, but you can rotate troops and you can bring some home, so you can do that. A lot was at stake here, and the Prime Minister did try very hard after the failure of the first Resolution that they tabled as US/UK/Spain simply saying 1441 was not fulfilled. And they could not get support for that and despite ministers going to Africa and so on and the US trying to press Chile and Mexico, they just could not get the majority for that. So the Prime Minister tried for this Chilean so-called compromise with the six points that would be required to be fulfilled if Blix was to be successful, including Saddam Hussein going on television, if you remember that discussion, but he was saying then that he could get the US to give us a few more days, but the target was still March, so this is the thing which drives me to my conclusion, that there had to be military action by March at the latest. Now, that, I think, closed down any prospect of a second

Resolution and then we were misled about what France was saying. I do not like this conclusion, but I think the facts lead you here when you scrutinise it all and, as I say, I can only assume that the Prime Minister thought that Saddam Hussein needed to be dealt with. This was an honourable thing to do and "I've got to use my influence and my persuasive powers to get us there". There is a legal problem then.

Q131 Mr Pope: Should he consider his position?
Clare Short: I think we should, as a country, get to the bottom of it and the lessons of it. That question is a separate issue.

Q132 Andrew Mackinlay: Am I correct in saying that the Cabinet did not meet from the time of the start of the summer parliamentary recess round beyond the Labour or Conservative Party Conferences? Is that right?
Clare Short: Yes. The Cabinet does not meet when Parliament is not meeting. This business of being asked if I wanted to raise anything and I said Iraq and the Prime Minister said not and then he said he would talk to me in Mozambique was before and after the summer recess period.

Q133 Andrew Mackinlay: So in terms of arguing there is Cabinet collective responsibility, it goes into deep freeze between the end of July and the third week in October?
Clare Short: Well, it does not meet.

Q134 Andrew Mackinlay: Just a ballpark figure, how long did the average Cabinet meeting last in your experience of six years of Government?
Clare Short: Something under an hour.

Q135 Andrew Mackinlay: And there are various subjects to discuss?
Clare Short: You start off with next week's business and there are other areas.

Q136 Andrew Mackinlay: Are Cabinet minutes—I was a town councillor—done like local authority minutes? Are there minutes circulated with "resolved" and "recommended" on them?
Clare Short: The minutes are very lean, but this is the deep part of the British tradition. They are very limited. They are there but the Head of the Civil Service sits there with a book writing everything down and there are two others, one for home and one for foreign because they change at the end of the table, so a much bigger record is kept which presumably comes out 50 years later or however many years it is.

Q137 Andrew Mackinlay: With the Queen Mother it will be a hundred years, I suspect.
Clare Short: They are lean.

Q138 Andrew Mackinlay: You have revealed some interesting things about the machinery of government, you have shown us some of the flaws in the thinking in some of the intelligence, but where I think there is agreement is that you actually said you did not think containment was working?
Clare Short: Containment was hurting the people of Iraq too much. We could not go on with sanctions.

Q139 Andrew Mackinlay: So you were frustrated by this. I did not want to interrupt you, you said it could not go on like this. You also recognised he posed a threat or would develop the weapons of mass destruction if he had not got them, though I take the point on that terminology. It really comes down to whether or not there should have been more time for Blix, in which case you seem to think the French and others would have fallen into line if there had been continued frustration by Saddam Hussein. Would that be correct?
Clare Short: I think we had to deal with it and we should have done our very best to keep the international community acting together, but we had to be willing to contemplate military action to resolve it. That was my position throughout and I still think that is right, we should not have just left it indefinitely with the nature of the regime and the nature of the suffering of the people. But I think the prize of having unanimity at the Security Council and getting 1441 and getting the dismantling of 60 ballistic missiles was very considerable, and we should have gone on for a bit longer to see how much more we could get.

Q140 Andrew Mackinlay: Can I be devil's advocate. It seems to me at some stage you have to blow the whistle and say, "The game is over, the time has run out". Are you not slightly confusing the decision to go war, which was taken in the late summer/autumn, as the deadline? Either we have unimpeded access for UN inspectors, full compliance or, in a sense, Saddam triggers the tripwire?
Clare Short: There was a sleight of hand over 1441. As I have said, assurances were given to the Security Council that there was not automaticity, the thing the French objected to, and if Saddam Hussein did not co-operate with 1441, it would come back to the Security Council and of course Blix came back with his reports. Our Prime Minister had got himself committed to the second resolution. I do not agree, 1441 was not in terms which said, "Comply now or there is military action."

Q141 Andrew Mackinlay: No.
Clare Short: Therefore the second resolution, therefore you are back to why not more time to do it right but with an absolute determination to take action. You have to take this point, if the real objective was to overthrow the Saddam Hussein regime rather than the WMD, then there are legal questions.

Q142 Andrew Mackinlay: Yes. But supposing there had been more time but still no second resolution mandating, where would you have stood then?
Clare Short: Then we would have had to have the advice of the Attorney General and we got that advice, very strangely, very late. By then there was

agitation in the Ministry of Defence that they would not go if it was not legal. The published Attorney's advice—and the day Robin Cook resigned from the Cabinet was the day we got it and he came and sat in Robin's seat—and I saw everything but that was all I ever saw and I did not see any longer papers from the Attorney General. He said there was legal authority for conflict without a second resolution. That caused surprise to some but I accept that. This is our system. If our Attorney General says that, that is the legal position. I still think we should have gone on to see if Blix could work, but once we had that advice we knew we could legally take military action even if it was impossible to get a second resolution in the Security Council. We did not know it until that date but from then on we knew it.

Q143 Andrew Mackinlay: It seems to me, although you were not Foreign Minister you were in foreign affairs in the broad sense, and it seems to me there would have been cataclysmic consequences for the Atlantic Alliance, for perhaps even the relationship of the United States with Europe, commitment to NATO, many other things, if the United Kingdom had at the eleventh hour said, "We are not going to play ball." The die was cast.
Clare Short: No, I am sorry, this is really important. That implies we had given our word earlier. I am absolutely clear we had to mean resolving it this time but it was not the eleventh hour and we had all worked together to get 1441 and to get Blix in, and we should have had more time and the UK could have been a really helpful player and helped to try to get the international community together and try to see if it could have been resolved together and if that had failed then it would have come to military action as we took, and that would have been a deeply honourable role. That is not what we did. So I do not agree that all those things were at stake. I think enormous harm has come out of what has been done. I think probably very large numbers of recruits to al-Qaeda have come out of what has been done.

Q144 Andrew Mackinlay: You raised the question of the moral justification for war, proportionality and last resort and so on, and the legal advice and so on, but surely the kernel of this matter is that Saddam at the end of the first Gulf War sought an armistice, it was granted subject to conditions, he never complied, so surely the legal and the moral basis is there, taking Thomas Aquinas on board. He abrogated the armistice terms and basically there was a search warrant. If a policeman turns up at your door and my door, you do not negotiate with him, you either give him unimpeded access and full disclosure or he has to force his way in.
Clare Short: The trouble with that argument is that he is a monstrous dictator who has inflicted enormous suffering on the people of Iraq and indeed endangered neighbouring countries and defied the UN, and the people of Iraq have suffered terrible and are suffering terribly. The teaching on the just war and the law on the just war says, "no other means". I think you could say it was a just cause, you

can argue proportionality because of the nature of the regime and so on, but we did not exhaust "other means" and in the teaching on the just war and politically that was a very big mistake. The determination to take the route you are on, "We are fed up, time is up, we are going to do it anyway" means our country was deceived about what the plan really was.

Q145 Chairman: Roughly how many meetings did you have with the chairman of the JIC or someone else briefing you on the Iraq situation?
Clare Short: With the chairman of the JIC I only went to that meeting when the groupings in the Cabinet were being briefed, until the War Cabinet was set up and he attended that daily. I saw representatives of SIC five or six times, something like that.
Andrew Mackinlay: Chairman, does that square with what we were told by the Security Intelligence Committee?
Chairman: That is one thing for the Committee to discuss.
Andrew Mackinlay: Can you put that to Clare because she might be unaware that the Annual Report says that the Intelligence and Security Committee says that, "Ministers confirm they were given the JIC papers which their private offices believed they needed to see. Officials in the Department drew papers to the ministers' department and reflected their ministers' views at JIC meetings."

Q146 Chairman: Do you dissent from that?
Clare Short: I saw the JIC papers, and they became more frequent. That is the assessment then of the intelligence. I was never asked to comment on them or feed into meetings of the Joint Intelligence Committee but I read all those papers.

Q147 Chairman: You read them?
Clare Short: I did not meet the chair of the Joint Intelligence Committee when I read those papers.

Q148 Chairman: When you met him, that was before the dossier of 24 September?
Clare Short: No, I do not think it was, I think it was afterwards. It was quite late on, the meetings of groups from the Cabinet. They must have given you the date of that.

Q149 Chairman: What briefing did you get before the 24 September dossier?
Clare Short: As I said, personally I was reading all the raw intelligence and the JIC reports regularly. And I had had individual briefings.

Q150 Chairman: Did you conclude there was any discrepancy between what you had heard and what you had read and what appeared in that document?
Clare Short: As I said earlier, it is spin, it is exaggeration of imminent threat. There is no dispute on the fact the regime is resisting the UN, committed to chemical and biological weapons and had ballistic

missiles with too great a range, it is how you present how imminent the danger is as a result of that. That is where I think the exaggeration took place.

Q151 Chairman: From your contacts with members of the agencies, did you have any indication of any dissent, any concern about exaggeration?
Clare Short: You have asked me that already. This dispute came later. Once the conflict started I attended the daily Cabinet but I ceased to have—well, I had a couple of personal chats in the margin, I suppose—those individual briefings. It was too late then.

Q152 Chairman: But the imminent threat appeared on the 24 September dossier. There were a number of occasions when you met these people, when you would have had the opportunity to express your views.
Clare Short: Indeed. As I said to you, senior people in the system said to me that a date had been fixed sometime ago.

Q153 Chairman: Did they express their concern about any exaggeration in the document?
Clare Short: No, we did not have that conversation. There was concern about whether a date had been fixed and there were people who were very keen on a second resolution.

Q154 Chairman: A very final question, are there any matters which you want to raise which we have asked you which you would like to leave with the Committee?
Clare Short: I would like to mention—and I have just mentioned it in the exchange here—the incompetence of ORHA and the failure to take seriously the Attorney General's advice prior to the passing of the Security Council Resolution which then authorised the coalition to act in ways that have not previously been seen as the powers of an occupying power. I think that is a very serious question which helps to explain the disorder we have in Iraq. There is also the very serious constitutional issue of how important is the Attorney's advice. I thought it was sacrosanct, yet it was brushed to one side. He wanted to negotiate a memorandum of understanding with the US so British people who were put into ORHA, British public servants, would be protected to comply with legality, but the US would not do it. I think that is another extremely serious question. The question of the Attorney's advice and what is his power and what is supposed to happen in our system when it has been given, needs further examination.

Q155 Chairman: The advice you are referring to is the limits of the occupying powers?
Clare Short: Absolutely, which was later leaked. I would like to draw your attention to it. I think it is another very serious set of issues.

Q156 Chairman: It is your judgment that those concerns have been overridden by the subsequent UN Security Council Resolution?
Clare Short: I am sure they have legally. Once the Security Council has passed a resolution, it has authorised the coalition to behave in ways which the advice said it could not. So there was an interim period when that advice was ignored. It seems to me this is extremely serious—systems of government, powers of the Attorney General, how are you supposed to operate as an occupying power—which I ask you to look at.
Chairman: You have been very helpful. I am sure the Committee will ponder and reflect on your concerns. Many thanks.

Tuesday 17 June 2003

Members present:

Donald Anderson, in the Chair

Mr David Chidgey	Mr John Maples
Mr Fabian Hamilton	Mr Bill Olner
Mr Eric Illsley	Mr Greg Pope
Andrew Mackinlay	Sir John Stanley

Witness: **Dr Gary Samore,** Director of Studies, International Institute for Strategic Studies, examined.

Q157 Chairman: Dr Samore, can I welcome you again on behalf of the Committee. You have helped the Committee on a number of occasions. For the record, you were a national Security Council proliferation analyst under President Clinton. You are now a senior fellow for non-proliferation with the IISS, and I believe it is correct that you were the primary author of the dossier *Iraq's Weapons of Mass Destruction: a Net Assessment, An IISS Strategic Dossier*, published just prior to the Government's dossier. Yours was published on 9 September, the Government's on the 24th. I think chronologically the CIA document came out very shortly afterwards. An outside observer would note a very remarkable similarity between these three documents. Is that because they were effectively drawing on the same source?
Dr Samore: With respect to information about Iraq's programmes prior to 1998 all three dossiers were drawn from very similar sources.

Q158 Chairman: That is the UNSCOM document?
Dr Samore: It is basically inspection documents from UNSCOM and from IAEA[1]. With respect to activities after the inspectors left in 1998, the British Government dossier and the American Government dossier draw from classified information that was made public which the Institute did not have access to and so therefore from that standpoint our information base was limited to publicly available information.

Q159 Chairman: And you did not draw on your personal contacts with members of the intelligence community?
Dr Samore: We shared drafts of our document with experts inside and outside governments and got personal comments back, but the Institute's dossier was not co-ordinated with any government agencies, either intelligence or policy.

Q160 Chairman: What about, for example, the number of mobile biological weapons laboratories which I believe were roughly the same in the CIA document and in the British document? What was your assessment of that?
Dr Samore: The information that Iraq was pursuing or might be pursuing a mobile biological weapons capability came out from one of the defectors, so it was publicly available information which had been

published, I believe, in the *New York Times*. In the course of my looking through documents from the various inspection reports I found reference to some of the interviews that UNSCOM had with Iraqi scientists in the BW programme where they also talked about the possibility of Iraq developing a mobile capability. I took that as an interesting correspondence of information that added credibility to what this defector claimed and that was one of the reasons why we included that in our dossier.

Q161 Chairman: From your general background what significance in your judgment did the Iraqi regime attach to the development and retention of weapons of mass destruction? Take it stage by stage, during the 1990s first, when you were in Washington.
Dr Samore: Everyone believed during the 1990s that Iraq's refusal to co-operate with the inspectors, both UNSCOM and the IAEA, and their persistent efforts to conceal and deny and only admit when pressed to the wall were an indication that Iraq was trying to preserve some undetermined capability and that that reflected Baghdad's view that the possession of or the ability to pursue nuclear, chemical and biological weapons and long range ballistic missiles was essential to Iraq's strategy and defence needs. Certainly if you look at the history of the Iraqi efforts going back to the mid 1970s there does appear to be a very persistent effort on the part of the Saddam Hussein regime to develop and master those capabilities.

Q162 Chairman: You say "defence needs". Some analysts claim they were rather wider ambitions in terms of their standing in their region, their prestige, rather than the more narrow defence needs. How do you interpret that?
Dr Samore: I accept that. If you look to the extent that we can understand Saddam Hussein's psychology, I think he wished to be a leader and a uniter of the Arab world and he believed that in order to serve that role he needed to possess a very strong military both in the conventional sense and also through the possession of unconventional weapons because from his standpoint potential enemies of the Arab world, be it Israel, be it Iran, be it the US, all possessed those kinds of weapons and so therefore it was necessary for him to possess them as well.

[1] International Atomic Energy Agency.

Q163 Chairman: Did it have the effect within the region which they hoped?

Dr Samore: Before the invasion of Kuwait and the disastrous loss afterwards there were many Arab citizens who saw Iraq as the best hope for the Arab world asserting its previous prominence in international relations. After the 1991 Gulf War, which really demonstrated the hollowness of Iraq's military capabilities, and then of course the subsequent years of inspection and sanctions and basically isolation, Saddam's ability to appeal to the broader Arab public as an Arab unifier was probably tarnished.

Q164 Chairman: Did that rationale extend to, say, the 12 months prior to the conflict and did it change in any way?

Dr Samore: It is hard to say precisely but what everybody agrees, including even the opponents on the Security Council to using military force, is that Iraq did not demonstrate the kind of proactive co-operation with Resolution 1441 that would have been required to meet the conditions that the Security Council laid out. Most countries who follow the issue reached the conclusion that, just as Iraq was seeking to hide something or preserve some capability during the 1990s, Baghdad was following a similar strategy in the year leading up to the war, trying to do as little as possible to co-operate with the inspectors and give up capabilities.

Q165 Sir John Stanley: As you know, we are particularly examining the information that was made available to Parliament and therefore to the British people as the justification for going to war against Iraq, and of course the Government's overriding priority war aim was, of course, to remove Saddam Hussein's weapons of mass destruction. I would like to ask you the same question in relation to the two key documents that were presented to the British Parliament and perhaps I could start first with the one produced in September, *Iraq's Weapons of Mass Destruction: the Assessment of the British Government*. We of course entirely understand that you do not have access to the intelligence sources which the British Government have but, from the very well informed position which you and your Institute are in, when you came to go through that document were there any statements in it in terms of the scale of weapons of mass destruction, the immediacy of the threat, the degree of linkage with terrorist organisations like al-Qaeda, which came out of the page at you and made you wonder whether there might have been a degree of exaggeration of the scale of the threat?

Dr Samore: As you say, I cannot comment on some of the specific information in both the British and American Government dossiers because I have not seen that information, so I have no way of judging it, but in terms of the overall conclusions about Iraq continuing to have a commitment to nuclear, biological and chemical weapons and having, at least to some extent, been able to revive or rebuild that capability in the period after the inspectors left in 1998, again, without being certain about to what extent that was possible, I think those general conclusions were shared not only by the British and American Governments but also by the French and other governments as well. There was a dispute over how you dealt with the threat but I do not think anybody that I know of believed that Saddam had abandoned his interest in building those capabilities and I think everyone believed that to some extent he was hiding some elements of a programme.

Q166 Sir John Stanley: As far as the second document is concerned, which has got the name "the dodgy dossier" because it appears now that the majority of it came not from intelligence sources but off the internet from the various sources that have now appeared in the press, and indeed in front of the Committee, are there any points in that document which you felt on reading it were immediately questionable?

Dr Samore: I am afraid I never read that dossier so I just cannot comment on it.

Q167 Sir John Stanley: Given what you said about you essentially sharing the conclusions of the British Government as far as their assessment of Iran's weapons of mass destruction is concerned, has it come as a surprise to you or not, given the lapse of time, that both during the war and since the war clearly the very determined and intensive efforts that have been made to find WMD, so far nothing material has been turned up?

Dr Samore: I think it is too early to make a final judgment. In terms of the absence of finding clandestine facilities for the production of nuclear weapons or long-range ballistic missiles, the general consensus was that they were unlikely to exist, so I do not think that is a surprise. To the extent that there has been a surprise, I think it involves chemical and biological weapons, and in particular I think there was a genuine expectation that Iraq would at least deploy in the field and probably use whatever chemical or biological weapons it possessed in the course of the war. If they had actually deployed such weapons it is likely that coalition forces would have stumbled across them just as they have stumbled across abandoned tanks and artillery pieces and so forth, so it does not appear to me likely that Iraq actually deployed chemical or biological weapons. Of course, it is still possible that there are hidden caches of such weapons and the Iraqi forces collapsed so quickly that they never really had a chance to move them into the field. I do not think we will get an answer to that until the current Iraqi Survey Group is really able to complete their work. I actually think they have been a bit late getting off the ground because Washington and London thought they were going to find chemical and biological weapons in the field in the course of the conflict. When that did not happen it has taken a while to set up an organisation that will have to do much more difficult work to try to trace through documents and interviews and so forth what kind of capabilities Iraq might have had, including, if not stocks of chemical and biological weapons then possibly the kind of equipment and material that would be necessary to produce them at some time in the future. I do not think we can make a judgment at this point to compare the real situation on the eve of the war with the various dossiers. I think we will have to wait for quite a few months before the Iraqi Survey Group finish their work.

Q168 Sir John Stanley: It is evident, most conspicuously in the case of the alleged Iranian supplies from Niger to Iraq, that there were those who were in the business of forging intelligence, perhaps because they had a political interest in trying to precipitate a military intervention. Can we ask from the standpoint of your Institute whether you believe that there were other attempts? Do you believe that the business of providing forged intelligence in order to try to precipitate a military intervention was happening on any significant scale or that there may be other items of intelligence which did have a forged provenance?

Dr Samore: I think that any information you get from defectors should be automatically suspect because defectors have such a strong interest in making up stories or exaggerating stories, if not for political reasons then perhaps for reasons of personal gain. You have to start with the assumption that anything you get from a defector is probably not accurate. Having said that, there are occasions when defector information proves invaluable when there are *bona fide* people who come out of programmes and provide extremely important information. That was certainly the case for Iraq in the early 1990s. There were a couple of defectors who came out of the nuclear programme and provided very detailed and accurate information that helped the IAEA to crack the secret of Iraq's nuclear programme. We treated with great caution in our dossier information from defectors. In some cases we did not even bother to cite it because we thought it was just not credible. In other cases where we were not quite sure we would cite it but make clear that the reader understood that we were not in a position to substantiate or validate the information that was provided.

Q169 Mr Olner: Basically what you were saying in one of the answers you gave to Sir John was that when the UN inspectors were not in Iraq between 1998 and 2002 he did indeed continue to keep building up his weapons of mass destruction.

Dr Samore: I would say that we made the argument in the dossier that, given Iraq's history of wishing to develop these capabilities and given some of the technical capabilities that were available to Iraq after 1998, especially in the chemical and biological area, it made sense to argue that Iraq probably had taken advantage of circumstances to begin to rebuild its capability. Of course, the Institute was not in a position to assert that Iraq had actually begun to produce chemical and biological weapons; that would require access to classified information. We argued that it would be a logical assumption that Iraq would, and then we tried to assess, assuming that they did, what could be the capabilities in terms

of the magnitude of the amount of agent they could produce and what kind of delivery capabilities they had and so forth.

Q170 Mr Olner: Then what you are really saying is that the missiles which were delivered up to Hans Blix were proof, if you like, that there had been further developments, particularly on the weapons launch side of things, in those four years?

Dr Samore: I think that is a very good example. In fact, I believe our dossier was the first to call attention to the al-Samoud as the likely direction that Iraq's missile programme had taken. In the absence of an ability to produce longer range systems it was clear, even during the days of the inspections before 1998, that they could use the al-Samoud in order to get a slightly extended range and of course that was a missile that not only was banned and was declared to Blix but also was used during the war.

Q171 Mr Olner: Just prior to the latest conflict starting it seemed that the weapons inspectorate were having a certain amount of success. Do you think Saddam miscalculated? Do you think he played chicken and got run over? He was rather late in saying, "Yes, I will co-operate after 12 years. I will start to co-operate properly"? Do you think that really was a mistake on his part?

Dr Samore: That certainly is one possible explanation. It was clear to me that Iraq was trying to provide just enough co-operation with the inspectors to keep the Security Council divided and to try to deny Washington and London a rationale for going to war, but not so much co-operation that they actually truly opened up the books and gave up whatever capabilities they were hiding. I think Saddam's effort to balance those conflicting objectives ended up being part of the reason why he was doomed.

Q172 Mr Olner: We have heard a lot about weapons of mass destruction as part of Saddam's armoury. Is there any intelligence that says that he would be willing to give part of the armoury up to third parties to use against the West?

Dr Samore: I have not seen anything.

Q173 Mr Hamilton: Dr Samore, do you think that the UN inspectors were given enough time to complete their task or do you think they were always destined for failure because the regime really did not want to disarm? You have partly answered the question but I am just wondering whether the arguments of many of the countries in the United Nations that wanted to see the inspections continue were the correct arguments, that eventually sooner or later Hans Blix and his team would have found the evidence that everybody has been looking for?

Dr Samore: I think that if the inspection process had been allowed to continue with the threat of force being ever-present, as it was, it is quite likely that there would have been further success, that the Iraqis would have been forced to make additional areas of co-operation and concession to the inspectors. However, at the same time I think it is very likely that Baghdad would have continued to bide its time waiting for the opportunity when it saw the political situation change so that it could try to circumvent the inspectors' authority and try to revise some of its programmes. From that standpoint it is hard to argue with the proposition that an invasion to change the regime is much more likely to be a comprehensive and enduring solution to the threat than efforts to try to sustain sanctions and inspections and containment. Of course, war has a lot of other threats associated with it and risks and dangers, but as a non-proliferation instrument it clearly is going to be more effective than inspections.

Q174 Mr Hamilton: Do you think, however, in spite of what you have just said, that a more limited military operation like, say, Desert Fox in 1998 would have been just as effective in trying to disarm Iraq?

Dr Samore: Even in the case of Desert Fox, and certainly what we now know based on what has turned out to be inaccurate intelligence about where weapons might be stored, I would have to say that there probably was not a very sound intelligence basis for that kind of pre-emptive strike, and even with those sorts of limited strikes, again, if you do not change the regime which has the basic motivation to acquire the capabilities it is basically just buying time.

Q175 Mr Hamilton: Can I ask whether you were surprised that the limited time that was eventually given for inspections failed to come up with anything on the sites that were disclosed in the September dossier?

Dr Samore: I am sorry—which limited inspections?

Q176 Mr Hamilton: The UN inspectors went in in November and finally left just before the conflict started, so they were in Iraq for barely four months, but they did have access to some of the sites that were outlined in the September dossier and yet failed to come up with anything.

Dr Samore: I think I am on record as saying that it would be very difficult for the inspectors to find anything because, to the extent that Iraq had retained stockpiles of chemical and biological weapons, they would both be small enough and probably mobile enough for them to move them around in a way that would make it very hard for the inspectors to find them. Absent timely intelligence it is very difficult for outside powers to gain that kind of timely intelligence.

Q177 Mr Chidgey: Dr Samore, I am sure you will know better than most of us that intelligence analysis is an art form at its best and certainly not an exact science. My understanding is that it is usually the case that because of the nature of war information intelligence analysts will provide a number of scenarios to explain the meaning of the information that has been gathered. You could call it best case, worst case or anything in between. If that is a reasonable way of looking at the work of our

intelligence services, were you surprised in any way or did you feel it was realistic that in the September dossier, summarising slightly, the British Government drew the conclusion that Iraq had a usable chemical weapons capability which had included recent production of chemical agents and Iraq could deliver chemical agents using an extensive range of artillery shells, bombs, sprays and ballistic missiles? That all sounds pretty dogmatic to me and I find it a bit ambitious, and I wonder if you would comment on the basis of the sort of intelligence that you have already described in the latter years was available.

Dr Samore: Certainly in the Institute dossier we were a bit more cautious in saying "probably" and trying to explain on which basis we had reached that conclusion but I think that the kind of confidence that you just described in the British Government dossier was very widely shared in western intelligence agencies. If you look at the US Government dossier it makes a similar assertion, that Iraq has begun to produce fresh chemical and biological weapons agents. I do not know on what basis they made that judgment because I have not seen the classified information but it was certainly a strong consensus among western intelligence agencies that Iraq did have chemical and biological weapons.

Q178 Mr Chidgey: Would that have been sufficiently strong to convince the British Government that they only had one option in terms of counteracting the threat, which was assessed as being imminent and far-reaching in terms of our British bases in Cyprus, which was to launch a war against Iraq, or could it be that the assessment had already been made that the only real way of ensuring the threat was removed was in fact to launch a war and therefore cherry-pick the information to justify that conclusion?

Dr Samore: Let me not speak about what the decision-making process is in the British Government because I just do not know what that is and I cannot comment on it but, speaking from the standpoint of what I think Washington's calculations were, I think that President Bush was persuaded that it was necessary for international and domestic political reasons to give Iraq a final opportunity to disarm in accordance with a whole string of Security Council resolutions. That produced Resolution 1441 and I think Iraq's failure to take advantage of the resolution and really demonstrate serious co-operation, starting with the September declaration which everybody recognised as being very incomplete, persuaded President Bush that Saddam Hussein was not going to be willing to solve the problem through co-operation with inspectors, and everything that happened after that December declaration reinforced, at least in the White House's mind, that it would not be possible to solve the problem through inspections and the only way to deal with the threat was to remove the regime through force.

Q179 Mr Chidgey: Could it not be argued though that the pursuit of Resolution 1441 was the pursuit of getting a cloak of respectability over the eventual policy aims of tackling the situation? You may recall at a previous time when you came to give evidence before us that you talked about the difficulties of finding quantities of chemical weapons. I remember very well that you said that anything less than a thousand litres was virtually impossible to find and yet one litre is sufficient to do incredible damage to people in the area. That must have impacted surely on the strategic analysts in Washington, let alone in London, about how to tackle this threat. I would just like your comment on whether you feel that would have been a paramount problem in the sense of, "If we cannot find the weapons and remove those maybe we should think about removing the person who is most likely to use them".

Dr Samore: My guess is that many officials in Washington were probably sceptical about whether the Iraq problem could be resolved through inspections and probably believed that the only really effective way to deal with the threat was to remove the regime. I am confident that many people thought that in Washington but, as I say, I think President Bush was persuaded that it was necessary to try the inspection round first. I really do believe that if Iraq had demonstrated serious co-operation to the point where the inspectors would have been able to report to the Security Council that they were satisfied that they were getting proactive co-operation in trying to resolve some of these very difficult issues, including finding very small quantities of material, it would have been very difficult for the coalition to justify the use of military force. It was Saddam's failure to co-operate with 1441 that, it seems to me, made it easier for Washington and London to justify the war on legal and political grounds.

Q180 Mr Chidgey: Could it not be that we were putting Saddam in a position where he was being asked to prove a negative; in other words, deliver up the chemical weapons that he did not actually have?

Dr Samore: He did not even try to prove a negative. I agree with your point that even if Iraq was fully and actively and totally co-operating there probably would always be some margin of doubt.

Q181 Mr Chidgey: Because you could not be sure you would find them?

Dr Samore: Yes, and especially given the previous decade of the Iraqi efforts to try to destroy evidence and conceal their activities, of course there would always be some uncertainty, especially given small amounts of material and how easy it is to hide. Baghdad did not convince anybody on the Security Council that they were making a serious effort to resolve the unaccounted for issues. From that standpoint you really do have to blame Baghdad as being the primary party responsible for the war.

Q182 Chairman: That is contradicted by one of our witnesses this morning who said that the Prime Minister and the President had reached an agreement in the summer that the war was going to come in any event. What comment do you make on that?

Dr Samore: I just do not have any information about conversations that took place between President Bush and Prime Minister Blair. I am sure great books will be written about this issue, but my reading of what I think was going on in Washington is that the critical turning point came with the early December Iraqi declaration which was seen in Washington as a blatant failure by Iraq to co-operate and, by the way, was seen by everybody I spoke to as being a clear indication of Iraq not taking advantage of a final opportunity to make a declaration.

Q183 Chairman: You talked of a consensus in Washington on chemical weapons, yet the Pentagon's Defence Intelligence Agency believed that there was "no reliable information" on whether Iraq was stockpiling chemical weapons. Can you comment on that?

Dr Samore: I have seen some of those excerpts and as I recall what it said was that they believed Iraq had chemical weapons but they did not know where they were located. They have no reliable information about where they are located.

Q184 Mr Illsley: Dr Samore, it is a pleasure to see you again. Perhaps I could just read a couple of quotes to you, and some of these might sound familiar: ". . . his military planning allows for some of the WMD to be ready within 45 minutes of an order to use them"; "the Iraqi military are able to deploy these weapons within 45 minutes of a decision to do so"; Iraq has "military plans for the use of chemical and biological weapons . . . Some of these weapons are deployable within 45 minutes of an order to use them", the famous 45 minutes claim. First of all, what types of chemical and biological agents and means of delivery do you think that 45-minute statement actually referred to?

Dr Samore: Of course I have not seen that raw information and I do not know the source of the information so I do not think I can extrapolate beyond what has been made public.

Q185 Mr Illsley: You have no information as to what it might hint at?

Dr Samore: No, I am sorry. I am just not aware of anything. I would say that if you make the judgment that Iraq has chemical and biological agents then it is very logical that they would have plans to deploy and use the agent. It would be strange to have weapons and not have plans to use them. As to the detail of whether it is 45 minutes or two hours or whatever, I think that is a particular detail that I cannot comment on but the idea that Iraq would have in place military plans to use their weapons seems to me to be the kind of obvious thing that you would expect and certainly was the case in 1991 when they actually deployed chemical and biological weapons in the field.

Q186 Mr Illsley: The 45 minutes would assume therefore that some weapons would have been prepared, manufactured or be held in readiness, maybe in dual use facilities? Would you elaborate on that 1991 aspect as well?

Dr Samore: What we can say about what we know about their deployment, which is not an awful lot, is that they had the agents separated from the empty munitions, from the artillery shells and rockets and bombs which were then filled once the order was given to deploy, because you would not normally store these things together, and then once they were filled they would be transported to the units that had authority to use them, and at least in the case of 1991 it is believed that those were some very select Republican Guard units. As to the current situation concerning the 45 minutes, I just do not have any knowledge about what further details are available.

Q187 Mr Illsley: But, based on that information from 1991 when perhaps the 45-minute claim was not as out of the ball park as we have been led to believe, perhaps it is a little bit more serious than some commentators have alleged? Could that be true?

Dr Samore: Again, I cannot comment on the 45 minutes *per se* because I do not know who the source of the information was and what the details were, but the fact that Iraq would want to strive to have some relatively short term capability to use chemical and biological weapons once a political decision had been made is very plausible to me. Whether it is 45 minutes or two hours, I just cannot make that judgment.

Q188 Mr Illsley: Following on from that, in your opinion would you say that the British Government did exaggerate the capability by alleging this 45-minute capability from the giving of an order? Assuming the weapons were in existence it is perhaps not such a big exaggeration.

Dr Samore: I cannot make that judgment. Perhaps you can. The only way to make the judgment is to look at the source of the information and whether that individual—and I am assuming it is an individual—had credible current access to Iraqi military planning and whether the kinds of details that that individual provided seemed to hang together and give his story credibility. Without knowing who the person is and what he said I cannot possibly make a judgment.

Q189 Mr Illsley: You just mentioned that in 1991 the warheads and the material were stored separately. How easy is it to do that and how easy is it to perhaps convert from a dual use facility to disguise the use of it? Is that capability available? Could Iraq have done that?

Dr Samore: Yes. Obviously the ease with which you can move to deploy filled chemical or biological munitions depends upon what steps you have taken beforehand, what kind of practice you have, for example, and also what kind of safety standards you are prepared to accept. Certainly in the case of 1991 some of the filling practices that the Iraqis used were

not up to the kinds of standards that we would expect in our armed forces, so it does depend in part on what kinds of shortcuts you are prepared to take as well as how much practice you have had. Again, that is another issue that I just cannot comment on, the extent to which American and British Governments believed they had information indicating that the Iraqis were keeping their practice and exercises, for example, with the use of chemical and biological weapons and whether that might have given governments more confidence that such weapons existed.

Q190 Andrew Mackinlay: To some extent this has been covered, but I looked at the dossier produced on 9 September and then we had the Government's assessment on 24 September, much of which it mirrored. They mentioned four references to the 45 minutes. You made no reference to it at all because you have repeatedly said you do not know. I was surprised, because they seemed to be so much a match and there is obviously in the community you circulate in a lot of sharing of information, that the Government or people who you talk to had not flagged this up with you because presumably a lot of this is nod and wink directions and so on. It is just generally surprising. I wonder if you can comment upon that, the fact that you guys professionally were unaware of the 45 minutes, you do not mention it at all, and yet it comes soon after the publication of your much heralded and highly regarded document.

Dr Samore: I assume that the 45-minute information was highly classified information and so it would be a crime for someone to share that with a private institute that is dealing just with public information. If someone had been willing to share it with me I might have used it.

Q191 Andrew Mackinlay: Are you surprised that you were unaware of it? Are you surprised that you folk have not rumbled this or been aware of it?

Dr Samore: No. I think there is a lot of very sensitive classified information that I would not expect people to feel they were free to share because it would violate their orders not to share classified information.

Q192 Mr Pope: In the foreword to this document, the British Government's dossier of September of last year, our Prime Minister, Tony Blair, said that Saddam continued in his efforts to develop nuclear weapons. In your assessment do you think that was an accurate statement then?

Dr Samore: I would put it this way. I deeply believe that Saddam Hussein retained an interest in developing nuclear weapons and we talked abut the kind of research work that Iraq could do in order to keep its nuclear scientist cadre active, and in particular we talked about doing work on nuclear weapons design and small scale experiments with various kinds of nuclear technologies. Our dossier expresses scepticism that Iraq could have made much in the way of significant advances, especially in terms of building large-scale clandestine facilities for the production of fissile material (which is very difficult to disguise), which would have required that Iraq purchase from overseas critical materials. Of course, as we now know from declassified information, the British and American Governments believed they had information of procurement activity, like the aluminium tubes or the uranium from Niger, which helped to convince them that Iraq's nuclear programme was very much active and alive and perhaps had gone beyond simple research.

Q193 Mr Pope: Would it be fair to say that Iraq were lacking that critical component of the fissile material but they had managed to assemble all the other components of nuclear weaponry?

Dr Samore: This is speculation because nobody knows for sure. I think it is very plausible that they did continue work on nuclear weapons design, which is the kind of thing they had not quite mastered in 1991 but were probably within a few years of achieving, and it is the kind of activity that would be very difficult for inspectors to find. We speculate in our dossier that Iraq has probably continued that kind of research work clandestinely and therefore did have the ability to build a nuclear weapon if they could somehow produce or otherwise obtain the key fissile material.

Q194 Mr Pope: This key fissile material is obtainable, is it not? Obviously, it is not easy to obtain but it is obtainable and the worry is that it could come from a former Soviet state or from a country like Niger which has exported fissile material in the past and has a track record of doing so. That is a plausible threat?

Dr Samore: I would say it is possible. We make the point that there is no case we know of where a country has obtained weapons-grade material in any large quantity from the black market, so this would be the first time it ever happened but it is certainly something one has to be worried about.

Q195 Mr Pope: On a more general issue, the whole issue of whether or not the US and the UK can find weapons of mass destruction in Iraq is a huge issue in the UK. Is it anywhere near as big an issue for the Bush administration or for the American public?

Dr Samore: Of course, I live here now so I am not sure I am the best person to tell you what is happening in the United States, but my impression is that it is not as big an issue in the States as it is here, I think in part because opposition to the war was much less in the US than it was here. In the United States my impression is that the investigation, the various measures that are under way by Congress, is focusing more on the question of what the intelligence community got right and what they got wrong and how to improve their performance in the future rather than allegations that the policy community somehow distorted or made use of the intelligence to pursue a particular political objective.

Mr Pope: Thank you, that is very helpful.

Q196 Mr Hamilton: Dr Samore, are you aware of any reliable evidence that supports the Government's claim that Niger supplied uranium to Iraq?

Dr Samore: Only what I have read in the papers, which is aside from what were obviously forged documents I have read some newspaper articles claiming there is other undisclosed information indicating that Iraq at some point in the past made efforts to acquire natural uranium from Africa. Since I have not seen that information I cannot tell you whether those press reports were true or not. Certainly the documents in question were, I think everyone agrees now, forgeries.

Q197 Mr Hamilton: There were reports also of the Iraqis trying to procure different types of supplies—vacuum pumps, magnet production lines, aluminium tubes, and so on. Do you think those reports, if credible, show evidence that they were trying to achieve a nuclear missile?

Dr Samore: Well, the tricky thing about all of those items that were listed in the various documents, which were based on classified information, is that they are all dual-use and so it is very hard to give you a firm conclusion. The only way we will ever really get the answer to that is by interviews with mid-ranking Iraqi scientists and officials who can explain to what extent Iraq had tried to retain a nuclear weapons programme. The tubes are a very good case. If you look at the tubes, the dimensions are too small to be very efficient as centrifuges although they are the right dimension for the rockets which the Iraqis claimed they were buying them for. At the same time, some of the precision of the tubes and finish of the surfaces is really inappropriate for rockets and much more useful for centrifuges, so I think we are left with a real technical mystery about why they were buying these tubes, was it for rockets, was it for centrifuges, was it for both? I do not think we will get the answer to that until the Iraq Survey Group has done a very thorough job of interviewing the scientists who did the work.

Q198 Mr Illsley: Was the Iraq Survey Group already in existence or has it been put together simply because weapons have not been found?

Dr Samore: I think that, as I said earlier, Washington and London genuinely expected that they would find chemical and biological weapons in the course of the war.

Q199 Mr Illsley: In the field.

Dr Samore: And in fact they had set up special groups to search for and secure such weapons. In the US case it was called the 75th Exploitation Team. They were given a list of sites which the US government believed could be storage sites for chemical and biological weapons. All of those turned out to be inaccurate and all turned out not to have such weapons. It was only then that Washington and London realised they were going to have to put together a much more sophisticated detective operation to look at documents, interview people, do further forensic testing, and that has taken some time, it has taken months to get that organisation up and running. Even now I think they are just beginning the work. If I can just add, for perfectly understandable reasons, Washington and London have been focusing their efforts in Iraq not on hunting for weapons of mass destruction or for associated equipment and materials but on trying to secure stability and defeat the remnants of the previous regime. It is perfectly understandable but unfortunately, as a consequence, we have probably lost a couple of months and the looters have probably cleaned out a lot of evidence. So it may be difficult to come to final conclusions in a number of those areas.

Q200 Mr Olner: They have not been looting mustard gas!
Dr Samore: So far, thank goodness no looters have walked away with any deadly materials.

Q201 Mr Hamilton: You were interrupted, did you want to finish what you were saying?
Dr Samore: I think it is quite plausible that looters could have walked away with dual-use equipment, the kind of things that could be used to make manufacturing equipment.

Q202 Mr Illsley: When you say looters, you mean part of the regime, people covering their tracks, not people going in off the street to loot for profit?
Dr Samore: My impression is that there is pretty extensive and widespread looting throughout the country of many different types, so they probably walked away with some of the clues.

Q203 Mr Hamilton: Can I move on to some of the missile issues because I think they are pretty critical to deciding what the threat from Iraq was to the rest of the world. Do you think it is true to say, as it does in the September Dossier, that following the departure of inspectors in 1998 that allowed Iraq to continue the development of its ballistic missile programme?
Dr Samore: It is clearly true in the case of the al-Samoud. At the time the inspectors left in 1998 the al-Samoud programme was not quite at the point where it could be produced and deployed. Obviously by the time the inspectors went back in the al-Samoud had been both produced and deployed in a version that exceeded the limits imposed by the Security Council.

Q204 Mr Hamilton: How much do you think the development of al-Samoud-2 showed that the regime was determined to circumvent the UN Security Council Resolution?
Dr Samore: I believe the Iraqi regime wanted to produce an infrastructure, a technical basis for producing longer range missiles which it saw as essential, particularly since most other countries in the region have such longer range missiles, and it saw al-Samoud both as a stopgap in terms of giving some military capability but also as providing the

production base once it felt the coast was clear once the restrictions were lifted in order to break out and build longer range systems.

Q205 Mr Hamilton: A few weeks before the invasion started, Iraq agreed suddenly to destroy all those al-Samoud 2 missiles. Was it a delaying tactic, was it a way of gaining positive publicity to say "Look, we are co-operating," while doing something else behind the inspectors' back, or was it genuine?
Dr Samore: That was a classic case where Baghdad was cornered and they really had no choice. If they had defied a direct order from Blix to destroy the al-Samoud, which UNMOVIC had decided exceeded Security Council limits, then that would have completely under-cut Iraq's position in the Security Council. I believe a number of countries on the Security Council made that clear to Iraq, that they had no choice but to accept the destruction of the al-Samoud. Of course, in reality the Iraqis did agree but only to the extent of scheduling destruction and I think that was Iraq hedging its bets. It is a good example of how Baghdad tried to have it both ways, to co-operate to some extent with the Security Council but also to try to preserve some capabilities against what they saw as threats.

Q206 Mr Hamilton: The September 2002 Dossier suggests it was not going to be long before the al-Samoud 2 missiles were capable of reaching Cyprus, for example, and the discovery of a test stand showed that they were working on long-range missiles with a range over 1,000 kilometres. Do you think that is credible?
Dr Samore: I honestly do not recall what the British Government Dossier says about the development of longer range missiles. I know that our dossier argues that Iraq was still years away from being able to build longer range systems, something that could hit Cyprus. Of course, that would not prevent them from doing research on longer range systems, including testing engines and so forth. I thought the evidence about the test stand was pretty compelling evidence to show that the Iraqis harboured plans to eventually build longer-range systems, but in terms of how long it would take them to get there it was still at a pretty early stage.

Q207 Mr Hamilton: Presumably building a test stand in itself is not evidence that the missiles are there; it is simply plans to produce those missiles in the future?
Dr Samore: And plans to test engines. The engines are only one component in missiles.

Q208 Mr Hamilton: Forgive my technical ignorance but is there anything from a test stand, any knowledge you can gain via analysing chemical deposits or whatever that would suggest that such an engine existed?
Dr Samore: I think in the case of Iraq probably not because they used the same kind of propellants and oxidisers for the full range of engines of different sizes, so my guess is that chemical residues probably would not tell you about the size of the engine.

Q209 Mr Maples: I wanted to come back to the intelligence question for a couple of moments. Dr Blix has been very critical of them and said that such intelligence he was given—and we understand why he was not told everything—when he followed it up did not lead to anything. You said yourself that the British and American troops out there have been searching sites that were mentioned in these Dossiers and found nothing. I think something like 700 sites have been notified or suggested by the United States and British intelligence services, and something like 100 of them have been searched—that is obviously newspaper reading—and nothing has been found. There does not seem to have been any evidence of the Iraqi army's willingness to use these weapons during the war either against invading forces or against Israel. Are you surprised that the intelligence has not turned out to be more accurate?

Dr Samore: The record of Western intelligence agencies collecting information on Iraq's various weapons programmes is very poor and in particular if you think about Western intelligence estimates prior to the 1991 War, all of the Western intelligence agencies completely missed a massive, secret nuclear weapons programme, they all missed the biological weapons programme. We did not really learn about that until 1995 with the defection of Hussain Kamal, so I think that reflects the inherent difficulty of collecting information against a very ruthless totalitarian regime with a very effective counter-intelligence capability which is trying to keep these programmes secret. So I have to say that I am not particularly surprised that it is hard to get very detailed, explicit, firm information about weapons of mass destructions programmes in countries like Iraq or North Korea, which are trying very, very hard to hide them. The same thing was true in the days of the Soviet Union. Our record of understanding military capabilities was often very, very weak.

Q210 Mr Maples: Perhaps politicians are inclined to place too much reliance on such intelligence as we get?

Dr Samore: I think we probably demand too much of our intelligence communities. It is very difficult for the head of the CIA to say to the President, "I just do not know, I do not have enough information to make a decision." That would probably be seen as an acceptable answer.

Chairman: Thank you very much indeed, as always, Dr Samore.

Wednesday 18 June 2003

Members present:

Donald Anderson, in the Chair

Mr David Chidgey	Mr John Maples
Mr Fabian Hamilton	Mr Bill Olner
Mr Eric Illsley	Mr Greg Pope
Andrew Mackinlay	Sir John Stanley

Witness: **Dr Thomas David Inch, OBE,** Former Deputy Chief Scientific Officer, MoD at Porton Down and former Chief Executive of the Royal Society of Chemistry, examined.

Q211 Chairman: We continue our inquiry into the Decision to go to War in Iraq. We welcome Dr Inch. Dr Inch, as a Committee we look to you for specialist advice on the scientific aspects of our inquiry, helping us to pose the correct questions on matters of science. We ask you to draw on your wide experience in this area. For the record, I should say that you were employed by our Ministry of Defence from 1965 to 1985 at Porton Down. Latterly you were Deputy Chief Scientific Officer with responsibility for all the basic chemical defence research. Before attending the Royal College of Defence Studies in 1985, you were, for a time, Deputy Director of Porton Down. You joined BP in 1986 where you were Vice President, responsible for BP's research and technology in the USA from 1990 to 1993. From 1993 until 2000 you were Secretary-General and Chief Executive of the Royal Society for Chemistry. There will be a number of technical questions that the Committee will pose to you. We know from your experience that your answers will be extremely valuable. Dr Inch, I have first a general question. The inspectors were absent from Iraq between 1998 until 2002. The assumption in the Government's paper is that during that time the regime continued to work on its programmes of prohibited weapons of mass destruction and missile programmes in violation of a whole raft of UN Security Council resolutions from the end of the Gulf War. How credible, from your experience, is that?

Dr Inch: Can I give a kind of disclaimer at the start? I have had no direct links with Porton or the intelligence community for about 15 years. So everything that I say is kind of public record material and common sense deduction. It is not quite true that I have not spoken to some of the people at Porton because I am still involved in the Royal Society working party on decontamination and detection in regard to anti-terrorist issues. As chairman of the advisory committee to the National Authority on the Chemical Weapons Convention, I deal, from time to time, with chemical weapons convention issues. But I have no direct links in terms of the intelligence on the Iraq situation.

Q212 Chairman: That is the disclaimer?

Dr Inch: That is the disclaimer. I think you have to take the information in the dossier very much with a pinch of salt. The intelligence behind the dossier may be quite good, but I think that my interpretation of what is written raises more questions than answers. In many general terms that reflects some of the problems of making good technical assessments of the bits and pieces of intelligence information that comes your way. Sometimes the scientific community is in agreement with the intelligence community; and sometimes the scientific community disagrees strongly with the intelligence community's assessments. Perhaps I can give two historical examples as it is important to understand this. In the early 1970s the US intelligence community reported that there had been an accident in Sverdlovsk in Russia and that there had been an accidental release of anthrax from which many people had died. At that time in the US the chief scientific adviser was not convinced by the intelligence information; he did not think that it all held together. The signs and the symptoms did not fit the intelligence report. After the Iron Curtain came down that same person went to Sverdlovsk and was able to make a thorough interpretation. The scientific community had missed one or two important facts and the intelligence community was absolutely right. The total picture that emerged post-event was very convincing. That is one plus to the intelligence community. Rolling on to the early 1980s, the US intelligence community claimed that a new form of toxic material—T2 toxin—was being used in Laos and Cambodia which was subsequently dubbed "yellow rain". The American intelligence community went public at that time, and the information reached the Secretary of State and the President of the United States who went public on that information. Subsequently there was enormous pressure on our intelligence community to support the arguments. In this country our scientific community was never convinced; nothing really held together; the materials in question were insufficiently toxic; and there was a whole raft of other information that just did not fit. Eventually it was proven to our satisfaction that yellow rain was simply the droppings from flocks of bees. That is a big negative for the US intelligence community who, in my view, made in their interpretation a whole range of fundamental errors in not carrying out the proper checks and studies. When you apply those two lessons, there are signs of dilemma and you have to look at some of the statements in the dossier to see whether you can make sense of them. The short answer is that I do not know that you will be able to unless you have the right raw data from which to make some kind of an assessment. I can give you some pointers from the report of the kind of things that worry me as I look through some of the reported statements in it.

Q213 Chairman: Please do.
Dr Inch: On page 18 of the report at paragraph 3 it says that the intelligence suggests that: "These stocks would enable Iraq to produce significant quantities of mustard gas within weeks and of nerve agent within months". From a technical perspective I find it very difficult to understand unless the intelligence was very firm, very clear and very precise why it should be possible to make mustard gas within weeks but it would take months to make nerve agents. If you have the facilities in place, the previous knowledge and so on, and the plants available, it does not seem to me that it takes more time to make one than the other. The question is: how good was the intelligence? That would be the kind of question that I would wish to probe to find out whether it was hard or soft material that we are looking at. There are other examples.

Q214 Chairman: It may be helpful to the Committee, if, having trawled through the dossier, you were to give us a separate memorandum with your concerns as a scientist about some of the matters that you find in the dossier.
Dr Inch: I can do that[1].

Q215 Chairman: If there are one or two startling examples you can give them now, but are you prepared to do that?
Dr Inch: Yes, I would be very happy to do that. There are some general matters on that point in terms of questions about some of the technical claims within the document.
Mr Olner: With regard to supplying that further information, does Dr Inch know the deadline for our work?
Chairman: Yes, of course. Dr Inch, we are conducting a rather speedy inquiry, so our clerk will give you the deadline.

Q216 Mr Chidgey: Dr Inch, it falls to me to examine this area of chemical and biological issues with you, mainly because I am the only Member of the Committee with anything approaching an applied scientific background. To quote Newton, the more I know the more I know how little I know. I am hoping that you can help us a little on this. In this series of question that I am going to ask you I shall be trying to get you to explain to us how readily you can convert, for example, from an industrial process—the processing of the basic ingredients that go into chemical and biological weapons—to military objectives to create weaponised material. I am quite deliberately using general terms so that you can be more specific. On the back of that, one of the issues that exercises me is just how stable is the weaponised material? How readily can it be stored, transported and placed within warheads and how

difficult would it be to detect those processes? There is the change from industrial to military use, the creation of weapons material, transporting it, making it ready for use, all those kind of technical, challenging issues for the scientists and engineers, which for a layman are probably a complete maze. Clearly the telltale signs behind all this are essential in trying to gauge the accuracy of the information that is being presented to us in a political format.
Dr Inch: First, I shall comment on the stability. Some chemicals are obviously more stable than others. There are problems, mainly with something like VX, but the other materials are fairly stable and I would have thought that they would have been stored and stabilised in adequate conditions. That is not a problem.

Q217 Mr Chidgey: What would those conditions be?
Dr Inch: To illustrate the point, the two countries with the big weapons stocks are the US and the old Soviet Union. Under the chemical weapons convention both countries are committed to destroying those stocks. It is going much more slowly than anticipated because of safety concerns. It will be 10 or 12 years before those stocks can be destroyed. Clearly, there is no real problem with the stability of them. They will not be in the same high quality as when they started, but they will still be very effective weapons stocks. That is the situation, I think, with anything held in Iraq.

Q218 Mr Chidgey: How easy would it be to be absolutely sure that the storage facility was precisely the facility for chemical or biological weapons? Could it readily be mistaken or disguised as something else?
Dr Inch: You asked about production as well and how easy it is to transfer from a civil to a military use. In recent years there has been a major change in manufacturing technology in the chemical industry. One still has the enormous petrochemical type complexes which are very dedicated to making one material by continuous procedure. But the pharmaceutical industry, for example, which also makes highly potent compounds, is in the mode of just-in-time synthesis. They make a few tonnes of material and then quickly move to something else. It is the same in a lot of industries these days; the equipment is designed to be flexible and used in a wide variety of ways. Once upon a time, when health and safety concerns around the world were not very important, one could probably detect a plant making a highly toxic material by the extra safety precautions. In the modern world everything is governed by very tight safety regulations and it becomes increasingly difficult to judge whether a plant is making something that is highly toxic or something that may just be toxic.

Q219 Mr Chidgey: Does that kind of health and safety regime apply to Iraq?
Dr Inch: It is pretty general industrial practice and the kind of equipment and so on is readily available and may be bought. It is the kind of engineering

---

[1] Ninth Report from the Foreign Affairs Committee, Session 2002–03, *The Decision to go to War in Iraq*, HC 813-II, Ev 2.

18 June 2003   Dr Thomas David Inch, OBE

practice that gets into the culture. One could still go against that, but the point I am making is that for many of the compounds involved there would be no difficulty in switching from one form of manufacture to another. Can I give you one other example because I think it makes the point very clearly? Under the chemical weapons convention, there are scheduled chemicals which are the highly toxic ones, and there is another class of chemicals called discrete organic chemicals which are also banned under the convention. The real inspection regime for those materials is only now getting under way. But I think that the OPCW[2] inspectors in The Hague believe that about 30% of the plants that they see worldwide, making discrete organic chemicals for perfectly legal purposes, have the capability to be modified very rapidly to make chemical warfare agents.

Q220 Mr Chidgey: My question on that particular point is whether, due to the way in which you describe the situation, we should not talk about dual-use facilities, but about multi-use processing facilities. In other words, the plants that you describe could do any number of things one of which is producing chemical weapons.
Dr Inch: One has to be a little careful. Dual-use chemicals are things like phosgene or hydrogen cyanide, in the kind of definitions that are highly toxic in their own right and could be used as a chemical warfare agent, although maybe not too effectively, whereas the facilities—you are absolutely right—are multi-purpose facilities rather than dual-purpose facilities.

Q221 Mr Chidgey: Given that situation, if you were in the position of trying to define whether or not Iraq was operating a chemical weapons warfare programme and you were presented with a site that was a pharmaceutical chemical complex, what would you be looking for? Clearly the plant itself is not sufficient evidence to say that it is definitely a processing plant for chemical weapons.
Dr Inch: Personally, I would have given as much attention to carrying out some environmental analysis on the plant as I would to the facilities, given the situation in Iraq. We read in the report that they have gone to great lengths to hide things. I do not believe that you can hide the fact that you had been making some toxic chemicals on that site. If a site had been declared as a chemical weapons producing site, or if the original inspectors at the end of the Gulf War knew it was a site, you would not find out the information, but if there was intelligence pointing to quite new production facilities that were being denied as production facilities by the Iraqis, then I believe that the trace analysis and so on of certain residues would probably give confirmation of whether or not that was a correct statement.

Q222 Mr Chidgey: On that basis, what is your view of the assessment that Iraq was continuing to produce chemical and biological weapons after the inspectors left in 1998?
Dr Inch: I have to say that I have no view. I do not think that there is any compelling evidence to say that they did, but again there is no compelling evidence to say that they did not. You really need to make a close inspection of the data available.

Q223 Mr Chidgey: Do you have a view on the assessment that Iraq had a usable chemical and biological weapons capability in breach of UN Security Council resolutions, which has included the recent production of chemical and biological agents?
Dr Inch: I have no view. I think you really need to judge the data. There are some other statements on the dual-use facilities. It says: "New chemical facilities have been built, some with illegal foreign assistance". Again, that is talking about the import of precursors and so on. I would have thought that that evidence needed to be pretty hard if it exists, and it should be quite clear. Under the various UN embargoes and under the chemical weapons convention now signed by over 150 countries and under the terms of the Australia group regulations, which is the western group which embargoes supplies of materials and products, Iraq would definitely be a "no go" area for any of those materials from any respecting western government. Under the convention it is the responsibility of national governments to ensure that there are no exports to places like Iraq. Otherwise the treaties and so on are not being properly implemented.

Q224 Mr Chidgey: Dr Inch, if you could attach to the note that you are going to give us on the dossier the specific questions to which we should seek answers in regard to this matter it would be very helpful.
Dr Inch: I shall try to do that[3].

Q225 Sir John Stanley: We are in some difficulty because we are taking a great deal of evidence the rest of today and again tomorrow. Your subsequent paper will be of great interest to us. Could you help us with some pointers? At the outset you said that there were some specific points where you felt that the Government's assessment should be treated with a pinch of salt.
Dr Inch: Yes.

Q226 Sir John Stanley: On the one example that you gave us in paragraph 3 on page 18, if I understood what you said correctly, you were saying that the Government were probably under-estimating the degree of threat rather than over-estimating it because from what you said you were suggesting that not only could the mustard gas be produced within weeks but that the nerve agent could as well. Did I understand you correctly? Is that what you were saying to us?

---

[2] Organisation for the Prohibition of Chemical Weapons.

[3] Ninth Report from the Foreign Affairs Committee, Session 2002–03, *The Decision to go to War in Iraq*, HC 813-II, Ev 2.

Dr Inch: I was not making any comment on that. What I was saying was that I would have thought that to be able to make that kind of statement in terms of weeks for mustard gas and months for nerve agents, that there must have been some pretty good intelligence that suggested where and how those two time scales were going to differ. That would be a question that I would want to ask: how good was that?

Q227 Sir John Stanley: Can you point out to us the particular paragraphs and points in the paper where you felt the comment should be treated with a pinch of salt?

Dr Inch: It was in those general terms really. It is probably easier to do it in writing, but I found that there were too many weasel-words in the report, as I read it. They could do this or they might do that and so on, rather than saying that the evidence was hard. That was some of the concern that I had.

Q228 Sir John Stanley: Perhaps I can follow on the point that Mr Chidgey was making. As you know, the Prime Minister, in the final debate that we had in the House on 18 March before we went to war in Iraq, set out very clearly the Government's view as to the scale of the potential CW, BW stocks that may still be in Iraq. Just for the record, the Prime Minister said in col. 762: "When the inspectors left in 1998, they left unaccounted for 10,000 litres of anthrax; a far-reaching VX nerve agent programme; up to 6,500 chemical munitions; at least 80 tonnes of mustard gas, and possibly more than 10 times that amount; unquantifiable amounts of sarin, botulinum toxin and a host of other biological poisons; and an entire Scud missile programme". Against the scale of those stocks—the implication behind that was that much of that was unaccounted for and might therefore still be around in Iraq—and from your scientific standpoint, are you mystified, as certainly those of us who are not scientists are, that after this length of time after the war, in the post-war period with the access that we have now had to the Iraqi scientists, and after large numbers of the people on the 50 most wanted list are now under interrogation, that we have still been able to turn up virtually nothing?

Dr Inch: I am totally confused by this intelligence, particularly about the missile stocks and so on. It is very difficult to see where it has all gone in such a short space of time, particularly when such movements, I would have thought, would have been monitored by our total air superiority. You cannot move that amount of weaponry around without seeing it, I would not have thought. The chemical basis is a different matter. There are even problems in interpreting the reasons for some of the chemical stocks. It is difficult to be certain of what the situation was there. For example, if you take the aflatoxins, which are signalled up strongly in the report, they are potent carcinogens and not particularly toxic and they were in dilute solutions, gas. It is given in litres rather than in solid form. It is difficult for me as a scientist to think why anyone would want to use aflatoxins as a chemical weapon.

If you have a slow carcinogen and were to use it on people who may have a nuclear capability, and you want to trigger a nuclear response that is the kind of chemical to use. When you have something that is slow acting, you only have to think of the possibility of using something like that that has insidious slow effects on the civil population to see what a country like Israel might think of that.

Q229 Sir John Stanley: Do you have any view as a scientist that these stocks are largely unaccounted for? Would it be relatively easy to hide them in some incredibly clever way so that we would be unable to unearth them? Presumably if they are to be hidden, there must be substantial numbers of people who must be involved in the hiding operation, so can you give any explanation as to why we cannot trace where they are?

Dr Inch: None at all. Handling this amount of material is not a trivial exercise. If you are trying to move it around quickly, I would find it difficult to conceive that some accidents did not occur in the process and you would not have had some kind of civil report of deaths from poisoning. That is extraordinary to me.

Q230 Sir John Stanley: Does it suggest to you that the scale of stocks may not have been anything like the scale as reported in the assessment?

Dr Inch: That is one conclusion. You have to ask how good is the housekeeping, and how good is the record keeping in the first place. I do not really know enough about the way that the Iraqis function, but you may remember the time we had major problems with our nuclear housekeeping. It may be 30 years ago now, but I remember that there were problems trying to make all our numbers add up and that is a much more sensitive issue.

Q231 Mr Illsley: Dr Inch, I have two questions. The first is that a few minutes ago you referred to the telltale signs after perhaps chemicals had been removed from a facility and that you would look at the environment of that facility to see whether production had been carried on there at any point. How long would that trace remain after the production had finished? Is there a timescale that can be measured in months or years?

Dr Inch: It depends on the facility and the atmospheric conditions and whether there was moisture and so on. If it is in a plant, in a building, I think you would find traces for a very long period afterwards. Our analytical methods now are so sensitive that it is difficult not to find some kind of traces that would give some indication.

Q232 Mr Illsley: Do you have any knowledge of the quality of the scientific community in Iraq in terms of their capability of producing chemical and biological weapons, and perhaps even nuclear weapons? I ask that question because one or two reports were received and logged in this country of mobile weapons facilities. Recently in the press the scientific community in this country now are beginning to think that the mobile weapons facilities were simply tankers to produce hydrogen for barrage balloons, which does not suggest the top quality weapons that we might have been led to believe were in Iraq if they are still producing vehicles to produce hydrogen for barrage balloons. Does the Iraqi community lag behind in terms of its expertise or do they have the capability to produce these weapons?

Dr Inch: They certainly have the capability to produce the weapons by conventional methods. Whether they have the technology to think in terms of mobile laboratories is a different matter. Last year, at this time, in preparation for the chemical weapons convention review conference, I was one of the co-ordinators at the conference in Bergen that actually looked at new synthetic technologies for chemical weapons. The idea was that other developing technologies may mean that anyone wanting to break out of the chemical weapons convention could get away with it undetected, so we looked critically at a whole range of techniques such as solid phase synthesis, combatorial chemistry and nanotechnology devices of one kind and another. The conclusion was that it was all possible, but it required a lot more work and the answer was probably not yet. If that was the kind of conclusion from the developed, western nations in terms of the state of technology, then it is pretty unlikely that anyone in the hierarchy could do it better than was already possible elsewhere. So in terms of the mobile situation for chemicals, I find it very unlikely. I am not sufficiently familiar with the biologicals although I realise and read that there has been great doubt, as you say, about those procedures too.

Q233 Mr Illsley: One of the theories put forward is that perhaps some of the WMD production facilities and the weapons themselves might have been loaded into railway carriages and/or lorries and transported into another country. Would they have the technology to do that as well? Could they just load the stuff up and transport it across the border in a train or in a lorry?

Dr Inch: I think that is possible.

Q234 Chairman: You mentioned the state of technology. Can you also comment on the quality of housekeeping in Iraq and the general reputation for Iraq in that field? Are they particularly conscious of health and safety?

Dr Inch: I could not answer that question. I have no knowledge of that. If you ask that question about Iran, I have better contacts. I am pretty sure that they are as good as we are and that they are getting as good as we are now at housekeeping. That is another issue, but on Iraq, no.

Q235 Mr Olner: Do you think it would be fair to say that because chemical weapons have been used by Saddam Hussein on Iran and on his own Kurdish population, and seeing that they have not signed the chemical weapons convention, that he was still pursuing acquiring chemical weapons and biological weapons?

Dr Inch: I really have no knowledge of that. It has always been of enormous advantage to him to create the impression that he was. Some people think that chemical weapons are more of a kind of bugbear on the battlefield than they are a weapon of mass destruction. The fact that someone thinks you have biological and chemical weapons means that any forces opposing you have to take all the necessary precautions. They have to wear the protective clothing; they have to have all the injections and suffer Gulf War syndrome and the rest of it. To force any potential opposition into that kind of posture has to be an advantage to anyone. If you go back to the Second World War, Sir Winston Churchill took strong steps to stop the Germans from using chemical weapons by pretending that we had things that we could return in kind, whereas that may not have been very true. At times there is a powerful argument for making people think that you have something that you do not have.

Q236 Mr Olner: And you suffer the consequences, of course, if people think you have them and take action.

Dr Inch: That is right.

Q237 Mr Olner: In some respects, with justification.

Dr Inch: Yes.

Q238 Mr Olner: On a technical point, how possible is it for chemical weapons or biological weapons production facilities to be maintained without detection? Chemical plants are very easy to see. How small can they be and how easily can they remain undetected?

Dr Inch: You can make chemical weapons in the garden shed if you wish.

Q239 Mr Olner: So you are saying that there is no possible way that we could easily detect that these were being produced?

Dr Inch: No, not on that kind of scale. That kind of scenario, of course, is always attractive to a terrorist organisation, but in terms of a state waging war, the quantities that you would make would be totally useless.

Q240 Mr Olner: Who do you think would know how safety conscious the Iraqis were? I believe that they would take enormous risks, because life is so cheap, to move those things about which we would not even contemplate.

Dr Inch: The UNSCOM inspectors must have a very good idea from what they saw previously as to what kind of safety precautions were taken. The safety status within the Iraqi production plants and laboratories and so on, must be very well documented.

Q241 Chairman: Our next witness is a former UNSCOM inspector.

Dr Inch: It must be very well documented.

Q242 Mr Maples: We and the public have been surprised that we have not found any of this stuff in Iraq. The numbers sound very big. I am just looking at the report again. It mentions 8,500 litres of anthrax, for instance. I have been doing the arithmetic in my head and that is not a very large volume of anthrax, only about 300 cubic feet or so. Are we talking about huge quantities of the stuff?
Dr Inch: No.

Q243 Mr Maples: If you split that 8,500 litres of anthrax into about half a dozen places, it would be very difficult to find.
Dr Inch: If my memory serves me correctly, in China there are something like 3 million chemical rounds left over from wars in days gone by that they are still trying to clear up. There are some big stocks around. So in those terms it is pretty small numbers.

Q244 Mr Maples: So they would be difficult to find?
Dr Inch: Yes. There are not big stocks. The point has been made around this room that with all the human intelligence now available, someone ought to be pointing the finger in the right direction.

Q245 Mr Maples: Without someone pointing their finger in the right direction it would be quite tricky?
Dr Inch: It would be quite tricky.

Q246 Mr Maples: On biological as opposed to chemical weapons, to maintain the production facility and a sample of the toxin that you want to grow or to culture, do you need to store it in large quantities? Or are manufacturing times quite short once you have decided to go ahead, and therefore all you really need to do is to maintain a production facility and a sample of whatever it is you want to grow.
Dr Inch: Apart from anthrax, most of the other biological agents they talk about are actually chemicals; they are toxins produced by biological species. Ricin is from the castor oil bean; the aflatoxins are fungal products—botulinum toxins and so on—and have to be treated like a chemical; they do not cause a disease but they kill you like a poison; they create a fever or something. They are really just chemicals by any other name.

Q247 Mr Maples: It is a manufacturing process?
Dr Inch: It is a manufacturing process.

Q248 Mr Maples: Whereas with anthrax you actually grow the culture?
Dr Inch: That is right and produce spores which is much more lethal. The ricin is a particularly interesting one as we have had a case in this country. It is isolated from the castor oil bean. The normal method of isolation, because of heat treatment, destroys the toxin during the process, so you have to adopt a slightly different extraction process to get the ricin out. The problem with ricin at the end of the day is that it is a powder which is not easy to disseminate. Western countries that evaluated ricin

during or at the end of the Second World War lost interest in it because of the difficulty of spreading it about. Those are some of the problems; why bother when you have mustard gas and nerve agents?

Q249 Mr Maples: The only one of Iraq's weapons that is discussed in this paper which is genuinely a biological weapon in the sense of creating a disease which is spread is anthrax?
Dr Inch: Anthrax.

Q250 Mr Hamilton: Dr Inch, earlier you said that you were surprised that there were no accidents in Iraq or no reports of any accidents when chemicals were being moved around. Is it such a surprise in a dictatorship where there is no free press that no reports were made public? It could be that there were accidents and that people were killed. Would you necessarily have known about it in a country like Iraq?
Dr Inch: No. That may be some of the information that is in the raw intelligence data which would be good supportive material.

Q251 Mr Hamilton: The intelligence services would know only if someone had told them. Presumably if someone was so disgusted by the death and destruction caused by the accident they may tell one of the western intelligence agencies. If that did not happen, how would we know? We would have had no surveillance.
Dr Inch: That is quite right, but as I read the dossier, there is information in there that tells us what Saddam was thinking and what he planned to do. That could have come only from intelligence sources, somebody telling the intelligence agencies that that was what was happening. If one were receiving that kind of information from within Iraq, one would expect to see within the documentation other similar information about some of the more practical details.

Q252 Mr Hamilton: Do you draw the conclusion from the fact that there were no intelligence reports, as far as you know—I accept that you were not party to those but none have come through to us of any accidents being concealed or otherwise—that the chemicals were not there in the first place?
Dr Inch: No, I am not drawing any conclusions. I am just saying that one would have expected to see something.

Q253 Mr Hamilton: Some of my colleagues have explored arguments about concealment, quantities and toxicity. I want to be clear in my own mind about the kind of quantities of chemical agents that are necessary. Obviously, it will vary depending on the agent itself, compared with the quantity necessary versus the toxicity. It is quite important. As my colleague John Maples was saying, if you can conceal a small amount of chemical agent in a very small place, but it has huge toxicity and can kill a lot of people, could that go some way towards explaining why we cannot find these agents.

Dr Inch: For battlefield use, for loading up into the missile systems you really need many tonnes of any particular chemical agent, irrespective of how toxic it is. You really have a major problem of dissemination and in the modern battlefield you have to get quantities down quite quickly against a protected force if you are to cause great damage. It is a different matter if you are attacking the civil population that is not protected, in which case a smaller amount would have an enormous effect. If the planning is for military use then large amounts of material are required. Of course, when he was poisoning his own people, much smaller amounts of material could be used and used effectively.

Q254 Mr Chidgey: You say many tonnes, but can you give us a figure? Is it thousands of tonnes?
Dr Inch: I think it is many hundreds of tonnes, if you are going to wage warfare against a military group with chemicals. If you are attacking a civil population, a few tonnes can do an awful lot of damage.

Q255 Mr Hamilton: Would you be prepared to make any guess as to why Saddam—I appreciate you do not know his mind but he may have been prepared—did not use chemical or biological agents in the invasion in March and April?
Dr Inch: I do not know what his tactics were. I have no idea. He did not use them in the Gulf War either.

Q256 Mr Hamilton: Could it have something to do with the difficulty of deployment, as you have just described?
Dr Inch: I do not know. At the time of the Gulf War, quite clearly he had quite large amounts of material. He did not deploy it then.

Q257 Mr Illsley: You were talking about chemical weapons when you said he never deployed them in the Gulf War?
Dr Inch: Yes.

Q258 Mr Illsley: The reason I ask that is that yesterday we heard evidence that tended to suggest that chemical weapons were deployed, but never used.
Dr Inch: That is what I meant. I am sorry if I said deployed. He did not use them in the Gulf war. They were available for use; and we know he had them for use because we destroyed a lot of them afterwards.

Q259 Mr Pope: Dr Inch, the most likely chemical weapons that Iraq had were presumably like mustard gas, phosgene and nerve agents. How quickly can they be deployed? What is the time frame from making a decision to use them to firing? The reason I ask is that the dossier refers to 45 minutes several times. That seems to me to be a really short time frame to deploy what must be a fairly complicated weapon. I do not know what the procedures are. How quickly can it be done?
Dr Inch: I do not know what the military procedures are. If you have your shells, bombs or missiles filled with chemical and they are ready for release, it does not seem to me to make any difference whether it is a chemical weapon or conventional artillery. It is ready to be fired.

Q260 Mr Pope: I worked on the basis that the missiles and the chemical agents that could be deployed within the missile would generally be kept separately and that it is not safe to keep them together. Therefore, there needs to be a technical procedure to insert the chemical agent into the missile and that takes a while.
Dr Inch: It depends on the weapon system. To illustrate the point, one of the major problems on the disarmament side is how long it takes to demilitarise and to destroy chemicals already loaded into bombs and other weapons. You need special facilities to handle the bomb or the shell. You have to drain it, clean out the chemical and destroy the chemical before you destroy the rest of the weapon. It is much more difficult to destroy chemical-filled weapons than it is for chemicals. A lot of chemicals are stored in the weapon system to be used or they have been in the past.

Q261 Mr Pope: What is the easiest way of deploying chemical weapons? Is it by dropping a bomb from an aeroplane? Is it by firing a missile such as a Scud, or would it be by a small battlefield weapon like a mortar shell, or spraying? What is the most common way of doing that?
Dr Inch: It is horses for courses. When the Cold War was on most of our worst-case evaluation was on the basis that the Russians would use a multi-barrel rocket, which is effectively mortar shells in a multi-barrel situation. Most of the worst-case planning was about how much chemical could be put down by using multi-barrel rockets. That is probably the most effective.

Q262 Mr Pope: One of the things we know about the Iraqi regime is that it had many of those rocket-type launchers. Going back to the 45 minutes, the dossier makes quite a lot of play about that. When I read the dossier the first time I thought that the idea that these kinds of chemical weapons can be deployed within less than an hour was extraordinarily worrying. Do you think that the Government overplayed that or do you think it was a reasonable assessment?
Dr Inch: I do not understand why it was put in. I cannot see the significance of it other than saying that it is a terrible situation. If you are at war, all weapons have to be deployable fairly quickly—unless they were suggesting at that stage that the chemicals were stored way back and that they had to be brought up.

Q263 Mr Pope: I think part of the reason why they put it in was because they were alleging a variety of matters. They were alleging that Saddam was developing a missile system that could reach our sovereign bases in Cyprus; they were alleging that he was a threat to his neighbours; they were alleging that he would be a threat to any allied forces that entered the region. The worry was that he could deploy those terrible weapons really quickly and there is not a long lead-in time. That is the politics and that is why they put in the claim that they could be deployed quickly. I want to get to the bottom of whether that is a reasonable thesis to put forward. Was it accurate to say that they could be deployed in that way?

Dr Inch: One of the pointers about the report is that one really needs to see the raw data that generated that claim. What was the true basis for saying 45 minutes? Is there some significance to that statement that most of us failed to appreciate at this time?

Q264 Chairman: The Government appear to have qualified the 45 minutes by saying "from the time of the order". One interpretation of that is wholly meaningless because the order would be given only at the point when the delivery system was ready.

Dr Inch: Yes.

Q265 Chairman: What significance do you attach to the addition of the words "from the time of the order"?

Dr Inch: I am afraid that I cannot say any more. I am just totally baffled by why it should be there. That is why I say again that one has to probe the raw data much more carefully to find out why it was there and what the significance was and what the military thinking behind it was.

Q266 Chairman: If it is meaningless, clearly the insertion of it could only cause confusion and lead to an impression of an imminent threat which may not be there.

Dr Inch: That is the only conclusion one can reach.

Q267 Andrew Mackinlay: In the great debate about the justification for the conflict, do you think that too much emphasis has been placed on ready-to-use weapons and not enough on the industrial infrastructure, the skills that existed and were available and were being exercised in pursuit of these weapons?

Dr Inch: I think we tend to forget at times, particularly when one looks at the dual-use chemicals and the kind of infrastructure, how critically dependent all societies are on the chemicals that we use, in our homes, in all our materials—everything is chemical. Of course, Iraq was a fairly sophisticated society with reasonable demands. With a petrochemical industry one would expect them to have a reasonably sophisticated chemical industry capable of producing many of these things. Many of the compounds concerned are not themselves petrochemical in origin, but are used to convert petrochemicals into other products.

Q268 Andrew Mackinlay: What you say is correct, unfortunately. It seems to me that we will have a great problem looking ahead to other despots. If we are trying to frustrate proliferation, for ever and a day we shall have increasing problems as regards dual use. States will claim a legitimate need to have them for the well being of their peoples and the development of their commerce and industry.

Dr Inch: That is absolutely right. That is why again under the chemical weapons convention there is an enormous drive to increase the inspection of discrete organic chemical facilities that I mentioned. There is something like 4,200 or 4,300 around the world and probably a lot more. So if 20 or 30% of those have the capability of being diverted to other things, you have a major inspection problem. That is one of the major concerns of the Organisation for the Prohibition of Chemical Weapons. How does one carry out worldwide effective inspection of those facilities, not necessarily because of states trying to break out of the convention, but because terrorists may try to subvert some of those activities?

Andrew Mackinlay: Would it have been easy for the regime to have hidden their WMD capacity just prior to the opening of the conflict, to have destroyed it or to have spirited it away? The nature of these things cannot be seen from satellite or other surveillance techniques. Is that correct? Could their disposal or despatch to other locations or hiding them within the state be done fairly easily?

Q269 Chairman: We are talking of a period of six months or so.

Dr Inch: What surprises me most is the intelligence information that went into the compilation of the dossier, the ideas about the number of sites and particularly the suspect sites that were used for the production of chemicals. However, over the past few weeks, when the inspectors have been inspecting, they have not found substantial evidence in terms of traces of materials that would be manufactured on those sites. They may not have found the weapons, they may not have found the bulk materials, but I would have expected there to be some evidence of the presence at one time of some of the chemicals concerned. That is much more difficult to hide if one is carrying out the analysis in the right kind of way.

Q270 Mr Olner: It may be small-scale manufacture.

Dr Inch: Yes, small-scale manufacture too, if you know what the site is.

Q271 Mr Olner: If by necessity it is small, it will be very difficult to find.

Dr Inch: You have to sample in the right place.

Q272 Andrew Mackinlay: It is possible that things have been discovered but for wider security interests they have not yet been disclosed because they are putting together a jigsaw puzzle and you want to corroborate what you are doing and find the trail.

Dr Inch: That could be possible.

Q273 Mr Chidgey: One issue that has become apparent in the post-war situation is a switch of emphasis to the importance of the interrogation of the scientists and engineers and so on involved in this programme, this delivery. Be that as it may, in that context, would it be absolutely standard practice for the administration in Iraq to have absolutely full records of what was being produced and where it was going as a matter of course? I am trying to get at whether it would have been feasible for a chemical weapons and biological weapons programme to be in production without a full record of what was happening being kept and there being monitoring? It strikes me that it would be very unsafe not to have that.

Dr Inch: There must be reasonable records. You have to know what you are making, where you are going to store it, whether it will go into the weapons, whether you are producing the warheads for it and so on. You have to have an overall plan. I do not know how else you would operate.

Q274 Mr Chidgey: That would not just have been held centrally, I presume. Presumably the manufacturing plants and processing plants would have had their own records too.

Dr Inch: They should have had their own records.

Q275 Mr Chidgey: It would have been country-wide?

Dr Inch: Yes.

Q276 Andrew Mackinlay: I have two more questions. One flows from a previous point. Yesterday, the former Foreign Secretary put to us a rhetorical question. He said he could not understand why the UN weapons inspectors have not been allowed back, certainly into the United Kingdom jurisdiction in Iraq. Is it true that the function of the diligent United Nations weapons inspectors would be different from those who are trying to pursue a trail of seeking these weapons? Another legitimate reason for not allowing them back would be that their narrow remit would frustrate the detective agency, as it were—I forget the terminology of the group that is in there now, the survey group, whose functions are different—and they would impede the work of the survey group if the UN weapons inspectors diligently went about doing what was their narrow remit.

Dr Inch: There are a number of areas here that trouble me. There is the problem of inspection post-event, the importance of understanding the industrial processes and whether or not they can be easily diverted. There is the problem of obtaining analytical data which is totally rigorous and indisputable. The people most experienced in that now are the inspectors who routinely carry out industrial inspections, the OPCW in The Hague. The United Nations groups under Hans Blix, was totally independent of that group and had a much wider remit. Now, the kind of special investigation teams are, I think, independent in both those groups. That is not to say that there is not some read-across and some collaboration—I do not know the detail—but it does raise a number of issues as to how you get, even at this stage, very authentic and authenticable information. There has been set up under the Chemical Weapons Convention a so-called group of designated labs. They are not easily maintained in terms of the quality of analysis they produce: 20 or 30 labs participate in the programme and only about a dozen at any one time are designated as being capable of doing a good job. Most are in Europe; one in Singapore, one in South Korea, one in China

and one in the United States. None unfortunately in Arab countries, so there is no kind of read-across there. There is no clarity at the moment, even if samples were to be found in Iraq, that the products would be actually going to some of those independent labs for analysis. Maybe the situation is clearer now than it was, but it is still a little confused and not well planned.

Q277 Andrew Mackinlay: If you were advising the British Prime Minister or President Bush as to how to pursue this as at this time, what vehicle, what grouping, what combination would you have been suggesting?

Dr Inch: I would have certainly tried to involve some of those international teams who sit in The Hague and I would also want to make sure that, for any final analysis, it went to the independent labs around the world which are trained up for those purposes.

Q278 Andrew Mackinlay: And you do not think it is happening at the present time?

Dr Inch: I believe that the United Kingdom Government have pushed for some of those things to happen but whether that is happening I do not know.

Q279 Mr Hamilton: Dr Inch, just very briefly to help my technical understanding. We have been talking about the delivery of chemical weapons on the battlefield. Can you just explain to me why those chemical weapons are not destroyed by the ordinance that is used to project them into the enemy territory.

Dr Inch: That is part of the design of the material. Some of them are reasonably stable. That is all part of the design and there is not a problem there.

Q280 Mr Hamilton: I presume that there is an awful lot of heat generated by an explosive device.

Dr Inch: They are low-explosive devices; they are not the big weapons; they are not high explosives. It is the minimum amount of energy required to disseminate the chemical.

Q281 Mr Illsley: Given the difficulties that the international communities faced in Iraq in that the inspectors have had difficulty finding weapons and, as we understand it, some part of the military were sent to search and try and locate weapons and they failed and the difficulties faced by the Iraq tear-away group, is inspection going to be a thing of the past as a way of monitoring weapons of mass destruction in role countries? Is it working as it should be or do we have to look for an alternative way of policing weapons of mass destruction?

Dr Inch: It depends which ones we are talking about in terms of the nuclear problem. Chemical is very difficult and, in a sense, the current policing activities probably internationally . . . Although they were intended originally to build confidence and they have gone some way to doing that but, as absolute deterrent, I do not think they work or will work. The problem that we now have on this kind of system is not so much the inter-state activity but the terrorist activity. Some of us believe very strongly that the only way to counter that is by much more national implementation of the inspection system and greater awareness amongst the legitimate citizens and the problems that could occur, but internationally because of the commercial confidentiality and the dual use of these materials, any legislation would be so draconian that I think it would be totally unworkable.

Q282 Mr Illsley: Finally, just a personal opinion given what you said this morning about not finding trace elements and the length of time it takes, do you think we are going to find any weapons in Iraq?

Dr Inch: I have no idea. I am totally open. I started by saying that sometimes intelligence get it right and sometimes they get it wrong and I think that we are still in that situation. From the Committee's point of view, I would have to take a much closer look at some of the data to see how much you believe.

Q283 Chairman: After lecturers by all the best scientists, we are still confused but at a much higher level of confusion. Thank you very much indeed.
Dr Inch: I will try and let you have a few notes on this[4].
Chairman: We look forward to your further memorandum.

---

[4] Ninth Report from the Foreign Affairs Committee, Session 2002–03, *The Decision to go to War in Iraq*, HC 813-II, Ev 2.

Memorandum submitted by Mr Terence Taylor[5]

Witness: **Mr Terence Taylor,** President and Executive Director, International Institute for Strategic Studies—US, examined.

Q284 Chairman: Mr Taylor, we welcome you again. You gave evidence to our last inquiry on weapons of mass destruction. You are a member of the directing staff for the International Institute for Strategic Studies; you are the President and Executive Director of IISS in the United States; you have much experience in international security policy matters as a UK Government official, both military and diplomatic, and for the United Nations, both in the field and at UN Headquarters; perhaps very relevantly, you led UNSCOM inspection teams in Iraq in the 1990s, had military field operation experience and in the development and implementation of the policies; and you were also a career officer in the British Army. I think you heard the final part of Dr Inch's careful evidence in respect of the role of weapons inspectors. Can you set out what your role was in the old UNSCOM and to what extent that was changed with the UNMOVIC.

Mr Taylor: It is a very interesting question. I was a chief inspector mainly employed for investigations into biological weapons and, for each of my missions, the detailed mission was given to me by the Executive Chairman and, for most of my time, that was Ambassador Rolf Ekeus who was in charge at that time. The missions were cleared in detail with him, for they varied in type. Some would be of the surprise inspection variety, some may be more routine in background investigation and others were destruction missions. I was involved in the destruction of the main biological weapons agent production site at al-Hakam.

Q285 Chairman: I recall that the Foreign Secretary said that certainly your successors, UNMOVIC, were not meant to be detectives but were ascertaining whether or not there was the degree of

co-operation from the regime demanded by UN Security Council Resolution 1441; is that different from your role then?
Mr Taylor: No, it is not different. Inspections will not make any progress without some co-operation from the Iraqi side—this was as true in 1990 as it was in 2002–03—so the onus was on Iraq to show and tell and not for the inspectors, to use Dr Blix's words, to play catch as catch can, but that is what we were doing for most of the 1990s, which is why it took four-and-a-half years of dedicated forensic investigation to find the evidence which forced the Iraqis to admit that they had a biological weapons programme. In other words, this was what is now called the "smoking gun".

Q286 Chairman: You were actually ready to sign off Iraq in respect of its biological weapons programme until there was this major defection.
Mr Taylor: That is not quite true. That is fundamentally untrue. Certainly after a number of years and a lot of effort by a lot of people of which I was just one, there was some wilting and thinking that perhaps we were not going to find anything. We were urged to keep going and, in March 1995, we had a breakthrough in that Iraq failed to account for 40 tonnes of growth media, which we knew they had imported. We knew the companies that had sent it to them, we had the transit documents and everything, so they could not deny that, in one year, they had imported 40 tonnes of growth media. This was far, far in excess, many, many times what Iraq would need for legitimate purposes.

Q287 Chairman: Let me provide a platform for Mr Hamilton. Can you comment generally from your experience during the 1990s on the degree of co-operation UNMOVIC received from the regime.

---

[5] Ninth Report from the Foreign Affairs Committee, Session 2002–03, *The Decision to go to War in Iraq*, HC 813-II, Ev 3.

Mr Taylor: UNSCOM in the 1990s. It was very familiar to that which UNMOVIC received in 2002–03. Generally, on my inspections we were allowed access. There were some difficulties sometimes, but they were usually overcome through negotiations. So, generally speaking at least on my part, there were no limitations on the access; I could go more or less where I wanted. Of course, they had a comprehensive concealment plan. They also were monitoring our communications and also they had penetrated UNSCOM from New York right the way through to Baghdad. So, we had this challenge that we had to face. We knew this and so we had to try to deal with this situation and we had to be very creative about how we went about our inspections, in order of course to achieve surprise.

Q288 Chairman: Were there allegations that UNMOVIC had been similarly compromised?
Mr Taylor: I have no hard evidence that that was the case, but the Iraqis have a very good intelligence and security service and it would not surprise me that they would try, but I have no evidence that they tried this.

Q289 Chairman: We have heard that one of the reasons why there was a reluctance initially to provide intelligence was the fear about the compromising of sources and the leakability of UNMOVIC.
Mr Taylor: I think that is a reasonable fear; I think it has substance to it; and the experience of the 1990s showed that very graphically indeed. I think that governments, when handing over sensitive information and wanting to protect their sources, would have to take that into account. I think it would be very imprudent to just simply hand over information; it would have to be sanitised in some way. I have to say that I have not seen any evidence.

Q290 Mr Hamilton: Mr Taylor, in your opinion, what significance do you think the Iraqi regime and Saddam Hussein himself of course attach to the development and retention of weapons of mass destruction during the 1990s after UNSCOM left Iraq in 1998 and immediately prior to the war and invasion in March of this year?
Mr Taylor: There was certainly no evidence that they had given up these types of weapons as a strategic priority. I think that central for Saddam Hussein was a nuclear programme. High importance was also given to the biological and chemical weapons. Throughout the 1990s, they tried everything that you could conceive of to hide as much as they could and to give away as little as possible. Once the co-operation began to fade away in 1997, by 1998 inspections were not achieving very much at all and I am sure you will recall that the western military efforts were focused on the Balkans at that stage, so Saddam Hussein and the regime felt that they were not going to be threatened by substantial use of force, hence the co-operation faded away. So, they would retain their

remaining capabilities. They had an objective of getting the inspectors out of the country. They were trying all sorts of means to do that. One can only conclude that one of the reasons for that was to retain their capabilities and, free of inspectors, it would be unwise to assume that they would stop doing what they were trying to do during the 1990s. We have to recall that, even when inspectors were there, they were, for example, caught importing missile parts. I had the galling experience of going to al-Hakam while they were continuing to build their biological weapons facilities before we had actually proved that this was the case. So, I think that any senior government policy maker would have to take this experience into account when making judgments about what happened between 1998 and 2002 and taking account of the Iraqi behaviour from the time the inspectors returned until March of this year.

Q291 Mr Hamilton: Presumably then, from what you say, you do not think that the regime ever came anywhere near close to deciding strategically to disarm itself of weapons of mass destruction. There was constantly the determination to develop those weapons whether biological, chemical or nuclear.
Mr Taylor: Yes, I believe that to be the case and I think you will recall that, in Dr Blix's reports, he repeatedly said time after time, I think in all his Security Council reports, his disappointment that they had not realised what was required of them. I think that of course they realised what was required of them but they were not prepared to do it, so they were trying to retain just as much as they could and only give away the minimum . . . I think that the pattern throughout from 1991 to 2003 was only to hand over information if the inspectors already knew it and that was true between 2002–03.

Q292 Mr Hamilton: Was therefore the last round of inspections from November 2002 until the conflict started doomed to failure from the start?
Mr Taylor: Not necessarily. Their chances of success were low, I have to say. It would require a strategic decision by Saddam Hussein himself. On 7 December when they presented their so-called full, final and complete declaration, this was the last chance for immediate compliance and I registered with great disappointment that that declaration was well short and my personal view was that, given the pattern of behaviour, inspections were very unlikely to succeed.

Q293 Mr Hamilton: In your opinion, Mr Taylor, was the only way left to disarm Iraq of its weapons of mass destruction, assuming that they did exist and you have more experience than most in that, through conflict of the type we saw in March?
Mr Taylor: I would not go as far as that. I think that if the Security Council had been fully united, 15 to zero, on threatening serious consequences, there was just a chance because one of the regime's paramount requirements was regime survival. In the end, Saddam made his third big strategic mistake which resulted in his overthrow, the first

one being the invasion of Iran, the second one being the invasion of Kuwait and you cannot do that three times. His strategic mistake was not declaring something extra in that full, final and complete declaration in December. If the Security Council held together in that final month if you like, there was just a possibility that, within the regime itself amongst the hierarchy, they might have seen a chance of survival by giving up at least a major portion of their weapons of mass destruction capability. So, I would not say that it was absolutely certain but I could sense that the use of force was more likely than not.

Q294 Mr Olner: From what you have just said, if the French position had been adopted and they had given the weapons inspectors forever and a day to find things, they would never have been found.
Mr Taylor: I think it very unlikely unless the Iraqis made a mistake and they were not likely to because they learned from their mistakes in the 1990s. I think that the inspectors in 2002–03 had a more difficult job because they [the Iraqis] learned from their mistakes. Like, for example, producing forged documents which they did to me, but we soon detected those, so they did not do that again. I doubt very much whether they would have. It [the UNMOVIC inspection process] would have taken years.

Q295 Mr Maples: As a result of something you said to my colleague Mr Hamilton—it is the same point in a way—I just want to make sure that I understood you correctly. UNMOVIC were never going to succeed without some level of Iraqi co-operation.
Mr Taylor: Yes, that is correct. The requirement was for the Iraqis to co-operate fully, absolutely fully. They could probably make some progress if there was more than minimal co-operation, but all there was was minimal co-operation.

Q296 Mr Maples: External intelligence from whatever British and American intelligence sources were prepared to give them and their own efforts on the ground would not have resulted in discovering Iraq's weapons of mass destruction without some level of co-operation from the Iraqis.
Mr Taylor: That is correct.

Q297 Sir John Stanley: From your very extensive background as a chief inspector, when you went through the British Government's assessment paper *Iraq's Weapons of Mass Destruction,* did it basically ring accurate to you or did you at a particular point feel there was anything that might be exaggerated or overplayed?
Mr Taylor: In its main substance, it seemed to me to be very accurate. Of course, I was not party to intelligence information myself, so I was judging it from open sources and from what I knew and from what I could judge. I suppose it is fair to say that I am an insider in many ways and, having studied the information in detail, I think that in main substance, the UK Government's dossier was

correct. On certain details of certain aspects of particular weapons, I really cannot judge because I can only assume that this came from very specific intelligence that I did not have access to, so I cannot really form too much of an opinion, I can only speculate about certain aspects.

Q298 Sir John Stanley: From that standpoint, are you, again with the huge background you have of trying to get access to the key people and so on in Iraq, given the fact that the war has now ended and given the fact that presumably we had identified previously who were the key people in the WMD programme—we have access to them and we have had access to other people within the government including a lot of the top people whom we have now picked up—are you surprised that we have not so far managed to unearth anything of any significance?
Mr Taylor: I am disappointed but, in a sense, not surprised because most of the people who have come into the hands of the coalition, either voluntarily or otherwise, were people like General al Saadi and Dr Rehab Taha and so on who never really gave us any new information at all and I do not know what interrogation is going on at the moment and what the results of those interrogations are, but it would not surprise me that they are not at the point of telling the coalition any details. Most of the information that was valuable during the 1990s came from mid-level and below people in the organisation who were either perhaps wrong-footed in some way or simply honestly answered the questions. I do not believe that a lot of progress will be made until the Iraq Survey Group, which has of course only just started its work and you have to remember that, up until now, we have had the military exploitation teams, some 200 people with very basic equipment who do not have the knowledge and depth of the programmes and the people they are talking to and so on, so only now is the Iraq Survey Group starting and my hope is that if the security situation can improve, that, if we do get the information in the end, it will come from the more junior members involved in the programmes, the lab technicians, store-men even and military people from the special security organisation who are responsible for protecting particularly filled munitions that might be ready for use, the inner core of the regime who are very hard to get at. Unless there is a big change of heart by some of the more senior members who are already in coalition hands and I do not know what bargaining is going on in that regard. There is the fear of prosecution as well, particularly by more junior members. They are worried that if they say, "I have been involved in biological weapons programmes" or something like that, they might be prosecuted. There are all sorts of complicated factors involved and maybe they worry about their families. If they do come into the coalition and do give information, then there are still elements out there that might make their lives difficult and their families' lives difficult. It is a very challenging situation and I think that it will take a little while.

Q299 Mr Chidgey: Returning to the September dossier, what is your view of the assessment that Iraq has useable chemical and biological weapons capability in breach of UNSCR 687 which includes recent production of chemical and biological agents?

Mr Taylor: From all the information available, I think it would be very surprising if they did not have operational biological and chemical weapons, very surprising indeed. They certainly had all the capability to do that. They never satisfactorily accounted for all the munitions, filled and unfilled, and they never satisfactorily accounted for all the material by a long way. We are not talking about marginal differences, we are talking about hundreds of kilograms, we are talking about hundreds of munitions, that is things like 155 mm artillery rounds and 122 mm rockets, air delivered bombs. It would be extraordinary if there were not filled weapons somewhere. How many is the challenge. For a number of technical reasons, they held a large number of unfilled munitions, chemical ones for example, and kept a limited number ready filled. This would be for storage reasons, for security reasons and for a number of other factors.

Q300 Mr Chidgey: So you do therefore believe that the discovery of the empty 122 mm munitions which have been found are the tip of the iceberg?

Mr Taylor: I believe so. There is a very large number unaccounted for which UNSCOM and UNMOVIC both agree. This is the problem with Iraq. They never answered the questions and it is not good enough to say, "We don't have any weapons of mass destruction" without accounting for hundreds of munitions which are things that are visible in large numbers and could be found if they say they were buried somewhere or were dismantled somewhere, there should be traces. Of course, with UNMOVIC with, at its height, only about 150 people and not all of them working on chemical weapons you have to remember, so we have a very tiny number of people doing this, so unless the Iraqis took them there and said, "Here it is", they were not going to find it.

Q301 Mr Chidgey: How straightforward is it in your view to conceal elements of chemical and biological weapons programmes within civil industrial facilities? Is it relatively easy, in your experience, to convert from clandestine CBW work to legitimate civilian work and then back again?

Mr Taylor: Yes. I would not say that it is easy, they have to know what they are doing, and the Iraqis certainly had some very good process engineers, chemical and biological, who really did know what they were doing. The main production site for biological agents, Anthrax and Botulinum which they turned into toxin, was actually a combined single-cell protein plant which made additives for animal food and they did that, and also a bio-pesticide plant, both in the same location, al-Hakam, but we had monitored the flow of materials into that place and it did not match up with what they said they were doing. They could

run a production run, clean it out and then a production run of weapons material. They may even bring in different staff to actually run the production lines. That was a regular feature. They also did it at al-Dawrah which was a foot and mouth vaccine plant, which was again one of their main production sites for biological weapons agents. What they would do there was move out the regular staff doing the vaccine production and bring in a staff to run a production line for two or three days and then go back to normal again. These were classic techniques by the Iraqis and with their chemical production—I was talking then about biological—they dispersed it. UNSCOM found a document where they had dispersed the capabilities amongst civil chemical plants so that they could produce the required chemicals' precursors to make chemical weapons in a number of different places. This is not speculation; this is hard evidence. We have the documents. All of those things I have said are hard evidence.

Q302 Sir John Stanley: Just continuing on the concealment issues, we have heard evidence from Dr Inch and indeed from yourself about the length of time residues of BW and possibly CW are likely to be around once production has taken place. We have heard evidence about the difficulty of moving some of this stuff around. I assume that applies particularly to BW. We have the evidence of the amount of volume of this that has been supposedly unaccounted for. The quotation I gave from what the Prime Minister said on 18 March: 6,500 chemical munitions, that is substantial volume; mustard gas, somewhere between 80 tonnes and 100 tonnes, suggesting again very large volumes. Against these issues like difficulty of moving, the longevity of the residues, the tonnage volumes and the fact that we now have access to a number of people and obviously a lot of the country, it does seem certainly mysterious to me that we have so far made so little progress in uncovering this. Is it a matter of surprise to you?

Mr Taylor: It is a matter of disappointment but perhaps I am not quite so surprised. I would distinguish between biological and chemical. The biological agent production is easier to hide, smaller facilities are needed and to clean up afterwards and so on. I am not one who believes that the residue is a problem in that regard. On the chemical side, if you have a highly dispersed and many different facilities for production of chemicals and where the Iraqis were probably restricted in having the number of field chemical weapons available for operational use. I am sure that was somewhat restricted. They had a record of putting munitions in hides in locations which you would not expect. If I were to give an example, they had, as a result of our breakthrough in 1995 in forcing the Iraqis to admit that they had a biological weapons programme and, after the defection of General Hussein Kamel al-Hassan, the Iraqis gave us a little bit more. They thought that the General was going to tell us more, so they gave us a bit more. Then they reported that they had deployed, in 1991, four sites with operational biological weapons and the command and control system to go with those. Three of those sites were just out in the desert, in the countryside—holes in the ground camouflaged and covered with tarpaulins. They were not meant to be left there for a very long time. This is the kind of pattern that I would expect. The stocks being moved around. The weapons of mass destruction stocks were guarded by the Special Security Organisation and probably for use by the Special Republican Guard where a very limited number of people would know where they are and where they would be hidden and they would be constantly and regularly moved as far as they could do in a certain erratic pattern. So, there is plenty of experience on the Iraqi side of having these flexible, mobile deployments both for operational weapons and for the facilities. I have noted it looking at the other programmes too, not just the Iraqi one. The old Soviet programme, for example, had production facilities in box cars which they moved around on the railway in order to make sure that they were not vulnerable and they managed to develop a system there. So, it is a feature where you have a regime that has run a clandestine programme and protected it very carefully, not only of course from the coalition oversight and the coalition operations, but they hid it from their own people and that is why it is so deeply recessed and so deeply hidden. That is another feature with the old Soviet programme. I remember a deputy foreign minister, of then what became Russia, saying that it was the best-kept secret in the old Soviet Union. It was so deeply hidden using dual-use facilities and nobody really knew where it was except for a very small number of people. The Iraqis were well capable of doing something like that given the very nature of the regime.

Q303 Sir John Stanley: Just one other important issue and this really goes back to your time as a professional soldier. If as a professional soldier you were given this sentence, which is the sentence in the Government assessment, I would like to understand how you would construe that as to what it actually meant. The assessment is and I quote, "Intelligence indicates that the Iraqi military are able to deploy chemical or biological weapons within 45 minutes of an order to do so." Can I ask you as a military man, how would you understand that sentence in terms of the capability facing you?
Mr Taylor: I would read it—and of course I do not know where the intelligence came from and I do not know about its accuracy—that that would have been based on the Iraqis having ready-filled biological and chemical weapons. The fact that they would have filled munitions would not surprise me. Unlike conventional munitions which would be ready to fire immediately, these munitions . . . If I think back on the way in which we used to handle our nuclear weapons because I was actually involved in one of the units that guarded the nuclear weapons and moved them out to their missile batteries and we had a very short time in which to do that. So, from that firsthand historical experience, I would imagine that there were special controls for these chemical

weapons and they were not placed immediately with the artillery batteries, with the 120mm multi-barrel rocket launchers or the artillery or with the air force base, so somebody had to do some kind of handover to get them into the hands of the people who were actually going to fire the munitions. I am entirely speculating but that is how I would account for the 45 minutes. Otherwise, if it was conventional ammunition, the ammunition would be ready with the batteries.

Q304 Sir John Stanley: Does that Iraqi military are able to deploy chemical or biological weapons within 45 minutes of an order to do so imply to you that the stocks of those munitions were within 45 minutes' drive of the artillery tubes or does it imply to you that the stocks might be quite a substantial distance away but that, from 45 minutes of an order being given, those stocks would be rolling out of wherever those stocks were held?
Mr Taylor: I think it is a normal practice for countries that have weapons of this type, special weapons, that there would be deep storage. When it came to possibly being used in a conflict, they would be moved to hides and temporary locations, probably being moved around, taking account of the deployment of the artillery. So, both would be moving and, so at a certain point through special instructions, then there would be a convergence and the two would come together and be useable. I would find that sort of timing not to be unusual. I would think it probably could be credible. I am not commenting on the quality of the intelligence.

Q305 Sir John Stanley: It is really interpretation because obviously this was what was given to the public. Are you saying that it does not necessarily imply that the stocks were going to be held within 45 minutes of the artillery tubes but that it would imply that the stocks were held some distance away but, from the moment an order was given, the stocks would be rolling out from wherever they were being held?
Mr Taylor: Yes and married together. I imagine that the term "ready to deploy" does not necessarily mean "ready to fire". I imagine that "ready to deploy" means that the ammunition is married to the delivery means.

Q306 Sir John Stanley: Married to it within 45 minutes?
Mr Taylor: I imagine that is what it means.

Q307 Mr Pope: The allegations that the Committee has heard against the Prime Minister in particular and against the Government in general are of the gravest nature. The allegation is that the Prime Minister has misled Parliament about the reason for going to war, that Iraq did not have chemical or biological weapons, that it was not an imminent threat and that the Government exaggerated the nature of the threat in order to provoke the conflict. Those are essentially the allegations that we heard yesterday. Obviously I cannot ask you to defend every word that has ever been uttered by a government minister but, in general terms, do you think that the Prime Minister has misled Parliament and the country over the nature of the threat that Iraq posed?

Mr Taylor: I have difficulty in answering the question completely because I did not have access to the intelligence, so I did not see the intelligence and so I cannot comment on that. I think, as you can probably tell from my earlier remarks, that there was substantial, I would say overwhelming, evidence, a mountain of evidence, that Iraq had research, development and production facilities and useable weapons and almost certainly operational biological and chemical weapons. If I were sitting in a position in early March 2003, that would be a conclusion and I think I would be irresponsible if I came to some other conclusion. By that, I do not mean that that automatically means armed conflict. I think that then the political judgment has to be made about that fact. I think it is interesting that all 15 members of the Security Council did not disagree that Iraq was hiding its weapons programmes. There was no disagreement about that. They did not disagree that Iraq was in breach of 1441. These were two issues on which there was agreement. There was disagreement about what you did about those facts. The general thrust—and I cannot comment on the quality of intelligence because I did not see it—of the Government's position alerting Parliament and the public to the dangers, the very real dangers, of the chemical and biological weapons and their delivery means and, in my personal view, the nuclear capabilities as well and one must not lose sight of that because my personal view is they are the most dangerous and most important that we should be worrying about, that if Iraq did not comply, it required serious consequences. Anything else would leave the region and the wider world in a more dangerous situation. I cannot think of any other way of putting it. However, on the 45 minutes and these other detailed questions, I cannot comment.

Q308 Mr Pope: There seems to be a difference between possessing a weapon and organising a programme to produce the weaponry and that Iraq appears to have been non-compliant in both areas. It not only had chemical and biological weapons but it also had programmes which it concealed from UNSCOM in the time that you were involved in it. Do you think it is a reasonable conclusion for the United Nations, or indeed individuals, to draw the worst conclusions from the fact that they concealed the programmes of manufacturing these weapons?

Mr Taylor: The catastrophic results that can arise from the use of these weapons, particularly in relation to biological and nuclear weapons, requires urgent and effective action. The chemical weapons are hideous and dangerous and we must not forget all along that the Iraqis used these weapons. This is a country that used these weapons on its own people of course and against Iran and, while we were inspecting, the Iraqi senior officers were quite clear that they saw great value in these weapons. Whatever others may think and I hear some voices say, "Well, chemical weapons are not so serious"

and so on, that was not the view of the Iraqi military hierarchy. They thought they were very important and absolutely vital to their survival and overcoming, particularly in relation to Iran who they saw as a potential adversary, being outnumbered by using this particular weapon to make up the difference. Do not forget that they did develop—there was debate about how far they went—VX which is the most lethal of chemical agents in any known arsenal anywhere in the world. Only the Russians and the Americans who are now dismantling their arsenals had this particular agent. So, they were not just doing the basic things with mustard agent and other things, they were going for leading-edge chemical weapons because they assigned high value to them.

Q309 Mr Pope: This is really helpful information. In the memorandum which you supplied to the Committee, you talked about the information attack on UN communications "at all points from our operations from New York to Baghdad." I wonder if you could elaborate on that. I was intrigued by that comment and I was not entirely clear as to what it meant.

Mr Taylor: I can only speak generally and I certainly cannot mention individual names and things like that, but I will just give you the range of the type of activities. It ranged from suborning people to steal documents from UN headquarters in New York and that would be true right through to Baghdad, having bugs obviously in hotel rooms where inspectors were staying and it also was found that there were listening devices inside the UNSCOM headquarters in Baghdad itself. They were monitoring our communications—we were open with those—but they were also monitoring the secure fax machines from which we sent back our assessments and our situation reports and we discovered that they were able to read those. We could only be secure with the use of, for example, laptop computers because they could read the communications sent on the linked desktop computers from the cables and so on if they had the right devices. Extraordinary measures would have to be undertaken if we were ever to achieve a surprise inspection. The UN and other international agencies will always make their best efforts to avoid these kind of things, but these are not national governments. They do not have classified information; they have protected information but not classified information in the way that one would have in a national government, in a ministry of defence, a foreign office or something like that. UNMOVIC, the most recent inspection agency, was obviously aware of the history, so I think they did take stronger precautions, but it is still a challenge when you up against the sophisticated and very determined information attack which I am sure continued, but it was very, very challenging. We managed to get round it in various ways, but I would rather not go into that.

Mr Pope: If I could just make a quick comment. I think everybody in this room is an elected member voted in favour of the conflict on 18 March.

Andrew Mackinlay: And would vote in the same way again tonight if a vote were taken.

Mr Pope: I just think that this kind of evidence is incredibly helpful. I personally feel better, having heard this evidence, about what I did on 18 March.

Q310 Chairman: Mr Taylor, you have made Mr Pope feel better today.

Mr Taylor: Chairman, that makes me feel better too, but that was not my objective!

Chairman: See if you can make Mr Mackinlay better as well!

Q311 Andrew Mackinlay: I notice that the gallant members of the press are not present; I look forward to the transcript which I certainly will use my best endeavours to ensure is of some interest to the press. Also, your very helpful memorandum and I will have to ask the clerk when it comes into public domain. I too found that very useful. Can I take you back. In relation to UNSCOM, you rightly pointed out the fact of the number of inspectors who were on chemical and who were on biological. In a sense, this is not new ground because Government ministers have said, "Look at the scale of Iraq, the size of France" and so on. They stated that point. I wonder if you could amplify upon what you were saying. UNMOVIC is presumably not appreciatively different. We do need to focus on the scale of these guys. They are a large country, a large territorial area, and, if you break them down into nuclear, biological and chemical, you are talking a relatively handful of people, are you not? Can you just beef up on that.

Mr Taylor: The effort has to be targeted and the Iraqis have to co-operate. Those are the two things that you have to remember. When I said UNMOVIC, remember that they are doing the chemical, biological and the missiles, and of course the International Atomic Energy Agency is doing the nuclear side, so there are more inspectors, but not that many, not a huge number.

Q312 Andrew Mackinlay: Anyway, I think we are all agreed that nuclear is the relatively easier part of the test.

Mr Taylor: I would disagree.

Q313 Andrew Mackinlay: Tell me why you disagree then.

Mr Taylor: The easy part to find or relatively easy part to find are the enrichment facilities and they were found pretty quickly by the UN Special Commission. Within a year, they had found them. What was never really uncovered were the components of the weapon itself, that is to say the non-nuclear bits if one might term it that way and I hope I am clear: the electrical firing circuits, the timing devices, the marraging steel, the lenses and all the bits except for the core in which you put the fissile material. The Iraqis had many years of working on these components. I think the opinion of the IAEA and others, and UNSCOM is involved also in it in some ways, because the IAEA are the experts in uranium enrichment and fissile material but you

need other people looking for weapon components. I think the judgment was that they were within two years, in 1991, of having an operational nuclear weapon. I was interested to see last December that Lieutenant General al Saadi, who is now in Coalition hands, actually confirmed that view; he said they were within two years—

Q314 Andrew Mackinlay: He actually confirmed that?

Mr Taylor: He said it publicly; I remember him saying that they were within two years in 1991. Well, what went on in 1991 after that . . . To be fair to the IAEA and, if you recall, I remember Dr Mohammed El-Baradei, the Director General of the IAEA, in his last statement when summarising the inspection effort said, "First of all, we had to reconnoitre the sites and then we focused on whether or not the Iraqis had restarted their uranium enrichment facilities" and that was the last Security Council Meeting before military operations began, so they had not actually looked for weapons components and we never had a full understanding of that. That is what worries me a great deal. I think you will find this thinking reflected in the International Institute for Strategic Studies dossier which they produced, which was slightly different from what the Government—

Q315 Chairman: Is this the one in September of last year?

Mr Taylor: Yes, this is the 9 September report. This dossier said that, if they managed to get the fissile material from somewhere else, in other words not through their own means of enrichment, they could have an operational weapon in less than a year, maybe in a few months. That was always something that worried those of us who thought about these issues. We worried about it all the time during the 1990s and I can remember thinking, at many meetings thinking and pondering over this when I was actually in the position of a commissioner. It is a real challenge to find that part of a nuclear programme. That is very difficult to find.

Q316 Andrew Mackinlay: I have a few more questions to ask in order that I understand this. In a sense as a parallel, you were telling us about the artillery pieces and the shells coming together in 45 minutes. It seems to me that what you have described, in terms of the components for a nuclear device, a lot of these could be over the decade manufactured in-house or, instead of being imported, they could be done in a very stealthily way because it is a long-term project and each individual component can then be dispersed and, basically in a relatively short time frame of a year, you can literally them together like Lego pieces, as it were, and all you need is the final . . . Basically, to a layman, that is what you are saying. It could be all be out there dispersed in various locations, so it is not put together but the potential is there.

Mr Taylor: That was from my personal point of view my biggest fear if nothing effective was done. If the only thing that was done was just more inspections and we went on like that for many months, of course troops would have to be withdrawn from the region, you could not keep them there, so the pressure on the Iraqis would have reduced and inevitably, as it did indeed in the 1990s and this is, I am sure, what the regime was hoping for, and then they would have all the parts, they would have all the people and then, in two years' time, we could have found Iraq with an operational nuclear weapon. That was my nightmare and, looking very carefully at all the information available, looking at their behaviour throughout from 1991 to 2003, I think that the Government were faced with doing a risk assessment of a very challenging kind. Only doing something that would not actually address this in an effective way was probably the most dangerous thing that one could do for the region in a strategic sense. It would alter the whole strategic balance in that region if that were allowed to happen. I know that there is a lot of talk about imminent threats and one can play with that, but I think that if Iraq were allowed to get to the point of having an operational weapon, pulling back is terribly difficult as we know from other cases.

Q317 Andrew Mackinlay: You heard me ask the previous witness—I sort of bounced it off him—that in fact the coalition forces or the survey group, although it has only just gone in, could already have discovered stuff and, from your experience, there is clearly some commonsense in not necessarily revealing this at this stage because you are on a detective exercise now whereas UNMOVIC and UNSCOM were not supposed to be on a detective exercise. Lots of things have happened since as it were and we are in pursuit of things, so you sensibly would not reveal and say, "Here, we have it." Politicians might want to do it because they are probably quite desperate from the point of view of the hunger of the public and press to be assuaged but, in terms of really pursing this, you would not declare it yet, would you?
Mr Taylor: No and indeed that did happen in the 1990s. When we first discovered what people now call the "smoking gun", the hard evidence that would convince the Security Council, all of them, 15 to zero, they have this programme and here it is. We did not make it public and in fact several months passed and then, on 1 July 1995, the Iraqis, because they knew that the Security Council was about to pronounce, admitted it. That took several months. I think that you have to be very careful when you are interviewing somebody which might lead you to somebody else which might lead you to somebody else. You cannot go public with the rest of the material, so it could take—

Q318 Andrew Mackinlay: If you had UNMOVIC in parallel with this, it would actually really screw things up.
Mr Taylor: Of course, they are set up to deal with an Iraqi Government that was meant to co-operate with them. Now we have a different government in Iraq, effectively it is the coalition, and it is a forensic and archaeological search, if I might use that term rather loosely, and it is a very different situation.

They are not faced with a regime that is determined to hide things but with a very different challenge in trying to uncover the truth about these weapons programmes which depends on the coalition forces being able to offer security to people coming in and people will only talk if they feel secure. UNMOVIC and the IAEA just cannot do that kind of thing at this point. Maybe at some time later, there may be a role for international organisations, particularly in long-term monitoring.

Q319 Chairman: Robin Cook, when we asked him yesterday, left us with the key question: why is UNMOVIC not going back? That is the most important matter. What answer would you give to him?
Mr Taylor: I would say that UNMOVIC is not structured to carry out this new mission, this fundamentally new mission, with a coalition in charge, with having to use all their intelligence resources and their interrogations of people coming in, offering security to them. They are about to deploy 1,200 and I think it could be up to 1,500 people, ten times the size of UNMOVIC, so it has to be led by the coalition and, with all the security implications, I think it makes it very difficult to include UNMOVIC as it is presently structured with the kind of people they have at the moment, they probably need some different kinds of people to do the missions.

Q320 Andrew Mackinlay: And the carrot/stick of immunity or immunity from prosecution, that is the carrot and stick, was at the disposal of UNMOVIC.
Mr Taylor: That is correct. So, I do not think it is practical at the moment.

Q321 Andrew Mackinlay: You mentioned VX and I know I should understand the gravity of it but you did flag that up. He was developing VX in the past. Do we know that he definitely did abandon that? Can you explain to a layman the gravity of VX as it were because you said that this was the highest . . .
Mr Taylor: It is a persistent nerve agent and, if it is properly produced, it is the most lethal nerve agent. It is delivered in liquid form, so it is persistent depending on the weather. In summer, it does not last as long, whereas Tabun and Sarin disperses very rapidly and it is much more concentrated. You need a smaller amount to achieve the same effect. In terms of the production of VX, of course Iraq denied they were producing it but UNSCOM was of the opinion that they did produce weaponised VX and eventually UNMOVIC in their deliberations, and Dr Blix came to the same conclusion, believed they had done that. The Iraqis did have technical problems with the stability of the agent, and as far as I can tell, but of course we do not know what went on after 1998, there were some views that they did overcome the stability problems, others that they did not. I think they had a storage problem. I do not think the quantities were that large. Again, they had the capability, they had the people with experience,

this was the kind of programme that they would restart given the opportunity when the pressure was off.

Sir John Stanley: I have just got one remaining question on the 45 minutes and then I would like to turn to uranium, if I may. On the 45 minutes, and this, I fear, will upset Mr Pope's radiant day, if I refer to the *Today* programme—

Mr Pope: That will always upset my radiant day.

Q322 Sir John Stanley: On the *Today* programme of 29 May, Mr Humphreys asked the Armed Forces Minister, Mr Ingram, this question: "Why was Tony Blair in a position back last year, last September, to say that these weapons could be activated within 45 minutes?", to which Mr Ingram replied: "Well, that was said on the basis of a security source information, single sourced, it was not corroborated". The Armed Forces Minister, by virtue of that reply, suggested that the 45 minutes claim might not be very well substantiated because it was based on a single source and that was how he sought to deflect it. I would just like to ask you, from your extensive intelligence background, would you regard it as being certainly less than satisfactory to have a major point like this single sourced and, therefore, without corroboration?

Mr Taylor: My background is more as a user of intelligence as policy for military operations. I am more of a user. I find it hard to comment without knowing the quality of the report and who delivered it. In the past there has been information that certainly I have knowledge of which has come from a single source which has proved to be correct. You cannot always find that corroborating evidence. Of course, as a user of intelligence one would always ask for that and try to get it. I really cannot comment on the specifics of this case without knowing where it came from. Usually, as a user of intelligence you do not know, it just gets delivered to your desk or through your communications, you do not actually know the source, so you have to rely on the intelligence service giving you an idea that it is good quality, medium quality or whatever.

Q323 Sir John Stanley: Can I just now turn to uranium supplies. The Prime Minister in his speech to the House on 24 September last year, column four, said: "We know that Saddam has been trying to buy significant quantities of uranium from Africa, although we do not know whether he has been successful". As we know, President Bush paid the British Prime Minister a great compliment by specifically referring to this in his State of the Union address on 28 January of this year when President Bush said: "The British Government has learned that Saddam Hussein recently sought significant quantities of uranium from Africa". Subsequently, of course, we know that Dr Mohamed El-Baradei, Head of the International Atomic Energy Agency, said that the claim about a uranium deal in Niger was based on forged documents. Can I just ask you, in your experience in Iraq, given the fact that there were undoubtedly people, possibly those inside Iraq but certainly people outside Iraq, who were very,

very keen that military intervention should take place in order that the Saddam Hussein regime should be removed, did you come across any other examples of forged intelligence being deliberately put in the way of the intelligence services, the British and the American intelligence services, in order to serve particular political objectives?

Mr Taylor: I am not aware of anything of that kind.

Q324 Sir John Stanley: You are not, right. Have you got any comments about the issue of whether or not Saddam Hussein was trying to acquire uranium from Africa?

Mr Taylor: I am not aware of any specific information indicating that was the case. I know what you have read out but that is all I know, I am afraid I cannot add to that.

Q325 Chairman: What other sources could the relevant fissile material be obtained from?

Mr Taylor: There is a wide range of countries. It is well known that the former Soviet Union states, that is Russia itself and the other now independent states, are areas of concern and that is why a lot of effort has been put in by the United States, through its Co-operative Threat Reduction programme, and by the European Union and Japan helping with the International Science and Technology Centres to try to do something about trying to stem the possible flow of radioactive material from that area. That is where the biggest single source of material lies, in Russia. A lot of effort has been made to try and limit that. One could go to a number of countries around the world where there might be sources. Relevant to this particular case, I do not have any specific information.

Q326 Andrew Mackinlay: So I fully understand it, your evidence earlier was that your anxiety is all the components over a decade could have been procured and/or created and probably attention not drawn to them and they could be dispersed for relatively swift assembly.

Mr Taylor: Yes.

Q327 Andrew Mackinlay: Then you only need the final ingredient, the material itself, and in the marketplace around the world, alas, that would be available. It only has to be available once anyway, does it not?

Mr Taylor: Yes.

Q328 Andrew Mackinlay: A relatively small amount for one device.

Mr Taylor: I would not pretend that it would be easy to get that kind of weapons grade material, it is difficult, but the apparatus that Iraq had and the amount of money in the hands of the regime certainly made it something that those responsible for security would have to worry about. What I cannot offer you is any specific evidence of that, or where it might be obtained.

Q329 Andrew Mackinlay: The thrust of the former Foreign Secretary's evidence yesterday was that containment was working. I do not want to put words into your mouth, but it seems to me the thrust of what you are saying is that you would question that, would you not, because containment would not give the security or satisfaction to you or I to know that this guy had not got the capacity once the pressure was off

Mr Taylor: We certainly could not be 100% sure it was working. Given the catastrophic possibilities of getting that wrong, I think you have to err on the side of caution. It is very important to do that in this particular case.

Chairman: Two final questions, if I may. The first one is on concealment. You said you were disappointed but not surprised that we have found nothing as yet. On the one side, clearly there have been many months in which Saddam Hussein has had the opportunity to conceal, and some who argue the possibility of trains taking the material elsewhere in Iraq or outside the country, some talk about many hundreds of miles of underground tunnels, learning techniques from the Yugoslavs and so on, that is agreed, but surely—I think Sir John made this point—with those in custody, no longer can there be the cement of loyalty to the regime, there must be many inducements offered—I think Clare Short said the farm in Texas or whatever. Would you not be surprised if one of the people in custody were not prepared to point out where this stuff is?

Q330 Andrew Mackinlay: Not publicly.

Mr Taylor: I suppose unless you have been in the same room with them it is hard to imagine, but I am not surprised they have not done that.

Q331 Andrew Mackinlay: If you arrested Geoff Hoon today or whoever, he or she would not necessarily be able to know all that is in their jurisdiction. It seems to me at the government level, whether it is a dictatorship or democracy, by the nature of things it is down, is it not?

Mr Taylor: May I just make a point?

Q332 Andrew Mackinlay: I was not trying to be flippant, I meant it as a genuine question. These guys would not necessarily know the exact details, locations, etc, etc.

Mr Taylor: If I could make two comments. One, the situation is nowhere near secure yet, the whereabouts of Saddam Hussein is not known. The nature of the regime was absolutely extraordinary and the threat that the regime internally and certain elements still exercise over people is extraordinary. This is one of the difficulties. Also, Sir, you are absolutely right, very few people have an overview of everything. Even the scientists at the senior level would certainly not know where the weapons were. They would know about research and development, they would know about possibly some production, they would know names of certain people, but the Special Security Organisation which had the responsibility and some elements of the Special Republican Guard were the people that really knew.

These were the hardest core part of the regime and that is really where I think those coalition members doing the investigation need to get to. The Iraq Survey Group really has not begun its work yet.

Q333 Chairman: This is the final point and I am not asking you not to be an analyst, but a psychiatrist. Here we have after November 8 of last year a resolution giving Saddam Hussein a final opportunity, with serious consequences if he did not co-operate. If he had destroyed those weapons of mass destruction, and he had an army building up on his doorstep, he had all these pressures on him, we know or at least we have heard that they are meticulous bookkeepers, so can you give any sort of explanation as to why under those circumstances he still prevaricated and still did not come clean?

Mr Taylor: I would not have expected him to come clean if it was to match earlier behaviour, but what I would have expected, which surprised me, was that he did not decide to deliver up something new, something substantively new, not to give up the whole programme. That might have been enough and would have made things very difficult.

Q334 Chairman: When Dr Blix was forced into a corner on this, I think, on the *Today* programme, he was trying to explain Saddam's failure by the possibility that pride was one explanation which he sought to give and the other was the prestige of the regime which would be damaged in the region. How plausible do you think that Blix explanation was?

Mr Taylor: That is a very hard one to answer. I think they are obviously factors you had to think about, but my personal view is that this was about regime survival and making strategic mistakes. As I said earlier, I believe this was Saddam Hussein's third strategic mistake in the brinkmanship that he played. For him, the weapons of mass destruction were of a very high order of importance and given the divisions in the Security Council, which were obvious at that stage, he felt he could play this game for much longer, but it still surprised me that he just did not deliver up something more, though I do not think he could be expected to deliver up all of his weapons at once in that way.

Q335 Chairman: Mr Taylor, there is the final question: are there any matters which you think we have failed to cover now or any points you would like to leave with the Committee?

Mr Taylor: Well, I suppose I am repeating something I have already said, but I think it is important that the Committee thinks about what was on offer as an alternative, and I am sure you are doing this, so forgive me for perhaps pointing out the obvious. Given that the Government was faced with having to go ahead with military action, whereas the alternative was that one could only see more inspections, I think if you were to do a rigorous risk analysis, a really rigorous one, looking ahead two years, and there is always a challenge about this term about 'imminent threat', but we are in a kind of new environment with weapons of mass destruction, particularly nuclear weapons, and if you look at other weapons programmes, like India, Pakistan, I am not saying they are anything like Iraq, do not misunderstand me, but rolling back those programmes is extraordinarily difficult, so in that sense it is imminent that something had to be done about Iraq's weapons programmes. Inspectors were only there because there were large numbers of troops in the region. There would have been no inspectors in Iraq in 2002 and 2003 had it not been for very large numbers of troops. I think the regime was gambling that they would not be able to keep them there for a long period and eventually they might survive to live another day and continue on and revive their programmes. I think I would ask the Committee that they do a risk assessment that takes account of these things.

Q336 Chairman: On that risk assessment, looking at the key dossier of September 24 of last year, from your background, do you see anything which struck you as being exaggerated?

Mr Taylor: Excluding the detailed intelligence assessments, and the 45 minutes is one and so on, I find it hard to make a judgment on that, but the main thrust of the dossier seemed to me to be the best course, the best recommendation that the Government could make to Parliament and to the public about the state of Iraq's weapons of mass destruction programmes, and not forgetting of course the other issues associated with the UN Security Resolution in Iraq, so I think the main substance of the dossier was, in essence, a good judgment based on the evidence available.

Q337 Chairman: Thank you. You have been extraordinarily helpful to the Committee members.
Mr Taylor: Thank you.

Wednesday 18 June 2003

Members present:

Donald Anderson, in the Chair

Mr David Chidgey	Mr John Maples
Mr Fabian Hamilton	Mr Greg Pope
Andrew Mackinlay	Sir John Stanley

Witness: **Dame Pauline Neville Jones,** examined.

Q338 Chairman: Dame Pauline, may I welcome you, again, on behalf of the Committee. I apologise for the delay. You probably heard that the Committee were meeting President Musharraf in another part of the building. We are delighted you are with us, particularly because of your own experience in the diplomatic service and again as having chaired the Joint Intelligence Committee from 1993 to 1994 and being political director and Deputy Under Secretary of State at the FCO from 1994 to 1996 you can help us particularly on process and areas of that sort. In their Annual Report for the year 2002–03 our colleagues in the Intelligence and Security Committee stated: "Ministers confirmed that they were given the JIC papers which their private offices believed they needed to see, and that officials in the departments drew papers to their Ministers' attention and reflected their Ministers' views at JIC meetings. The Ministers also said that they themselves sometime requested sight of specific papers". It went on to say: "The JIC Chairman, in his review of performance 2001–02, noted need to produce starker papers, which could then aid Ministerial decision-making". From your experience of the Joint Intelligence Committee is it reactive or proactive? Who effectively decides the work programme of the Committee?
Dame Pauline Neville Jones: The work programme of the Committee is a rolling work programme. It is something which is, I would say, largely in the hands of the professionals. I say "largely" because at the end of the day all civil servants work for ministers. This is not done in a vacuum. Clearly two things are taken into account, one is what are the strategic priorities of the Government: there both the policies and objectives of the Ministry of Defence and the Foreign Office are absolutely key to the priorities which the JIC ought to reflect. Secondly, obviously it takes into account in its own tasking the shared intelligence relationship with our other main partner, the United States, and there is no point in duplication. What you have then is strategic priorities to reflect in the work you do, then decisions that are taken on how the work is then tasked within the British machine to supply information to and assessment of intelligence which is important to the attainment of those priorities. That is a process in which a lot of people are involved. This is a process that involves the intelligence service themselves, in my day the intelligence co-ordinator. The exact pattern and who holds this job has varied slightly from time to time, but whoever it is it is a key figure.

Q339 Chairman: From your experience would ministers have a direct input into those priorities?
Dame Pauline Neville Jones: I would have said that the relationship between the Chairman of the Joint Intelligence Committee and the Prime Minister was central. I was also at the same time the Deputy Under-Secretary in charge of Defence and Overseas Secretariat so I saw a good deal of my Prime Minister wearing both those hats. You would know, and I do not think you would need to ask, what the preoccupations were and where the emphasis on the work needed to be put. There would be a formal process in which the work programme would be approved. In my day the Cabinet Secretary was the most senior official who would ultimately take responsibility for what those underneath his charge were doing. Certainly my Cabinet secretary certainly did take an interest in the tasking—that was Robin Butler.

Q340 Chairman: Who prepares the assessment?
Dame Pauline Neville Jones: Let us go on to that?

Q341 Chairman: Who prepares the assessment and who has the input at the initial stage and then at the later drafting?
Dame Pauline Neville Jones: You can see what I am trying to paint for you. There is a structure which works within a framework of agreed priorities and an agreed work programme. The work programme that derived from that tasking is something which the Joint Intelligence Committee as a committee has a primary role over. It will decide on the basis of what it knows about the Government's priorities the work it has done in formulating its programme and what at any given moment it ought to be looking at, and there is a rolling programme. A typical meeting of the Joint Intelligence Committee, which meets once a week, certainly in my day, would be composed of probably two kinds of papers, most of them would relate to items of direct topical interest which were alive in foreign policy terms. There might also be however alongside that a longer term piece of work which the intelligence services had been engaged on, which was designed to give you a broader view of some of the longer term trends in a given field, which informs the general scene. When the Joint Intelligence Committee takes a paper and is preparing to put an assessment up to ministers it will already have a draft in front of it. That draft which have come from the assessment staff. The assessment staff are drawn from various departments in Whitehall,

those departments which have a particular expertise and interest in foreign affairs. It is a mixture of the departments and the agency people themselves. They do the initial drafting. They are the people in that sense who receive, I would hesitate to call it raw material but more basic material from the agencies. Nothing comes out of the agencies, as I understand it, and this is something that the agencies need to be asked, nothing comes of the agency that has not been assessed. They do not put up raw material, blind without themselves having taken a view on how reliable this is, what its provenance is and whether it is something that ought to see the light of day or not. The assessment process is one where taking the evidence that you from covert sources you would then say, "what does this mean?", against the background of what we already know, what we can further know from overt sources and what our common sense tells us about what this situation looks like. You are at all times in the assessment process testing the material that comes from covert sources against what you know from overt sources and against your judgment. Your judgment is obviously informed by your understanding of the situation and knowledge. There is rigorous analysis. The people who are engaged in this game are some of the best that Whitehall can offer. Talent is put there because everyone understands, I think, if you put stupid people in there you will get stupid papers. It is something where I think the quality of the analysis and the quality of the debate is actually high and it does credit to those involved. The same thing takes place at the Joint Intelligence Committee itself. If there is a bias in the system the bias is towards care, which means you are cautious, which means, if anything, you are conservative. You do not venture to put something in and to make what you know will be regarded as an important judgment or indicator unless you have a reasonable degree of confidence, that that is something that is on solid ground. Having said that, it is always a matter of judgment.

Q342 Chairman: Clare Short told the Committee yesterday that as Secretary of State for International Development she had to ask for JIC assessments. Is that unusual? How does material get to ministers?
Dame Pauline Neville Jones: In my day the product of the Joint Intelligence Committee which was put in book form was sent to all members of the Cabinet. That was a regular thing. The Cabinet machinery sent it to the department. It would go the private office. I cannot tell you what the private office would have done with it. The piece that you read out to me is obviously capable of being construed in at least two ways, one is that they thought they should see all of it, they saw all of it, or they only thought they should see some of it because they did not think they were in a ministry that was particularly interested in this kind of thing, or ministers had higher priorities so they only saw selected items. That is something that I cannot know. It was certainly supplied to them.

Q343 Chairman: How are ministers comments conveyed back? Are ministers comments actually asked for?
Dame Pauline Neville Jones: Ministers comments are not asked for. From time to time ministers, particularly if they are responsible in those portfolios, are obviously more likely to take an interest in and ask for further work. It is perfectly the legitimate for a minister to say, "this is very interesting, can you give me some more on this?", either because they find it very relevant or odd or "how do you reconcile this with this?" That is something that clearly the Committee would want to respond to. What do ministers do with all this knowledge? I do not know whether it operates now, and that is something that you would need to ask somebody whose experience in Government is more recent than mine. But in my day the Cabinet Committee system was very important and the OPD of the day was an absolutely vital piece of the machinery which took the proposition, the particular issue or crisis or set of issues that really needed close ministerial attention among the ministers who were actually in OPD—that tends to be foreign affairs, defence and treasury ministers and these days I am sure overseas development. The Prime Minister chairs that meeting, it is a formal meeting, it is fully minuted. A lot of the information supplied by the JIC is therefore part of the background material against which the members of that committee would then be considering the policy issues. In a sense that is how it affects the decision-taking of government.

Q344 Mr Chidgey: Dame Pauline, just on that point, I think I have the right parallel here, in her evidence to us Clare Short said that Cabinet Committee, who I think are defence and foreign policy, had not met for as long as she can remember. I bounce that back off you about the importance of the Cabinet Committee?
Dame Pauline Neville Jones: I can only say that this Government appears to operate differently.

Q345 Mr Chidgey: Thank you. Yes, we have noticed that. In the context of the JIC reports and who sees them, in your day did special advisers of the FCO or in Number Ten see the JIC reports?
Dame Pauline Neville Jones: I do not know the answer to that question, I cannot absolutely say. In my day it was the case that special advisers on the whole did not sit in private offices. The relationship between a minister and a special adviser I think is between the two of them, and they do operate differently. There was no single, set pattern in my day. As a general proposition it would be true to say that the special adviser would be in a different office and not in the private office, which in my day would have been exclusively civil service staffed.

Q346 Mr Chidgey: It is quite likely then. You probably cannot answer my next question, I wanted to know whether in your day did you ever have comments from special advisers on JIC reports other than through their ministers?

Dame Pauline Neville Jones: No. Frankly I would not expect special advisers to see this. This is usually top secret, code word stuff. It is actually meant for people who are effectively privy councillors. I think that one could expect this material to be closely guarded in a private office. It should not be stuff that is flung round.

Q347 Mr Chidgey: Again in your day was the JIC obliged to take account of ministers comments? In practice to what extent were those comments, if received, acted upon?

Dame Pauline Neville Jones: Put it this way, JIC would have regarded itself as professional advisers to the government, supplying them to the best of its ability an assessment of the situation as they saw it. If a minister said, "I would very much like to know more about that particular area", or "this would seem to me to mean the following, is that right?" That is the sort of question which would be quite within the purview of the Committee to answer. I think if the minister was to say something rather different, which is, "I do not know why you have not brought this out more", which gets into the questioning the validity of the assessment I think that would raise more problems because at the end of the day people have to stand behind the assessments they have made. You cannot just brush these questions off, I would expect them to examine that and on the whole if they have done their work properly they will stand behind what they have already assessed. I am not saying any work is perfect but what I am saying is that those judgments, certainly in my day, and I do not suppose there is any reason to be different now, were arrived at after very careful consideration. There was a lot of beating of the material and people going over it very carefully.

Q348 Mr Chidgey: Was there any formal set procedure for resolving any disagreements that could arise in this process between ministers and JIC?

Dame Pauline Neville Jones: I did not experience it so I cannot answer what we would have done if a minister had come along and said, "I think what you are producing is absolute rubbish". It just did not happen. The resolution of disagreement inside the committee was going on until we agreed. Usually the case was if you did not agree then on the whole, if I can put it this way, you were inclined to go for the more conservative of the interpretations. As I said to you earlier on the Committee's default position was, it was conservative.

Q349 Mr Chidgey: Did Number Ten play any particular role in the process? Today we have the special advisers at Number Ten.

Dame Pauline Neville Jones: I do not ever remember anybody from Number Ten in the sense that I think you are using it, ever intervening in the assessments or the Committee's procedures, no.

Q350 Mr Chidgey: It is really a question of whether the JIC assessments are essentially neutral, you have more or less said where there was any doubt they would tend to be conservative would it have been the norm for a JIC assessment to propose a particular line, whether it be with a "small c" or not?

Dame Pauline Neville Jones: No, I do not think so. It is not JIC's role to propose policy. One thing I ought to say, because what I have described to you in a sense is the peace time method. In the run up to a crisis clearly the machine goes into a higher gear and committees called CIGs meet, they are committees of specialists and drawn from the ministries, who do short-term stuff. If you have a developing crisis you might have an assessment every single day to see where that takes the new material. There you have a much more rolling and running flow of information and that will shoot up the system quite fast. At the end of the day the Joint Intelligence Committee, particularly the Chairman, is responsible for the integrity of that flow of information.

Q351 Mr Chidgey: Assuming you are not in the highly critical situation where you are reviewing on a daily basis and it is a steady process of assessment would it be the norm for the assessment of a particular piece of information or intelligence to give several explanations as to why that might have been uncovered, whatever it might be, it could have a military significance, it could have a civilian significance, it could have any number of degrees of significance which the assessors would have to evaluate. I am sure that must happen quite often. Would it be the case that in the assessment there would be possibly several scenarios given to explain what was happening, several options, the best or worst case?

Dame Pauline Neville Jones: There are several ways that you can assess material. The way that it was done in my day was when a single assessment came up we did not offer alternative explanations of life, nor do we do something else, which is have what I would describe as competitive assessment. Here I think we do differ from the Americans. We on the whole had a machine which built up the picture on the basis of each stage itself being satisfied, you could say the consensus method. The consensus method has its own penalties and shortcomings but that is the way we do it.

Q352 Mr Chidgey: Occasionally you would have contradictory information, would you not, as part of the process?

Dame Pauline Neville Jones: Yes. Then you have to decide. What I am saying is you do not put up it is either this or this, you do take a position on it, you do decide which of those two things is the one that you follow. What would then happen is that the assessment itself will explain that the indicators are not clear. It will not just say, this is what we think without explaining the basis of that judgment. It will indicate if in fact the situation is fairly fluid and the signals are mixed. That sort of thing would be made absolutely clear so nobody would be in any doubt about the clarity of the background against which these judgments are being made. That is a very, very important part of being absolutely straight with people about the firmness with which they can base themselves on what the assessment material is telling them. What we do not do, is to say, there is this or this and you can choose. What we do not do is have different bodies competing with each other for interpretation or indeed intellectual competition inside the JIC. Those are differences between our method and the Americans.

Q353 Mr Chidgey: The final question from me, again using your own experience, do you feel the FCO has adequate resources within itself to question the assumptions and the analysis of the JIC reports?
Dame Pauline Neville Jones: That is a really hard question to answer. The FCO is part of the system. What you would be saying if you put that question is, is a part of the system equipped to challenge it? The answer is yes. With it I think is a different issue. I would say as a general proposition that what comes out of the central machinery of government in this area, and I think it applies to the authority of a lot of the co-ordinating committee of the Cabinet in my day, is not something that the departments on the whole are going to argue with. It is the nature of government, you go into the centre, you come to a position through an OPD paper, whether it is at official or ministerial level, in a sense that is the line. The JLC is an information process, it is not a policy-making process. It is very much underpinning that policy-making process and if you are both part of the information machine that feeds the policy process and you are part of the policy process you have to stand a very long way back indeed to say, "after all that", and I have been part of it, "I do not actually think we are making sense".

Q354 Sir John Stanley: First of all, for the record, in response to one of the points you made in reply to Mr Chidgey, you did not say this but it might possibly be implied and misconstrued from the answer you gave on the issue of the security of JIC assessments. Although you are, of course, entirely right in saying some of those assessments are top secret, code word perhaps you would confirm that JIC material has quite a wide range of security classifications—
Dame Pauline Neville Jones: Absolutely.

Q355 Sir John Stanley:—and quite lot of material on a rather wider circulation has a much lower security classification.
Dame Pauline Neville Jones: Absolutely correct.

Q356 Sir John Stanley: The point I would like to put to you is this, it arises out of a press report but given the fact that 10 Downing Street, according to this press report, has confirmed the existence of this document I want to raise it. It appeared in the

Independent on 9 June. That is a report to the effect that JIC produced a six page report in March of last hear in which it allegedly reached the conclusion that there was no evidence that Saddam posed a significantly greater threat than in 1991. The press report states that this particular JIC report was suppressed. I do not invite you to comment on whether it was suppressed or not because I have no means of knowing and secondly that is an issue the Committee will be able to pursue at other hearings. What I would like to ask you from your wealth of experience inside the JIC, are you aware of any occasions when you had those responsibilities inside JIC in which a particular JIC assessment was suppressed?
Dame Pauline Neville Jones: No. It all depends on what suppression means. Does it mean that JIC produced something and that was found to be inconvenient by somebody else and therefore was quietly put away or does it mean that the Committee itself took a view on a report it had produced and decided that it was not going to put it forward for whatever reason. I do not know what that means. I am trying to think whether in my day we ever decided not to put a piece of work up that we had previously been working on. I cannot confirm to you that we never took a decision not to put something up. Were we to have taken that decision I think it would have been on the grounds that there was something wrong with the work inside it, that is to say we were not satisfied with the conclusions we had reached. This does happen, it happens with some of the longer-term work, by the time it has risen to the top it was already out of date, life had overtaken it. Sometimes you do say people are not going to be interested in this, it is wasting their time and sometimes you do not deal with it or you go away and take the bit that is of real interest, that is the bit that people really need to understand. I cannot confirm that we did not ever say, let us not put this piece of paper up. I can certainly confirm to the best of my recollection so far as I know no piece of paper, no assessment that we put up was subsequently put in a locker and not circulated I did not experience that.
Sir John Stanley: That last question was the one I hoped you would answer and thank you for answering it very clearly.

Q357 Mr Maples: Dame Pauline, I wonder if I can go back to something that Mr Chidgey raised, which was that Clare Short told us that OPD, or whatever it is called in this Government, Defence and Overseas Policy Committee, never meets. I do not think she meant literally never, but it never discussed Iraq and when the Cabinet discussed Iraq it would do so in a very casual sense of asking the Foreign Secretary to say what happened in New York last week. It was never discussed with papers which set out options. Although there were security briefings from time to time there was never a discussion in OPD or the Cabinet with papers of this issue. In your experience is that unusual? Does that surprise you?

Dame Pauline Neville Jones: Not entirely, no. I think it is the case, and of course as Deputy Secretary of the Cabinet I used to go to Cabinet to take the minute on foreign affairs, I did have sight of Cabinet discussion on foreign affairs. It is certainly the case that I think increasingly, if I might put it this way, Cabinet is a meeting into which business is reported but very often not actually discussed in any detail.

Q358 Mr Maples: If it was not discussed in Cabinet would you expect it to be discussed in the Cabinet Committee?
Dame Pauline Neville Jones: Absolutely. That is the distinction. The Cabinet Committee is the place for discussion. The conclusion of Cabinet Committees are reported, if the system is working properly, into the full Cabinet by the Prime Minister with the lead minister usually coming in behind giving further explanation. It is not usually regarded as a forum for debate but it is certainly an opportunity for discussion or for questions. Something which is often legitimate for Government to talk about is: "How do we handle this in public? What are the implications for the Parliamentary aspects of it?" It would be regarded as an item of business, but a deep, in-depth discussion of the policy issues would be elsewhere.

Q359 Mr Maples: You would have expected such a discussion with papers to have taken place in a Cabinet Committee? That is the surprise.
Dame Pauline Neville Jones: Absolutely. I would expect that.

Q360 Mr Maples: What Clare Short went on to tell us was that the way that these decisions were made were that OPD did not meet and decisions made, in her words, "by a small, close entourage of the Prime Minister". She named the people in it, only one of whom is a career civil servant, David Manning, and the other three were the Director of Government Information Service, Alistair Campbell, a Baroness Sally Morgan and Jonathan Powell. She said what was happening was that these people were making the decisions and this was being reported directly to Cabinet. If it is normal to do this through OPD then that would be unusual. Do you see any weaknesses in doing it like this and not having a full discussion with papers in OPD or if this is a perfectly sensible way to approach major foreign policy issues.
Dame Pauline Neville Jones: It is certainly different from the regime that I knew. I think, I will put it this way, there is the danger that you do not get properly recorded decisions and properly analysed decisions. That is a problem. There is also the question of accountability.

Q361 Mr Maples: I want to move on to the process by which the weapons of mass destruction publication was produced by the Government. We have asked the Foreign Secretary and he has given us some answers and I wonder whether this is usual. The questions you have been asked about

how JIC normally operates and its output is not usually published and the unusual thing about this is we have a series of intelligence assessments being presumably edited and then published. What the Foreign Secretary told us was the drafting was coordinated by the Cabinet Office assessment staff working with representatives of the Department. The final draft was approved by JIC, who said there were separate drafts, it has a long history of a rolling draft process. Then he said that ministers and special advisers offered comments during the drafting process in the normal way. At the end of the day the whole thing was approved by the JIC. Clearly during this process there is political input into this, because it is going to be published, one understands that, were you ever involved in a case where the output was eventually published in one form or another? Does this strike you as a normal and sensible way of doing it or would it have remained in the hands of the Foreign Secretary and JIC?
Dame Pauline Neville Jones: So far as I know this is an unprecedented situation, it certainly did not happen in my time. I was trying to think whether it had any happened previously. We are obviously faced by a new situation and I think it is always right to recall why all this happened. I recall being one of the people, despite my background in the JIC, who said I think we have to have more evidence. Here I speak as a voter. It is not easy to ask people to send their sons and husbands into military conflict on the basis of evidence which the Government says, "it is too secret for me to be able tell you what I know". I think that is a very difficult proposition in a democracy. It did seem to me at the time that a way did have to be found for material of which the Government disposed, which had clearly convinced it there was a real threat, could be made available so that the rest of us could understand what that was and why we were being told this was so serious. The issue at the time certainly seemed to me how you did that in a manner compatible with the protection of the sources, which is crucial. That is so far as I know an unprecedented thing to try and do. The process that is being described is one which also in a sense has no precedent. What emerges from that account obviously is that the process went through the professionals, it went to ministers and possibly the political staff, it then came back to the JIC eventually for their—the word I have heard used is "endorsement". One of the issues is how like the version put up was the final version that went out? What we do hear from the professionals is that they were prepared to stand behind that assessment. I can only conclude from what that they believed that assessment as it finally emerged had integrity. How much it varied, how much there was further argument after the first assessment, how much the judgments that emerged thereafter were different from the ones that went in I simply do not know. This is why I think the work of these committees is very valuable because there are lessons to be learned from this. Let us hope we do not have to do this again but we are now in a world where we

have a hidden enemy and the chances of us having to take military action again on the basis primarily of information coming from covert sources certainly cannot be discounted. Therefore I do think it is very important that the lessons are learned about how to get information out in future. Clearly there is a very fine line between showing the evidence and making a case. It is where showing the evidence turns into making the case where the system has to take a very, very strong grip on itself.

Q362 Mr Maples: Can I just take you into another aspect of the same thing, in the Executive Summary of the Report it says: "as a result of the intelligence", which they obviously got from JIC, "we judged that Iraq has continued to produce chemical and biological agents". In 1998 in the run up to the Desert Fox operation the then Foreign Secretary, Robin Cook, Minister of State published a paper which went with a covering letter to all Members the Parliament and it was considerably more cautious it said: "Saddam has almost certainly retained some BW production equipment, stocks of agents and weapons. Some CW agents and munitions remain hidden. The Iraq chemical industry mustard gas almost immediately. Iraq could procure the necessary machinery and material", that was about his nuclear programme. That seems to be it still has the capability, it has a few stocks, it has the capability, it has the ingredient there, the precursors but here we are four years later saying: "Iraq has continued to produce chemical and biological weapons". Does that seem to you to be a substantive shift of opinion to go from one to the other? Does it seem much less cautious or not?
Dame Pauline Neville Jones: I would say those two statements can only be justified by their being a change in the situation. They are different. They are different. Clearly one is saying there is a capability there. The straightforward reading of that statement is it is not particularly active capability but certainly people in that situation could clearly start making it again. Do not forget once you have that capability, particularly biological, it is quite quick to get it going again. Chemical is one that does not degrade, although biological degrades quite quickly chemical does not degrade so quickly. There are some real puzzles about what happened to stocks which the UN inspectors believe were left behind. I think there are some puzzles that are not yet properly uncovered. If you put those two statements together one is a much more active statement than the other and does suggest that there is a different situation.

Q363 Mr Maples: If you had been the Chairman of the JIC on both occasions and these were put to you based on what you just said it would seem you could only feel you could justify both statements by saying there had been a change in intelligence in between the two, some new information?
Dame Pauline Neville Jones: Yes, I think that is exactly what I would have to conclude would justify the difference.

Q364 Mr Pope: Dame Pauline, just to go back to Mr Maple's line of questioning about the September dossier, I would be really interested to know what your view is as to whether or not on the one hand it could be argued that the publication of the dossier leads to a very real danger that the security services will end up being politicised, that drags them into a party-political area that they have never been in before, and probably do not want to be in. On the other hand if we have a situation where the intelligence that is being given to the Prime Minister is that Britain really needs to take military action to protect and defend our own interests and yet that military action does not command support for the wider public or critically on the floor of the House of Commons, and it is worth bearing in mind that even if a small number of Labour MPs voted against the Government on March 18 Tony Blair probably would not be Prime Minister now. In those circumstances do think it is justified to have done what they did?
Dame Pauline Neville Jones: I have already made it clear I think that the publication of evidence was justified, in fact I think necessary. I do not think that it right, as I said to you, that voters should be asked to send the army into battle on the basis of not knowing why. The issue is was the "why" correct. I think that is a justified process but you need to take certain precautions. This is where we need to learn lessons. I do not think that that process *per se* carries the danger of the politicisation of the intelligence services. It gives them a degree of exposure to public discussion and debate which I would not want to see happen often. I do not want to see our intelligence services get into the limelight and become political footballs or perform the roles, which does happen in the United States. If we start letting our intelligence services constantly into the limelight I do not see how you erect barriers of the kind that will prevent that happening. I am very comfortable with, and I do think it is much preferable that services of that kind are actually below the line of publicity, I think it safeguards their integrity. Therefore these situations should be exceptions. The business of them producing reports—here was this demand. It was right for the ministers to ask the professionals to put the dossier together, we would have liked it even less if they had done without the help of the professionals. My working assumption when I saw that dossier and read that dossier, which was greeted I seem to remember with considerable scepticism, and I remember going on television and defending it, for two reasons: I assumed that on the basis of my information and of its methods that what was there could be relied on. Secondly, I also assumed that it was a selection, I never expected everything that the Government knew and everything the intelligence services were able to bring up by way of assessed information would be shown to us. We would get an assessment which contained a fair representation of the underlying information but would not itself be the total weight and volume.

Q365 Chairman: Has anything you have learned since induced you to modify that view?

Dame Pauline Neville Jones: I am now probably in a situation where I would like to see my assumption tested, yes. I do not assume that it will come out any different but I think there are various issues here, one is clearly what happened to the information after it left the JIC. I also think, and I say this with all due respect to my successors in this craft, that it is so extraordinary not yet to have found any weapons of mass destruction that I do think the question has to be asked was—for reasons, which I am sure have nothing to do with the integrity of the people involved—was the intelligence after so many years when we have not had inspectors in there, and the sort of direct access we have had previously somehow off beam? It cannot be ruled out that over time our sources, which we certainly accepted—and I believe the Prime Minister when he said this "45 minutes" came from a trusted source, that is how it had been assessed. I do wonder whether one does not need to go back not only to the question of how the material was handled when it came to the compiling of evidence for public consumption but also how reliable the base was underneath. That is a more profound question. I think this an important one to satisfy oneself on and we need to know and intelligence services need to know if their information is not well based.

Q366 Mr Pope: This is precisely the area I wanted to investigate with you, were you satisfied when you were the Chairman of JIC about the quality of intelligence that we received about Iraq and how much of our intelligence is derived from the USA and therefore is there not a danger that if somebody makes a mistake with some of the raw data and that is passed on it just becomes treated as gospel. There is a danger there, is there not?

Dame Pauline Neville Jones: You have put it yourself, clearly there is a danger. When I was in the JIC it was the time of the imposition of the no-fly zones. From the flow of information we had coming on those issues we had good reason to have reasonable confidence in that information. If you asked me the question, was I at any stage uneasy about the quality of the information I cannot put my hand on heart and say, no. I do think, and I think this is probably for the Committee, it is an issue for people in the intelligence world and what they do to test the reliability of information over time, particularly in situations where your access is through sources on the ground whose ability to have up-to-date and close information is lessoning.

Q367 Mr Pope: Obviously there is a huge amount of intelligence shared between the United Kingdom and the US, what level of credibility and what level of independent checking is there of information that comes from the US? Is it taken as being absolutely right or is there a system of checking it? What level of credibility would you generally give information from an allied power?

Dame Pauline Neville Jones: The two system have always maintained their independent assessment. While I was there the rule was we assess independently and we assess information coming from the other side of Atlantic. So far as I know that was not breached. I think the system answer to your question is there is independent assessment. I think that is important to both sides. It is better for both sides to have each tested it and, of course, those assessments are compared. We do have knowledge of each other's assessment but they stand independently of each other. It is not the other side's lot that goes to your ministers, it is your assessment that goes to your ministers. It is a joint policy, that is the other thing one has to bear in mind, there is a real life background to all of this. The Iraq policy has been a joint UK/US policy for a very long time and one has to fit that whole scenario into that fact.

Q368 Mr Hamilton: On 24 September, as we have discussed, the first dossier on Iraq's weapons of mass destruction was published and it met with some cynicism and I saw you defend it on television, and you did a good job. What I wanted to ask was, how would you have expected that dossier to have been drawn up? What would the procedures have been when you were in charge of JIC?

Dame Pauline Neville Jones: I thought about that and I thought to myself I am extraordinarily glad that I did not have to do this. I think clearly the question that you would have had to ask yourself is what is the evidence of what kinds of threat? You would have to identify what it is that you are talking about by way of threat and I would have wanted to go back a long way. What I would not have wanted to do with something as important as this was take recent material and put it together in an essay for public presentation. This is where the pressures of time do become a very real factor in life. What I would have wanted to do was go back a bit. I am not sure I would have gone back as far as I suspect in doing a post-mortem it would probably now be right to do. I would have wanted to go back a bit to see the consistency of the evidence and whether we really had an audit trail of evidence that did not have breaks in it so that you did not somehow suddenly get a period when those previous judgments did not seem to be supported or where there were gaps in the picture, because that would have made me worry. I would have wanted to do a lot of work behind that dossier to be really satisfied what I was putting up and I could point to evidence behind it. I am painting an ideal world, I know, those people were under great pressure and whether they were able to do that I do not know. That is how you would want to do it. That would be one of the lessons that you would try to draw for any future occasions.

Q369 Mr Hamilton: Can I ask you if you had come to the conclusion as Chairman of JIC that somebody in the Government was trying to exaggerate elements of the intelligence information to support the case for war with Iraq what would you have done?

Dame Pauline Neville Jones: I would have done what the Civil Service Code prescribes, I would gone to see my line manager, who would have been the Cabinet Secretary, and I would have put my anxieties to him. That would have been the right thing to do. I would have expected on something as important as that for him to have reflected that to the Prime Minister. The relationship between somebody in that position and the Prime Minister is close enough that I think that any occupant of that position would feel able to go to the Prime Minister and say, "I am worried". There is a procedure and it is certainly in those circumstances one that should be used.

Q370 Mr Hamilton: Is there any sense in which it is a function of any of the agencies of Government, especially intelligence agencies, to support a policy of the Government? Has this ever happened?

Dame Pauline Neville Jones: No. I think it is the function of agencies the put advice to the Government that is honest and reliable and as timely as they can make it. It is not for the agencies to be part of the policy-making process.

Q371 Mr Hamilton: Can I finally refer to something that you said earlier, the fact that it is rather worrying that weapons of mass destruction have not yet been found in Iraq. Could there not be another explanation, most people are saying it is because they are not there. Surely there could be an explanation, I wonder if you accept this or not, that it is not the priority of the occupying forces at the moment to look for those weapons. It would be convenient when they are found but the priority is to get the country up and running again and therefore they are not really spending any time and energy on it. As we know Saddam's regime hide those weapons very carefully in order to make sure that the UMNOVIC inspectors were foxed at every turn.

Dame Pauline Neville Jones: I ought to be quite clear on this subject, I used the word "yet" I used it advisedly because I do not draw the conclusion because they have not been found they will not be found or do not exist. I am surprised they have not been found, I am surprised. What I cannot help feeling is if they had been more operational they would have found something by now. I do not exclude there are explanations of the kind that you put forward or others. I do not think you send your soldiers out to exercise in chemical suits if you are trying to pull a fast one. I do think there was a real belief and I do think that there was a real capability. I think the issue is, how active was it? How much of it was there, and what is the explanation for not having yet found any?

Q372 Mr Hamilton: Would you accept the fact that because those weapons of mass destruction have not been found yet increases the cynicism of the British public as to the causes of the war?

Dame Pauline Neville Jones: It does. That is why it is very important to establish what really went on. I want to say one other thing, none of this, in my view, should be taken as making one conclude that weapons of mass destruction are not a very serious threat. They are. When the Prime Minister lays emphasis on the seriousness of that threat one should not disagree with him, he is absolute right.

Q373 Chairman: You said that our soldiers would not have been sent out in chemical kits unless we believed in it. It is also true that there were chemical kit suits found belonging to the Iraqi forces?

Dame Pauline Neville Jones: Yes, absolutely. These are factors that give you pause and that is you why should not conclude we now know everything we need to know, I do not think we do.

Q374 Andrew Mackinlay: Listening to the most recent exchange it did occur to me perhaps even you might have fallen into the chasm of that of a number of my politician colleagues and perhaps even members of the press in making the assumption that weapons of mass destruction have not been found, it did occur to me there is a scenario I want to bounce off you that if evidence had been found as we speak or the survey group is finding it now whilst there is a compelling case and a democracy for the Prime Minister to rush to the House of Commons and say, "got it, here it is", it would not be the most prudent thing if you are trying to find the trail and find the lot, is it not?

Dame Pauline Neville Jones: That is a perfectly fair point. I rather interpret some of the things the Prime Minister said in the House the other day that he has evidence of evidence, if you see what I mean. That is why I hesitate to draw hard and fast conclusions that "now" does not mean there will not be.

Q375 Andrew Mackinlay: All will be revealed.

Dame Pauline Neville Jones: Having said all that I still think there are really important things we need to try to get to the bottom of.

Q376 Andrew Mackinlay: I almost admit to a degree of jealousy, you mentioned privy councillors and I always thought that was a bit old, a bit humbug. Nevertheless I am persuaded for the purposes of this afternoon there are privy council terms and I also recognise that me as a Member of Parliament is not privy council—I am apparently not good enough to share some of this documentation, I can even live with that—but then I hear these people called special advisers, I think I have a degree more legitimacy than they have, what I can make out it is a fact, you have some concern about this. What the minister decides to share with his special adviser, whether or not the special adviser follows him into a meeting room, your former colleagues cannot say, "who the heck is he?", or "is she seeing that?" It does seem to me there is a major point of not just principle here but security and also ultimately, this is not perhaps a concern for you, respect for Members of Parliament, we are trustworthy. What say you on that?

Dame Pauline Neville Jones: There are two related but separate things here, one is the decision-making process where there is formal accountability from civil servants through ministers. I think the other is security clearance. Who is part of the decision-making process and who has access are two different things. I would hope, I do not know, I would hope that special advisers who had access to this material had the appropriate clearances. I believe that somebody who was working as closely to the Prime Minister would have been vetted. I would think it surprising there would not have been a vetting process. My working assumption would be they were cleared.

Q377 Sir John Stanley: Dame Pauline, I want to carry on a bit further the very important conduct of government issues that have been raised so far in the course of this inquiry and carry a bit further the exchange to which my colleague John Maples referred to earlier. The exchange continued into the role of the Foreign Secretary, which is highly germane to this Committee. Just for convenience can I for the record and both to assist you just give you the transcript of a short exchange which took place on this point yesterday with Clare Short. "Mr Maples: And decisions were being taken by a very small group of people close to the Prime Minister, none of whom, apart from him, are elected? Clare Short: Yes. Mr Maples: So there were no ministers involved in that part of it? Clare Short: That is right. Chairman: Did you know about the role of the Foreign Secretary at this time? Clare Short: The Foreign Secretary would have a close relationship with the Prime Minister and the entourage, but I think the decisions were being made by the Prime Minister and the entourage and the Foreign Secretary was helpful. He went along with those decisions, but I think the decision-making was sucked out of the Foreign Office which I think is a great pity because there is enormous expertise about the Middle East in the Foreign Office and certainly the Foreign Office has the expertise to understand what is necessary to achieve the second Resolution. Chairman: You are saying that the Foreign Secretary was helpful. Are you suggesting that he was ancillary and the decision was elsewhere? Clare Short: I am suggesting that he was extremely loyal to the Prime Minister and his decisions." The key question I would like to ask you, Dame Pauline, from your time when you, of course, were serving in Foreign Office prior to the start of the last Gulf War, what is your view of the position of the Foreign Secretary of this country in circumstances where the Defence and Overseas Policy sub-committee of the Cabinet was not meeting and where, as is claimed hereby the former secretary of state for international affairs the key decision making is being taken by the Prime Minister and his immediate entourage at Number Ten?

Dame Pauline Neville Jones: That is a really difficult question. Clearly the theory answer is that the Foreign Secretary was part of OPD, and OPD decisions would decide the policy and it would then fall to the various departments to implement bits of that policy relevant to them. Therefore were the Foreign Office conducting diplomacy towards the Middle East it would be in the lead in getting the resolution through the UN. If you do not have a formal structure making those decisions you are then dependent on the relationship, as Clare Short indicated, between the Foreign Secretary and the Prime Minister, do they talk to each other on the 'phone? You are also dependent on communication between officials, which I imagine is what happened, officials like David Manning, whoever it may be, would make sure that the private secretary or the Foreign Secretary himself knew what had gone on so that he was well informed. There are two separate things, what is the input into the decision-making? It is not to be excluded after all there can input from the Foreign Office in a more informal way than through OPD, even in the system that is being described. The expertise in putting the UN resolution through is something that the Foreign Office does not need help on. Where the decision-makers at the centre would need help would be the Foreign Office's assessment and the chances of getting that resolution through and how to do it and therefore their decision-making should be influenced by that information and by that assessment. One of the questions would be how the Foreign Office's professional judgments on the sustainability of the policy would be pursued or how the targets that have been identified could be best reached, and so on. All of that would be an important part of the likely success of the policy, because the policy has to be the right policy and we also have to implement it in a way that gets you there. If you do not have a committee operating it certainly means the way in which that advice is put into the centre and the way in which the decision coming out of the centre is implemented is clearly, to put it mildly, less easy to track.

Q378 Sir John Stanley: Like you I am wholly familiar with the system which you described to the Committee and one has had a lot of experience of Cabinet sub-committee meetings, I would like to ask you whether or not you agree that in a system where these key policy decisions are effectively being carried out by the Prime Minister and his immediate entourage, as claimed by the former Secretary of State for International Development, in such a system where there is a great deal of dependence on what is happening verbally and a great deal of dependence on the personal relationship between the Foreign Secretary and the Prime Minister do you consider that that might be a form of decision taking that at least has a higher risk of going wrong than one through the structure of Cabinet sub-committee meetings, the presentation of paper and genuine discussion and debate on policy options between ministers?

Dame Pauline Neville Jones: I think the caveat has just been mentioned, I do not know this to be the case so I am operating on this hypothesis. It does not necessarily lead to a worse discussion, the discussion will depend on the quality of the people in the room, to be really brutal about it, so it does not mean that worse policy is made. It does mean that that policy is less imbedded in the government as a whole because a whole series of other participants are not there and therefore bounded by it. One. Two, I suppose it is, as I say, less easy to track. We do not know whether there were records made of these meetings, in that sense they would not be an official document. A written record is very helpful to people and the written record can go across the road as well. The third thing that you are pointing to is ultimate accountability. These are obviously issues for the functioning of Government. I do not think by itself it means there was worse policy there.

Q379 Mr Maples: I wanted to ask you a few things about the dodgy dossier, which was published in January 2003, the preamble to that dossier says: "This report draws upon a number of sources, including intelligence material", when the Prime Minister spoke to it on 3 February in the House of Commons he said: "We issued further intelligence over the weekend about the infrastructure of concealment". It seems clear it was based in part on intelligence material yet we are told by the Foreign Secretary the document was not cleared by the JIC. Would you like to comment on that? These are all on the record. These are facts.

Dame Pauline Neville Jones: This is supposition on my part, I imagine what happened is this was a document that was largely put together at Number Ten, if not wholly put together at Number Ten. Number Ten at this stage after all of the proceedings, and we are now late into a long process of information stream and policy formulation in this area, would itself have access to work already done by the intelligence community. I think a straightforward reading of what is being said is that elements of that material were incorporated in a piece of work which was largely composed of material from other sources. It is certainly true to say that it contains intelligence material. The Government has subsequently made it clear that was not the bulk of what was there, that came from an open source, quite an interesting open source, it was quite an interesting dossier. I think it is probably fair to say that one was led to understand that the source of that material was rather closer to Government than it turned out to be at the time.

Q380 Mr Maples: If one is going to use intelligence material it seemed that the Government has now agreed that it has got into some trouble with this dossier because it came off the internet. We have a rather interesting paper from Dr Glen Rangwala at Newham College, Cambridge[1], he said that it comes

from three sources off the internet, he tracked them, punctuation mistakes occur in both versions, he says pages six to sixteen are just a straight script. The Government seems to have acknowledge this has got them into difficulties and of course the lack of credibility that document contains reflected on the other ones and if had not been for that people would have been more inclined to take the Government's word on the other one. Do you think that any document which in future is published and draws on intelligence material should be run passed JIC to see what they think about it?

Dame Pauline Neville Jones: I would be reluctant to see JIC getting into the game of endorsing and acting as an imprimatur to information that the Government is putting out. I do think this kind of thing I hope will be an exception. I think it loses its value if it becomes run-of-the-mill and it has a series of other undesirable consequences . My answer to is you is no. What I do think is that if a mixed document is put out in the future, and one can see circumstances where that would be a perfectly sensible thing to do, it is made absolutely clear what comes from where. That seems to me to be the key thing, you have to own up about your sources.

Q381 Mr Maples: We asked the Foreign Secretary some questions about this and he said that the document was prepared or started off by a thing call the communications and information centre which reported to the Prime Minister's director of communications involved through a number of stages. No ministers were consulted in the preparation of the document, no FCO ministers or FCO special advisers were consulted on the document, which seems to bare out what you were saying. Number Ten officials, including special advisers, asked for some editorial changes. Interestingly, according to Dr Rangwala when this document was first put up on the internet the names of you authors were in the file as well but within half an hour they were taken off. He got the names of the authors and they turn out to be a Foreign Official called Paul Hamill, I do not know who he is but presumably he works for David Manning in Number Ten and three people, all of whom work for Alistair Campbell, one of whom is his secretary, another of whom is the news editor of the Number Ten website, and somebody called John Pratt, who is a junior official from the Prime Minister's strategic communications unit. Do you share my amazement that the second document in this chain, the first one is a very serious piece of work, whether it turns out to be right or not is a very serious piece of work based on intelligence through JIC, with input from ministers and will go through a long evolution that we then have the second instalment in this series put out by effectively the Downing Street communications unit with no input from the Foreign Office at all, the intelligence is not cleared with JIC and it is put into the public domain as though it is as serious a document as the first one. Do you think the Government is corrupting its own process?—

[1] Ninth Report from the Foreign Affairs Committee, Session 2002–03, *The Decision to go to War in Iraq*, HC 813-II, Ev 30.

Dame Pauline Neville Jones: It is a serious mistake. I agree with what you said that it discredits the earlier material, it is a mistake. I think you should not do cut and paste jobs.

Q382 Andrew Mackinlay: Can you throw some light on this, from your experience being in the Cabinet Office, a senior position, your relationship with the security intelligence community, is there an equivalent of lobby term whereby folk of your level, that echelon, or people who link up the security intelligence services do talk to journalists. Journalists have said to me, they might be bragging, "Funny, Mackinlay, you cannot talk to them, we talk to them all of the time", even allowing for a bit of exaggeration and then we have had this man who is going to appear before us, Gilligan, and also you people do meet. What were the ground rules? What was the convention? Does lobby system exist? Who is allowed or permitted to so talk?

Dame Pauline Neville Jones: As far as I know there are no ground rules. The head of the services would speak for his service. I think Eliza Manningham-Buller does, I think on the whole it is customary not to have a high profile in MI6. Basically and fundamentally these are not people who talk to the public and personally I do not think they should or to journalists. There clearly was turbulence inside the machine and some people have been talking, I do not know who, and I do not know if they are representative. Personally I do not draw any conclusions from that because I simply do not know. I would not draw general conclusions about attitudes inside the services on the basis of conversations that appear to have taken place between some journalists and some individuals. It is dangerous to draw that conclusion because you do not know what they represent, what their motive is and whether to put any weight on it. I think, I really do think there are ways of finding out through this process of getting to the bottom of it. I am not happy about that, I think it stirs the pot and it creates heat. I do not think it gives us light.

Q383 Andrew Mackinlay: As a general rule you do not think it happens.

Dame Pauline Neville Jones: I do not think it happens, this is a loyal and professional culture and very important it stays like that.

Q384 Chairman: Because the BBC intelligence correspondent presumably would have certain sources but in your time these would not have been officials with the lobby terms that Mr Mackinlay talks about.

Dame Pauline Neville Jones: We are a democracy and people do communicate. This is not the way this kind of information should be filtered out because it ends up with precisely what we now have, no real information which damages reputation and destroys trust. I do not think it is helpful. I do not think this represents anything very general.

Q385 Chairman: This Committee will have to make recommendations at the end of the inquiry, you drew the clear distinction between showing the evidence and making the case. What lessons should there be learned? What recommendations would you commend to this Committee?

Dame Pauline Neville Jones: I certainly would not say that this exercise of putting evidence in front of public in circumstances that were necessary should never be repeated, I would not draw that conclusion. What I would draw is that safeguards need to be put in place about how that is done, which includes the integrity of the system in which it is produced, I am not saying that it was not, I do not know, that is what you are trying to find out, so if this is work done by the intelligence community it would be clear that this is work done by the intelligence community and no one else. I think the second thing is, I go back to what I said earlier on, I think that if the intelligence community is going to be called upon to do this, and I think it is a tough thing for them to be asked to do they themselves need then to conduct the kind audit of their material to be absolutely confident that what they are saying is really very well based. This is not a point that relates to future exercise so much as in this instance. I do think that the information base about Iraq policy is both sufficiently controverted and there is sufficient doubt among those who are themselves professionals and take a close interest in government that I think one has to the take the audit trail back further into the material itself. That is I think what the other Committee will be doing. I think there are things which are peculiar to this situation which they need to do and then there are certain recommendations for any future occasions which perhaps the Committee will want to consider

Chairman: Dame Pauline, thank you very much.

Thursday 19 June 2003

Members present:

Donald Anderson, in the Chair

Mr David Chidgey   Mr Bill Olner
Mr Eric Illsley   Mr Greg Pope
Andrew Mackinlay   Sir John Stanley
Mr John Maples

Witnesses: **Mr Andrew Gilligan,** BBC Defence Correspondent, and **Mr Mark Damazer,** BBC Deputy Director of News, examined

Q386 Chairman: We continue today our inquiry into the Decision to go to War in Iraq and I welcome as our witness Mr Andrew Gilligan, the BBC Defence Correspondent. Mr Gilligan, you have asked that you be accompanied by Mr Mark Damazer, the BBC Deputy Director of News, in case any questions of editorial policy were to arise during the course of our inquiry. They may not do so and then obviously, Mr Gilligan, you are the main focus, because some might say that it is in on your report that much of the current controversy has arisen. I was just a little amused to note that of course you came from a stable mate of *The Daily Telegraph,* namely *The Sunday Telegraph,* and *The Daily Telegraph* stated on 6 June in respect of you: "In 1999, after five years at the paper"—that is *The Sunday Telegraph*—"Gilligan was poached by the *Today* programme's then editor, Rod Liddle, with a brief to cause trouble." Is that your understanding of your brief?
Mr Gilligan: Not entirely, no. I think my brief was to—

Q387 Chairman: Not entirely.
Mr Gilligan:—report—

Q388 Chairman: Partly or . . .?
Mr Gilligan: Well, I think the role of any reporter is slightly to probe and ask questions a bit.
Andrew Mackinlay: Sometimes that causes trouble.

Q389 Chairman: Is there something equivalent to the lobby in respect of the agencies? Is there a way, if not of deep throats, of scheduled regular briefing of newspaper and media correspondents?
Mr Gilligan: There is nothing as formal as the lobby. There are no regular meetings. There are, to my knowledge, few, if any, group meetings. The agencies do have officers whose particular job is to talk to journalists, and certain journalists have those people's contact numbers.

Q390 Chairman: These are journalists who are specifically designated for matters with the press.
Mr Gilligan: Yes. They are serving intelligence officers as well, actually.

Q391 Andrew Mackinlay: They are intelligence officers?

Mr Gilligan: Yes.

Q392 Chairman: They are intelligence officers. What sort of matters are given to the press by those individuals?
Mr Gilligan: It is difficult to discuss that actually.

Q393 Chairman: Are they defensive briefs when matters are raised, criticisms are made of the agencies? Are they in-house matters, such as the cost of the headquarters? Or are they matters like 45 minutes in JIC reports?
Mr Gilligan: In some ways, albeit in a more low key way, they act a little like press officers. Sometimes you can go to them with questions on an issue which has come up, like, for instance, the cost of computerisation or of buildings, and they operate a kind of response service like that to certain journalists. The 45-minute question did not in fact come from, if you like, the designated press spokespeople of any of the agencies.

Q394 Chairman: Would you expect it to come in these irregular briefings?
Mr Gilligan: I do think that when other journalists with intelligence contacts, presumably including these same people, these designated spokespeople, went to their contacts for corroboration of my story, then it was corroborated and we saw similar reports appear in several newspapers in the days after my story.

Q395 Chairman: When you talk about these contacts, these are serving members of the agencies who talk to the press informally.
Mr Gilligan: Yes, some of them talk to us informally, some of them talk to us with official sanction.

Q396 Chairman: But those who talk to you informally are doing so against their professional code and their terms of engagement.
Mr Gilligan: No, I think that the agencies, like any other organ of state and, indeed, any other organisation, sometimes have a need to maintain relations with the press. That is really all they are doing. A lot of the time it is authorised so they do not fall out with their professional code.

Q397 Chairman: You are saying that the agencies give licence to some individuals to talk informally to the press outside these regular meetings.

Mr Gilligan: That is correct, yes.

Q398 Chairman: Are you saying that the meeting you had with that individual, unnamed, was so authorised?
Mr Gilligan: I would not like to characterise how the meeting . . . whether the meeting fell within that authorisation or not. I can tell you a bit about my source. I mean, essentially, the particular meeting from which this story arose came about at my initiative. I have known this man for some time. He is quite closely connected with the question of Iraq's weapons of mass destruction and I asked for a meeting with him. We have met several times before, we have spoken on the phone from time to time. We have both been rather busy over the last six or seven months for obvious reasons, so this was the first free moment I had to ask for a meeting with him.

Q399 Chairman: So this individual meets you on a fairly regular basis.
Mr Gilligan: I would not say that regularly, no. I mean, it was something like a year since I had last seen him face-to-face when we met, but I have spoken on the phone in the interim.

Q400 Chairman: Clearly what he told you on this occasion by definition was not authorised.
Mr Gilligan: It is simply impossible for me to know whether it was authorised or not. That was not a question I discussed with him.

Q401 Chairman: But the Chairman of the JIC has repudiated what you have said.
Mr Gilligan: The Chairman of the JIC. The Joint Intelligence Committee is not the same thing as the intelligence agencies. I mean, they are represented on it, of course, but the Chairman of the JIC is a civil servant not an intelligence official.

Q402 Chairman: Well, all the civil servants.
Mr Gilligan: He is a civil servant in the non-secret part of the civil service as distinct from the secret part.

Q403 Andrew Mackinlay: Not so secret, though.
Mr Gilligan: Not so secret, no.

Q404 Chairman: Are you aware of anyone within the services who has complained at what has been published?
Mr Gilligan: Complained to us?

Q405 Chairman: No, complained through any formal channels to their line management.
Mr Gilligan: No, but I would not expect to be. I am aware of disquiet within the intelligence community over the Government's handling of intelligence material related to Iraq, not just on this particular issue of the September 24 dossier but on others.

Q406 Chairman: From this one individual?
Mr Gilligan: No, from several individuals. From a total of four different people.

Q407 Chairman: Four different people. And these are individuals who see you from time to time.
Mr Gilligan: That is right.

Q408 Chairman: Contrary to their terms of engagement.
Mr Gilligan: Not all.

Q409 Chairman: So some are allowed by the agencies to speak to you about their concerns about government.
Mr Gilligan: When we meet, we never quite discuss things like whether the meeting is contrary to their terms of engagement or not.

Q410 Chairman: But you know it is, surely, if they tell—
Mr Gilligan: Assumptions are made.

Q411 Chairman: If they tell a press officer that there has been undue interference, this must surely be contrary to any terms of engagement of a public servant.
Mr Gilligan: In my experience, the intelligence agencies do sometimes do things in a calculated fashion, and maybe some of these contacts were such contacts.

Q412 Chairman: In a calculated fashion.
Mr Gilligan: They are not unlike any other part of government, in that they sometimes want to get a message across.

Q413 Andrew Mackinlay: That is rather making Reid's point, is it not? Rogue elements.
Mr Gilligan: No, I do not think it does.

Q414 Andrew Mackinlay: I am sorry to interrupt but it just occurred to me. Reid came into my mind then.
Mr Gilligan: I do not think you should assume that these are necessarily rogue elements. I do not think that has entered into it.

Q415 Chairman: You think they are doing a public service, do you, by leaking their views to you?
Mr Gilligan: I have no opinion on what they do to me; I am just grateful for the information as a journalist.

Q416 Chairman: Grateful for the information.
Mr Gilligan: Yes.

Q417 Mr Maples: I wonder if we can just establish not who these people are, because I am sure you are not going to tell us that, but where they are coming from. I have been looking at the transcripts of your appearances on the *Today* programme, May 29 and June 4. On May 29 you started by saying, "I have spoken to a British official who was involved in the preparation of the dossier," and you say, "I want to stress that this official and others I have spoken to . . ." Then on June 4 you say that, while the quotes came from a single source, ". . . four people over the last six months in or connected with the intelligence community have expressed concern . . ." etcetera. What I want to try to establish is: are these people all, or are some of them, actually currently working in one of the intelligence agencies? Or, when you say a British official, do you mean someone in No 10 or on the JIC assessments staff? Could you try to establish where these sources are coming from?

Mr Gilligan: First, I want to make the distinction between the specific source for this specific story, which is a single source, and the three other people who have spoken to me generally of their concern about Downing Street's use of intelligence material over the last six months. They spoke to me about the allegations made of links between Saddam and al-Qaeda. They spoke to me about the so-called "dodgy dossier", the one produced in February, and they spoke to me about this dossier. The story that began the fuss came from the single source. I really cannot characterise the source any further than I already have done because it would compromise him.

Q418 Mr Maples: No further than that he is a British official. I think it makes a huge difference to us to know how much credibility to attach to this. If it was somebody who actually works in SIS or on the JIC assessments staff involved in this, that is clearly one thing, but if it is somebody telling you some office gossip, that a few people up there are unhappy about this, that is clearly different to us. When you say "a British official"—and this is presumably the person who gave you the 45-minute story—can you not tell us which part of the Government that person works in?

Mr Gilligan: I have described him as one of the senior officials in charge of drawing up the dossier and I can tell you that he is a source of longstanding, well-known to me, closely connected with the question of Iraq's weapons of mass destruction, easily sufficiently senior and credible to be worth reporting

Mr Maples: Could you say that again: an official of longstanding involved in . . .?

Q419 Chairman: A source of longstanding.

Mr Gilligan: A source of longstanding and I described him in the broadcast as one of the senior officials in charge of drawing up the dossier. That is how I would leave it.

Q420 Mr Pope: Is this the September dossier?

Mr Gilligan: Yes.

Mr Maples: One of the senior officials in charge of drawing up the dossier.

Q421 Chairman: And a source of longstanding.

Mr Gilligan: A source of mine of longstanding.

Q422 Mr Maples: But the other three people spoke to you, you said, about the al-Qaeda links and the "dodgy dossier" but they also spoke to you about these weapons of mass destruction dossier.

Mr Gilligan: No. As I say, the other three people spoke generally to me about their concerns about the use of intelligence material on Iraq by the Government. One spoke to me about the link being

made by the Prime Minister between Saddam Hussein and al-Qaeda. He was kind enough to leak me a document on that link which said that there was not one or there had not been one lately. Another spoke to me—

Q423 Andrew Mackinlay: He actually gave you the document?

Mr Gilligan: He let me read it. Another spoke to me about the "dodgy dossier", the February dossier, produced by the Government, plagiarised or partly plagiarised from internet sources and to tell me of his concern about that. The third person was the source of this story and the fourth person was somebody who has come forward since the story was broadcast to talk about similar issues.

Q424 Chairman: Just one point on that. The individual who left you the document, what was the classification for that document?

Mr Gilligan: He did not leave it with me, he sat with me while I read it.

Q425 Chairman: And what was the classification of the document you saw?

Mr Gilligan: Top secret.

Q426 Chairman: So the source in the intelligence agencies is showing a top secret document to you, a journalist. Did you ever consider what his motive might be?

Mr Gilligan: It was fairly unusual—indeed, it is unprecedented, for me anyway—to have received a document of that classification. Clearly consideration of motive is part of any story. My understanding of this person's motive was concern at claims, which this person felt were exaggerated, being made by the Government about links between Saddam Hussein's regime and al-Qaeda for which there was little evidence.

Q427 Chairman: And it could equally well have been someone who did not get the promotion he wanted or who had some sort of grudge.

Mr Gilligan: I think it is unlikely. Of course it is always a possibility, but I think the possibility I have given is more likely.

Q428 Mr Maples: Two of the other three, so to speak, talked to you about the al-Qaeda links and the "dodgy dossier" but not about the weapons of mass destruction dossier.

Mr Gilligan: That is right.

Q429 Mr Maples: The source of your story, I think you used the phrase or they used the phrase, "to make it sexier" about the weapons of mass destruction dossier, came from, you said, a senior official who was one of the people in charge of drawing up the dossier, but you feel you cannot tell us whether he was a civil servant or worked for the intelligence agency.

Mr Gilligan: I cannot add anything to what I have already done because it would compromise him, I am afraid.

Q430 Mr Maples: Okay. I mean, I understand that but obviously I want to press you as far as I can, but that person is a currently serving official.
Mr Gilligan: Yes.

Q431 Mr Maples: Then you say somebody else, the fourth person of these four, is somebody who subsequently came forward.
Mr Gilligan: That is right.

Q432 Mr Maples: To you and has talked to you again about . . . I do not want to put words into your mouth. Which of these issues did they discuss with you.
Mr Gilligan: He in fact drew my attention to a story in *The Independent* and said that the story was "spot on"—those were his words. The story was about the demand by the intelligence services at MI6 that any future dossiers, any future government dossiers, should make it clearer which of the words were derived from intelligence material and which were the product of, you know, re-writing or sub-editing inside government.

Q433 Mr Maples: Was that in relation to the weapons of mass destruction dossier or the "dodgy dossier"?
Mr Gilligan: No, you will remember there were a couple of stories that appeared a week after the 45-minute story broke about the intelligence agencies laying down ultimata to the Government. The source, my source, the fourth source, drew my attention to these stories and said they were correct.

Q434 Mr Maples: By the time that happened, the "dodgy dossier" had been published as well, had it not?
Mr Gilligan: Absolutely. Yes.

Q435 Mr Maples: What I was trying to get at is: was that unhappiness that was expressed to you by the fourth source in relation to the September dossier or the February one or both?
Mr Gilligan: Both.

Q436 Mr Maples: In relation to these two dossiers, what has emerged so far to us is that it is very difficult for us to evaluate the truth or otherwise of the weapons of mass destruction dossier because it is obviously based on intelligence material and we have not seen the originals. The "dodgy dossier", on the other hand, we now know most of it came off the internet, even including punctuation mistakes, and seems to have been generated almost entirely inside No 10. I wonder if you can help us about how that came about. We are told in a formal answer by the Foreign Secretary that no minister—whether that includes the Prime Minister or not is not clear—saw or played any part in the preparation of the "dodgy dossier" or saw it before it was published—and I could come across that exact quote. When it originally appeared on the internet, apparently it had four names attached to it, three of whom worked for Alastair Campbell and one who is a

Foreign Office official who works in No 10. Can you tell us any more about how that document was produced and by whom it was produced?
Mr Gilligan: It was issued under the Prime Minister's imprimatur. He said on the 3 February in the Commons, "We issued further intelligence over the weekend about the infrastructure of concealment. It is obviously difficult when we publish intelligence reports but I hope the people have some sense of the integrity of our security services. They are not publishing this or giving us this information and making it up; it is the intelligence that they are receiving and we are passing it on to people." That is what the Prime Minister said in the Commons about the "dodgy dossier" the week after it was issued.

Q437 Mr Maples: We asked the Foreign Secretary some formal written questions, one of which was: "On what dates were drafts put to ministers?"—this is on the "dodgy dossier". His answer was: "No ministers were consulted in the preparation of the document." Can you corroborate that.
Mr Gilligan: I have no information either to confirm or deny that. My involvement in the "dodgy dossier" story was being told, along with others, by Glen Rangwala, who was a politics lecturer at Newnham College, Cambridge, that he had spotted similarities between the dossier and this PhD thesis. Unfortunately *Channel 4 News* beat me to the story. Then, after it, to be told of the intelligence services' concern about the way this dossier had been produced. The claim made to me was that the services had not been consulted. I do not know about ministers.

Q438 Mr Maples: It is the same person, Dr Rangwala, who says that when the document first appeared on the Downing Street website it had four names attached to it as people who were the authors. The identity of the authors is as follows: Paul Hamill, a Foreign Office official; John Pratt, a junior official from the Prime Minister's strategic communications unit; Alison Blackshaw, Alastair Campbell's PA; and Murtaza Khan, the News Editor of the No 10 Downing Street website. Do you know whether that is correct or not?
Mr Gilligan: No, I do not. I did not see the dossier on the internet before those names were removed.

Q439 Mr Maples: Was your impression from the people who talked to you that this was almost a freelance operation by Alastair Campbell's people?
Mr Gilligan: There was concern expressed to me about the role of No 10 in the production of the dossier and there was concern expressed to me that the final draft had not been shown to the intelligence agencies or to the JIC. That was essentially the limit of what my source told me about the "dodgy dossier". They are not garrulous people, these people.

Q440 Mr Maples: We know now that quite a large part of this came from this PhD thesis but Dr Rangwala points out a couple of changes. Whereas the author of that thesis had said that a particular Iraqi security organisation had as part of its role to "monitor foreign embassies in Iraq", that became in the "dodgy dossier", "spying on foreign embassies in Iraq." On the same page Ibrahim al-Marashi had written that Mukhabarat had a role in "aiding opposition groups in hostile regimes" but in the dodgy dossier that becomes "supporting terrorist organisations in hostile regimes". Are these the sort of things that people were drawing to your attention as their complaints, their concerns?

Mr Gilligan: Yes, among others. That was also one of the things which led me to invest credibility in my source for the 45-minute claim, because it seemed to fit with the pattern of behaviour by Downing Street that had already been established in the "dodgy dossier".

Q441 Mr Maples: So the person who gave you the 45-minute story had been involved in these other things and talked to you about those.

Mr Gilligan: No. I invested great credibility in my 45-minute source for a number of reasons but one of the reasons was that Downing Street had already been shown to have embellished, to have "sexed up", if you like, material.

Q442 Mr Maples: Over the "dodgy dossier".
Mr Gilligan: In the "dodgy dossier".
Mr Maples: Thank you very much.

Q443 Chairman: You have said that the agencies were laying down ultimata to the Government. What did you mean by that?
Mr Gilligan: Would you remind me of the context again.

Q444 Chairman: It was a phrase which I wrote down as you were saying it, that the agencies were "laying down ultimata".
Mr Gilligan: Yes, that is right. That was something that was reported, as I mentioned, by the *Independent* and the *Guardian* in the week after the 45-minute story broke. I cannot remember the exact words of the reporting but it was in terms of: the agencies have asked the Government to make a clearer distinction between material derived from intelligence and material derived from Downing Street or government with regard to your sub-editing in any future dossiers. That was it.

Q445 Chairman: That is in respect of the January dossier rather than—
Mr Gilligan: It is in respect of all future dossiers.

Q446 Chairman: But it arose after the publication of the January dossier.
Mr Gilligan: The story emerged after the row over the September dossier, the 45-minute story. You will remember that the Prime Minister answered some of the criticisms expressed at the time by promising, I think, a third dossier, and I think this was in relation to that promised future dossier.

Q447 Chairman: Was this suggested to you as well by your sources?
Mr Gilligan: As I say, an intelligence source contacted me and said, "The story in *The Independent* is spot on."

Q448 Chairman: Right. Were these ultimata meant to be in written form?
Mr Gilligan: I do not know.

Q449 Sir John Stanley: Mr Gilligan, could I go back to what you describe as the 45-minute story and to what you said on the *Today* programme on May 29. We are referring here not to the so-called "dodgy dossier" but to the assessment of September 2002. You said this: "I have spoken to a British official who was involved in the preparation of the dossier and he told me that until the week before it was published the draft dossier produced by the intelligence services adds little to what was already publicly known." He said, "It was transformed the week before it was published to make it sexier. The classic example was the statement that WMD were ready for use in 45 minutes. That information was not in the original draft. It was included in the dossier against their wishes because it wasn't reliable." Mr Gilligan, we have specifically put that issue to the Foreign Secretary and we have received the Foreign Secretary's response. The question we put to the Foreign Secretary was this: "Was the wording of the 45-minutes claim given on page 19 of the document *Iraq's Weapons of Mass Destruction* exactly the same as it was in the intelligence assessments applied to the Government? If not, was it accompanied in the intelligence assessment by qualifications not included in the public document?" The answer we have received from the Foreign Secretary is this: "The same report was reflected in almost identical terms in the JIC's classified work. There were no further caveats used." The question I put to you is this: against what has been clearly stated now by the Foreign Secretary, are you saying that the Foreign Secretary is lying to this Committee? Or will you now acknowledge that your source was incorrect in saying that the 45-minutes claim was not based on a genuine assessment of the JIC, fully approved through the JIC process?
Mr Gilligan: I note the words "almost identical" in the Foreign Secretary's response. I would simply say that it is not my business to say whether the Foreign Secretary is lying or not. All I would say is that I invested strong credibility in my source, who is a person of impeccable standing on this issue, and whose complaints have been reflected in something like seven or eight newspapers and other media outlets, including other BBC outlets, since my original story and his complaints have also been reflected by named, on the record, former intelligence officers from Australia, from the United States, and also, to some extent, by other Members of the House.

Q450 Sir John Stanley: You are making, Mr Gilligan, a very, very serious allegation against the integrity of the JIC. The entire—

Mr Gilligan: I am not making any allegations.

Q451 Sir John Stanley: I am sorry, may I just go on. You are making, in my view, a very serious allegation against the integrity of the JIC, all the members of the JIC and, most particularly, against the integrity of the JIC Chairman. You are saying that the JIC Committee and its Chairman, under pressure, which you are implying is political pressure from, presumably, 10 Downing Street, "sexed up" their original assessment at the last moment and introduced material which according to your source was unreliable. You are effectively saying that the whole of the JIC system, including the Chairman, connived in a political embellishing of a JIC assessment for political purposes. I cannot think of anything more damaging by way of an accusation to make against the professional integrity of those who serve on the JIC.
Mr Gilligan: I would repeat, as I have said throughout, I am not making any allegations. My source made the allegations. We were reporting the charge of my source, who is a figure sufficiently senior and credible to be worth reporting.

Q452 Sir John Stanley: I accept you are reporting your source, but you and your organisation chose to give this matter publicity in this country and around the world to the effect that the JIC system, including the Chairman, was effectively a party to including unreliable intelligence assessments material in a document going round under the JIC's imprimatur. I put it to you that is a very, very serious allegation to give the sort of publicity which you have given.
Mr Gilligan: As I have said, the JIC did not enter into my report. I reported the source as saying there was unhappiness within the intelligence services, disquiet within the intelligence services. The JIC and the intelligence services are not the same thing. The JIC is a Committee of the Cabinet Office and the intelligence services are represented on it, but they are not the same thing.

Q453 Sir John Stanley: Can you say whether your source suggested that any other pieces of the text that were put in at the last minute, presumably following its approval to the JIC system, other than the references to 45 minutes, were inserted at the last minute before the document was made public?
Mr Gilligan: He was quite cutting about the claim that uranium had been sought from Africa.

Q454 Sir John Stanley: Are you suggesting, apart from being quite cutting, that that was a last minute addition as well?
Mr Gilligan: I am not sure. No, I do not think I am because I do not think he quite said that. He was of the opinion, however, that that was unreliable information.

Q455 Sir John Stanley: In terms of your evidence to this Committee, the only piece of evidence which you are specifying was allegedly made at the last minute subject to a political requirement to "sex it up", to use your phrase, is the 45 minute claim?

Mr Gilligan: That was the only specific piece of evidence that my source discussed, yes.
Sir John Stanley: Thank you.

Q456 Mr Olner: So the rest of the evidence that was in the dossier was reliable? By implication, if your source said he was not happy about the 45 minute thing then he was happy with the rest of it.
Mr Gilligan: The fact that my source was not specifically unhappy with other elements of the dossier does not necessarily mean that other elements of the dossier were reliable. Of course it might mean that, but I do not think anything can be drawn from it either way.

Q457 Mr Olner: Who from Number Ten asked for the dossier to be changed?
Mr Gilligan: I asked this. The source's claim was that the dossier had been transformed in the week before it was published and I asked, "So how did this transformation happen?", and the answer was a single word, which was "Campbell". I asked, "What do you mean, Campbell made it up?", and he answered, "No. It was real information"—this is the 45 minute claim—"but it was included in the dossier against our wishes because it was not reliable. It was a single source and it was not reliable." He also said that Downing Street officials, he did not name anybody else, had asked repeatedly if there was anything else that could be included on seeing the original draft of the dossier which was considered dull.

Q458 Mr Olner: After having heard evidence on this Committee yesterday, I think the 45 minute thing is irrelevant in a way because if an armament is found it can be used immediately.
Mr Gilligan: Irrelevant to what?
Chairman: Let us get onto the subject.

Q459 Mr Olner: I thought it was a relevant question to ask.
Mr Gilligan: The 45 minute claim is important because it went to the heart of the Government's case that there was an immediate threat from Saddam, it was not a mere detail and it was one of the most headline grabbing parts of the dossier. The 45 minute claim was far from irrelevant to the case the Government made against Iraq.

Q460 Mr Olner: Not the Government's headlines, your headlines, the media headlines.
Mr Gilligan: Yes, but it was clearly designed to elicit those sort of headlines. As I say, the implication of 45 minutes was that Iraq was an imminent threat.

Q461 Mr Pope: Just on this issue of the 45 minutes, I want to be very clear about what your source is alleging. Is your source alleging that the 45 minutes did not exist in the assessment that was inserted by Alistair Campbell?
Mr Gilligan: I will quote his words again. He said, "It was real information. It was the information of a single source." My source did not believe it was reliable. He believed that that single source had

made a mistake, that he had confused the deployment time for a conventional missile with the deployment time for a CBW missile. He did not believe that any missiles had been armed with CBW that would therefore be able to be fireable at 45 minutes' notice. He believed that claim was unreliable.

Q462 Mr Pope: But that view was not necessarily shared by the Joint Intelligence Committee because they did have, albeit a single source, evidence of the 45 minutes.
Mr Gilligan: That is right, absolutely, yes.

Q463 Mr Pope: Has your source made any wider allegations or expressed concerns about Number Ten in general and Alistair Campbell in particular interfering in intelligence assessments?
Mr Gilligan: He expressed concern that Downing Street had spoiled its case against Iraq by exaggeration. I want to make it clear that my source, in common with all the intelligence sources I have spoken to, does believe that Iraq had a weapons of mass destruction programme. His view, however, was that it was not the imminent threat described by the Government.

Q464 Mr Chidgey: On that very point, we took evidence earlier in the week from Clare Short. Would you have a view on whether or not your source might have been briefing her on this issue?
Mr Gilligan: No.

Q465 Mr Chidgey: It seems rather similar.
Mr Gilligan: It is a hypothetical. I just cannot comment on it.

Q466 Mr Chidgey: Can I draw you back to the uranium from Africa claim. You said that your source's response to that issue was "crisp". Did you have any more detailed discussion with your source? Could you share with us how your source analysed that particular issue and came to the conclusion that his remark should be crisp?
Mr Gilligan: My source believed that the documents on which the allegation rested were forged.

Q467 Mr Chidgey: That has been proven subsequently, has it?
Mr Gilligan: Yes. I believe it was a letter from a minister who had left the Niger government several years previously.

Q468 Mr Chidgey: Forgery at what point? There have been some stories in the press that the forgery occurred in the UK.
Mr Gilligan: These people do not tell you everything, they are pretty taciturn.

Q469 Mr Chidgey: It is clearly a very serious matter if somebody in our intelligence services should have forged the documents that we are referring to.
Mr Gilligan: That has never been an allegation that we have made or that my source made.

Q470 Mr Chidgey: Have you any indication from your source of where the forgery is thought to have occurred?
Mr Gilligan: No, I am afraid not.

Q471 Mr Chidgey: Have you any information at all about how it came to be included in the dossier, who picked it up and who presented that information, forged or otherwise?
Mr Gilligan: I did not go into it in sufficient detail.

Q472 Mr Chidgey: It seems surprising that this suddenly dropped out of the air at a stage when there was not enough time to check it.
Mr Gilligan: I did not go into that in sufficient detail with my source to answer that question, perhaps I should have.

Q473 Mr Chidgey: Do you think it is possible that it could have been a deliberate plant by somebody?
Mr Gilligan: I have got no evidence on which to base that view.

Q474 Mr Chidgey: It is possible, is it not?
Mr Gilligan: I have got no view.

Q475 Mr Chidgey: Moving on, we have had a lot of very interesting information from you regarding the intelligence community's view of what was passed in the presentation of the February dossier. Is it your view that they are generally angry about that, is that what has motivated them to speak out now about the September dossier, even though it happens to be through sources such as yourself?
Mr Gilligan: Specifically about the February dossier?

Q476 Mr Chidgey: Yes.
Mr Gilligan: Anger is too strong a word; I would use the world disquiet.

Q477 Mr Chidgey: Do you think it might stem not so much from the way the information has been used in this particular case but from the fact that it is a sort of change in the relationship between the intelligence services and the Government of the day and the Prime Minister attempting to bring the Parliament, the Government and the country behind him on this view that we would have to prosecute this war? He has possibly gone further than any previous Prime Minister in setting out the case using intelligence information. Is this maybe the sort of cultural change to the issue that is causing the disquiet amongst the intelligence services in that they are not happy that the previous information that was only shared with key members of Government is now being perhaps slightly sanitised and shared with the nation?
Mr Gilligan: I think that is in part fair. We do need to stress, this story took on the life it did because everyone else's intelligence sources were saying the same things as mine were saying to me. One of the complaints made by some of our intelligence sources, not just mine but across the press, was that

intelligence services are secret and they do not like necessarily having their work exposed to the public gaze. Yes, I think that is partly fair.

Q478 Mr Illsley: What you are saying is that your source told you that the 45 minute claim was unreliable, is it not?
Mr Gilligan: Yes.

Q479 Mr Illsley: So the claim existed in intelligence terms but it had not been corroborated and was unreliable.
Mr Gilligan: Yes.

Q480 Mr Illsley: Basically whichever committee holds an inquiry into this will have access to the raw data and they will find that claim somewhere in the intelligence reports from the intelligence community.
Mr Gilligan: It was not a claim that was in any way made up or fabricated by Downing Street. Another one of the reasons why this story took on the life that it did was that Downing Street denied a number of things which had never been alleged. They denied, among other things, that material had been fabricated. Nobody ever alleged that material had been fabricated.

Q481 Sir John Stanley: Mr Gilligan, in one of the responses you gave to Mr Pope your answer raised serious doubts in my mind as to the technical knowledge of your source in this area. You said in answer to Mr Pope's question that your source based his view about the unreliability of the 45 minutes claim on the assumption that the Iraqi WMD would be delivered by ballistic missiles. I want to point out to you that the Government did not make its 45 minutes statement on that delivery assumption. If you refer to page 19 of the September assessment, the crucial sentence reads, "Intelligence indicates that the Iraqi military are able to deploy chemical or biological weapons within 45 minutes of an order to do so." Encompassed within weapons is not just merely ballistic missiles, it would be artillery pieces and so on. I must make the point to you that if your source, as you have given in evidence so far to the Committee, was basing his assumption of unreliability on ballistic missile delivery, that is not the proposition which the Government put out in the September document.
Mr Gilligan: It was not ballistic missiles, just missiles. It is not my source who raised the issue of missiles, it was the intelligence source which was the original source for the 45 minute claim as delivered to the intelligence community. That original source of the 45 minute claim, he was the one that spoke about missiles. Maybe he was technically incompetent. Maybe that is a further reason for doubting his accuracy.

Q482 Sir John Stanley: So you are now acknowledging that your source was technically not competent?

Mr Gilligan: No, not my source, the source of the original allegation to the intelligence services, the Iraqi source. I think he has been described as a senior general or something like that in the *Financial Times*. He was the one that spoke about missile delivery, not the source of my story.

Q483 Sir John Stanley: Can I say to you that anybody who knows about this business would say that anybody who couched an assumption about a 45 minute threat based on a missile delivery system, whether it be a cruise missile delivery system or ballistic missile delivery system, would be certainly exposing themselves to suggestions of unreliability. The key issue here is the Government did not make any such claim. The Government put it in terms of weapons and very relevant here, of course, are artillery systems, where you have potentially a very much shorter timescale that is available to you between an order to deploy and making those available, for example, to artillery troops.
Mr Gilligan: The use by the original intelligence source to the Government of the missile as a means of delivery was one of the very reasons why my source did not believe it.

Q484 Sir John Stanley: Yes, but I think the point I am putting to you is that if the assessment had been made that Iraq had a WMD capability particularly in the chemical weapons area, given the known availability of large numbers of artillery troops, a lot of which were deployed forward, providing the Government were satisfied that the chemical weapon capability in particular was there then the 45 minute assumption would not be unreasonable from a technical standpoint anyway.
Mr Gilligan: The claim related to missiles. That was the claim of the original Iraqi intelligence source. We have the Defence Minister's word for it that he was the sole source for that claim. So it must relate to missiles whether it was said in the dossier or not.
Sir John Stanley: Thank you, Mr Gilligan.

Q485 Mr Chidgey: In earlier evidence, Mr Gilligan, the question of 45 minutes has been more or less considered to be irrelevant in terms of modern battlefield operations using chemical weapons. It is to be expected that within 45 minutes of being properly deployed chemical weapons would be in use from giving the order, so the 45 minutes question is taken as read. I just wonder whether there is a distinction here between the favoured method of delivering them, a battlefield scenario, which would be a mortar rocket launcher, and somebody talking about missiles. Has anyone checked what the translation is from Iraqi into English and the distinction between a missile and a rocket?
Mr Gilligan: In order to deploy any form of weapon at 45 minutes' notice it would need to have been relatively openly held, it could only have been relatively lightly concealed. One of the other things which led me to invest credibility in my source was the fact that no such discoveries had been made. As I say, the contention of the intelligence community's original source was about missiles, but if any

weapons of any description, be it rockets, missiles, crop spraying aircraft, aerosols, had been held at 45 minutes' notice the likelihood is that they would have been found by now.

Mr Chidgey: That is a secondary issue.

Q486 Mr Pope: I am just not convinced by the argument which says the absence of any evidence is proof that there is an absence of weapons of mass destruction. The claims that your source has made are of the gravest nature, which is that the Government in the September dossier exaggerated the threat posed by Iraq so as to persuade Parliament to vote for war. There were two specific claims, one about the 45 minutes and one about uranium from Africa. We have already heard that it is possible to deploy certainly chemical weapons at 45 minutes' notice. It may not be possible to deploy a missile, but it is not impossible to deploy a whole range of chemical weapons at 45 minutes' notice. The claim about uranium, which may not have veracity but at the time was an extremely plausible claim which was widely accepted in the intelligence community, that is that Niger was a country which had proliferated uranium and it was certainly known that Saddam Hussein was trying to purchase uranium, is not an unreasonable claim. Therefore, the general claim that your source has made that the Government exaggerated their case against Iraq has not been made unless you can give the Committee further evidence of exaggeration.

Mr Gilligan: My source said, as many others have said, technical experts and so on in the field, that if any weapons of any description had been held at 45 minutes' notice they would have been found by now, almost certainly because they could not have been particularly deeply concealed. If they had to be deployable at that short notice they cannot have been particularly deeply concealed. That is the testimony of my source and that is the testimony of many others in the field.

Q487 Chairman: You have conceded that we were talking about a source which must have given that information prior to September, possibly in May or June and there has been ample time and opportunity since that time for concealment, destruction or whatever. So the source could have been correct at the time it was given.

Mr Gilligan: My personal view is that I think it unlikely and illogical that Saddam, faced with an imminent threat to his regime, his very existence, would give up his weapons immediately before a war is about to start.

Q488 Mr Illsley: Is there any indication of the date of the particular piece of intelligence which refers to 45 minutes? The reason I ask that is because we have heard conflicting evidence as to Iraq's former capability of deploying weapons in that it has been suggested to us that in 1991 Iraq did deploy chemical weapons on the battlefield but did not use them. I think that has since been contradicted. Could it be

that that piece of evidence is a piece of evidence dating back to the 1990s and simply been regurgitated later?

Mr Gilligan: I do not know, I just have not got the evidence to answer that, but I would hope not because it is 12 years old.

Mr Illsley: A lot of what we are looking at is 12 years old.

Q489 Mr Pope: I have a few questions on a different topic. Yesterday the Committee was told by a former chairman of the Joint Intelligence Committee that people who work for the agencies do not speak to the press and indeed should not speak to the press, but you have told us today that you have up to four sources who do. Does that not lend some credibility to John Reid's claim that there are "rogue elements" in the intelligence services briefing against the Government?

Mr Gilligan: No. The person I spoke to on the 45 minutes story was in the absolute main stream of this issue and could not be in any way described as a rogue element. I do not think it should come as a shock to anyone to learn that some people do talk to the press sometimes, even when they are not supposed to.

Q490 Mr Pope: We are politicians so we are unlikely to be shocked by people speaking to the press, but there is an issue here about people in the security services not just talking to the press but acting as a press officer, ie verifying factual information. What we have here are people who work in the agencies briefing against the Government's policy to members of the press. That is an entirely different issue.

Mr Gilligan: It is impossible for me to say the motives, but what I can clearly say is that it went on in an extremely widespread fashion. Other reporters in the BBC were told the same, at least two or three other reporters in the BBC, TV News, *Newsnight*, the security correspondent. Equally, reporters on *The Times* were told it, a reporter on *The Guardian* was told it, a reporter on *The Independent* was told it, a reporter on *The Sunday Times*, the *Observer*, *The Independent on Sunday*, they were all told the same thing. It is not an isolated occurrence.

Q491 Chairman: Could they have been drawing on the same source?

Mr Gilligan: I think even Downing Street has acknowledged that the sources were plural. In that famous John Reid interview he spoke about "rogue elements" in the pleural and "bad apples" pleural, so I think it must have been more than one.

Q492 Mr Olner: But your one became four.

Mr Gilligan: No. As I explained before, the specific story was from the single source. The other three were over the last six months over various other stories.

Q493 Mr Pope: It is a widespread practice for people who work in our intelligence services to brief journalists, the effect of which may be to undermine Government policy.

Mr Gilligan: I have no opinion and I have no evidence to judge whether the intelligence agencies were seeking to undermine Government policy. It is not my role as a journalist to make that judgment.

Q494 Mr Pope: I was not suggesting that the agencies were undermining Government policy, I was suggesting that people who work for the agencies on a widespread basis brief journalists.

Mr Gilligan: Again, it is not my role to judge either the agencies or the people working for them.

Q495 Mr Pope: You have just given us a list of newspapers that were briefed.

Mr Gilligan: But that is just a fact, that happened.

Q496 Mr Pope: And is it still happening?

Mr Gilligan: It is impossible to adduce the motives of all this.

Q497 Mr Pope: I am not trying to adduce the motives, I am pointing to the fact that people who work for the intelligence services on a regular and widespread basis brief journalists and that is an on-going practice.

Mr Gilligan: That does seem to be the fact of the case in this story because, as I say, it has been going on for several weeks.

Q498 Andrew Mackinlay: The document which you read with the intelligence officer present, which document was that?

Mr Gilligan: It was a defence intelligence report from the defence intelligence staff terrorism analysis cell, DITAC, dated about 13 January from memory. It was about links between Iraq and terrorist organisations and it said, among other things, again this is from memory, that there had been links between Saddam and al-Qaeda in the past but they had foundered due to incompatible ideology. That was shown to me in response to the Prime Minister's allegations that there was a link between Iraq and al-Qaeda.

Q499 Andrew Mackinlay: Where did you see this document? I am not being facetious. Was it in the hostelry, was it in his office, was it on your territory? Where did you see it? Paint a canvas for me as to where you would have seen this.

Mr Gilligan: It was in an office.

Q500 Andrew Mackinlay: Your office?

Mr Gilligan: I did not say that.

Q501 Andrew Mackinlay: I do not blame you. If people are prepared to talk to you then you cannot say, "I don't want to talk to you". Was this in his office?

Mr Gilligan: I cannot say any more because it would compromise the source.

Andrew Mackinlay: You have helped us on something which is at a slight tangent to the main inquiry. As so often happens in inquiries, some other important things have emerged. Clearly, as I believed prior to this hearing, intelligence officers do talk to the press.

Q502 Andrew Mackinlay: Do you sometimes solicit the information or do they approach you folk, in your experience?

Mr Gilligan: Both is the answer.

Q503 Andrew Mackinlay: And they have your telephone numbers and you have theirs?

Mr Gilligan: Yes.

Q504 Andrew Mackinlay: So you can pick up the phone and say, "I want to bounce this off you", and they might say, "No comment", or they might say, "It sounds credible", and sometimes they go to extraordinary lengths and say, "Come and have a cup of tea and I'll leave something on the desk, I won't leave the room." That is a possible scenario, is it not?

Mr Gilligan: That is right. It is normal journalistic contact.

Q505 Andrew Mackinlay: I want to come to this business of the missiles that you were talking about a few moments ago. I think what you were saying was that your source indicated to you that he felt that the intelligence source was flawed but that this was the intelligence.

Mr Gilligan: That is exactly right.

Q506 Andrew Mackinlay: He was not flawed but he was saying the intelligence was flawed.

Mr Gilligan: That is right. He was describing the information provided by the original intelligence source, i.e. the Iraqi General, if it was an Iraqi General, to the British source or the Americans or whoever got it in the first place.

Q507 Andrew Mackinlay: I cannot really see what the beef is. This business of the 45 minutes deployment, in a sense we will never know, will we? Clearly the intelligence was there. There was sufficient intelligence there to say that there was a possibility of this being credible. I have to tell you, if I may share this with you, I do not think this 45 minutes question crossed my radar screen and it certainly was not a material factor in how I voted. Even if there were legislators and members of the public who were really exercised by this 45 minutes issue, after listening to the evidence yesterday and indeed to yours today, I cannot see how it was not corroborated by a second intelligence source but it was sufficiently credible. Bearing in mind this translation, and presumably intelligence sources come via a rather circuitous route rather like a Chinese whisper, some of it might have got lost there. Is that fair?

Mr Gilligan: All I can do is pass on to you what my source said. He said that he was concerned about the authority of this source and about its reliability. The

45 minutes claim did make a pretty big splash at the time. There were two main stories out of that dossier, the first was nuclear and the second was about 45 minutes.

Andrew Mackinlay: The other story is the al-Qaeda linkage. I think most people thought from day one there was no linkage. On a number of occasions I have willed the Foreign Secretary and the Prime Minister to say there was no linkage and they did not do that. I thought their rather coded phrases meant that there was no linkage. I am surprised you have asserted today that Mr Blair said there was a linkage with al-Qaeda.

Chairman: Can you give us its source?

Andrew Mackinlay: I do not think he ever did that. I think he should have been candid and said there was no linkage.

Q508 Chairman: Can you give us the source of the linkage between al-Qaeda and Iraq because certainly the Prime Minister, to my recollection, told the Liaison Committee on or about 9 July of last year that there was no linkage?

Mr Gilligan: Shortly afterwards, I think at Prime Minister's Questions, certainly in the Chamber anyway, I have not got the exact reference, he quite clearly said that there was a linkage between al-Qaeda and Iraq.

Q509 Andrew Mackinlay: Let us not labour the point. It would be useful if you could point to what you think was this fairly unequivocal statement. I did not there was one, but I might have missed it.

Mr Gilligan: I can give you the Hansard reference.[1]

Q510 Andrew Mackinlay: I am not trying to embarrass you. You felt that Blair was doing this on one occasion or more and I am at a loss to know when he did it. I was hoping he would go the whole hog and say there was no linkage.

Mr Gilligan: If you would like, I can write to you or I can give you the Hansard reference.

Mr Illsley: His junior minister made it directly to me in a debate on Iraq on the floor of the House.

Chairman: We can follow that up as a point of fact.

Q511 Mr Maples: I have a couple of things I would like to ask you about. It has been suggested to this Committee by various witnesses that the 45 minutes issue is kind of irrelevant because if they had weapons they probably would be used within 45 minutes. It seems to me that the relevance of this is it shows this is not just a weapons programme, they have actually got some weapons they can use. Is that how you saw the incentive to bring this 45 minutes question forward in your report?

Mr Gilligan: That is how my source put it. The 45 minute claim is an important one, he believed and I believe, because it did make the case that there were actual weapons with chemical or biological tips ready to go. My source's belief on this is that they had not managed to weaponise CBW. His actual quote was that they had not got useable weapons at

that point. They had obviously weaponised in the past but they had not got useable weapons at the point of the issue of the dossier. What he said is that, "I believe it is 30% likely that there was a CW (Chemical Weapons) programme in the six months before the war and, more likely, that there was a BW (Biological Weapons) programme, but it was small because you could not conceal a larger programme. The sanctions were actually quite effective, they did limit the programme."

Q512 Mr Maples: Like my colleague, I supported the Government over this and I would again. If you were trying to make the case to an audience with doubts about this and you were thinking how this was going to play in the press, this seems to me to be a very important claim to bring forward because I think you said to us it did provide the headline for a lot of reporting.

Mr Gilligan: I remember it was the headline in the *Evening Standard* that day and I am pretty sure it was the headline in several of the other papers the next day. I want to make the point that the 45 minutes and the uranium issues were the only specific two items of the dossier which we discussed, but he was unhappy with the general tone and tenor of the dossier as well. His words were, "Most people in intelligence were not happy with it"—that is the dossier—"because it did not reflect the considered view they were putting forward." It is as much a matter of language, phraseology—As you know, an intelligence report of any description is pretty unexciting to be honest. It is couched, it is full of caveats, it is full of conditionals.

Q513 Chairman: Have you seen such reports?
Mr Gilligan: Yes.

Q514 Chairman: In what circumstances have you seen JIC reports?
Mr Gilligan: In historical circumstances and in the Public Records Office and once again when one was shown to me.

Q515 Chairman: The Public Records Office, you mean of 30 years ago?
Mr Gilligan: Yes.

Q516 Mr Maples: What he was really concerned about was he felt that somebody was trying to make this report more newsworthy than it would otherwise have been and if that was the intention then it was hugely successful.

Mr Gilligan: It did make rather a lot of news. That is essentially it, that is exactly it. He started off by talking about the general tone and I pressed him for specific individual problems in the dossier, but it was a matter of the tone as well. It is the belief of some of my sources that there is a slight—this goes to the heart of the question that Mr Chidgey was asking— cultural conflict between the world of intelligence, the rather cautious and arid world of shifting different bits and pieces of information, trying to make something out of them, and the world of politics.

[1] Ev 80.

Q517 Mr Maples: I am sure you are aware, but in November 1998, after weapons inspectors had been thrown out of Iraq and before the Desert Fox bombing operation, the Foreign Office, under the signature of the then Minister of State Derek Fatchett, did write a letter to all Members of Parliament and published a three page document on the current situation with Iraq's WMD programme, obviously drawing on intelligence sources and it was very much more cautious than this document. It said, for instance, that "the Iraqi chemical industry could produce mustard gas almost immediately and limited amounts of nerve agent within months". Saddam almost certainly retained some BW production equipment, stocks of agents and weapons. In the dossier that we are talking about it says, "As a result of the intelligence we judged that Iraq has continued to produce chemical and biological agents." Do those two statements strike you as they strike me, as different, the latter one being much stronger?
Mr Gilligan: Yes. One of the other things that again led me to believe the credibility of my source was that only a few weeks before the publication of the September dossier, the Blair dossier, Whitehall officials had been describing it to the press as rather uneventful. I remember Mike Evans, the defence editor of *The Times*, wrote a story at the end of August in which a Whitehall official was quoted as saying that the dossier would not be revelatory. Richard Norton-Taylor, who is the security editor of *The Guardian*, both those people very long standing journalists in their field, wrote a story at the beginning of September, about a week after Mike Evans, saying that the dossier would no longer have a role because there was nothing to put in it, that was sourced to a senior Whitehall source, and then three weeks after that the dossier appeared and it was more revelatory than those accounts had it. So something had changed in that three week period.

Q518 Mr Maples: When your source said to you it was the general tone of the thing and as a result of you pressing him he gave as an example the 45 minutes issue, what he seems to be saying is an attempt was being made to make this document much more newsworthy than it would otherwise be and strengthening up claims like that which on the face of it do not seem to be a huge difference in wording, but "continued to produce" is different from "continues to have a capability to produce", these are the sort of things we are talking about.
Mr Gilligan: The words of my source was that it was transformed in the week before it was published to make it sexier. Given all that you have said and given the other things I have described, I think that is a credible allegation.

Q519 Sir John Stanley: Mr Gilligan, in answer to Mr Mackinlay's question you said that you had been shown a defence intelligence staff document in an office building which was a document that rebutted what the Government had said about a linkage

between al-Qaeda and Saddam Hussein. Was that document the document classified "Top Secret" to which you referred in your earlier evidence?
Mr Gilligan: Yes, it was.

Q520 Sir John Stanley: Can you remember whether the classification of that document was just top secret or was it a top secret code word?
Mr Gilligan: I am afraid I cannot.

Q521 Sir John Stanley: The office you referred to, was that office on Ministry of Defence premises?
Mr Gilligan: I cannot answer anything about this as it would compromise the source.

Q522 Sir John Stanley: When you had your discussion with your source in the context of the 45 minute claim, are you saying to us that that was the same source with which you had the office conversation and were shown the top secret document in relation to the al-Qaeda linkage issue?
Mr Gilligan: No, it was a different source. As I said, there were four altogether on this issue of Iraq and the use of intelligence material on Iraq.

Q523 Sir John Stanley: Coming back to the source for the 45 minute claim and the suggestion that that claim was unreliable, did that source convey that to you verbally or was that based on offering you sight of a different document?
Mr Gilligan: No, it was conveyed verbally.

Q524 Sir John Stanley: Did you ask for any documentary evidence?
Mr Gilligan: I cannot remember. I think I might have done more in the hope than expectation.

Q525 Sir John Stanley: So the whole of the 45 minutes claim rested solely on non-documentary evidence from your one source that you have been referring to?
Mr Gilligan: It rested on several things. As I said, it rested on the comparison between what those Whitehall officials told the newspapers at the end of August or the beginning of September and what subsequently emerged in the dossier. That seems to indicate a change. It rested on the authority and credibility of my source, which is substantial; it rested on what he said. It rested on the events which had taken place in Iraq after the end of the war, the failure to find weapons of mass destruction. It rested on a statement by Donald Rumsfeld and it rested on the Government's previous admitted track record of embellishing material in intelligence dossiers, as was shown with the February one. So it rested on a number of things other than the single word of my source, but the single word of my source was the centre of it.

Q526 Sir John Stanley: Going back to the meeting you had in the office at which you saw the top secret documents in relation to an al-Qaeda linkage, was the document volunteered to you or did you solicit it?

Mr Gilligan: Again I think I had better not say because I think it would be too much of a compromise to my source, I am sorry.

Q527 Sir John Stanley: And does your employer, the BBC, give you any guidance as to your personal potential position in being in a position where you may be soliciting highly classified material?
Mr Damazer: Mr Chairman, may I answer that?

Q528 Chairman: Yes, I think this is a matter of policy which you can probably answer, Mr Damazer.
Mr Damazer: All of our journalists who deal with sensitive stories of this kind would have access to the BBC's own legal advice. Andrew, being one of the more experienced journalists in defence and intelligence matters, would be aware of the broad background of the Official Secrets Act and would be able to avail himself of legal advice at any point in any story that he was pursuing.

Q529 Chairman: And what is the specific advice in respect of the handling of classified UK documents?
Mr Damazer: In the context of this story, that did not arise. As Andrew has suggested, there was no transaction involving a document.

Q530 Chairman: Surely the document was shown?
Mr Damazer: We are talking about the 45 minute allegation?
Mr Gilligan: That was a separate story.
Mr Damazer: I beg your pardon, but I thought you were referring to the 45 minute story. In the context of the 45 minute story, there would have been no need to worry about transactions involving documents because there were no transactions involving documents.
Chairman: And in respect of the other matter?

Q531 Sir John Stanley: Can I just clarify this. The whole discussion, I am quite certain the witness was quite aware of it, the discussion in relation to the document was solely in the context of the document which Mr Gilligan has said related to the rebuttal of the Government's claim about linkage with al-Qaeda.
Mr Damazer: In the context of the al-Qaeda documentation, I would not have been involved and would not have expected to have been involved in a direct conversation with Andrew about the legal risks, if any, involved in pursuing that story. I would have to say on a day-to-day basis I would expect our journalists to be in receipt of information which could potentially be embarrassing and damaging to a number of government agencies and not merely government agencies. It is part and parcel of what we do in the news-gathering of a story. There clearly has to be a sensible estimation of the degree of risk involved in each of those transactions and for the vast majority of them it is established that the risk is very low. In this specific instance, there would have been a discussion, as there was with the 45 minute story, between Andrew and his immediate editorial line management who would have plenty of experience in doing investigative stories. That is one of the *Today*

programme's specialities and they would have immediate access to a lawyer if they felt that the risk was sufficiently large that they needed to have access to a lawyer.

Q532 Chairman: So we are told that a top secret document was shown to one of your employees. What is the advice given by the BBC in such circumstances?
Mr Damazer: Each circumstance will vary. Would I allow any of our journalists to be in receipt of top secret documents? Of course I would if I felt that the document was properly procured, that is to say, that there had been no bribery or malfeasance and the document contained information which was appropriate to publish, and then of course I would think that it was the job of our journalists to pursue such information and to publish it in an appropriate way.

Q533 Mr Illsley: When you say "bribery or malfeasance", does that exclude payment or include payment?
Mr Damazer: There is no blanket for the way an individual transaction of documents and information which leads to a story should or should not be considered to be appropriate. What I can say, on sensitive stories, is that BBC journalists are not only expected to be aware, but they have line management who can check with them about the basis on which information has been derived. There may very well be circumstances in which the transaction is accompanied by a meal, some hospitality, some arrangement of some kind. I would not expect serious documentary evidence of this kind to be the kind of documentary evidence for which there was a cash transaction.

Q534 Mr Illsley: Could I ask you, Mr Gilligan, did you pay for any of the information you referred to?
Mr Gilligan: No.

Q535 Mr Illsley: You have referred to four sources of your own, receiving top secret documents in an office, having sight of intelligence reports, and you have referred to a number of your colleagues in different newspapers who also have their own sources. Basically what you are saying is that the intelligence services leak like a sieve basically.
Mr Gilligan: No, I am not saying that.

Q536 Mr Illsley: Well, you could forgive me for thinking that. Anybody reading today's evidence would draw the immediate conclusion that our security services have easy access to journalists.
Mr Gilligan: No, I am not going to have words put into my mouth. I think the intelligence services leak from time to time, like many other branches of the state, but probably less so than many others.

Q537 Mr Illsley: Would you say that your access to your sources is relatively easy and it does not really take a lot of digging to get the information you need?
Mr Gilligan: Well, I am sorry to be boring, but it really does depend and it is impossible to generalise.

Q538 Andrew Mackinlay: It has struck me, listening to this evidence, that a lot of your fellow journalists in other news outlets will be saying, and indeed sources of yours and theirs in the intelligence and security service, "What a rotter Gilligan is. He has really spilt the beans. Those of us who speak to journalists are going to have to clam up", and I imagine, as we are talking, there are memos going out, saying, "Don't speak to anybody". It did occur to me that you have probably killed off these geezers speaking to anybody like yourself for the immediate future and also other journalists will also have their sources clamming up. The other thing is that I would have thought you would have compromised your source because if the intelligence outfits cannot find out who this person is from what you have said, I would have thought we might as well pack up and go home. One day you spoke to them on the telephone and obviously went into their offices and photographs were done in the offices, they know the documents, et cetera, et cetera, but it struck me that this is all a bit clumsy unless, and this is the question I am coming to, unless there is a culture in the intelligence and security services where they will stick together. In other words, they will not at this moment be pursuing who spoke to you and showed you these top secret documents, in which case it does raise the issue of whether they are a law unto themselves if they do not like the Government.
Mr Gilligan: Again as I said at the beginning, I cannot really offer a characterisation as to whether this was authorised or not. You have said that this story might shut things down, but what it actually led to was a sort of flurry of disclosure to lots of other newspapers and broadcasters and I just think people are going to have to draw their own conclusions about this, as about so many things in this sort of secret world.

Q539 Andrew Mackinlay: The other question I want to ask you is this: I might be wrong, but certainly Members of Parliament have had unsolicited, on occasions, top secret documents land on their desks and I know on at least one particular occasion Mr Plod came round. You will gather I appreciate your views, but I think it is a nonsense the Official Secrets Act in many respects and one of them is that actually to see top secret documents can be deemed an offence. Is that your understanding as a journalist?
Mr Gilligan: I think probably something like three-quarters of the national media would be banged up if seeing documents was an offence.

Q540 Andrew Mackinlay: I am sure you are right on that and I share your view of cynicism, but I think that is the law, is it not, Mr Damazer?
Mr Damazer: There are circumstances in which obtaining and publishing top secret information would be considered to be a prosecutable offence.

Q541 Andrew Mackinlay: I did not say publication of, but just actually to have sight of.
Mr Damazer: I am not certain about that and I would need to refer back to the books in order to answer that.

Andrew Mackinlay: The only thing that many Members of Parliament will be concerned about, and you might share this view, is that there clearly is this continuous dialogue, relationship between the journalists, and I understand what your duty is, and that of the security and intelligence services, yet Members of Parliament cannot see these people, we are not supposed to know who they are, and then the Security and Intelligence Committee go away in a white van or something or other. There really is something very wrong.
Chairman: It is an interesting comment, but not for this witness, I think.

Q542 Mr Chidgey: If I can just take us back, Mr Gilligan, to some comments you were making, it seems, a long while ago now and back to the discussion we were having with you around the 45 minute claim, can I just check with you first to see if I have understood this correctly. Was it the same source to whom you were speaking who discussed the credibility of the 45 minute claim, the uranium from Niger claim and the one who discussed the capability of Iraq in its chemical weapons programme, was that the same source?
Mr Gilligan: No, there were four different people, as I say.

Q543 Mr Chidgey: The reason I ask that is because I particularly wanted to ask you a little more about the preparedness of Iraq on the chemical weapons front. You said that there was, was it, a 30% chance that they had small quantities?
Mr Gilligan: Yes, this is a quote from my source and I will give it to you again. "I believe it is 30% likely there was a CW programme in the six months before the war and more likely that there was a BW programme, but it was small."

Q544 Mr Chidgey: When you say "small", can you quantify that?
Mr Gilligan: Small enough to be heavily concealed.

Q545 Mr Chidgey: Yes, but there is a difference between having a sufficient chemical weapons arsenal for a particular type of military action and, if you like, a country-wide action. It depends what the Iraqis were preparing for.
Mr Gilligan: He did not quantify that, I am afraid.

Q546 Mr Chidgey: Did you at any time discuss with any of your sources, as you might have done as a journalist, what the intelligence services foresaw as to what would happen next? I will give you an example. Did you discuss with them at all whether or not Saddam Hussein may have a plan B in the event that if war was inevitable, he would immediately leave the country with most of his family, his entourage and a huge amount of cash, which would not just happen instantly, but there would have to be planning about that, and whether or not there was any indication that, as was subsequently reported, there were plans to move chemical weapons out of the country and just ship them out to somewhere else, moving them around the world in converted cargo vessels? Were there any of those sorts of discussions?

Mr Gilligan: I was personally quite concerned about what might happen next because I was in Iraq during the war. It was the subject of a lot of anxious speculation among the journalists there. I was in Baghdad. This was not something discussed by my source, I am afraid. Clearly there are a number of hypotheses and we can go through them if you want, but I do not think my hypothesis—

Q547 Mr Chidgey: No, I want to stick fairly close to the terms of the inquiry. The real issue I have here is that you did make a comment earlier on that one of the reasons which verified the views which you have expressed was that we had not found any evidence of weapons of mass destruction. I want to test with you that one of the options was that they actually had been removed and removed from the battlefield before the war even got underway.

Mr Gilligan: I said earlier, and this is really a personal view, I think it would be illogical to do that in the face of an imminent existential threat.

Q548 Mr Chidgey: Not if you have decided you are going to leave the country, and you might have planned already to take billions out of the bank.

Mr Gilligan: I think it is a bit difficult to say because there is just no final certainty on this issue.

Q549 Mr Chidgey: But it did not just happen, it must have been planned. That is the point I am making to you.

Mr Gilligan: It is just a little bit difficult to get into this kind of hypothesis on what is almost certainly insufficient evidence. Saddam may have dispersed or abandoned the programme because of the activities of the UN rather than because of the imminence of the war. He may never have had a particularly big programme, but wanted to maintain strategic ambiguity in the belief that that would deter potential aggressors, a sadly mistaken belief obviously because that was exactly the thing that encouraged the United States to attack it. He always had manoeuvrability—

Q550 Mr Chidgey: It does rather reinforce the point made by Mr Pope earlier that just because we have not found them does not mean they do not exist.

Mr Gilligan: All I would say is that none of these things can be said with any certainty.

Q551 Mr Chidgey: Precisely.

Mr Gilligan: And certainly cannot be said by my source or by anyone else in the intelligence community and I would not wish to characterise my source.

Q552 Mr Chidgey: So the only degree of certainty that your source has or had was that he did not believe the 45 minutes?

Mr Gilligan: No, as I say, my source was reasonably sure, as are all the other intelligence people I have spoken to, that Iraq had a WMD programme of some description, but it was smaller and less of an imminent

threat than that claimed by the Government. That was the view of my source and the view of several other people's sources in the rest of the media and indeed other sources I have spoken to, intelligence and non-intelligence.

Q553 Mr Olner: Given that the 45 minutes is in no doubt because it was in both documents, was your source really wanting to highlight it to get at the Government or his immediate boss who was not listening to him?

Mr Gilligan: I just cannot describe that kind of motive. I just have no evidence to do that, I am sorry.

Q554 Mr Olner: I cannot understand where a non-story became a story because the 45 minutes was in both documents. If you have got one intelligence officer doubting the data which other intelligence officers have gathered, that does not seem to me to be something that perhaps should be laid at the door of Number Ten.

Mr Gilligan: When you say both documents, you mean the JIC assessment and then the public document presumably. Without knowing the contents of the JIC assessment, it is difficult for me to comment on that, but I can say, I think, that, as I said before, one of the concerns of my source was about the tone of the whole production, the Blair dossier. It is perfectly possible for the same evidence, for the same essential 45 minute intelligence to be presented in different ways. In the JIC dossier, and I have not seen it, it might have been hedged about with all sorts of caveats, it might have appeared buried very deep in the paper somewhere—

Q555 Chairman: And it may not.

Mr Gilligan: Indeed, absolutely, whereas in the Blair dossier my source's complaint was that its importance was given undue prominence. It appeared no fewer than four times in the Blair dossier, let's not forget.

Q556 Mr Pope: Did you approach your source over the 45 minute claim or did he approach you?

Mr Gilligan: No, I initiated the meeting, but not specifically over the 45 minute claim. As I said, I initiated the meeting to discuss Iraq generally.

Q557 Mr Pope: And it was he who raised the 45 minutes then?

Mr Gilligan: He spoke of his concern that the dossier had been sexed up, that "it had been made sexier" were his words, and then I asked for specific examples.

Q558 Mr Chidgey: You did?

Mr Gilligan: Yes.

Q559 Chairman: Can I sum up the position as this: you approached, on your initiative, a source in the intelligence services?

Mr Gilligan: Yes.

Q560 Chairman: Is that correct?
Mr Gilligan: Absolutely, yes. Well, I would characterise this source in the same way as I characterised him on the programme.

Q561 Chairman: You took the initiative in calling to see him. You had met this individual on a number of occasions in the past?
Mr Gilligan: Yes.

Q562 Chairman: You were in an office and clearly you referred to notes, so you took extensive notes of that conversation?
Mr Gilligan: Yes, I took notes certainly, yes.

Q563 Chairman: How extensive are your notes?
Mr Gilligan: I am not really sure. What I was referring to was a summary of what was broadcast.

Q564 Chairman: But did you make contemporaneous notes of the conversation?
Mr Gilligan: Yes.

Q565 Chairman: For how long did that meeting take place?

Mr Gilligan: A couple of hours perhaps, an hour and a half.

Q566 Chairman: So the man of probity, you have mentioned, was prepared to come to you for a couple of hours at your instigation and give you that sort of information over that period?
Mr Gilligan: Yes, that is right.

Q567 Chairman: Because he felt deep unease?
Mr Gilligan: Well, that is what he said. I can only tell you what he said.

Q568 Chairman: And such deep unease that the man of probity did not use any official channels to voice his disquiet?
Mr Gilligan: I do not know whether he did or not.
Mr Illsley: That is not strictly true because you just said that you arranged a meeting generally on Iraq, not specifically about the 45 minutes.

Q569 Mr Illsley: Because you asked this man to come to you.
Mr Gilligan: Yes, we talked about a number of things to do with Iraq. I was genuinely curious as to where the weapons of mass destruction were. We talked about other things too, we moaned about the railways for five minutes.
Chairman: I think we have covered the ground and thank you both very much.

Extracts from Hansard and from a Downing Street briefing, forwarded by Andrew Gilligan, BBC Defence Correspondent.

Extract from Prime Minister's Question Time, House of Commons, 29 Jan 03, Hansard col 871

Mr. Iain Duncan Smith (Chingford and Woodford Green): May I join the Prime Minister in paying tribute to the constituent of the hon Member for Bradford, West (Mr Singh), who was, as the hon Gentleman said, nothing less than a hero?

On Monday, the Secretary of State for Defence said that the evidence of links between Saddam Hussein and al-Qaeda was "not strong." However, last night, President Bush said that Saddam Hussein aids and protects terrorists, including members of al-Qaeda. This morning, the Prime Minister's official spokesman appeared to agree with the President and disagree with the Secretary of State for Defence. Does the Prime Minister agree that those who believe that the threat from Iraq must be confronted and not ignored must speak with a clear and consistent voice?

The Prime Minister: First, I answered questions on this in detail at the Liaison Committee. I have explained that we do not know of evidence linking Iraq to al-Qaeda in circumstances concerning the 11 September attack. However, I chose my words very carefully in front of the Liaison Committee: we do know of links between al-Qaeda and Iraq; we cannot be sure of the exact extent of those links. Every member of the Government has adverted to that.

Extract from the Prime Minister's official spokesman briefing, 29 January 2003

Asked if the Prime Minister believed that the intelligence which Colin Powell had said he would publish would demonstrate a conclusive link between Iraq and Al Qaida, the PMOS pointed out that the Prime Minister had indicated during his session with the Liaison Committee last week that Al Qaida operatives were being sheltered in Iraq. As he had stated, "There was some intelligence evidence about loose links between Al Qaida and various people in Iraq". Put to him that the Prime Minister had not mentioned the fact that Al Qaida operatives were being 'sheltered' there, the PMOS pointed out that given the way the Iraqi government operated, Al Qaida would not be allowed to remain there unless the Iraqis wanted them to be there.

Thursday 19 June 2003

Members present:

Donald Anderson, in the Chair

Mr David Chidgey	Mr Bill Olner
Mr Eric Illsley	Mr Greg Pope
Andrew Mackinlay	Sir John Stanley
Mr John Maples	

Witness: **Mr Andrew Wilkie,** Former Senior Intelligence Adviser to the Australian Prime Minister, examined.

Q570 Chairman: Mr Wilkie, may I welcome you on behalf of the Committee to assist us in our inquiry on the decision to go to war in Iraq. You were a defence analyst with the Australian Office of National Assessments, ONA. You resigned on 11 March of this year in protest at the Australian Government's support for military action against Iraq. Is that correct?
Mr Wilkie: That is correct, Chairman.

Q571 Chairman: It is only fair to say that we have had a letter from your former employers[1], the ONA, giving some background and I think it proper that you be allowed to comment on that letter. First, can you help the Committee on the ONA. Is it equivalent to our Cabinet Office assessment staff, is it equivalent to the SIS? What is the broad equivalent in the UK system?
Mr Wilkie: Chairman, I do not know that you have an exact equivalent. The Office of National Assessments is our senior intelligence agency. It is a completely independent agency, although it is closely associated with our Department of Prime Minister and Cabinet. It is the gateway for all intelligence and assessments through to our Prime Minister and the senior ministers, the members of our National Security Committee at Cabinet.

Q572 Chairman: That is helpful. Let me then put to you, so you can give your own observations, various parts of the ONA letter. We are first told, and I suspect your answer to this is likely to be very clear: "Mr Wilkie's views on intelligence about Iraq and its WMD programmes do not reflect the views of the Office of National Assessments". That must be true.
Mr Wilkie: Yes, that is true, that my views are quite at odds with the views of the Office of National Assessments and, in fact, the views of most of the government, I suspect.

Q573 Chairman: They then go on to say: "His recent work in ONA as a senior analyst principally concerned illegal immigration and related transnational issues". Is that correct?
Mr Wilkie: No. I have heard such assertions previously and, in fact, on the day I resigned on 11 March the Office of National Assessments released a

statement to that effect. I believe that what I perceive as the government's attempts to sideline me in this issue are inaccurate. If I could just outline—

Q574 Chairman: But is it true that your work prior to your resignation was principally concerned with illegal immigration?
Mr Wilkie: No, that is not true. It is true that my work included illegal immigration.

Q575 Chairman: Prior to your resignation on 11 March, according to this information from your former employers, you produced only one written report about Iraq, an assessment in December of last year of the possible humanitarian consequences of military intervention. Is that true?
Mr Wilkie: That is correct.

Q576 Chairman: Thank you. They go on to say that you were one of several analysts who, as the Iraq crisis intensified, were asked, and offered, to be available to provide additional analyst capacity on Iraq when needed. Is that true?
Mr Wilkie: That is correct.

Q577 Chairman: On your return from two weeks' overseas travel, 11–27 February, researching immigration and transnational issues, you were rostered to be part of analyst teams in ONA's watch office on Iraq. Is that fair?
Mr Wilkie: That is correct, Chairman.

Q578 Chairman: Was the object of your overseas travel immigration and transnational issues?
Mr Wilkie: That is correct.

Q579 Chairman: They go on to say that you resigned before contributing to any assessment as part of an analyst team. Is that fair?
Mr Wilkie: That is correct.

Q580 Chairman: Thank you. Like other ONA analysts you had access to a range of current and stored intelligence reporting on Iraq, but on Iraq's WMD programmes access within ONA to some important relevant material was restricted, "those with access to that material did not include all those on the watch office roster and did not include Mr Wilkie".

---

[1] Ninth Report from the Foreign Affairs Committee, Session 2002–03, *The Decision to go to War in Iraq*, HC 813-II, Ev 52.

Mr Wilkie: It is correct that a very small amount of intelligence was not included in my compartment, if you are familiar with that term, but the rest was.

Q581 Chairman: So the purport of this is that in the one report you produced in December you were mainly concerned about the matters, until your travel leave, and then from 27 February until your resignation on 11 March you had access to much information but not to the most sensitive.
Mr Wilkie: Not that very small amount of some of the most sensitive.

Q582 Chairman: But you did not have access to the most sensitive?
Mr Wilkie: Yes.
Chairman: Thank you. I think that probably covers the background of it. Mr Maples?
Mr Maples: Perhaps we could ask Mr Wilkie to state his own credentials for the Committee.

Q583 Chairman: What are your credentials in respect of Iraq?
Mr Wilkie: I would appreciate the opportunity just to say something in addition to that letter from my former employer.

Q584 Chairman: Yes. It is only fair that you be allowed to say that. I understand that you have a written statement which might take ten minutes. That is not the practice of the Committee, as was the case with the former Foreign Secretary, for example, but that statement could be added to the documentation in the Committee's ultimate report[2]. If there are just one or two matters from that, that you would like to highlight, as long as it is brief we are prepared to hear that.
Mr Wilkie: In fact, I will put the statement to the side. I would just draw on a couple of points from the first page or so in response to that letter from the Office of National Assessments.

Q585 Chairman: Go ahead.
Mr Wilkie: Most of what it includes is accurate. However, it does not include a number of things which, when considered, give quite a different impression for the Committee about what my association with the Iraq issue was. For a start, because of my military background—I was 21 years in the army finishing as a lieutenant colonel of infantry—I was expected in ONA to be familiar with any issue that was likely to result in a war. For that reason, even though I was working as a transnational analyst, I covered Kosovo and I covered Afghanistan.

Q586 Chairman: What was your military role in those conflicts?
Mr Wilkie: I was employed as a military strategic analyst effectively in the strategic analysis branch, not the transnational issues branch. Hence, it was in that role that I was on standby to work on Iraq. I have also worked specifically on weapons of mass

destruction, which I think is a very important point that has been omitted from that letter. Specifically, in 1998 I prepared the ONA assessment for government on WMD in terrorism and I attended the Quadripartite Working Group on WMD held in the UK at Cheltenham, at GCHQ. More recently, I represented ONA at the Annual Australian Intelligence Agency's WMD Working Group held at the Australian Secret Intelligence Service's training facility. Finally, in my role as the senior transnational issues analyst I had access to virtually all of the Iraq database because my work involving global terrorism and people movements was very related to Iraq. I would not wish that single report I wrote to be under-estimated. That was the benchmark report for the Australian Government on the potential humanitarian implications of a war in Iraq, which required me to explore in some detail Saddam's regime and what his capabilities were, including his weapons of mass destruction capability. It was not just talking about refugee flows, it was talking about how the war might be fought and, hence, what the humanitarian consequences might be as it played out.

Q587 Mr Pope: Mr Wilkie, you said in an article in the *Sydney Morning Herald* that: "The fictions about Iraq's weapons programmes could be a best selling fairytale". In the British Government's assessment, which I am sure you are very familiar with, the British Government came to the conclusion that: "Iraq has a usable chemical and biological weapons capability in breach of UN Security Council Resolution 687, continues to attach great importance to the possession of WMD, has ballistic missiles, has the capacity to deliver chemical, biological agents". How is it that all of the United Kingdom's intelligence services working together have come to that conclusion and you have come to a completely different one?
Mr Wilkie: Mr Pope, I found, and I still find, the British Government's September dossier fundamentally flawed for a number of reasons. Specifically, the way it has attempted to fill the intelligence gaps on Iraq with a number of what I would call finely tuned assumptions that seem to match the British Government's pre-determined commitment to support a war. In particular, the dossier makes something of that range of WMD-related materials that were unaccounted for at the end of the UNMOVIC process. Just talking specifically about that for the moment, if I could, I think over-playing the unaccounted for weapons was quite misleading because, for a start, there is still a question mark over exactly what was unaccounted for. I do not think UNSCOM ever tried to say "there are exactly X tonnes of precursor" or whatever, all they were trying to say was "We cannot account for it". When you consider that not even the Iraqis know what they have produced, the Iraqis do not know what they used in the 1980-88 Iran-Iraq war, they could not quantify what they had destroyed out of the UNSCOM process, I think there is a great question mark over exactly what was there. Even if there was something left of that unaccounted for

---

[2] Ninth Report from the Foreign Affairs Committee, Session 2002–03, *The Decision to go to War in Iraq*, HC 813-II, Ev 4.

material, I would dispute the assertion in the dossier that much of that even exists to this day. I am sure you will appreciate that the ability to produce very pure chemical and biological agents and the ability to stabilise it are critical elements of having this stuff survive for any period of time and the Iraqis had a terrible track record of trying to produce pure agents. I do not believe that the assertion in that dossier is accurate or is substantiated by hard evidence, that is a better way to put it. The assertion that the Iraqis had perfected the art of stabilisation of chemical and biological agents I think is an unsubstantiated assertion. That is the first intelligence gap, what could not be accounted for. I think the other important intelligence gap is what mischief the Iraqis might have got up to in the period between the inspectors leaving and that four years before the new lot of inspectors arrived. Much is made in that dossier of the rebuilding of facilities that had been associated with the WMD programme. Much has been made of new facilities that had been built. I do not think it presents any sort of credible argument or produces any sort of hard evidence that these facilities actually went the next step and started producing chemical and biological agents.

Q588 Mr Pope: It is a public document, so it is not going to be possible to put in it the raw intelligence data. Can I just quote one line because I think this is an interesting point. It says: "Intelligence has become available from reliable sources which complements and adds to previous intelligence and confirms the Joint Intelligence Committee assessment that Iraq has chemical and biological weapons". That is on page 18 of the report. The allegations here are of the utmost gravity. I just want to know what your view is. Is it your view—I do not want to put words into your mouth—that the British Parliament was lied to by the Government to persuade a reluctant Parliament to vote for a war, or is it that the intelligence assessments that the Joint Intelligence Committee made were themselves inaccurate? Both of those are really serious charges.
Mr Wilkie: You have touched on a number of important points there and I will probably lurch straight to your final point about what do I think happened. I am not saying that Iraq did not have a WMD programme. There is so much evidence that has been accumulated over so long that I do not think there is any doubt that Iraq had some sort of WMD programme. The day I resigned on 11 March, I went on the public record and said a lot of things, including the fact that I judged Iraq's WMD programme to be disjointed and contained. The issue here is how big was the programme, what did the intelligence agencies think the scale of it was, what did they tell government and what was government saying publicly. I think there are a number of parallels between the way it was handled in the UK and the way it was handled in Australia. In both countries the intelligence agencies quite rightly judged that Iraq had a WMD programme. I think they generally provided a reasonably measured assessment of what the scale of that

programme was. They may have over-estimated it to a point, and I suppose the fact that nothing has been found so far does suggest that they did over-estimate it to a point. In fact, when I said it was disjointed and contained maybe even I over-estimated, and I thought I was being the minimalist. I think the problem was the way that the British and Australian Governments took those reasonably measured assessments and exaggerated them for their own purposes. Words used, such as "massive programme, imminent threat", I do not believe were words ever offered to governments by their intelligence agencies.

Q589 Mr Pope: What then is the motive of these governments? When they first said on 18 March they would commit our troops into war, and American troops entered as well and Australian forces, and some of those troops did not come back, I voted for it on the basis that Iraq had a weapons of mass destruction programme which was a credible threat to the region and to my own country and it needed disarming by force. Clearly you do not share that assessment. I cannot imagine any country, let alone the United States, Australia and the UK, would enter into a war lightly. What do you think their motive was?
Mr Wilkie: This really does go to the heart of it, I suppose. I have taken a fairly hard line position on this and I feel this very strongly. I felt it strongly enough that three months ago I walked out of a job I loved, I have been ostracised by people, including some of my friends, and three months later I am unemployed and here in London trying to explain myself. It has been very difficult for me. There has been no good side to this for me. I believe that in Washington, London and Canberra, the governments exaggerated the WMD threat to mask their real reasons for going to war. These are views that are based on the sort of assessments I read and the raw intelligence I read and so on, I did not make these up. I believe that the US was most interested in going to war in Iraq for a range of strategic reasons, such as rearranging the Middle East and moving the centre of gravity from the country with the most amount of oil to the country with the second most amount, trying to safeguard their global ascendancy, stamping their authority on the Middle East to try and gain access to strategic oil reserves. I think there was a range of US domestic reasons. The Republicans had done so well in the US mid-term elections on the back of dealing with the Iraq issue. Let us not forget that the history here is since the 1991 Gulf War there had developed in America a very strong underlying anti-Iraq sentiment, the government was pushed into a corner and sooner or later had to deal with. I think in Australia, the government was motivated more by supporting the US at any cost, more so interested in that than in WMD. I am not suggesting for a moment that WMD is not an issue. WMD was an important consideration in all three capitals. All I am saying is it was not the only consideration, it was not the most important consideration, and the resort of all three governments to use WMD and links with terrorism

as the two main pillars of this war was misleading. Remember that in the UK and in Australia, intelligence agencies were not just providing intelligence assessments on Iraq, they were also providing the three governments with assessments on Washington. It is no secret that we inform our governments about each other to help our decision making. There was no secret in Parliament House in Canberra, and I do not believe there was any secret here in London, about what the broad range of drivers were behind the US desire to go to war. When you superimpose that understanding of what Washington was wanting to do over my other claim of exaggerating the WMD issue, frankly I think it looks a little mischievous.

Q590 Sir John Stanley: Mr Wilkie, in your interview on the *Today* programme in this country on 4 June you said: "I am satisfied that governments have exaggerated Iraq's WMD capability. Governments in all three capitals have exaggerated Iraq's links with al-Qaeda. The governments in all three capitals have exaggerated both the general risk of WMD terrorism as well as the specific risks of Iraq passing WMD to al-Qaeda. The governments have exaggerated what their intelligence communities have offered them". Do you have a copy with you of the September assessment?
Mr Wilkie: The dossier? No, Sir John.

Q591 Sir John Stanley: But you are obviously very, very familiar with it indeed.
Mr Wilkie: Yes, I am.

Q592 Sir John Stanley: If wonder if we can have a copy in front of you. Obviously we cannot go through this page by page inviting you to substantiate your accusation of exaggeration, although if you wish to do that on a paragraph by paragraph basis I am sure the Committee would be interested to receive your memorandum. Just taking the Executive Summary, the Executive Summary, as far as I can see having just reread it very quickly, does not make any reference to the phrase that you used, "massive programme". It talks about a "current threat" and I know the words "imminent threat" have been used by some British politicians, but I am not sure that the phrase "imminent phrase" actually appears in this document. Certainly I do not see any reference to "massive programme". Just taking the couple of pages of the Executive Summary, could you tell us what is the wording there that you feel is unjustified against your information as to what intelligence was available?
Mr Wilkie: Okay. Before I look specifically at the Executive Summary, Sir John, I just want to remind us all that there was an awful lot more to the three governments trying to justify this war than just this dossier. In fact, I think the most emotive statements were probably oral statements in our Parliaments and so on, people standing up and saying what they said. One of my concerns with this is this has been marketed effectively as the product of the Joint Intelligence Committee. When I read this, and I have seen a number of JIC papers—in fact JIC papers

often come to ONA in draft for comment by us to help in the process of developing the JIC, I think it is a good process—it is very, very different from the sort of measured position that would be put forward by the JIC or any other intelligence body. The JIC is made up of the heads of a number of agencies, so by design it is seeking to achieve a compromise amongst a number of organisations. JIC papers, as you are probably aware, are full of terms like "could" or "uncorroborated evidence", "suggests" or "probably". Contentious issues are either dropped or they are heavily qualified, there is a certain style to it, whereas this is almost like a business development professional has been involved or a marketing professional because all of those qualifications are dropped out. This goes to the heart of my claims about exaggeration.

Q593 Sir John Stanley: Could I ask you to go back to my question, if you would be kind. This is a very important document for the Committee. You made this accusation of exaggeration and this is the base written document of the British Government, this was the one and only document which was an authentic document and stated to be derived from JIC sources, unlike the "dodgy dossier". From the Executive Summary, what wording in this do you consider is an unjustifiable exaggeration against the intelligence that you knew?
Mr Wilkie: I will ask for a moment just to read and think, if you do not mind. I am sure you will appreciate that this is a very quick look.

Q594 Sir John Stanley: I assume before making the claims you have made you have studied the document minutely. I hope so.
Mr Wilkie: The front end of it is loaded with historic information. That is a little misleading to say, and it is not just in this document but elsewhere and, in fact, my own Prime Minister used the term, "Iraq has form. It has fired ballistic missiles at countries, it has used chemical weapons on Iran and on the Kurds" and so on. That front end is referring to an Iraq of pre-1991, an Iraq that was virtually a different country from the Iraq we were facing in March 2003, a country with a genuine national WMD programme and that was acting terribly belligerently. It leads you along a little when you start like that. I know you have to start with history, I do not have a problem with you starting with the history, but it does tend to lead you along a little, just like in this document in a number of places all of the boxes and so on that talk about, "This is how you make a bomb, this is what bombs can do" and there is a photo in here of the gassed Kurds and so on. It is leading people to a certain conclusion. In paragraph four—

Q595 Chairman: Of the Executive Summary?
Mr Wilkie: Of the Executive Summary. There is reference there to the intelligence that obviously cannot be revealed in the document, and obviously it cannot be revealed in the document. This is one area in which I think the coalition case against Iraq has been flawed in that there has been a reliance on

what I have described in the Australian media as "garbage-grade" human intelligence from Iraqis opposed to the regime desperate to encourage intervention in Iraq. I saw at ONA human intelligence being used and attention being paid to it when on other issues it would have been discarded as uncorroborated, as questionable and so on. The reason this is relevant to your question, Sir John, is here is a simple statement saying, "We have got all of this intelligence".

Q596 Sir John Stanley: Are you claiming that the British Government in this context was using garbage-grade human intelligence as well as the Australian Government?

Mr Wilkie: No. All I am saying, Sir John, is that in Washington, in London and in Canberra, the intelligence agencies encountered an awful lot of this garbage-grade human intelligence, which in some cases was clearly garbage and produced by people who were trying to encourage an intervention in Iraq. When you have got intelligence agencies under pressure to come up with a smoking gun, there is a temptation to pay more attention to this than you perhaps should. It has been well reported in the media how Mr Rumsfeld set up his own intelligence body in the Pentagon who were perhaps paying too much attention to this. I think some of the garbage-grade human intelligence contaminated the assessments in London and Canberra. I am not at all critical of the intelligence agencies, I think they did a pretty good job on this subject in the face of some political pressure, they did a pretty good job of sifting through this and coming up with reasonably measured intelligence assessments on Iraq. My problem is that those assessments were always a step short of the comments being made by the political leadership in London and in Canberra, there was a gap between the two. If I could go on to paragraph six, the first dot, the statement there that Iraq "continued to produce chemical and biological agents". That links through later in the paper to a number of references, as I said earlier, to the rebuilding of a number of chemical and biological facilities and some new ones. I do not believe there is a case presented in there that these places were actually producing anything. In fact, there is a lot of the word "could", "it could produce that, it could produce this". When I cross-reference that point I have just made with the Fallujah II castor oil and phenol plant, not far from Baghdad, the weapons inspectors in late 2002—there is a lot in here talking about Fallujah II—not long after this was published said that the Fallujah II plant was not functioning. There is another reference in here to—I cannot recall off the top of my head—a serum laboratory. There is media reporting that the day this dossier was released journalists went to that laboratory, were shown around it by the Iraqi Government and, again, it was not functioning; they described the fridge as being empty. I think we are being asked to take a leap of faith from that statement, "they are producing it". There is a gap between that and the claims that some of these facilities have been rebuilt. Even in your document you make the point, quite

rightly, that all of these plants that are built are all dual use facilities. For example, at Fallujah II it was castor oil for brake fluid, serum laboratories try and develop things for agriculture and so on. While I am picking flaws in this document, I think the way it has treated dual use facilities is one of the flaws. It is no good to say that this country has a range of dual use facilities. I could get in a cab and within a few miles of this building I could probably find dozens of dual use facilities. I could find hospitals with laboratories, I could find industrial plants that can make chemicals, within not many miles of here I could find stockpiles of chlorine, the critical ingredient of some chemical agents. Just as there is a disconnect in this document between "these facilities have been built" and the claim that they are making weapons, there is also a gap between "there is a range of dual use facilities and material in Iraq" and "it is being used to make weapons".

Q597 Sir John Stanley: I think also when you jump into your cab you might be saying to yourself, "At least in this country, as in my own country, we do not have a government which goes around using WMD against its own people" and that is rather different from a country like Iraq under Saddam Hussein.

Mr Wilkie: Sir John, of course you are quite right. This is probably the point I want to emphasise, a very important point: I am not pro-Saddam obviously. Saddam is an evil man, he had to be dealt with. My concern is that we were too quick to go to war before all of the other options had been exhausted. We spent years trying to get Hans Blix back into Iraq and no sooner had he got there than we were trying to get him out. We were left with a feeling that—

Q598 Andrew Mackinlay: We wanted him in unconditionally.

Mr Wilkie: Sorry?

Q599 Sir John Stanley: Just continue briefly on the Executive Summary.

Mr Wilkie: I will come back to the 45 minutes issue.

Q600 Sir John Stanley: You are going to refer to the 45 minutes?

Mr Wilkie: I will refer to that last, if you do not mind, Sir John. On the second page, the first dot, these pesky mobile laboratories. There is a great debate over whether these trailers are or are not mobile laboratories and whether it is one, two or three. I do not care whether it is ten or 20 trailers, the point is we are talking about things, we are talking about finds that are so small in scale and are so far short of this serious and imminent threat. I think what we have found so far is much closer to my claim that it was a disjointed and contained WMD programme and not the sort of big national programme that was sold to us as the justification for the war. Below the line on that page, they are talking about the uranium from Niger. I know there has been some speculation about this but my understanding from having worked in the intelligence community is that the fact that the CIA disputed the uranium from Niger, that was known in the CIA early in 2002 and was shared with allied intelligence agencies through the normal intelligence sharing processes. As far as I am concerned the fact that that uranium claim was false would have been known by the British intelligence services months before this document went to press. Similarly, talking about the other materials here, I think it is probably referring to the thousands of aluminium tubes. The International Atomic Energy Agency had doubts about the purpose of those tubes from 2001, had doubts shared with the intelligence agencies, certainly in Australia at ONA and I would assume confidently also within your own intelligence agencies. That was a concern over a year before this document was published. There are serious deficiencies just in the Executive Summary. So I do not speak all day on this, if I could jump to the 45 minutes. I do not believe that there is any solid intelligence to back up that claim. I do not know what report that was based on, I am not claiming to have seen it. If there is a piece of raw intelligence, a piece of human intelligence I assume, saying 45 minutes, I would suggest that it is some of this garbage-grade intelligence. Can I suggest that we take a step back for a moment. We are getting into the detail and there are looks of disagreement around the board. The bottom line here is that in Australia, and I understand in the UK, people were sold the need for war on the basis of Iraq's WMD programme and on the basis of the likelihood of them passing WMD to terrorism. What has been found is so short of that claim, and what is likely to be found now is unlikely to be this large national programme.

Q601 Mr Chidgey: Just sweeping up what is left on the dossier, I take it that you do not believe that the dossier is a balanced assessment of Iraq's capabilities?
Mr Wilkie: No.

Q602 Mr Chidgey: You would not have endorsed the view that on chemical weapons Iraq has a usable weapons capability which has included recent production of chemical agents, as in the dossier?
Mr Wilkie: I do not believe there is enough evidence to know for sure that Iraq had been manufacturing chemical and biological weapons recently.

Q603 Mr Chidgey: So presumably you would not agree with the statement that: "Iraq can deliver chemical agents using an extensive range of artillery shells, free fall bombs, sprayers and ballistic missiles"?
Mr Wilkie: The issue here is one of degree, not of absolutes. I am saying they had a programme, I am saying they may well have some weapons, I am saying they may well find something. My chief concern was the way that what I judged to be a limited threat was exaggerated by the governments in three capitals. I think there are some elements in here which are just unbelievable. For example, the L-29 aircraft and the talk in here about that being used as a platform for spraying chemical and

biological agents, that just does not make sense to me. To convert a plane like that for that purpose is a very difficult and expensive project, why not just put them in a cheap ballistic missile if they are going to deliver them that way?

Q604 Mr Chidgey: Can I just come on to that because I wanted to ask you specifically, and again I am quoting from the dossier, one of the claims in it is: "Iraq's military forces are able to use chemical and biological weapons", it is weapons we are talking about, "with command control and logistical arrangements in place. The Iraqi military are able to deploy these weapons within 45 minutes of a decision to do so." You would not agree with that? I am asking the question particularly bearing in mind your military experience, I want you to think in that context, of what it takes to be able to give the order, have the weapons system ready in a battlefield scenario. It does not actually say anything here about launching missiles to Cyprus, for example.
Mr Wilkie: One thing that strikes me about that 45 minutes claim is for that to be accurate Iraq would have needed to have had everything weaponised.

Q605 Mr Chidgey: Everything? It is a capability, it does not say throughout the whole country, or whatever.
Mr Wilkie: Knowing how the military works in any country, particularly in a country like this, if they are going to have rounds in the air, or rockets in the air, in 45 minutes then I believe the actual WMD warhead, if I can call it that, already needed to be weaponised.

Q606 Mr Chidgey: I understand what you mean.
Mr Wilkie: Basically you liquid fuel a rocket, talk about it, press the button and your 45 minutes are up.

Q607 Mr Chidgey: What about rocket launchers, that is not liquid fuel as far as I know? I am not a military man.
Mr Wilkie: My only point here, and I am probably not articulating this particularly well, is for a country to have the capability to use WMD within 45 minutes then its WMD already has to be weaponised.

Q608 Mr Chidgey: The shells have to be filled?
Mr Wilkie: Yes.

Q609 Mr Chidgey: And the shelves actually too.
Mr Wilkie: You are talking about the shells virtually sitting next to the 155 artillery pieces or whatever.

Q610 Mr Chidgey: So what is the significance of that in this analysis?
Mr Wilkie: What is the significance of it?

Q611 Mr Chidgey: Are you saying that you would have known that they were filled, or what?
Mr Wilkie: I think there is a huge gap between the claim saying that a factory has been rebuilt which could manufacture an agent and the claim that a

country has weaponised and deployed its weapons of mass destruction. I do not believe there was enough hard evidence to paint a picture of Iraq having a developed capability out there.

Q612 Mr Chidgey: But this dossier is based on intelligence assessments, it was not invented.
Mr Wilkie: No. I am quite sure that the people who produced a lot of this in its first form did a great job, they came up with what their judgment was. I suppose one of the reasons why I am of interest to a committee like this is my judgment is at odds with the stated judgments of so many in the intelligence agencies, one of which I used to work for. How did I come up with a judgment so different? I cannot explain that, it was my approach to the issue. I think I was much more critical, particularly of the human intelligence, and, in fact, that might have had something to do with the fact that I did do work on people smuggling to Australia, an issue which is characterised by appalling human intelligence. Maybe because of the work that I had been involved in I had a slightly different approach and I was much more critical compared to some of the agencies.

Q613 Mr Chidgey: Can I pick that point up. Obviously we have taken evidence from a number of people already this week and a lot of that has hinged on how intelligence assessments are processed. I would just like your views, if I may. My understanding from the evidence we have taken is the raw intelligence can be very broad brush and some of it can be very contradictory. Do you take the view that working on that basis, the assessment, the analysis, that is produced from the intelligence might result in several different options of what the intelligence might mean? The classic case, of course, is dual use, or should we say multi use, chemical processing. One of the options is it is producing liquid soap or whatever, or it might be producing lavatory cleanser, or whatever, but it could also do this. You have to go a step beyond that surely to be able to analyse what the most likely use of that facility is. Do you see what I am getting at?
Mr Wilkie: Yes.

Q614 Mr Chidgey: You cannot rely just on the fact that there is a pharmaceutical or chemical plant, or whatever, which has a range of uses, you have to go further and have more intelligence to tell us what it is most likely being used for or most likely to be used for. This is where the options come in. Could you give me some idea how you would address that as an intelligence analyst and what sort of reporting procedure you would then—
Mr Wilkie: It is pretty simple really, is it not? At the end of the day you build a picture of someone's intention and their capability and you build that picture trying to get as much intelligence and as much different sources of intelligence from different sources, technical means and human means.

Q615 Mr Chidgey: Fine, that is great. You take a different view in your analysis, your assessment, from most of the intelligence community. Is that

because your analysis of the evidence comes up with a different conclusion or because you do not believe that sufficient intelligence was there to come to the conclusion that was reached?
Mr Wilkie: I think the latter was an important issue in me making the judgment I did. I did not think there was enough intelligence to justify some of the claims, and I have mentioned some of them in this dossier. I suppose ultimately I had interpreted things differently from some of my peers. I might point out that on the issue of Iraq, I think in the intelligence agencies there has been a range of views for a long time. A strength of the British system is the JIC where ultimately a compromise has to be reached to go to government, and ONA is sort of like that in that it is the single gateway.

Q616 Mr Chidgey: Does that not suggest that the British system which has resulted in the various dossiers is quite a robust system and, therefore, more trustworthy?
Mr Wilkie: I do not know that the British system is better than the Australian system.

Q617 Mr Chidgey: I did not make that comparison.
Mr Wilkie: I think they are both pretty good systems. The proof is in the pudding, so to speak. These systems came up with an assessment on Iraq that we should expect a certain WMD programme on a certain scale and it is not there. We can talk about a whole lot of stuff but at the end of the day it is not there, it has not been found. Is this a good document in retrospect? No, in retrospect it is a lousy document because this document led us to expect that the troops would go into Iraq and encounter and uncover a huge WMD programme.

Q618 Mr Chidgey: Is your argument, therefore, that this document is not representative of the intelligence assessments that were used to produce this document?
Mr Wilkie: I see where you are coming from. I think this document is a step beyond what I would expect the JIC to produce. I know that is a big claim and I base that on the work I have seen of the UK JIC. It is too unambiguous. It paints too confidently a picture of Iraq's WMD programme.

Q619 Mr Chidgey: Have you ever seen an intelligence assessment, say a JIC document in this case, resembling anything like this in your career?
Mr Wilkie: No.

Q620 Mr Chidgey: You have never seen anything as positive and as upfront?
Mr Wilkie: No, and I would not expect to because, as I was saying earlier, by design the JIC is seeking to achieve a compromise from all of these agencies and all of these peoples and it tends to produce things very cautiously.

Q621 Mr Chidgey: So it is unique in your experience?

Mr Wilkie: Yes. I have never seen such an unambiguous strong case put out that is labelled as an intelligence document.

Mr Chidgey: Or drawn from intelligence sources. Thank you.

Q622 Andrew Mackinlay: I genuinely do not understand one thing you are saying. To summarise: the charge here is that the government on one individual matter may have interfered, and there is also the so-called "dodgy dossier", but nobody has suggested here in the United Kingdom that the security and intelligence services have been politically pliable. There is a complaint allegedly by members of the security and intelligence services that, in fact, what they fed out might have been exaggerated but nobody has suggested that the security and intelligence services have been pliable. I listened very carefully to what you said and the inference that I got was that both the Australian security and intelligence services and the United Kingdom security and intelligence services had been pliable. By that I mean that you are comprehensively dismissing that document. I think that has been your thrust. Nobody has suggested in the United Kingdom that that September document is flawed or is a piece of propaganda. There are allegations about the validity and veracity of that 45 minutes thing, whether or not it should have been in, whether there was a corroborative source and so on. We have got to deal with the "dodgy dossier", and I understand that in five minutes nearly everyone fell about laughing. It is a matter for my political cousins in the House of Representatives in Canberra, but are you really suggesting that the security and intelligence services of our respective countries could be lent upon to produce that because I think that is incredible and nobody else has suggested that?

Mr Wilkie: Do not put words in my mouth.

Q623 Andrew Mackinlay: No, I would not want to do that.

Mr Wilkie: What I am saying is that the finished product, what I have got in my hands, does not have the feel of a carefully crafted, measured intelligence document. It feels as though it has been—I think the term used was—"sexed up".

Mr Maples: It has been used here.

Q624 Mr Chidgey: Developed.

Mr Wilkie: It has got a polish on it. It is very subtle. It has got a polish which makes the situation less ambiguous than it was.

Q625 Andrew Mackinlay: That is an incredible claim, Mr Wilkie, because nobody else, not even the people who criticised the Government's stewardship of this, not even people making serious allegations against the Government as regards what they put in the public domain, is suggesting that the document you have before you is anything other than a product of the security and intelligence services through the system, save the inclusion of one particular aspect, namely the 45 minutes thing, which is something that we are looking at

thoroughly and I would understand you might have a view on that. You are coming up with a suggestion and you have used terms like "feel" but you say you cannot find a word for it, and indeed you cannot because there is not a scintilla of evidence you can produce to this Committee this afternoon to rubbish that document save in those particular matters which I have referred to, the 45 minutes and so on. It is a matter for the folk back in Canberra but you seem to be including your folk back home in this. What is your evidence to suggest that security and intelligence services have acquiesced by their silence in a comprehensive and wholesale doctoring of evidence by two governments? It is just too fantastic for words.

Mr Wilkie: Mr Mackinlay, you are putting some words in to my mouth.

Q626 Andrew Mackinlay: Am I?

Mr Wilkie: Chairman, if I could just respond.

Q627 Chairman: Answer that and then I want to move on, please.

Mr Wilkie: I am not accusing the British intelligence and security services of anything I am accusing the British Government, along with the US and Australian Governments, of exaggerating the Iraq WMD threat and the associated terrorism threat. I have no concerns about—

Q628 Andrew Mackinlay: What is your evidence of that exaggeration?

Mr Wilkie: What is my evidence?

Q629 Andrew Mackinlay: Yes.

Mr Wilkie: The evidence is that what has been found in Iraq is nowhere near what is described in this book, that is my evidence. I think that is the clearest evidence anyone could produce to this Committee.

Q630 Andrew Mackinlay: You and I do not know what has or has not been found in Iraq yet, do we?

Mr Wilkie: What I do know is that whatever has been found in Iraq so far is short. You are asking me to present the evidence and that is the easiest challenge anyone can throw at me. The evidence is that we were promised a war on the basis of this big WMD threat but it has not been found and whatever is likely to be found now is going to be miles short of what the war was sold to us on.

Andrew Mackinlay: You do not know that, do you? We are going round in circles.

Q631 Mr Olner: Just on the back of what Andrew was saying, the whole substance of your argument, Mr Wilkie, is that your colleagues did not agree with your scenario, you took your bat away, you would not play, and you are now saying because they have not found any you were right. What about if they do find it all next week?

Mr Wilkie: We were promised—I do not know if the word "massive" was used in this document, I do not think it was—we were told orally and sold the war on the basis of a massive programme presenting an imminent threat.

Q632 Mr Olner: But you forget the history that he has used these weapons on Iran, he has used these weapons on his own people in the marshlands and what have you. We still control a no-fly zone, our planes still get shot at by Saddam. I have to say that even if he had enough weapons just to fill this room, I think he would gladly use them against the West.
Mr Wilkie: But we were not sold the war on the basis of enough weapons to fill this room. In all three capitals we were sold the war on the basis of a massive programme. There is a book here listing—
Andrew Mackinlay: Non-compliance with inspectors, unimpeded access for inspectors were the two material factors. Let me bounce this off you—
Chairman: Mr Mackinlay, we really must keep some discipline on this. To pick up on what Mr Mackinlay says, the basis of 1441 was non-compliance. I would like to get Mr Olner, then Mr Illsley and then back to Mr Maples.

Q633 Mr Olner: I really want to ask Mr Wilkie, can we as politicians, can the general public in Australia, America and Great Britain, trust our intelligence agencies again?
Mr Wilkie: Mr Olner, we have got to be very careful here not to shift the blame to the intelligence agencies.

Q634 Mr Olner: I am not shifting the blame, you are putting the blame there.
Mr Wilkie: I am not blaming the intelligence agencies.

Q635 Mr Olner: I assume the data that the Australian Government saw and the American Government saw was derived in the first instance from the intelligence agencies?
Mr Wilkie: You are quite correct, but my concern is the way reasonably sensible and measured assessments were exaggerated.

Q636 Mr Olner: Did you make that point to anybody in your department before you left? When you first became aware of this, did you say anything to anybody?
Mr Wilkie: That is a fair question. No.

Q637 Mr Olner: Why?
Mr Wilkie: That is a fair question and I welcome the opportunity to answer that. I did not voice my concerns in the Office of National Assessments. The reason was that just as I started to realise that my judgment about Iraq was so at odds with ONA's corporate line, if I can call it that, at the same time I came to understand I had to put up and shut up or do something about it, and I decided to do the latter, to do something about it.

Q638 Mr Olner: How much support did you get from amongst your colleagues? Did you get any support whatsoever or were you the sole, lone voice?
Mr Wilkie: I need to be careful how I answer that because the moment I say there are a few people in ONA who agree with me fully there will be a witch hunt around ONA trying to find out who these people are. I will answer that by saying the feelings through the Australian intelligence agencies reflects the feelings in the Australian community, which are everything from strong support for the war through to very, very strong opposition. I still have a number of very close friends in ONA who have been very supportive of me personally and both parties are sensible enough to know to keep the work stuff separate.

Q639 Chairman: That was not the question. The question was whether you were the lone voice in voicing this opposition or whether a number of your colleagues were saying that they agreed with you, not whether they sympathised with you personally.
Mr Wilkie: I was the only one who did what I did, obviously. ONA is a good organisation and people are allowed to speak their minds and on issues like this people do disagree all the time, but they tend to operate below a threshold.

Q640 Chairman: Again, that is not the question. You were asked did anyone else suggest that information had been misused by governments?
Mr Wilkie: No-one has voiced that in ONA.

Q641 Mr Illsley: Mine is a very narrow question. You mentioned a few minutes ago that the allegation that uranium was being purchased from Africa was known to the Australian intelligence services back as far as 2001, did you not?
Mr Wilkie: No. There has been some media reporting on this that has been reasonably accurate. The CIA had sent someone to Niger in early 2002 who had gone back and reported that they had concerns about the claims. My understanding is that information was shared through the normal intelligence sharing arrangements between the countries, so it was known in ONA and would have been known, I assume, in your own intelligence services. The 2001 reference was to the fact that the International Atomic Energy Agency had some concerns about the claims of that vast quantity of piping since late 2001.

Q642 Mr Illsley: We have heard a lot of evidence about the claim of 45 minutes, which I do not want to go back into, but could it be that this document has been compiled from pieces of intelligence which are quite old? I draw attention to the 45 minutes claim because we have heard conflicting evidence that perhaps weapons were deployed in the first Gulf War in 1991 and it occurs to me that perhaps this document has drawn on pieces of intelligence which are quite old. Would that be possible?
Mr Wilkie: It is possible. I am speculating now. It may be claims like the 45 minutes were as much a reference to Iraqi army war fighting doctrine as reality. If people ask me what the proof is, if that was an accurate comment then I would have expected coalition forces to have found weaponised chem bio agents.

Q643 Mr Maples: One of the things you said very early on was that this document does not read like a JIC assessment, it reads more like a marketing document or a political document, which in a sense it is because it was published by the Government but, we are told, based on the JIC assessments. What is quite interesting is that before the *Desert Fox* operation at the end of 1998 the Government, the Foreign Office, also published an assessment which was much shorter, a three page assessment, of Iraq's then weapons capability and what struck me was that the tone between the two documents was very different. I would just like to read you the passages on chemical and biological weapons and I would ask you how they strike you. "Iraq would be capable of regenerating a chemical warfare capability within months. Some CW agents and munitions remain hidden. The Iraqi chemical industry could produce mustard gas almost immediately and limited amounts of a nerve agent within months. This and some deionisation could be done covertly." On BW: "Saddam almost certainly retains some BW production equipment, stocks of agents and weapons. In any case, Iraq has the expertise and equipment to regenerate an offensive BW capability in weeks". Whereas this document says: "Iraq has continued to produce chemical and biological agents". They are separated by four years but I wonder whether the tone of the 1998 document that I have read to you sounds more like a JIC assessment than the 2002 document? It sounds more qualified to me.
Mr Wilkie: I would agree, there is a different tone to it, yes.

Q644 Mr Maples: You think that to talk about "could" and "has the capability to have some ingredients or store some weapons he made before" is perhaps a more realistic assessment?
Mr Wilkie: Yes.

Q645 Mr Maples: You said you saw some of the raw intelligence that went into Australia's assessment of this, which was presumably very similar to the intelligence that went into this. Are any of your misgivings about this document, and presumably whatever the Australians used, based on what you saw as evidence? You said you think this document goes beyond the intelligence evidence. Is that based simply on the fact that it does not sound like a JIC document to you, or is it based on having seen some of the raw intelligence yourself and therefore believing that this document goes beyond that?
Mr Wilkie: I did see some raw intelligence which led me to create that term "garbage-grade". It just looked like nonsense being said by someone trying to win favour with someone or trying to encourage a US intervention. In regard to the post-1998 material in here, what strikes me is just how much reference there is to facilities and so on, they keep saying they are being rebuilt but do not present any intelligence or any case to take it from "it has been rebuilt and is probably producing castor oil" to "it

is producing agents and those agents have been weaponised at this site and they are being moved to these areas and so on".

Q646 Mr Maples: The key phrase in the Executive Summary, it seems to me, is: "As a result of the intelligence we judge that Iraq has continued to produce chemical and biological agents". That goes considerably beyond the 1998 statement. What I am trying to get from you is did you see the intelligence of what collectively we think has happened between 1998 and 2002 and in what sense does it either justify or not justify the statement that "Iraq has continued to produce chemical and biological agents"?
Mr Wilkie: I do not believe that there was adequate hard intelligence to justify the claim.

Q647 Mr Maples: This is intelligence that you saw?
Mr Wilkie: Yes. Sorry, the turn of phrase was?

Q648 Mr Maples: ". . . continued to produce chemical and biological agents".
Mr Wilkie: I do not believe there was enough evidence to prove that they were producing chemical and biological weapons.

Q649 Mr Maples: When you say you do not believe, the evidence that you saw would not justify that?
Mr Wilkie: What I saw did not convince me that was the case. What is my evidence? The fact that I am not concocting this just now, I said this on 11 March when I resigned, I went public then with my judgment about how I thought WMD was being overplayed. The other important bit of evidence was—I was waving this around earlier—if that was accurate I think we would have found something by now.

Q650 Mr Maples: What I want to understand is whether your judgment that this goes beyond what was justified by the intelligence is based on having seen the intelligence or simply that the tone of this is rather different?
Mr Wilkie: No, no, I am sorry. It is an informed judgment based on me having seen intelligence and I now judge that that statement was overstating it. Can I just say something in fairness to the intelligence. I am sure you all know this but intelligence is not an exact science, there is a certain amount of black magic and black art and at some point someone has got to sit down and say, "I have read all this and I judge this". I am not necessarily criticising the intelligence official who said, "I judge that", I am saying I judge something different.

Q651 Mr Maples: But your assessment, your judgment of this document and your actions were based not on a feeling that this does not sound right but were based on having seen hard intelligence information which you believed did not justify the political conclusions that were being reached?

Mr Wilkie: Yes.

Q652 Mr Maples: I do not want to put words into your mouth, correct me if I am wrong, but it was on the basis of that that you resigned your job and your career.
Mr Wilkie: Yes.

Q653 Mr Maples: You have given up your career because you believed that the raw intelligence that was available did not justify the political conclusions that were being based on it?
Mr Wilkie: I am happy for you to put those words in my mouth because that is what I would say. My decision to resign was based on my judgments that were informed by my access to hard intelligence and assessments provided by ONA and ourselves.

Q654 Chairman: I think the Committee would sympathise with anyone who resigns on a point of principle like yourself, but you concede that you did not see all the evidence?
Mr Wilkie: No, I did not see all the evidence. I do not think anyone has seen all of it, the database is huge.

Q655 Chairman: You concede that you were effectively a lone voice in the intelligence establishment in Australia?
Mr Wilkie: As far as I am aware, yes.

Q656 Chairman: Your judgment differed from that of your superiors?
Mr Wilkie: Yes.

Q657 Chairman: Perhaps I could refer you to the dossier, *Iraq's Weapons of Mass Destruction*, which you have in front of you. If you would look at the Executive Summary, paragraph six was the key judgment: "As a result of the intelligence we judge that Iraq has continued to produce chemical and biological agents". You dispute that?
Mr Wilkie: I dispute that.

Q658 Chairman: If you would turn over the page, you see under seven: "These judgments reflect the views of the Joint Intelligence Committee". So you also differ in your judgment not only from your own Australian intelligence community but from the British intelligence community?
Mr Wilkie: Absolutely.
Mr Maples: I would just say it does say "reflect", it does not say "are the views of the JIC".
Chairman: Thank you very much, Mr Wilkie.

Witness: **Mr Ibrahim Al-Marashi,** Research Associate, Center for Non-proliferation Studies (CNS), Monterey Institute of International Studies, examined.

Q659 Chairman: Mr Al-Marashi, may I welcome you on behalf of the Committee to this inquiry into the Decision to go to War in Iraq. Your background as I see is this. You are a Research Associate at the Center for Non-proliferation Studies (CNS) of the Monterey Institute of International Studies. Your research focuses on the diffusion of nuclear, biological and chemical weapons and missile technologies in the Middle East, particularly Iraq and Iran. You received an MA in Political Science at the Arab Studies Center at Georgetown in 1997. You have also attended the University of California Los Angeles, and have worked for the Harvard University Center on a project classifying captured Iraqi state documents. You also have been a researcher on Iran-Iraq affairs at the US State Department, Congressional Research Service and National Defense University. You are now a DPhil student at St Antony's College, Oxford. Your work as I understand it was drawn upon largely for the second dossier without your authorisation.
Mr al-Marashi: That is correct.

Q660 Sir John Stanley: Mr al-Marashi, I would like to ask you a number of questions in relation to how, without, we understand, your consent, you came to make such a very substantial contribution to the so-called "dodgy dossier" entitled *Iraq: Its Infrastructure of Concealment, Deception and Intimidation*. We do not have the transcript of the evidence session that we took yesterday from Dame Pauline Neville-Jones, though it may be here in the room a little later on, so you will forgive me if I have to do this from memory but it was a point on which I was able to have a word with Dame Pauline Neville-Jones afterwards. Referring to the sources for the "dodgy dossier" and your own contribution, she made a comment which will be in the transcript that it transpired that the source was much better known to the British Government than was originally thought and understood. Can I ask you: in the period prior to the publication of your thesis did you receive any approaches from any of the staff at Number 10?
Mr al-Marashi: No, I was never contacted.

Q661 Sir John Stanley: Which people in the British Government did you know?
Mr al-Marashi: I have never known anyone in the British Government.

Q662 Sir John Stanley: Do you know how they knew you so well, because clearly they had come to recognise that you were a source of considerable expertise in this area?
Mr al-Marashi: The only way I can infer they got hold of this article was that not only is it published in the *Middle East Review of International Affairs* but there is also an on-line version. If one were to do an internet search of Iraqi intelligence agencies on any of the web browsers my article is the first to come up. Basically, it was one of the first articles ever written compiling all the open source information on Iraq's intelligence agencies, so on any kind of internet

service this would be the first article that would come up. I had reason to believe that the internet version of this article was consulted for the dossier released in February 2003 because grammatical mistakes made on the internet version ended up in this February 2003 document so, because of the mistakes I made that showed up on the internet version, they ended up in the document, *Iraq: Its Infrastructure of Concealment, Deception and Intimidation.*

Q663 Sir John Stanley: Can I just ask you, because it appears in a paper which we have received from Dr Glen Rangwala[3], who presumably you do know,—
Mr al-Marashi: Yes.

Q664 Sir John Stanley: —and probably consulted you before he submitted this memorandum for the Committee: in his paper to us he names four officials in Number 10 who were basically the authors of this document. Can I just ask you for the record whether you know them and whether they had made any approaches to you at any point: Paul Hamill, Foreign Office official, John Pratt, a junior official from the Prime Minister's Strategic Communications Unit, Alison Blackshaw, Alastair Campbell's personal assistant, and Murtaza Khan, News Editor of the 10 Downing Street website?
Mr al-Marashi: No, I have never met or spoken to any of the four people you mention.

Q665 Sir John Stanley: The subject of your thesis was basically the structure of the Iraqi Security Service in the very early 1990s. Did it come as something of a shock to you that you found so much of your thesis being drawn upon in a document which purported to give the current organisational structure of the Iraqi Security Service, even though your own thesis was related to the period ten years previously?
Mr al-Marashi: The ultimate aim of this project, the article that I wrote, was to accompany a thesis dealing with the 1991 Gulf War. Not only that, but I am a historian by training. I use historical methodology. The article I wrote for the *MERIA* journal was supposed to be a history of Iraq's Intelligence Services. It was supposed to give an overview but basically the bulk of the material came from the 1991 Gulf War. I tried to make it as up to date as possible but not for the purpose of serving as a policy brief for something that would influence the decision to go to war, as this document did. I was quite shocked to see it end up in this dossier. That was not my intent, to have it support such an argument to provide evidence necessary to go to war.

Q666 Sir John Stanley: As has been widely reported, the Government has chosen to make an apology to the heads of the intelligence agencies for producing a document which purported to have some degree of authority from themselves when that was not the case, and has provided an assurance that will not happen again in the future. Has the Government made any expression of regret or apology to you for the plagiarisation of your thesis?
Mr al-Marashi: I have never been contacted directly, either by phone call nor in writing, since February 2003 up to the present.

Q667 Sir John Stanley: Do you think you might be owed an apology?
Mr al-Marashi: I think the least they could do is owe me an apology.

Q668 Chairman: Can we now apologise for them?
Mr al-Marashi: The time is quite past but I would have to say that the biggest fear I had out of this whole story breaking out was that I am an Iraqi myself and when I wrote this article I did not think it would get much of a circulation, maybe 5,000 people at the most, people in the Middle East academic community. What the events have done to me around February and March was that basically they connected me to the British case for going to war and, having relatives in Iraq with my last name connected to me in the UK would have been disastrous for them. I have already lost two relatives to the Saddam regime. Any connection now between me and the UK Government and the case for going to war would have had a disastrous effect on my family back home. That was my biggest regret out of this entire affair. Given the personal stress I have gone through, I think the least they could have done was offer me an apology.

Q669 Sir John Stanley: Were there any reprisals made against any of the members of your family in the period between the publication of the "dodgy dossier" and the removal of the Saddam Hussein regime?
Mr al-Marashi: I have not been able to establish contact with my family. I cannot say 100%. In fact, I was intending to go back to find out the fate of my family, but I cannot say I am 100% sure if there were reprisals. Given the fact that my family was politically suspect in the past, it is likely that they could have been suspect or there could have been reprisals. There is always that possibility.

Q670 Sir John Stanley: When you say you sadly have lost two members of your family to the Saddam Hussein regime, are you saying to this Committee that they were imprisoned or are you saying they were murdered by the Saddam Hussein regime?
Mr al-Marashi: They were taken after the 1991 revolt in the south of Iraq. We found out about their fate through an Amnesty International report. They had disappeared and it was only after an Amnesty International report was released that we saw their pictures and the report that we knew that they were imprisoned and their fate is unknown, so that is all I can say, that their fate is unknown.

Q671 Sir John Stanley: Again, just for the record, because various suggestions have been made that there were those in the business who were seeking to plant information in the British Government's way

---

[3] Ninth Report from the Foreign Affairs Committee, Session 2002–03, *The Decision to go to War in Iraq*, HC 813-II, Ev 30.

and indeed in other Governments' way that might have been helpful to make the case for war against Iraq, can the Committee assume that you were a wholly unwitting and unwilling participant in this particular publicity exercise by the British Government?

Mr al-Marashi: Yes, you can assume I was completely unaware of the events and that I was never contacted by any government body.

Q672 Chairman: But you have actually worked for the US State Department?

Mr al-Marashi: I worked as an intern in 1996.

Q673 Chairman: And you have also worked at Monterey which is very closely linked to the intelligence community in the US.

Mr al-Marashi: No. The Monterey Institute is adamant in using only open source material. They keep distance from any intelligence agencies but the whole foundation of this organisation was to provide information to inform the public debate by using open source material. They strictly keep away from any kind of formal allegiances to any intelligence organisations and they do not use any intelligence information in any of the literature that the centre produces.

Q674 Chairman: You are a historian by training?

Mr al-Marashi: Yes.

Q675 Chairman: But did the article—correct me if I am wrong on this—appear in 2002?

Mr al-Marashi: That is correct.

Q676 Chairman: Was that broadly correct in terms of the structure of the intelligence community in Iraq at the point of publication?

Mr al-Marashi: It was as accurate as I could possibly make it as of September 2002 using open source materials.

Q677 Chairman: So it was updated beyond 1991 to 2002?

Mr al-Marashi: That is correct.

Mr Pope: I must say the details of this as it unfolds become more and more extraordinary. We have been told that the four junior officials in Number 10 were responsible for downloading this off the internet and then copying and pasting it. You said at the beginning that if you had tapped into a search engine yours was the top piece of research that came up, so they did not even look very far. It must have been a busy day in the office and they just took the first one.

Mr Illsley: We are not casting any aspersions on the quality of your work.

Q678 Mr Pope: No. It is just the detail that I was taken with. How did you find out that this had happened to your work and how did you feel when you discovered it?

Mr al-Marashi: I found out through an e-mail by Glen Rangwala from Cambridge. He asked me if I had collaborated with this dossier. I said I was not

even aware of this dossier. In fact, he was the one who sent me the text of the dossier I have here, so it was not until he had sent it that I was made aware of this document. I was made aware of the similarities. I did not take any action beyond that. I just compared the documents, knew there was a plagiarism, but I just left it at that. Given the fact that I had relatives back in Iraq I do not want to bring attention to this. The story developed a life of its own in the UK and so by Thursday, I believe it was February 7, I saw the story break on the internet and then it took off from there.

Q679 Mr Pope: Your work was altered as well. It was not just that they downloaded it; they used it without your permission, they did not attribute it to you. All these things are bad enough, goodness knows, but they also altered some aspects of it, did they not?

Mr al-Marashi: That is correct.

Q680 Mr Pope: Do you know whether those alterations were accurate or not?

Mr al-Marashi: I will show you, if I look at the key wording. No; the alterations were not accurate and those alterations changed the meaning of the intent of my piece. The key sentence in the section where we are talking about the Iraqi Intelligence Services—and when I say "we", that is—they took the information on the Iraqi Intelligence Services from my article and included it in the dossier. Key wording such as—

Q681 Chairman: Do you have a page number?

Mr al-Marashi: My text is not numbered.

Q682 Sir John Stanley: Starting at page 8?

Mr al-Marashi: It says, "The Directorate of General Intelligence" and then there are these bullet points, "Its internal activities include . . . Its external activities include . . ."

Q683 Sir John Stanley: Yes.

Mr al-Marashi: Again, from the first bullet from "Its internal activities include . . .", "spying"—I used the term "monitoring". I guess there is a thin line between those two words but I tried to use more neutral language. The key modification made was in the second section, "Its external activities include . . ."—"supporting terrorist organisations in hostile regimes", where I believe I used, "aiding opposition groups in hostile regimes". There is a big difference between "opposition groups" and "terrorist organisations". I was always one to believe that the link between Iraqi intelligence and terrorist organisations may have been quite active in the past but links between Iraq's security apparatus and terrorist organisations—there has not been evidence that there has been strong co-operation in the last decade, nor has there been strong evidence of Iraqi co-operation with al-Qaeda. By changing it to this word you are kind of distorting the intent, that is, "supporting terrorist organisations in hostile regimes" makes one infer that they could be supporting, let us say, groups like al-Qaeda. That is one key example of modifying the text. There are other examples where they not only plagiarised but they put it in the wrong place. If you look at the section "Military Security Service",—

Q684 Chairman: The page number?
Mr al-Marashi: It is towards the end. My draft is not numbered.

Q685 Chairman: Page 14, I am told.
Mr al-Marashi: Where it says, "Military Security Service", this section is wrong. The Military Security Service described here is actually the Iraqi General Security Service, so not only did they plagiarise large chunks of this but also the content of the report is wrong, at least in this section. They got this section completely inaccurate.

Q686 Chairman: It is actually incompetent. The other one was a distortion. This is just an incompetent transference.
Mr al-Marashi: Yes.

Q687 Mr Pope: Just to recap, they pinched your work off the internet, they took it without asking you, they used it without your permission and they altered some sections of it to change the emphasis and in other areas they incompetently got it completely wrong.
Mr al-Marashi: Yes.

Q688 Chairman: Is that a fair summary?
Mr al-Marashi: That is fair.
Mr Pope: I must say, I do think that maybe one of the recommendations we will make at the end of all this is that you get that apology.

Q689 Mr Illsley: Just to clarify the timescale of this, you did bring it up to date from 1991 to the present time, so it is a historical overview basically?
Mr al-Marashi: Basically, yes. The emergence of the Iraqi security apparatus from the creation of the Iraqi state in the 1920s to the present.

Q690 Mr Illsley: And you had no contact at all with anybody from the British Government?
Mr al-Marashi: No.

Q691 Mr Illsley: Are you considering making a complaint or raising the issue or in your present circumstances with regard to your family are you just wanting the matter to go away?
Mr al-Marashi: It really depends on my trip to Iraq and finding out if my family did suffer any reprisals.

Q692 Mr Illsley: Are you likely to be in any danger when you return to Iraq?
Mr al-Marashi: To be honest, not now with the regime pretty much eliminated. I would not say I would be in danger by going back, but I have to admit that, even though I was in California during the time when this story broke, even my own personal security I did feel was at risk. During the years of the Iran/Iraq War and the 1991 Gulf War Iraqi intelligence had contacted my family on

numerous occasions asking for our family to provide contributions to the war effort. Basically, they were conducting illegal activities, raising funds, so we knew that the Iraq Intelligence Services knew of our family and their location and our address in California at the time of the Iran/Iraq War, if not the 1991 Gulf War. The fact that they had our address on file and that my name had come up in the press again, even my own family in California feared for our personal safety. That was when the Iraq security apparatus was intact. Given that it has been for the most part dismantled I feel a bit more secure.

Q693 Mr Illsley: So not only was this an exercise in incompetence; it was so reckless as to have put lives in danger?
Mr al-Marashi: I would say that is fair to say.

Q694 Mr Maples: I just want to come back to the alterations. Dr Rangwala has been in touch with us, as you know, in a note, and he mentions another one too, which was where you had said in your report "monitoring foreign embassies in Iraq" and in the British dossier that became "spying on foreign embassies in Iraq". Is that a third example?
Mr al-Marashi: That is correct.

Q695 Mr Maples: The main one that you mentioned, where the British Government says "supporting terrorist organisations in hostile regimes", and your original, I believe, was "aiding opposition groups in hostile regimes"—those strike me as two very fundamentally different things. Maybe the Iraq Government was doing that as well, but what you were saying was that it was aiding opposition groups in hostile regimes?
Mr al-Marashi: That is correct.

Q696 Mr Maples: Nowhere in your document did you suggest that the Iraqi Government was helping terrorists, or did you?
Mr al-Marashi: No, because I could not really find open source evidence to provide that information. For example, the Iraqi Government was helping a rival wing of the Ba'ath Party in Syria. That rival wing of the Ba'ath Party in Syria is not a terrorist organisation; it is an opposition group to the regime of Hafez al-Assad, so by that definition the Iraqi intelligence was aiding an opposition group in a hostile regime. That was the intent I had. Any links between terrorist organisations—I just could not find evidence to include them in this article and for that reason I refrained from stating it like that.

Q697 Mr Maples: That is not just altering the sense of what you said. It is saying something completely different.
Mr al-Marashi: That is correct.

Q698 Mr Maples: Which, of course, suited the British Government's case extremely well, to try and paint Iraq as even worse than it really was.

Mr al-Marashi: That is correct.

Q699 Mr Maples: You have obviously studied in the course of what you are doing a lot of government documents; you have worked inside the State Department; you have worked in a very respected think-tank; you are doing a DPhil at Oxford, presumably in some aspect of international relations, and you must see a lot of government papers. Have you ever seen anything like what we have come to affectionately know as the "dodgy dossier" before?

Mr al-Marashi: No, I cannot say that in my past history of working with government organisations, think-tanks, etc, I have seen something so hastily put together that was not checked for even grammatical mistakes, never mind factual mistakes. This kind of document is unprecedented in my experience.

Q700 Mr Maples: When this was presented in the introduction it says, "This reports draw on a number of sources, including intelligence material". I do not actually have the quote with me, but when the Prime Minister introduced the document in Parliament he actually said something slightly stronger than that, but again, what we were led to believe was that this was based on intelligence material. Having read it, how much of it do you think is based on your article and there were two other articles, were there not, a Mr Boyne and a—

Mr al-Marashi: Ken Gause, that is correct.

Q701 Mr Maples: Among the three of you how much of this document do the three of you account for?

Mr al-Marashi: I highlighted the similarities between my article and this dossier here. I found 19 paragraphs that were taken directly from my article. A section such as the Presidential Secretariat here was taken directly from Ken Gause's article, virtually unchanged. If I could estimate I would say that 90% of this intelligence dossier was taken from the three articles, by myself published in *MERIA* and the two articles in *Jane's Intelligence Review*, virtually unchanged.

Q702 Mr Maples: We have been told by the British Foreign Secretary that no minister saw this document before it was published. We do not know whether that includes the Prime Minister or not, though he is a minister, but does that surprise you, that no minister would see a document like this before it was published?

Mr al-Marashi: It would surprise me because I think a minister would have the experience to see some kind of inconsistency in the document or something a bit suspicious about it, so it does surprise me that a document that was eventually handed over to US Secretary of State, Colin Powell, that he would present to the UN—you would think that at least one minister would have seen this document.

Q703 Mr Olner: You are an expert on Iraq and perhaps, if anything, what you ought to be really annoyed about is that it has suddenly been christened the "dodgy dossier" because it could well be that your document was very accurate and was a very good document and that is why it was used. On the broader aspects of Iraq, do you have any opinions at all on the quality of the intelligence of the US and British intelligence agencies on Iraq?

Mr al-Marashi: The quality, no, because I have never had access to British or US intelligence on Iraq.

Q704 Mr Olner: So you have got no views at all on that?

Mr al-Marashi: No. All my research is done through open source materials. The advantage I had was that I had these captured Iraqi intelligence documents to examine but those are also open to the public domain, so I cannot really assess or evaluate US or British intelligence on Iraq for that matter.

Q705 Mr Olner: How do you think the US gathers its intelligence on Iraq?

Mr al-Marashi: Probably through a variety of sources, where there are signal intercepts. The reason I could say that signal intercepts were used for gathering intelligence is that, looking at the Iraqi intelligence documents, I know they were constantly aware of the Americans' eavesdropping equipment, so they were quite aware, the Iraqi side, that the US had the capability of eavesdropping on their communications, as well as informers, people within the Iraqi Government, as well as probably from the Iraqi opposition groups, based on those three sources, as far as I know.

Q706 Mr Olner: Was there any linkage at any time between UNMOVIC and intelligence-gathering and what-have-you?

Mr al-Marashi: Between UNMOVIC and intelligence gathering? I am not in a position to say.

Q707 Mr Olner: There is no way you can speculate on it?

Mr al-Marashi: It is highly doubtful that UNMOVIC had any connections with intelligence as far as I know, given the past repercussions of the alleged US connection between the intelligence community and UNSCOM in the past. Given the fact that that had such repercussions, I would be sceptical at least that the were collaborating, that is, US intelligence and UNMOVIC, this time around, as far as I know.

Q708 Mr Pope: As an American of Iraqi origin, do you think, leaving aside the dossier that included your work, that the British and American Governments made a convincing case for the war?

Mr al-Marashi: I think the emphasis was in the wrong place. I think without a doubt that the regime of Saddam Hussein should have been removed, if not eliminated, in 1991. My regret was this over-emphasis on trying to implicate the Iraqi Government with the stocking of a weapons of mass destruction arsenal that could threaten the security of Europe, for example, as was argued in the September 2002 document. It was exaggerated and the repercussions of that in my opinion are that now US and UK forces are in Iraq, they are scouring for any traces of weapons of mass destruction when in my opinion they should be scouring Iraq for any evidence of mass graves. I think the emphasis is in the wrong place. The UK and the US are trying to find any members of the former Ba'ath regime and make deals with them if they can provide weapons of mass destruction when in fact many of them were criminals linked to the emergence of these mass graves, that they led to brutal human rights conditions in my native country. I think this whole emphasis, sowing this war as a war against the proliferation of weapons of mass destruction, was a bit misleading, and the fact that we have, I think, now forgotten the brutal nature of this regime and the fact that the mass graves that are showing up are not getting as much attention or are not causing outrage are because in this sense 10 Downing Street has pretty much put itself in the corner by arguing the case for war solely on the basis of weapons of mass destruction.

Q709 Mr Pope: Which, of course, is one of the differences between the US Government's position and the British Government's. We almost entirely based our case on WMD. One of the aims of the Americans and the British forces occupying Iraq at the moment is to de-Ba'athify the party. One of the things that we all noticed about Iraq was how the Ba'ath Party had seemingly infiltrated almost every aspect of Iraqi life. It was all-pervasive.
Mr al-Marashi: That is correct.

Q710 Mr Pope: Is that a realistic goal? I think we would all think it is a sensible thing to want to do but how realistic is it?
Mr al-Marashi: It is extremely realistic. The Ba'ath was prevalent in all areas of society. In fact, there is an Arabic word for the Ba'thification of society, *Taba'ith*. It is a process of infiltrating the Ba'ath into political parties, any kind of formal political organisation, any kind of educational organisation, any kind of sports organisation. It was standard government policy. They had a specific word for it. The process of extricating the Ba'ath from Iraqi society is going to be quite a difficult one and the problem is that any kind of professional in Iraq, whether he was a doctor, a lawyer, an engineer, had to be affiliated to the Ba'ath Party; if not a member, a sympathiser. There are different ranks. You can be a member or a sympathiser to get ahead in Iraqi society. It was all-prevalent and infiltrated every layer of society in Iraq.
Mr Pope: That is very helpful. Thank you.

Q711 Andrew Mackinlay: I had two or three questions here which you have largely covered, but one thing which does occur to me is this. You are not suggesting that he did not have weapons of mass destruction; you just think there was over-emphasis to some extent probably in terms of volume? Why do you think Saddam did not give unimpeded access, because his regime might have survived, it might have been sufficient, certainly here in the United

Kingdom and perhaps even in the United States administration, to at least spin it out longer? Why did he not concede more towards the end? It has always struck me as very strange.
Mr al-Marashi: In my opinion Saddam perhaps did not believe this, that they could have found evidence of him maintaining some kind of infrastructure for reconstituting his weapons of mass destruction in the future, what they call a breakout capability. The fact that perhaps UNMOVIC might have been coming close to finding out at least the infrastructure, that is our evidence, with the state of the paper evidence, or scientists, for that matter, who could have provided the key to uncovering these weapons of mass destruction, Saddam could have realised this and tried to prevent this. The fact of the matter though is that Iraq's weapons of mass destruction had never been used outside of Iraqi borders. There may have been a few cases of these weapons of mass destruction reaching outside Iraq's borders, but for the most part Iraq's weapons of mass destruction were a threat to Iraq's people. They were a threat to the Kurds, they were a threat to the Shi'a of Iraq, they were used against the Iranians once they crossed over their border. Definitely Iraq had weapons of mass destruction which were a threat to the Iraqi people and to the region. Whether they were a threat to the security of Europe or to the world is another issue. In my opinion I still do not think that Saddam fully 100% disarmed, given the billions of dollars that he invested in this programme. My opinion was that he destroyed his arsenal, destroyed any concrete evidence that he had the actual physical weapons, but there were clues that he was pursuing these weapons after the 1991 resolutions. Just in the last couple of years there was the case of an Indian company called NEC providing chemical precursors to Iraq. This was within the last year, so he had the substances. He was in pursuit of the substances. There was the discovery by UNMOVIC of 12 artillery shells that could deliver chemical weapons. They did not have the actual warheads filled but the fact of the matter is that they could have delivered the weapons if Saddam decided to do so. As well as keeping the necessary scientists, he had the manpower—or I should say the womanpower; most of Iraq's biological and chemical weapons experts were women—and there were clues that he was keeping at least some kind of residual chemical weapons capability or biological weapons capability. The key is, was it a threat as, let us say, the September 2002 dossier tried to depict? I would say no. I would say it was an exaggeration.

Q712 Mr Illsley: As far as you are aware, you were not known to British intelligence at all, were you?
Mr al-Marashi: As far as I was aware, no.

Q713 Mr Illsley: So your piece could not have been sought out by these people directly? They would not have known to go to your document?

Mr al-Marashi: No.

Q714 Mr Illsley: And yours was the first document listed on that particular site? If I went to the internet now your document would still be listed as the first one?
Mr al-Marashi: Yes.

Q715 Mr Illsley: Alongside how many other similar documents on a trawl of the internet?
Mr al-Marashi: How many similar documents to this? Having scanned the literature on Iraq's intelligence agencies exhaustively, if there is anything on Iraq's intelligence agencies that is in print I would know about it. I would say three documents in total deal with this breakdown of the structure of Iraq's security apparatus. There are three documents out there—Sean Boyne's, which is a two-piece article produced in *Jane's Intelligence Review*, Ken Gause's and my article. I would say that three articles in the press, and they are widely available, are devoted to Iraq's intelligence services.

Q716 Mr Olner: In answer to Mr Mackinlay, when we were talking about weapons of mass destruction, you did say that you felt that Saddam and his regime were still manufacturing or had still got stockpiled small amounts perhaps. Is not one threat the fact that yes, he has got them, even if he only has a small amount, and another of the threats was that he would willingly give them to terrorist organisations to use against the West or whatever?
Mr al-Marashi: No, I do not think that is a valid argument. Saddam would not even give them to his own military, never mind to a terrorist organisation. The control of these weapons were only trusted to the Special Security Organisation, which is not even a military unit; it is a political security intelligence organisation. It was only this organisation that could have deployed chemical weapons. The regular military could not, or did not have the authority to, deploy them. The command and control of these weapons was very tightly controlled. Based on his past precedent of using these weapons, I highly doubt that he would have given these weapons to an agency that he would have no control over. If he did not even trust his own military it is highly doubtful that he would give it to an organisation where he would have no control over it and that he would suffer the repercussions if the link was found. The argument that Iraq would have given these munitions to terrorist organisations I think is very hard to prove.

Q717 Mr Olner: Given your greater knowledge than ours on the Iraqi regime, and what you have just described about this dictator megalomania and what-have-you, do the Iraqi people now believe that he has gone and gone for good?
Mr al-Marashi: No. I could say as a fact that the Iraqi people still will not fully believe that he has disappeared unless they see his body. He had an all-pervasive presence in Iraq but he would rarely make a public appearance. He would rarely appear in public. What has changed? They still have not found

any conclusive proof that he is dead, so the Iraqi people are still convinced that nothing has changed since this war began.

Q718 Sir John Stanley: Apart from very visible things like missiles, most of the case for suggesting that Saddam Hussein had a major WMD programme rests on the figures reported to UNSCOM in terms of the unaccounted-for stocks of chemical precursors and so on. Do you have any reason to doubt those figures, which are the base line figures, the 1998 figures, or do you think they were hugely exaggerated? If you work from the basis that those UNSCOM figures, going back to the regime's declarations, were basically correct, do you believe there was a massive destruction programme? That in itself is quite reasonably detectable in some cases, certainly where CW is concerned, or do you think that there has been some incredibly successful, massive, hiding away operation? How do you account for the disparity between the scale of the programme in these unaccounted-for figures and here we are at the end of the war, access to all the scientists, etc, and we have come up with pretty well zilch?
Mr al-Marashi: It could be a combination of both, that a good part of the actual programme, stockpiles and so forth, could have been destroyed. Large scale destruction can be detected but basically not everything can be detected. Not all destruction can be detected. Concealing these weapons was something that the Saddam regime was very good at. They had 12 years of practice at doing so. They used any kind of facility in Iraq to conceal these weapons, any kind of civilian facility, the place that an inspector would be least likely to look a weapon could be hidden or any kind of precursor or necessary infrastructure or necessary machinery could be hidden in, let us say, a civilian facility. He had done that in the past. It could be a combination of destroying a good part of the arsenal or material and hiding the rest, but the fact of the matter is that he could have used any facility anywhere within the boundaries of Iraq to hide these weapons.

Q719 Sir John Stanley: But if you take the UNSCOM figures as broadly correct, if you take the assumption, which seems to be a reasonable one, that Saddam Hussein was not conspicuous about voluntarily going around destroying weapons of mass destruction, if he had a big destruction programme, surely he would have produced evidence of that when asked for when the pressure really came on and he was facing an invasion? What you are saying points to a very successful large scale concealment programme which sooner or later ought to be uncovered.
Mr al-Marashi: That is correct. There is a formal technical term for this process. It is called the concealment apparatus. It was believed that the head of the Presidential Secretariat of Saddam Hussein, the person who was just captured yesterday, was in charge of that. I really wait to see in the next week or so what kind of information he will provide but literally for the first time since this

war began the US forces have captured somebody who could really provide evidence on whether or not these weapons were actually hidden and to what extent. Whether he is going to be induced to co-operate and so on remains to be seen but, as I say, since this war began the first person who has been captured who has had a hand in concealing these weapons is in US custody and the evidence he provides will be the final key to providing evidence to the extent of Saddam's weapons of mass destruction programme.

Q720 Chairman: On that concealment apparatus, I have heard, for example, that there are several hundred miles of underground tunnels, that there are possibly tunnels under lakes and so on, that Iraq has had 12 years of practice in concealment with a number of experts from outside, including Serbian experts. Can you tell us a little more about that process of concealment?
Mr al-Marashi: It is not only underground tunnels but there were bunkers that Serbian—this was during the time of the former Yugoslavia that provided aid on these kinds of underground facilities, so there is a vast infrastructure of underground facilities in Iraq, and it has not, as far as I know, been publicly released how much of that underground structure has been uncovered or inspected. Those would be very likely places where such weapons could be hidden.

Q721 Chairman: Finally, I would like to build on a question which Sir John asked. You have researched extensively in the captured archives. Is it fair to say that the Iraqi regime was extremely meticulous in its bookkeeping?
Mr al-Marashi: Any incident, no matter how minuscule, was recorded in the Iraqi intelligence files. I will just give you an example. A soldier deserted to Saudi Arabia. They even knew he had six bullets in the cartridge of his Kalashnikov rifle. This is how minutely Iraqi intelligence kept track of matters. If they could keep track of how many bullets are in a Kalashnikov rifle it is most likely that key documentation or evidence of Iraq's weapons of mass destruction programme or any other kind of programme or human rights abuses were documented in Iraq. It was a bureaucracy that kept a record of almost anything that was of any significance or insignificance in Iraq.

Q722 Chairman: So in the light of that characteristic how can you help the Committee in this way? Here we have in November of last year a unanimous Security Council Resolution 1441. We have the forces of the coalition beginning to build up at his frontiers. There was a final opportunity if he did not co-operate. If he had destroyed those weapons it

would surely have been easy to produce those meticulously produced records, surely easy to produce the scientists who did it. What conclusion do you draw from that?
Mr al-Marashi: In fact, they would produce documents but then, again, the time it takes to link the paperwork to the actual destruction process, there was the key problem. They could produce any kind of documents necessary but how do you prove it?

Q723 Chairman: But these are documents to show, if it be the case, that he had destroyed all his weapons. If he had done so, surely those documents could have been produced to say, "Look: I am clean".
Mr al-Marashi: They could have been produced.

Q724 Chairman: So why were they not if he had in fact destroyed them?
Mr al-Marashi: The whole 12,000-page document that he handed over to the UN was this kind of effort, to provide the documentation that he had destroyed them.

Q725 Chairman: Yes, but by general consent the documents which were produced on December 8 were wholly irrelevant in terms of the fact that they were old documents, there was nothing that could show the process—
Mr al-Marashi: But it shows the point that he did try to produce paperwork to prove that he was complying. The fact was that it was not believed. He could have produced documents that would have provided evidence to say, "Look: I have destroyed this much amount of anthrax", but then the inspectors would have gone and would have had to take that paper and see the physical evidence of that destruction, so if he was faking this kind of evidence it would eventually have been uncovered.

Q726 Chairman: Can you give any plausible explanation as to why, if he had destroyed those weapons, at a point when he had the international community united, when he had the coalition forces building up, he did not produce the proof?
Mr al-Marashi: To understand why he did not do that? No.

Q727 Chairman: Before thanking you, could I also say a big thank-you for making such strenuous efforts to come to the Committee, as I understand you were a victim of the rail system and you did take a taxi, I think, for a large part of the journey.
Mr al-Marashi: Yes, that is correct.

Q728 Chairman: Thank you for that and thank you for your helpful evidence.
Mr al-Marashi: My pleasure.

Tuesday 24 June 2003

Members present:

Donald Anderson, in the Chair

Mr David Chidgey   Mr Bill Olner
Mr Fabian Hamilton   Richard Ottaway
Mr Eric Illsley   Mr Greg Pope
Andrew Mackinlay   Sir John Stanley
Mr John Maples

Memoranda submitted by Foreign and Commonwealth Office[1]

Witnesses: **Rt Hon Jack Straw,** a Member of the House, Secretary of State for Foreign and Commonwealth Affairs, **Sir Michael Jay KCMG,** Permanent Under-Secretary of State, Foreign and Commonwealth Office, and **Mr Peter Ricketts CMG,** Director General, Political, Foreign and Commonwealth Office, examined.

Q729 Chairman: Foreign Secretary, may I welcome you again on behalf of the Committee and with you Sir Michael Jay, the Permanent Under-Secretary, who we shall be meeting again in a different inquiry this afternoon, and Mr Peter Ricketts, the Director General, Political. We have considerable ground to cover in a short period of two hours and, of course, on Friday we look forward to seeing you, Foreign Secretary, in private session with senior officials. Can I appeal to you, Secretary of State, and to colleagues, that if we are to make progress on the range of ground that we need to cover we need both questions and answers to be reasonably concise. Foreign Secretary, hoping to set a good example can I begin this way, there have been the two dossiers, the September dossier and the early February dossier, we are promised by the Prime Minister another dossier, when will that come?
Mr Straw: You have been promised another dossier by the Prime Minister? When did he make that particular—?

Q730 Chairman: If I can find the relevant reference, this was on 1 June: "What I have said to people is over the coming weeks and months we will assemble this evidence and then we will give it to people".
Mr Straw: I am quite clear that the Prime Minister has not made a formal pledge to publish, as it were, a third dossier. What he has said is precisely what you have just said in respect of further evidence of the existence of weapons of mass destruction. He also said that this will be made available as and when it becomes available. As I think you know from the evidence which you took last week, in particular from Dr Samore and Mr Taylor, there are reasons why the Iraq Survey Group took some time to get going and it will be some time, I cannot say how long, before there is further evidence to put in the public domain.

Q731 Chairman: Would you expect that to come only at the end of the work of the Iraq Survey Group.

Mr Straw: Not necessarily. Again, I think both those people who gave evidence explained why a running commentary on the evidence which we hope is going to be collected may not be feasible or possible because you will be interviewing one person and you will want to corroborate what they are saying and to check back against other sources. The more likely probability is that this will come at the end of the process. As soon as there is information available which with our coalition partners it is judged safe to put in the public domain it will be put in the public domain.

Q732 Chairman: When that is done in whatever form what lessons will have been learnt about the use of intelligence-based material?
Mr Straw: I spelt that out effectively in both statements I previously made in evidence to this Committee and in some of the questions and answers which I have given. The process which was followed for the first dossier, which was the published on 24 September, was the right process and that was checked and double-checked by senior officials and was not signed off until the Chairman of the JIC was satisfied with it. We have spelt that out. Yes, ministers, officials and special advisers were involved in commenting on it but the veracity and the integrity of the document was very firmly a matter for the Chairman of the Joint Intelligence Committee. As you know the arrangements for the production of the so-called second dossier, which effectively was a briefing paper for the press, were not satisfactory, even given the status of the document, and lessons have been clearly learned in respect of that.

Q733 Chairman: What are those lessons?
Mr Straw: As Sir Michael has already made clear to the Committee, instructions were given very quickly after the failure of a proper procedure came to light to ensure that this sort of thing did not happen again. The lessons are very straightforward; you have to follow very clear procedures for any documents of that kind. Let me just explain this, at

---

[1] Ninth Report from the Foreign Affairs Committee, Session 2002–03, *The Decision to go to War in Iraq*, HC 813-II, Evs 61, 64 and 70.

a time of huge demand for media, 24 hour media coverage of a kind that is more intensive now than at any other time, there are all sorts of background papers being produced at any one time which necessarily are not going to go near ministers or senior officials (quite right too) provided all they are doing is replicating what is already in the public domain. The mistake that was made there was it was a briefing paper which then included intelligence and it was not subject to proper procedures nor proper checking. All that said and notwithstanding the very substantial error that the sources of the document were not attributed at all and that there were changes made, for example "opposition groups" to "terrorist organisations", the accuracy of the document I do not think is seriously at issue but of course it has been an embarrassment to the Government and lessons have been learned.

Q734 Chairman: So far as the first document is concerned, September 24, which went through the proper processes, have any complaints being made by any senior intelligence officials about the use made by those documents?
Mr Straw: None whatever to my knowledge.
Chairman: Thank you.

Q735 Sir John Stanley: Foreign Secretary, one of the central issues is whether the degree of immediacy of the threat from Saddam Hussein's regime that was conveyed to Parliament and to the wider public was justified on the basis of the intelligence information that was available to the Government. Central to this was the references in the September dossier to the 45 minute readiness of WMD to the Iraqi Armed Forces. As you know, Foreign Secretary, in the evidence the Committee has taken so far it has been alleged in Mr Andrew Gilligan's evidence, from the sources to which he referred, that the 45 minute element was a last minute insertion made for political presentations purposes and he associated that with the name of Alistair Campbell (who is before the Committee tomorrow). Would you like to respond to that allegation?
Mr Straw: It is completely untrue, it is totally untrue. I can go into more detail in the closed session, and will obviously be going into more detail before the Intelligence and Security Committee. Chairman, I wonder if I may be allowed to make this point in response to Sir John, so far as we can ascertain by word searches and so on, neither the Prime Minister nor I or anybody acting on our behalf has ever used the words "immediate or imminent" threat, never used those words, in relation to the threat posed by Saddam Hussein. What we talked about in the dossier was a current and serious threat, which is very different. The Prime Minister said on 24 September, the day this dossier was published in the House: "I cannot say that this month or next, even this year or next, that Saddam will use his weapons". What we did say was that Saddam posed a serious threat to international peace and security. That is the exact wording from the Prime Minister's introduction to this document. Interestingly that judgment, not that there was an

imminent or immediate threat but that there was a current and serious threat is also shared by the Security Council. Essentially what has been going on here is that some of our critics have tried to put into our mouths words and criteria we never, ever used. We did not use the phrase "immediate or imminent". Impending, soon to happen, as it were, about to happen today or tomorrow, we did not use that because plainly the evidence did not justify that. We did say there was a current and serious threat, and I stand by that judgment completely.

Q736 Sir John Stanley: Foreign Secretary, the Government did refer to the fact that Iraqi weapons of mass destruction were available for deployment within 45 minutes of an order to use them and you made that statement yourself in your House speech of 21 February. The question I wish to put you is that the US Government showed no lack of readiness to pick up British intelligence information which they believed would be helpful to their particular case of justifying military intervention in Iraq. As you well know the British information in relation to uranium supplies to Iraq from Africa actually made it into President Bush's State of the Union address in January this year, even though it was subsequently found to be based on forged documentation. You have told the Committee—and all of the evidence we have suggests this is wholly correct—that at no time did the Americans ever touch with a barge pole the 45 minute statement being made by British ministers. That would seem to suggest that within the American intelligence and the political community they thought the intelligence basis for that statement was extremely unsound.
Mr Straw: Can I first of all say on the issue of the uranium yellow cake, the information that was subsequently found to be forged did not come from British sources. A number of people have suggested that it did, it simply did not come from British sources, nor was this information available at all to the British intelligence community at the time when this first document was put together. Of course the words were chosen carefully, we did not say that Iraq had obtained quantities of uranium, what we did say, this is page 6, is that Iraq had sought significant quantities of uranium from Africa despite having no active civil nuclear power programme that could require it. As I hope to explain in the closed session on Friday, that information came from quite separate sources. Some background to that was that it is beyond peradventure that Iraq had at an earlier date imported 270 tonnes of yellow cake in the past, not at the time, that was not referring to that. So far as the 45 minutes is concerned I will check but I think that this intelligence was shared with the Americans.

Q737 Sir John Stanley: I did not question whether it was shared. It is striking that in the entire public statements of President Bush's Government there is not one single reference to that very, very important statement being made by the British Government?

Mr Straw: With great respect, I do not happen to regard the 45 minute statement having the significance which has been attached to it, neither does anybody else, indeed nobody round this table, if I say so with respect. It was scarcely mentioned in any of the very large number of debates that took place in the House, evidence to the Foreign Affairs Committee, all of the times I was questioned on the radio and television, scarcely mentioned at all.

Q738 Sir John Stanley: It was highlighted in the foreword by the Prime Minister.
Mr Straw: Of course but so were many other things highlighted in the foreword. This is a perfectly legitimate avenue of enquiry for the Committee but it is quite important for people to appreciate the 45 minute claim that these weapons would be ready to deploy, some WMD would be ready to deploy—no reference to missiles, by the way, as some of your evidence-givers have suggested, none whatever—was part of the case. To suggest that was the burden of the case is frankly nonsense. This has only taken on a life of its own because of the subsequent claims that this particular section of the dossier was inserted in there not as a result of the properly acceptable procedures for intelligence but as a result, as Mr Gilligan claimed, that Alastair Campbell had put that in there apparently from nowhere. That is totally and completely untrue. I also wanted to say this, because it is very important to get this into perspective, the case for seeking the first resolution for the Security Council, which we eventually got on 8 November, then seeking to hold Saddam Hussein to the terms of that resolution and then when he palpably failed to do so, deciding to take military action stood regardless of whether this evidence of the 45 minutes was available or not. It is significant because if you look at all of the statements that were made in the House and elsewhere, certainly in the lead-up to the war, the 45 minute section was not mentioned. Why? Because there was other evidence, overwhelming evidence, open source evidence which was available which was subject to no dispute.

Q739 Sir John Stanley: Can I ask one final question in relation to the second dossier, the dodgy dossier? There are a number of questions I would like to put to Sir Michael perhaps this afternoon if other colleagues do not take them up. Foreign Secretary, when you came before the Committee on 4 March you were asked by Mr Mackinlay: "Who authorised the dodgy dossier in that parlance?" You replied: "On the issue of which ministers approved it it was approved by the Prime Minister". Just for the record, when you gave your response to the Committee in answer to our questions when you said: "No ministers were consulted in the preparation of the document", can you just confirm you meant no Foreign Office ministers were consulted in the preparation of the document?
Mr Straw: I was drawing a clear distinction between the Prime Minister and ministers. No minister in Government was consulted about the document, apart from the Prime Minister.

Q740 Sir John Stanley: Apart from the Prime Minister. We now know that as far as the dodgy dossier was concerned it came very largely off the internet, words were changed to give it more drama and when the Prime Minister made his first reference to the document on 3 February said this in the House: "I hope that people have some sense of the integrity of our security services. They are not publishing this or giving us this information and making it up, it is the intelligence that they are receiving and we are passing it on to people". Everybody who heard that in the House and outside can have been left in no doubt whatever that this second document was an authentic, intelligence-based document, approved by the JIC, when as we now know that was nothing of the case. The question I have to put to you, and you are answering on behalf of the whole Government, because you are the only minister who is appearing—the Prime Minister, regretfully, is not appearing in front of this Committee—I have to ask you this in relation to what the Prime Minister said in the House on 3 February either the Prime Minister seriously misled the House as to the nature of the second dossier, the dodgy dossier, or the Prime Minister was himself seriously misled by his advisers as to the content and the sources of the document? Which was it?
Mr Straw: It was not either, Sir John. I do not accept the nature of that question. There is no question of the Prime Minister acting in the way that you have suggested. There are three parts to this second dossier, the briefing paper, part one and part three were based on further intelligence available to the British intelligence services. As far as I am aware the veracity of what was said in those two sections has not been challenged at all.

Q741 Sir John Stanley: Not JIC approved?
Mr Straw: I have made it clear from the moment I found out about this document, the procedure for putting it together was completely unsatisfactory. Let us put that aside. That is one issue. The second issue is notwithstanding the fact that the procedure was unsatisfactory did this second dossier say things which were not true. The answer to that is so far as the first and third sections were concerned is they said nothing that was untrue, it was both the first and the third sections, although they were not properly attributed, which were properly sourced and based in intelligence. The problem arose in respect of part two, which as everyone now knows was taken from a PhD thesis on the internet and there were some amendments made and this part was not properly attributed. It was not intelligence, it was about a description of the security apparatus of Saddam. A lot of the information even in the first dossier was taken from open sources, including things like UNSCOM and IAEA reports. The changes made should not have been made. If we pick up the key change that was made, where it says on page 9 of the dossier that the external activities of one of the security organisations includes "spying on Iraqi diplomats abroad", I think the original wording was "monitoring and supporting terrorist organisations in hostile regimes", the original

wording was "opposition groups in hostile regimes". Those changes should not have been made but both statements happen nonetheless to be true. In respect of terrorist organisations, the most serious of changes being made, you do not need to go to the internet to know that the Iraqi regime at every level was actively right until the last supporting the Iranian-based but Iraqi-financed and supported terrorist organisation MEK, which everyone in this room voted to be banned as a terrorist organisation three years ago and was actively supporting rejectionist terrorist groups in Israel and the occupied territories, Hamas, Islamic Jihad and Hezbollah, again which everyone in this room voted to ban as terrorist organisations.

Q742 Mr Hamilton: Foreign Secretary, can I move us back to March 2002, there was an expectation at that time, and that was partly fuelled by statements from ministers, that the Government would publish a dossier on Iraq's weapons of mass destruction; in the event nothing was published until the 24 September document. The Foreign and Commonwealth Office itself acknowledged there was a Joint Intelligence Committee dossier at round that time on Iraq in March 2002. On 16 April in the House of Commons in an exchange with you the MP for Halifax, Alice Mahon, said: "Will the Secretary of State say whether he intends to publish the dossier that was in the news a few weeks ago containing the evidence of mass destruction?" I assume she meant weapons of mass destruction. You replied: "No one should be in the least doubt about Iraq's flagrant violation of United Nations Security Council resolutions, we do not have to wait for the publication of a dossier". Then, of course, in September the dossier was published. My question relates to the March dossier itself, and what I wanted to ask you was whether the March paper was based on existing intelligence or had new intelligence come to light round that time?

Mr Straw: I am glad I said that because it was true and it makes the point that yes, of course, we published the September dossier for a reason, which was better to illustrate the threat posed by Saddam Hussein. I remember in some of those exchanges at the time I brought to the House to try and convince some of the doubters just over 200 pages of a very public dossier, which is the last report of UNSCOM, published on 29 January 1999. I just have to say that my starting point for getting into this was not the intelligence but it was open source information, plus statements made by many others on the record about the nature of the threat. I cannot recall exactly which document you are referring to but what is the case is that there were a series of assessments in respect of threats to the Middle East, including Iraq, which were coming through in JIC papers and if it were a JIC paper they tried to reflect a current assessment. We can also give you more detail about this on Friday.

Mr Ricketts: In March a draft was produced drawing on JIC material with other material as well, much less detailed than the eventual September

dossier but it was decided not to publish at that time and to build up a fuller picture, which eventually emerged in the September dossier.

Q743 Mr Hamilton: If I am not mistaken, Mr Ricketts, ministers really did indicate at the time something would be published and yet there was a decision made not to publish at that time.

Mr Straw: Yes. There was no secret about the fact that we thought we ought to publish a compendium of information at an appropriate stage about the nature of the threat posed by Iraq. When early last year there came to be a significant debate about the Iraqi threat at that stage as well as looking at intelligence papers I started to look at open source information. One of the reasons, it goes back to a question raised by Sir John, if you look through what I have said and the way I have argued this, and indeed the Prime Minister, we have tended to argue it on the basis of a great deal of open source information because there you are not asking people to take on trust what you are saying, you will say this stuff is available, just as in the House much later my main argument was based round the final report from UNMOVIC of 6 March. Yes, there was a discussion about how we brought the information together and at what stage it was appropriate to publish it. I am pleased that we did not publish the matter earlier because at that stage the question of what international strategy should be adopted in respect of the threat posed by Iraq was still itself open to discussion. By 24 September the strategy was very much clearer, the whole of the international community was clear that the first stage of this strategy was to go back to the United Nations Security Council and to get what became Resolution 1441, putting Iraq on notice about active and immediate cooperation.

Q744 Mr Hamilton: Would it be fair to say that what changed between March and September last year in terms of publishing a dossier was the fact that you had begun to examine all that open source information and were determined that that is what should be included as much as Joint Intelligence Committee assessments?

Mr Straw: It was more the political environment. I will say that I did publish information about the threat from Iraq. I cannot remember exactly when but certainly for some weeks, if not months, I would have had this information and I made it available, because it was a public document. For example a memorandum to the Parliament Labour Party when there were first concerns by colleagues about the nature of the threat—

Q745 Mr Hamilton: Can I move on to September dossier?
Mr Straw:—5 March 2002.

Q746 Mr Hamilton: Moving on to September 24 dossier, a number of assertions were made in here, why were they so rarely repeated in debates and statements by Government ministers between the publication in September 24, 2002 and early 2003?

Mr Straw: Which ones do you have in mind?

Q747 Mr Hamilton: For example we have talked about the 45 minutes. Some of the points that the Prime Minister makes in his opening foreword here were then not subsequently repeated?

Mr Straw: I said in answer to Sir John and to the Chairman the 45 minutes has been given a life of its own, which was not justified from this document nor by the ebb and flow of the political argument about the key issue before this Committee, the decision to go to war. However, this document did reflect our overall concerns about the nature of the threat and the truth is that we did make use of exactly the same arguments. If you pick up the Prime Minister's introductions, this is page 4, he talks about the threat to international peace and security, "when WMD are in the hands of a brutal and aggressive regime like Saddam's is real". He talks about the fact that in an inter-dependent world major regional conflict does not stay confined to the region in question, which is why we use the phrase, "a threat to the United Kingdom's national interests", aside from the fact that the illegal al-Samoud missiles, which we thought existed, identified here, which did indeed exist, with a range of 650 kilometres had a sufficient range to attack our direct assets in Cyprus, because those assets are less than 650 kilometres from the edge of Iraq. If you then go over page one, Mr Hamilton, you will see that the case set out there is exactly the case which we continue to use, namely that Saddam Hussein had used chemical weapons before; he had developed overt, nuclear and biological capabilities as well; he was very secretive; he concealed these; he was a significant threat to the region and to international peace and security and he was in open defiance of a succession of mandatory Security Council resolutions going back over 12 years to 1991. That was exactly the case he made. Of course we drew on the same arguments. At the same time it is certainly the case that we did not keep referring back to this as though this was the only evidence available, because palpably it was not. As the debate moved on the significance of this dossier was overtaken by other evidence entirely open. Once we got 1441 this judgment was shared by every single other member of the Security Council, including the other three Security Council members with extensive intelligence services of their own, China, France and Russia—Germany came on to the Security Council in January. The issue after 8 November was about Saddam's failure to meet the two tests set in 1441, not this because this pre-dated 1441, those two tests were a complete and accurate disclosure of all of his WMD capabilities and complete and immediate cooperation with the inspectors. He failed both tests.

Q748 Mr Hamilton: Finally, Foreign Secretary, can I ask you, and accepting everything you just said about the way events overtook the publication of this document, did you at any time from the publication of this document until the conflict itself started have any doubts about the accuracy of the information that was published on September 24?

Mr Straw: None whatever, and I said that in answer to questions and answers, nor do I now. Some of what is in here has been proved by events, none has been disproved.

Mr Hamilton: Thank you.

Q749 Mr Chidgey: Foreign Secretary, staying with the dossier I would like to ask you some particular questions about the section dealing with chemical agent production facilities in Part 1.

Mr Straw: Is this the 24 September one?

Q750 Mr Chidgey: Yes. I appreciate that your Department were responsible for Part 2 and Part 3, and not for Part 1 but no doubt you are familiar with it and signed it off at the time.

Mr Straw: Which page are you on?

Q751 Mr Chidgey: Page 19. You will note that there is a comment to say that UNSCOM had been responsible for the destruction of the main chemical weapon production facility at al-Muthanna, and it had not been rebuilt but "other plants formerly associated with the chemical warfare programme have been rebuilt", and that included the chlorine and phenol plant at Fallujah 2. It also says, "In addition to their civilian uses, chlorine and phenol are used for precursor chemicals which contribute to the production of chemical agents". I want to make you aware of the language here, if I may, so that we can come back to it further on in my questioning, again in paragraph nine the document talks about other dual-use facilities being rebuilt, new chemical facilities being built, including the Ibn Sina Company at Tarmiyah, where the production of chemicals that were previously imported were now being produced because they were needed for Iraq's civil industry. Then we have a later reference to say that at the al-Qa'qa' complex a phosgene plant had been repaired. There is an important here, it says: "While phosgene does have industrial uses it can also be used by itself as a chemical agent or as a precursor for a nerve agent". On page 21 is perhaps the most balanced comment in this section, where you talk about the problems of dual-use facilities and you say: "Almost all components and supplies used in WMD . . . are dual-use . . . any major petrochemical or biotech industry . . . will have legitimate need for most materials and equipment". Then it says, without UN weapons inspectors it is very difficult to be sure about the true nature of those facilities. At this stage I would like to ask you four discrete questions that might help us on the Committee to understand the relationship between the dual-use and the chemical industry and weaponising. Can you tell me whether there was any assessment made or were you aware of any assessment made of the production of the chemicals chlorine, phenol and phosgene needed to meet the requirements of Iraq's industry? Was there any assessment made of surplus production or devotion of production to the military for their use in WMD? Has any assessment been made that you are aware of or was any assessment made of the quantities of these chemicals that would be needed to produce the sort of stocks of WMD that would have been sufficient to allow the Iraqi Army to mount a sustainable and credible military action against any attack from the coalition forces? If there was what sort of quantities are we talking about? My final question at this point is, was there an assessment made or are you aware of that gave a view on the degree of the threat posed by Iraq's WMD capability to our coalition forces, embracing in all those four questions, were the scientific community involved in making those assessments? Did the Cabinet Committee agree with the assessments made by the scientific community or their contribution?

Mr Straw: My interim answer is fairly short. Because of their technical nature I will have to submit a paper[1]. May I say, this may be for the convenience of the Committee, we will do our very best and we will try to respond very quickly to your questions to get these back by Friday. If it is for the convenience of the Committee I am perfectly happy for the opening part of the evidence session on Friday to be in public to deal with issues like this.

Q752 Mr Chidgey: I will move quickly on because I know other colleagues want to make their contribution. Can I turn back to the dossier, I have just discussed with you this particular part on chemical production facilities, which seem to be fairly even-handed, if we now look at the executive summary the language seems to change to me, if you look at page 5, paragraph 6 we now have a statement that the judgment is that Iraq does continue to produce chemical and biological agents. It has military plans for the use of chemical and biological weapons and some of these weapons are deployable—we know about the 45 minutes. My point is that we go from the difficulties of interpreting dual-use into a definite statement that Iraq has these weapons. Then when we move on further towards the front and we look at the foreword we now see that the language is even stronger. We now see that assessed intelligence has established beyond doubt that Saddam has continued to produce chemical and biological weapons and there is no doubt a threat of serious and current—

Mr Straw: Which page?

Q753 Mr Chidgey: This is the foreword by the Prime Minister. I am really looking to know, do we know who actually drafted the executive summary from the body of the report and then the foreword because the language does seem to change?

Mr Straw: Is that the question?

Q754 Mr Chidgey: That is the question. Do you see my point?

Mr Straw: Yes. The Prime Minister signed the foreword.

Q755 Mr Chidgey: Is this Number 10? Is this the JIC?

Mr Ricketts: One point, the whole document, including the foreword, was shown to and approved by the Joint Intelligence Committee, so the foreword was not some and separable part of the document that was written elsewhere, it is was all cleared through the Joint Intelligence Committee. What you are seeing in the executive summary is the assessment and the judgment that our intelligence community brought. Having looked at all of the various factors you drew attention to in the body of the document the JIC exist to make a judgment to ministers and that is the judgment they came to.

Q756 Mr Chidgey: There is reference in the foreword to the assessed intelligence, can you tell us how current that intelligence was at the time?

Mr Ricketts: This document drew on the most up-to-date intelligence that was available to us.

Q757 Mr Chidgey: We have already received evidence from previous witnesses to say it was very difficult to get current intelligence from Iraq.

Mr Straw: It was on the most up-to-date intelligence available, I promise you that.

Q758 Mr Chidgey: My final series of questions is again referring back to chemical production and what has happened since the conflict to try and resolve these issues, we have already had the confirmation of the problems of dual-use in the petrochem and biotech plants in regard to WMD production. The dossier highlights the new facilities at Tarmiyah. The point is this, the new facilities are critical, as we understand it from the evidence that we have taken, that is because the trace elements of any WMD production remain for a considerable period on the site. Clearly plants that were previously dismantled by UNSCOM would still be contaminated even though production had not taken place for some years. With a new site and a new plant if WMD production had taken place in that new plant that could be confirmed quite readily by the trace elements that exist. These are the questions for you, if I may, have inspections and testing been launched since conflict at Tarmiyah and the other new plants? If so, what progress has been made and what has been found? When are the full results expected? Did the UN inspectors visit Tarmiyah in the months immediately before the conflict? If so, what did they find?

Mr Straw: Again, Mr Chidgey, I will get you written answers as quickly as possible[2].

Q759 Chairman: Do you think you could get those to us by Friday?

Mr Straw: I hope so. I will not know until I make enquiries. May I just make this point, Mr Chidgey, as far as I know, and again I will take scientific advice on this, your categorical statement that evidence exists where there has been CBW for a long time is not necessarily supported, it depends to what extent the facilities have been cleaned up.

[1] Ninth Report from the Foreign Affairs Committee, Session 2002–03, *The Decision to go to War in Iraq*, HC 813-II, Ev 72.

[2] Ninth Report from the Foreign Affairs Committee, Session 2002–03, *The Decision to go to War in Iraq*, HC 813-II, Ev 72.

Q760 Mr Chidgey: I appreciate that.
Mr Straw: Either Dr Samore or Mr Taylor were very clear in their evidence that with these dual-use facilities, which the Iraqis were unquestionably operating during the period of the UNSCOM inspections, they were adept at completely cleaning these facilities so they were sterile in between the production of CBW agents.

Q761 Mr Chidgey: That is not the opinion of all the experts. Can I ask you one final question: have any inspections been undertaken of those sites that I mentioned post-conflict?
Mr Straw: We will find out and come back to you[3].

Q762 Mr Olner: Can I ask, basically on a similar theme to Mr Chidgey, why do you think Saddam did not either provide evidence of destruction of weapons of mass destruction in accordance with UN demands or once military action had started why did he not use them?
Mr Straw: The most credible explanation as to why he did not comply was that this was consistent with his previous behaviour of lying to and cheating the international community in order that he preserved his capability, and that the most rational judgment made on the basis of Saddam's behaviour by the middle of March was that the anxieties of the international community about the fact that he had concealed chemical and biological weapons programmes and was beginning to try to put together a nuclear programme were indeed very well-founded. I know everybody here, with the exception of Mr Chidgey, voted for the Government resolution on 18 March, but I have to say that the question for those who took a different view is what position would we now be in if with all this evidence of non-compliance and of covert programmes, only revealed as a result of defections and the most intensive subsequent inspections, and with the incontrovertible evidence we also knew of the building up of their missile programme in the period after the inspectors had left, if we had suddenly walked away and allowed the inspections to dribble away, which happened before and would have happened again once the military pressure was off, what would have been the position now in the Middle East? You would have had an emboldened Saddam causing immense disruption to regional peace and security there. Your second question, Mr Olner, was why did he not use chemical and biological weapons during the campaign? We do not know is the answer. The assumption was that he would use those and, as I think either Mr Taylor or Dr Samore said, since the assumption was that he was likely to use them, the provenance of these weapons would be found during the course of the military campaign. I can only speculate why he chose not to do it. It may have been that having made serious undertakings to some people in the international community that he did not have this material, he decided not to use it and to continue to

have it concealed, but am I satisfied about the basis for the judgment that the Security Council made on 8 November and that we made on 18 March? Yes.

Q763 Mr Olner: How confident are you that the interrogation of Iraqi personnel will produce these concrete results in the weeks and months ahead?
Mr Straw: I am hopeful but—

Q764 Mr Olner:—But not confident?
Mr Straw: I say hopeful. You choose your words, I will choose mine, and I am hopeful. First of all, what we are looking for is further corroborative evidence. The case was justified on 18 March on the basis of evidence then available, let's be clear about that. Again, as some of your witnesses have explained, there are immense difficulties, particularly at this time, in creating a safe, secure and confident environment in which the right people feel confident about talking about their involvement in programmes. I am told by people from Iraq that the sense of fear that Saddam could still be somewhere is very strong. There is a real anxiety by people that if they offer information they could still be subject to intimidation or worse by people still loyal to Saddam. I also have to say that arrangements have not finally been made to offer immunity to appropriate people in return for evidence and of course where you are offering immunity you also have to make sure that it is done in a sensible and sensitive and relatively transparent way otherwise the evidence could be the subject of concern that it has been tainted the other way, in other words, the people giving evidence are simply providing what their interrogators want to hear in return for immunity, so these are complex issues.

Q765 Mr Olner: How far away are we from that immunity being granted?
Mr Straw: I cannot give you a precise answer just now. I will try and get you one for Friday[4].

Q766 Mr Olner: Can we try and move on a little bit because it is well documented that the Iraq Survey Group got off the ground a little bit slowly, given that there were other priorities that I agree needed to be attended to first. Now it is up and running, how many personnel are there and what type of skills have they got? Is this a big operation or just an add-on operation?
Mr Straw: It is up to 1,300 people now and I will bring in Mr Ricketts in a second, mainly US with some UK and Australians.
Mr Ricketts: The total number is going to be 1,300, they are building up to that now, of which there will be at least 100 British personnel with a wide range of skills necessary for looking for WMD.

Q767 Mr Olner: Foreign Secretary, how much importance do you think the Government should attach to having plans and things in place to ensure that the verification of any weapons of mass

---

[3] Ninth Report from the Foreign Affairs Committee, Session 2002–03, *The Decision to go to War in Iraq*, HC 813-II, Ev 72.

[4] Ninth Report from the Foreign Affairs Committee, Session 2002–03, *The Decision to go to War in Iraq*, HC 813-II, Ev 72.

destruction finds are done completely away from and completely independently and completely transparently of the global community?

Mr Straw: If we are talking about physical evidence, it is obviously very important that any evidence that is found is subject to rigorous, independent examination. Of course we all recognise that. That said, I think that recent events show that the concern by the coalition is simply to arrive at the truth and nothing else and that is what we are seeking to do. It is as frustrating for us as it is for everybody else. There is a separate issue about the direct involvement of the IAEA and in particular UNMOVIC. As you will be aware, the terms of Resolution 1483, the latest Security Council Resolution on Iraq, said words to the effect that the Security Council would re-visit the role of UNMOVIC and the IAEA in Iraq, and again your two witnesses Dr Taylor and Dr Samore gave you quite good explanations as to why they thought the current environment was not an appropriate one for the civilian inspectors.

Mr Olner: Thank you, Chairman.

Q768 Mr Illsley: Foreign Secretary, you just mentioned that the issue after 1441 was disclosure and non-co-operation as opposed to the threat posed by weapons of mass destruction. Are you now telling the Committee that the decision to take military action was based on disclosure and co-operation rather than the threat?

Mr Straw: I did not put it in that way. If I may say so, that is the wrong way of looking at it. It was because the international community said there was a threat from Iraq to international peace and security posed by its proliferation of weapons of mass destruction, its missile systems and its failure to comply with a succession of Security Council resolutions, that it then imposed new obligations on Iraq which were the inspections. The two key tests under 1441 were a complete disclosure, which they failed to provide on 9 December, and then full, active and immediate co-operation with the inspectors, which they also failed, but of course, as events moved on, the focus came on these two tests because they were the tests under operational paragraph 4 of what amounted to a "further material breach". You will remember that under op 4 "further material breach" was a failure of disclosure and other failure "actively, completely and immediately to comply." In the absence of their meeting these two tests under operational paragraph 13 the Security Council had warned Iraq that they faced further serious consequences.

Q769 Mr Illsley: At the end of the day I think you said the same thing, that the two tests, the two key issues, were disclosure and non-cooperation, as opposed to the evidence of weapons of mass destruction.

Mr Straw: If you look at the resolution of the House that was agreed by a very big majority on 18 March, it was carefully drafted, as it were, to take people through a series of propositions. We recalled the terms of 1441, the fact that it posed this threat, we

noted that 130 days since 1441 Iraq had not co-operated as required and was, therefore, in further material breach and had rejected the final opportunity to comply, and then we went on to deal with other issues. That was the sequence. Inevitably, as an argument evolves the current issue changes. What is crucial here, Chairman, is whether Saddam had capacity, was rebuilding his capacity, for chemical and biological weapons production and was seeking to re-establish his nuclear programme was simply not an issue by this date, the Security Council had accepted that. I attended five successive Security Council debates and that was not an issue. France and Russia did not stand up and say, "Oh, they have not got this stuff". When President Chirac gave his celebrated interview on 10 March he accepted that they had chemical and biological programmes, that was not an issue. The issue by the beginning of March was what do we do about the fact that—again, it was not an issue—he was in further material breach of 1441 and it then became an argument about containment versus military action, that is what it came down to.

Q770 Mr Illsley: Just coming back to the intelligence evidence and a very general question. How satisfied were members of the Government with the intelligence that they had in relation to Iraq? I ask this because one of the themes which seems to run through the evidence we have received so far is that there were requests for the evidence to be "sexed-up", there were perhaps suggestions that some of this evidence was quite old and, in fact, the 'dodgy dossier' had been initially written based on materials available in 1991. That was an historically based document. How happy were ministers with the quality of the raw intelligence data and the assessments from that data?

Mr Straw: First of all, let me make it clear that there was never any request for the so-called "sexing-up" of either dossiers, certainly not of the first dossier, none whatever.

Q771 Mr Illsley: Is there any truth in the fact that it was sent back six or seven times to the intelligence community to be rewritten?

Mr Straw: To give you chapter and verse on it, and I have been doing the same thing with the Intelligence and Security Committee, to give you exact numbers I would have to come back with the information on Friday. It is not about these things being sent back, it is an iterative process where various drafts are shared. All the time documents go through all sorts of drafting. I made comments, other ministers made comments, officials made comments. It is not a question of anybody saying, "This must go back. This will not do", the process was not remotely like that. It was here is a document, does it present the best case on the evidence which was being sourced and adjudicated by others, namely the JIC? That was the process. Was I satisfied with the intelligence?

Q772 Mr Illsley: Were you happy to use it?

Mr Straw: I was satisfied that the available intelligence justified the judgments that were made. Would I, in an ideal world, have preferred more intelligence? For sure, because the only reason we had to rely on intelligence was because of the highly secretive and mendacious nature of the Iraqi regime. That meant that we were reliant on a series of sources, but let me say, and again I will go into more detail about this on Friday, from time to time I would say in respect of a piece of intelligence that I had received, "What is the background to this? I want to know more about the nature of the source". On occasions, I would talk to the seniors of those people directly involved and so on. I think I have been reading and taking account of intelligence now for long enough, and anyway have a questioning mind, not just to take stuff that is put in front of me. Can I put this last point which is a really important part of our system. The reason why we have a Joint Intelligence Committee which is separate from the intelligence agencies is precisely so that those who are obtaining the intelligence are not then directly making the assessment upon it. That is one of the very important strengths of our system compared with most other systems around the world. Mr Ricketts can tell you more about that because he was Chairman of the JIC until two years ago.

Q773 Mr Illsley: Just coming back to the 45 minutes claim, and I know this has been done to death over the last few days. You said yourself that this has taken on a life of its own. I think one of the reasons for that is the prominence given to it by the Prime Minister in the foreword where it is highlighted in a very vague way, and this is why I come back to the quality of the intelligence, that weapons could be deployed in 45 minutes. There is no explanation of which weapons, whether they were weaponised, whether the weapons would have to be weaponised, what the term "deployment" means, whether that means deployed on a battlefield or from the battlefield or transported to the battlefield. There is a complete vagueness there. At the end of the day the suggestion is that if weapons could be deployed in 45 minutes they could be found pretty quickly during a battle or during the investigations afterwards. It has been suggested to us that the reliance on this 45 minutes claim tends to suggest that it would have been very easy to find such weapons if they actually existed, if they could be deployed in such a short space of time.

Mr Straw: With respect, Mr Illsley, I think that is with the benefit of some hindsight. People reading this document when it came out treated the 45 minutes claim in the way which was intended, as part of the evidence, but in no sense the whole burden of the case, not remotely. I would just refer to the fact that when the BBC's Mr Andrew Gilligan gave a report on this document on, I think it was, the *Today* programme, he said "To be honest, the document is rather sensibly cautious and measured in tone as a whole". He then goes on to say "There are a couple of sexy lines designed to make headlines for the tabloids, like the fact he can deploy within 45

minutes if the weapons are ready and he could reach British bases on Cyprus", both of which we actually knew, so they were not deployed because they were sexy lines. What Mr Gilligan was saying here was that in any event this information was known. I personally did not know it but then, of course, my sources are not quite as good as Mr Gilligan's it turns out.

Q774 Mr Illsley: I am coming on to that.

Mr Straw: It was news to me. Historians looking at this—I guarantee—when they go from September through to March, the decision to go to war, will make a judgment about what was in the minds of people and as at each stage people were shifting their opinions, in this particular example I gave in favour of going to war, and they will say, "Look, the fact that he had developed weapons, some of which were deployable within 45 minutes, was part of the overall case but in no sense the absolutely key element for it", not at all. The key element for me was much bigger than whether he could deploy them in 45 minutes, 60 minutes or 15 minutes. In any case, if he has got the weapons—it is a statement of the obvious—they are deployable within a certain period. The key thing for me was this guy had developed chemical and biological weapons and a nuclear programme against the will of the international community, he had used chemical weapons against his own people, he had hidden a biological and nuclear programme and then stayed in defiance effectively having pushed out the inspectors at the end of 1998, even though there remained this much unanswered business for the inspectors. Having done that, there was important evidence that he had not stopped his programmes but used that pause in terms of surveillance by the international community to build up his programmes. That was the argument, and then we gave him chance after chance after chance before we took military action to comply peacefully, and he failed to take those chances.

Q775 Mr Illsley: Finally, Foreign Secretary, were you concerned about the evidence the Committee received recently about the easy accessibility journalists seemed to have to intelligence sources?

Mr Straw: The first thing I would say is that our intelligence services, the security service and the secret intelligence service—MI5, MI6 and GCHQ—have people at every level in them of the highest integrity and professionalism, and I have no evidence whatsoever to suggest that anybody in those agencies is other than totally loyal to the Crown and committed to their job.

Q776 Chairman: That was not the question.

Mr Straw: I thought it was, I am sorry.

Chairman: The question was are you satisfied—

Andrew Mackinlay: Telephone numbers of journalists, that sort of thing.

Q777 Mr Illsley: It is the ease of access that journalists have to intelligence sources. I am not questioning the loyalty of intelligence services or whatever, although that is obviously a question.
Mr Straw: It remains to be seen, I would rather not speculate about Mr Gilligan's sources, but that was the answer to the question.
Chairman: We will pursue that further in private.

Q778 Mr Maples: Can I take you back for a couple of minutes to the so-called "dodgy dossier" and when that was first published on the internet. The names of the authors were given and I would like to take you through who they were and what their functions were. They were somebody called Alison Blackshaw, who is Alastair Campbell's PA; is that correct?
Mr Straw: I am sorry?

Q779 Mr Maples: There were four authors named in the file when the document was first put onto the internet. They were taken off pretty quickly afterwards but I want to take you through who they are and establish what their functions are. Alison Blackshaw was named as one. Is it correct that she is Alastair Campbell's PA?
Mr Straw: She is Alastair Campbell's PA, sure.

Q780 Mr Maples: Murtaza Khan was another. I understand he is the news editor of the Downing Street website and he works as part of the Strategic Communications Unit.
Mr Straw: I do not know him but I believe so.

Q781 Mr Maples: So he works essentially for Alastair Campbell as well?
Mr Straw: I think so.

Q782 Mr Maples: John Pratt, who I understand is a junior official in the Number 10 Strategic Communications Unit.
Mr Straw: If you say so, I do not know these people.

Q783 Mr Maples: He presumably works for Alastair Campbell as well. And a Foreign Office official you maybe can tell us about called Paul Hamill who at that time was working for the CIC which was at that time reporting directly to the Head of the Strategic Communications Unit as well, so all these four people were one way or another working for Alastair Campbell?
Mr Straw: One way or another, yes.

Q784 Mr Maples: Would it be fair to assume that Mr Campbell knew what they were doing?
Mr Straw: You will have to ask Mr Campbell that but he was supervising the operation of the CIC in his office.

Q785 Mr Maples: So he was supervising the production of this dodgy dossier?
Mr Straw: Mr Maples, there is a key problem about your question which is that as far as I know these four people were not involved in the production of the dossier.

Q786 Mr Maples: Then why were their names published with the original document as authors?
Sir Michael Jay: I do not know the answer as to why their names appeared on the website when the document was published. If I could just say a word about how the document was produced, Mr Maples. A group called the Iraq Communications Group, which is a group of senior officials which Mr Campbell chairs, commissioned a briefing paper for use with the media from the Communications Information Centre, the CIC, during the course of January. The CIC was charged with putting that document together and in order to do so sought information from different parts of the Whitehall machine, and that document was then put together by the CIC within the CIC.

Q787 Mr Maples: But you told us in answer to our questions that it reported to the Head of the Strategic Communications Unit, which is Mr Campbell, is it not?
Sir Michael Jay: The CIC reports to Mr Campbell.

Q788 Andrew Mackinlay: What does CIC stand for?
Sir Michael Jay: It stands for Communications Information Centre.

Q789 Sir John Stanley: Might I help Mr Maples on this very precise point. I am most surprised, Sir Michael and indeed Foreign Secretary, that, as I understand it, you have denied authorship by or the involvement of these four people. Just for the record may I say I have this morning before the meeting of this Committee spoken personally to Dr Rangwala whose memorandum is before the Committee[5]—
Mr Straw: I have a copy of it, yes.

Q790 Sir John Stanley: And he has informed me that in the few hours before the authors of this document were erased from the internet the computer names under which this document was saved, it was saved in the first instance under the name of Mr Paul Hamill, the Foreign Office official, then by Mr Pratt, then by Alison Blackshaw and then by Mr Khan, and he has hard copy evidence of that.
Mr Straw: I have seen that, Sir John, however in terms of the detailed operation of the CIC but these are questions you will have to ask Mr Campbell.

Q791 Mr Maples: We will. I just want to put this to you because I think it is terribly important it goes to fundamental subjects which I want to raise with you. Mr Hamill presumably you do know about because he is a Foreign Office official?
Mr Straw: I do not know Mr Hamill personally.
Sir Michael Jay: He is a Ministry of Defence official.

Q792 Mr Maples: He is not a Foreign Office official?
Sir Michael Jay: I understand he is a Ministry of Defence official who was working in the CIC.

5 Ninth Report from the Foreign Affairs Committee, Session 2002–03, *The Decision to go to War in Iraq*, HC 813-II, Ev 30.

Q793 Mr Maples: He is described on the FCO website as the Head of Story Development, which seems an appropriate title. One is tempted to ask why does the Foreign Office need a Head of Story Development, or the Ministry of Defence for that matter?
Sir Michael Jay: I imagine this was a function that he held within the CIC.

Q794 Mr Maples: The CIC needed a Head of Story Development?
Sir Michael Jay: The CIC is a group of officials drawn from a number of government departments.

Q795 Mr Maples: If that was his function it seems to me they got the right guy to do the job! The reason I raised these, Foreign Secretary, is when people like me read this dossier on weapons of mass destruction we believed it. We thought the Government is putting this out, it is based on JIC material, and we believed the Government. Even your opponents believe you when you say things like that. Then when we find the same Government, or the official closest to the Prime Minister, is capable of producing what can only be described as an amateurish, irresponsible and, quite honestly, fraudulent document in the dodgy dossier, do you understand why it then makes us suspect every single little difference in wording in these documents?
Mr Straw: Mr Maples, I understand why you make the claim; I do not accept what you say. I have already said that the way in which this document was produced was unsatisfactory and it should not have happened in this way, and it should have been subject to proper procedures. It is an episode which has been a very great embarrassment to the Government precisely because it has enabled those—not you, may I say—those who opposed military action in any event to seize on the idea that somehow the other evidence, which was the burden of the case, was not entirely accurate. But what I just invite you to say is leaving aside for the second the fact that the provenance of the document was not made clear, which was one of a number of aspects of the unsatisfactory nature of its production, can you point to parts of the second dossier which were and are now factually inaccurate?

Q796 Mr Maples: Yes, according to Mr al-Marashi, whose thesis was stolen for most of this document, on page 40 of his evidence he says there was a clear misunderstanding of the military security service, and in fact what is being described in the document as the military security service is something else. So, yes, I can point you absolutely to something where he, who is the expert whose evidence was used, says you are wrong. "Where it says, "Military Security Service", this section is wrong. The Military Security Service described here is actually the Iraqi General Security Service". So, yes, I can point to something that is absolutely wrong.
Mr Straw: That does not sound to me to be a hanging offence, if I may say so.

Q797 Mr Maples: Can I move on.
Mr Straw: Excuse me.

Q798 Mr Maples: All I wanted to raise this for is to say why people like me suspect every little difference in the wording of the main document. I want to come to a couple of those. In November 1998 the Foreign Office wrote letters to all Members of Parliament before Desert Fox and attached to it what was obviously an intelligence assessment and on the last page of it, paragraph 9, it says: "The Iraqi chemical industry could produce mustard gas almost immediately and amounts of nerve agent within months. Saddam almost certainly retains some WMD equipment." Dame Pauline Neville Jones and an official of the Australian intelligence agency told us said that that sounded like the kind of material that JIC produced, it is "could", "might" "maybe", and it has got ambiguities in it. When we come to this document that you published at the end of last year, it says: "We judge that Iraq has continued to produce chemical and biological agents. Some of these weapons are deployable within 45 minutes". All those shadings of doubt and ambiguity have gone. To make the leap from one to the other there must surely have been some new piece of intelligence in those four years that led you to go from "could" and "would" and "might" to "has" and "does". I want to know if you saw a piece of intelligence between November 1998 and September last year which led you to make that, frankly, fairly radical reassessment of the information that you published.
Mr Straw: I can go into detail on Friday about the flow of intelligence which I saw over a period. This document, I think, is very corroborative of the case that we made on 24 September and subsequently. It was signed by Derek Fatchett and Doug Henderson, and I understand approved by my predecessor and consistent with other things my predecessor was saying at a much later date, including in the early part of—

Q799 Mr Maples: I am not arguing whether it is true or not, I am just saying the language is completely different.
Mr Straw: The headline above paragraph eight says, emphatically—you said this comes from intelligence, I take your word for this—"Saddam will rebuild his WMD unless he is stopped".

Q800 Mr Maples: Four years later you are saying he has.
Mr Straw: Palpably four years later he has certainly not been stopped. Indeed, far from stopping the building—

Q801 Mr Maples: I was being very precise in my question to you.
Mr Straw: I am being precise in my answer.

Q802 Mr Maples: No, you are not actually, or you are answering a different question. Your document says that he is capable of doing these things and he will do it unless he is stopped. Four years later you are saying he has done it, he does have the capability.

I am asking you if you saw a piece of intelligence which justified the move from somewhat tenuous conclusions to absolutely unambiguous conclusions.
Mr Straw: What we saw over a period was intelligence evidence which arrived at an assessment which was then accurately reflected in this document.

Q803 Mr Maples: Are you saying that the JIC document used language like "Iraq has continued to produce chemical and biological agents", it did not say "may have done" or "has the capability to"?
Mr Ricketts: This document was drafted in the JIC structure and approved by the JIC, so responsibility for it was taken by the Chairman of the JIC. This is certainly drawing on JIC judgments and, as I said earlier, the point here is this is a judgment, it is a clear statement of our judgment.

Q804 Chairman: Were any of the ambiguities altered in the progression from the JIC initial report to what ultimately appeared?
Mr Ricketts: This document was drafted in the JIC and, as far as I am concerned, this is the judgment that the JIC came to.

Q805 Mr Maples: We had evidence from a former Chairman of the JIC, Dame Pauline Neville-Jones, that this is not the kind of language that a JIC assessment would use, that actually it is strengthened up considerably. What is more, for instance in the body of the document it says: "The JIC concluded that Iraq had sufficient expertise to produce biological warfare agents", but in the summary you say: "It has produced biological warfare agents." In the bit about 45 minutes, it says: "Intelligence indicates that the Iraqi military are able to deploy" and in the summary it says: "These weapons are deployable within 45 minutes".
Mr Straw: Hang on a moment, it does not say that, Mr Maples, it says that: "As a result of the intelligence, we judge that Iraq has . . ." and then goes on to say some of these weapons. The qualification for those is very clear. You made a very large claim a moment ago that what was in the second dossier published at the end of January was substantially inaccurate and that has damaged confidence in the Government, but the only thing you have been able to point to—

Q806 Mr Maples: You challenged me to point to anything and I instantly pointed to one thing.
Mr Straw: I just say this: some of those things, like the references to "opposition groups" should not have been changed to "terrorist organisations", but it happened, they have been changed to "terrorist organisations". That document, in that respect, was 100% accurate. If the only factual inaccuracy that you can point to is that where it said "military security service", it should have said "Iraqi general security service", then I rest my case.

Q807 Mr Maples: You challenged me to find anything.

Mr Straw: I would have thought—

Q808 Mr Maples: I am coming to this document and saying, for instance, it seems that where you say about biological weapons "JIC concluded . . .", that seems to me to be stronger than what it says about the 45 minutes which is: "Intelligence indicates that the Iraqi military are capable of deploying within 45 minutes". It says that on page 19. Those seem to me to be different. That has a ring of truth about it that is the kind of thing an intelligence assessment would say, but that is not reflected in the summary. The summary is much more certain and draws no distinction between the nature and the quality of the intelligence assessment on those two things.
Mr Ricketts: Perhaps if I could just respond in my capacity as another former Chairman of the JIC, Mr Maples. I do not find anything in the language of this at all surprising in terms of the judgments that the JIC reach. I do notice at the end of the Executive Summary there is a clear statement in paragraph seven: "These judgments reflect the view of the Joint Intelligence Committee." That seems to me to be absolutely clear, the JIC take responsibility for the judgments set out in the Executive Summary.
Mr Maples: I have to say "reflects the views" is exactly the kind of wording which high quality officials like yourself and Sir Michael use in documents when we know that does not actually mean these are the words of JIC or this is a document that they have produced. I am afraid I am running out of time but there is lots more.

Q809 Chairman: Can you respond in answer to what "reflects the views" means?
Mr Ricketts: I feel entirely confident that the JIC took ownership of this document, took responsibility for it and stand by it.

Q810 Mr Pope: Foreign Secretary, in respect of the September dossier you told us a little while ago that it was an iterative process, that drafts were going backwards and forwards, ministers would put little notes on, small changes would be made, it was an updating process. Mr Gilligan told us when he came before the Committee last week that his source, who he also told us was involved in drawing up the September dossier, said that the dossier was "transformed" in the week prior to publication, so between 17 September and 24 September the dossier was transformed. Was that the case?
Mr Straw: It went through a number of drafts. To say it was transformed—As I said, where documents like this have been prepared, a core is prepared and it then goes out for comment. There had been previous drafts and this particular draft, which I think started its life sometime in early September, went out, it went out for comment and I had a look at it. The thing I can say perfectly publicly is that I thought it should make more reference to earlier inspections because having read this document I thought it should have a wider audience, referring to UNSCOM's final report of uncompleted disarmament tasks through late 1998, things like that, suggestions. I think one of my colleagues

suggested that there should be a foreword. That is what happens. I think the implication of what Mr Gilligan was saying was that the judgments were changed, but that was not the case.

Q811 Mr Pope: The implication is worse than that. Can I just read you what he said. He said: "My source's claim was that the dossier had been transformed in the week before it was published, so I asked 'how did this transformation happen' and the answer was a single word, the word was 'Campbell'." What I want to know is, is that true? Can you refute that?
Mr Straw: Yes.
Mr Ricketts: What that implies is that the entire Joint Intelligence Committee would accept that their judgments, set out in earlier drafts, would be transformed at the request of a single official and then still regard the document as their own, and that certainly does not reflect anything that I know about the integrity of the Joint Intelligence Committee process.

Q812 Mr Pope: Could I Just move on to the decision-making process in the run-up to the conflict because Clare Short gave us some quite interesting evidence last week. She told the Committee that: "There was never an analysis of options, there was never an analysis on paper before any Cabinet Committee or any meeting, it was all done verbally. It is quite a collapse of normal British procedures for decision-making". That seems quite a damning indictment from somebody who was a member of the Cabinet at the time.
Mr Straw: That was not the case. I have set out in answers to the further series of questions, which I think you have had this morning, the degree of examination and debate that took place in Cabinet. Contrary to what Clare said first of all, it is not the case, as I think she said, that the Cabinet had gone into deep freeze between the end of July and mid-October, that was not the case at all. When Parliament was recalled for 24 September there was a special session of the Cabinet on 23 September which dealt with a couple of current items but the discussion was dominated by Iraq. In addition to that, I have also set out that she made a point, or I think Dame Pauline Neville-Jones did, about the fact that DOP had not met since June 2001. That is correct but in its place there is a ministerial committee with wider membership, which I think met 28 times between the beginning of the military conflict and the end of April. Can I just come back on this. Nor is it the case, as Clare claimed, that all the discussions which were held in smaller ministerial groups (some of them, yes, relatively informal) were without papers and, for example, it is simply untrue that there were no papers that analysed the military options. Of course what is the case, can I just explain this, which is a reconciliation between what Clare was saying and what I have just told the Committee, is that some of these decisions had to be and some of the discussions had to be very tightly held, and there was a reason for that, which is that we were involved in very intense diplomatic

activity throughout the period from the middle of July and if you were involved in intense diplomatic activity to start with, and it was with our partners in the United States and with other partners in the Security Council, you have to ensure that these discussions are tightly held. The communications you have with diplomatic partners itself are almost always confidential and often secret. In addition to that, we had to ensure that the military options were very tightly held too, not least so that none of its detail could filter its way to Saddam, so that was the reason.

Q813 Mr Pope: One of the things that Clare said to us was she described it as an entourage in Number 10 (comprising Sally Morgan, Jonathan Powell, Alastair Campbell, David Manning) that was in charge of day-to-day policy-making, and what I am putting to you in light of the written answers you have supplied to us this morning[6] is there was a gap between when the DOP last met, which was two years ago, and when the War Cabinet, the *ad hoc* Ministerial Committee on Iraq, started meeting, which was on 19 March this year, so we have got this very long period of time when there was no Cabinet committee meeting and what Clare was suggesting was in that period of time the day-to-day decisions were being made by an unelected cabal of people in Number 10.
Mr Straw: It is untrue. There has always been an entourage in Number 10 for as long as Number 10 has existed and people need to chill out about that. At any time there are people who are not in Number 10 who get concerned about the entourage. That is true if you look at recent history with Mrs Thatcher and also if you go back to the staff in Number 10 at the time of Harold Wilson, Harold Macmillan, Winston Churchill, Lloyd George, and so it goes on. As far as the Cabinet was concerned, Robin Cook provided the complete answer to what Clare was saying which was that there was the most intensive discussion week by week by week. I have given the answers here. The Cabinet discussed Iraq at every Cabinet meeting between 23 September 2002 and 22 May 2003, which is 28 meetings. In addition to that, I do not think Parliament has ever been more closely involved in a process leading up, as it turned out, to military action than this Government has involved Parliament on this occasion. I have done a list and I am happy to put it before the Committee, but leaving aside routine opportunities for interrogation of Ministers like first order Questions and Prime Minister's Questions, I took part in five debates or statements or evidence sessions between September and the end of November on Iraq and then seven before military action took place. It really was the subject of the most intensive scrutiny. The implication of what Clare was saying was that somehow there were decisions being made without reference to Ministers. That is simply untrue. Apologies, Mr Chairman, for taking a little bit of time on this but I think it is important to see the sequence of things here. In July, as the issue of Iraq

---

[6] Ninth Report from the Foreign Affairs Committee, Session 2002–03, *The Decision to go to War in Iraq*, HC 813-II, Ev 70.

had become a much bigger issue in the international arena, the question before Ministers was how do we get this issue before the United Nations, and that required the United States President to make that decision. There was not actually any argument, whatever position people subsequently took, about whether we went to war or not, there was nobody inside Cabinet nor in the country that did not think it was a sensible approach. There was a very intensive level of diplomatic and other activity to secure that. However, by 12 September President Bush went to the General Assembly and made this very fine speech at which he committed himself to the UN route. The next stage was delivering that Security Council Resolution. Again there was no argument about this, everybody wanted this. There was very intensive discussion to get the Security Council Resolution; we got it by 8 November. Then there was the issue of getting the Iraqis to comply. You know the story there, but alongside that there was the issue of military deployments. Of course what happened, as would happen in any government I guess, is, yes, we looked at military deployments and these were additional considerations made in meetings in which some or all of the people you mentioned were present. They included Number 10 officials plus others including the Chief of Defence Staff, the Prime Minister, the Defence Secretary and myself, often heads of agencies, sometimes Mr Ricketts or Sir Michael Jay as well. Then those decisions were reported to Cabinet. Then—and this is in a sense the defect in Clare's analysis—as soon as decisions were ready, announcements were made to the House of Commons. On 18 December there was an initial announcement made by Geoff Hoon in the House of Commons about potential military deployments and he made a series of further statements as well.

Chairman: Mr Pope, would you make this the final question please.

Q814 Mr Pope: My final question is on a different topic and it is questioning you in your role as the Minister responsible for some of the intelligence services. Mr Gilligan told us that it was a commonplace for people in the intelligence services to give information to a variety of newspapers and to himself. I put the question to him do people who work in intelligence services on a regular and widespread basis brief journalists and is that an ongoing process and he said: "That does seem to be the fact of the case." Is that the fact of the case and are you happy as the Minister responsible that there appears to be widespread briefing by members of the intelligence services to journalists?

Mr Straw: I do not believe that to be the case. I know a number of people personally who are members of the intelligence services, aside from those I am responsible for more widely. They are people who go to immense lengths to ensure that the trust that is invested in them is not compromised. It is true, as Mr Gilligan confirmed he knows this to be true, that because of the intense interest that the public and the media have in intelligence agencies, they have some arrangements which are entirely official for—

Q815 Mr Pope:—These are unofficial. Maybe they are the rogue elements that have been talked about.

Mr Straw:—for the briefing of the press, and of course we take seriously any allegations of this kind. I just want to put on the record that having been responsible over the last six years first for the security service MI5 and now over the last over two years for SIS, MI6 and GCHQ, I think the overall level of the quality of staff, their integrity and their commitment to their work is second to none.

Q816 Chairman: When you see us on Friday perhaps you could provide the instructions to personnel in respect of contacts with the press.

Mr Straw: I am happy to do so.

Q817 Andrew Mackinlay: I want to ask you this: you said that the dodgy dossier was an acute embarrassment to the Government; it was also an acute embarrassment to those of us who supported the Government in the division lobbies, and would do so again tonight for other reasons. But it was an acute embarrassment and therefore we are legitimately angry. I thought we rather stopped Sir Michael's flow because he was opening out just what was the genesis of this document, who handled it and I really want to go back to that, either through you, Foreign Secretary or Sir Michael, directly. Who handled this, who were the authors, and did it go to the Prime Minister in his Red Box to be signed off? Did the Prime Minister see it?

Mr Straw: I think the short story, a perfectly obvious point and I will bring Sir Michael in on the particulars, is there are people who believe there is some kind of conspiracy behind this document which, as I say, was unsatisfactorily produced but, as I say, which is also very important, nothing in it of any seriousness is inaccurate but, yes, of course it is still an embarrassment.

Q818 Andrew Mackinlay: Of course, I understand.

Mr Straw: : There was no conspiracy behind it. It was not remotely in the Government's interest to produce a document with this provenance. To put it in the vernacular, it was a "complete Horlicks" in terms of the way it was produced.

Q819 Andrew Mackinlay: So how did it come to be produced?
Mr Straw: It should not have happened.

Q820 Andrew Mackinlay: How?
Mr Straw: It happened because it happened.
Andrew Mackinlay: I want to know who did it, why, who commissioned it and to whom did it go?

Q821 Chairman: A simple question.
Mr Straw: Mr Campbell commissioned it, I understand. The request went into the system and then it went back to him.

Q822 Andrew Mackinlay: Did it go to the Prime Minister? Do we know that?

Mr Straw: He will have to tell you. It was authorised by the Prime Minister. The other important thing to bear in mind about this, and in a sense this is the foundation of the error, is that it started its life as a briefing paper, as a background briefing paper, and, frankly, if what had happened to it was that in addition to parts one and three, whose provenance was clear, they said "Here, by the way, off the Internet is a PhD thesis from this fellow, we think it is correct but for a wider audience, here it is", end of story. At the time it got remarkably little coverage. It was touched on by the newspapers but, as far as I know, not covered at all by the broadcast media.

Q823 Andrew Mackinlay: I think, Foreign Secretary, you miss a narrow but important point and it really goes back to Sir John's question. Let us assume for the purpose of our discussion for the next minute or two that the broad thrust of it was correct, but it is the status it was given, the trailer he gave it in Parliament. Sir John said either the Prime Minister misled Parliament or he was misled, and you said it was neither and went on to say that broadly the contents were correct, so I want to put that aside. What was the Prime Minister told? Did he sign it off?
Mr Straw: I was not present. As you know, this did not come to Foreign Office ministers so I was not present when it was "signed off".
Andrew Mackinlay: Was Sir Michael?

Q824 Chairman: Who was it?
Mr Straw: Neither was Sir Michael.

Q825 Andrew Mackinlay: He might know. Presumably somebody asked.
Mr Straw: You can ask Mr Campbell tomorrow.

Q826 Andrew Mackinlay: Foreign Secretary, you must have said to the Prime Minister—I can imagine it—because you meet him regularly, "We have a problem on the 'dodgy dossier'", he would have put his hands behind his back, gone back in his chair, as he does, because I have seen his body language, and he would have said, "But, Jack, I made the assumption that it came up through the normal channels". Am I right?
Mr Straw: I cannot recall that conversation with him.

Q827 Andrew Mackinlay: Precisely.
Mr Straw: I cannot recall that conversation but I think it was an entirely reasonable assumption by him if he made that assumption that it had come through the normal channels. He, after all, is the Prime Minister. Just as I made that assumption. You must wait to see Mr Campbell's statement which I hope to be with you later on today, and his evidence.

Q828 Andrew Mackinlay: What does Sir Michael want to say?
Mr Straw: As I say, it was a series of innocent errors, nothing venal at all.

Q829 Andrew Mackinlay: That was really good but let us hear from you, please, Sir Michael.

Sir Michael Jay: I do not have a great deal to add to what the Foreign Secretary has just said.
Mr Straw: You are a good man.
Sir Michael Jay: I am sure that Mr Campbell will be able to give you more detail tomorrow on exactly what the mechanism was on which the document was produced. What I would just like to stress is that it was commissioned as a briefing note, a briefing paper to be used with journalists, and it was prepared on that basis. The Foreign Secretary has said, even prepared on that basis, clearly when it was put together in the CIC, as it was put together in the CIC, then sources should have been attributed to it and the fact that the sources were not attributed to it was a mistake. As I understand it, it was then used by Mr Campbell on a flight to Washington in order to brief journalists.

Q830 Andrew Mackinlay: Okay.
Sir Michael Jay: I think that was exactly what happened. They are questions really to ask him.

Q831 Andrew Mackinlay: I do not want to labour this point, Foreign Secretary, but you referred to part one and part three of that dossier, Mr al-Marashi when he gave his evidence said: "If I could estimate I would say that 90% of this intelligence dossier was taken from the three articles, by myself published in *MERIA* and the two articles in *Jane's Intelligence Review*, virtually unchanged". It seemed to me he was quite emphatic. He looked at two other contributors.
Mr Straw: I am sorry, I have not done contextual comparisons but I just make this point: much of what is in here also reflected information that was publicly available in other sources. This was corroborative and what we knew publicly from documentary sources but also from Saddam's behaviour.

Q832 Andrew Mackinlay: Can I come to yellow cake. It is now agreed ground that the Niger document's were falsified, we do not know by who, but Dr El-Baradei has said publicly that he repeatedly asked the United States and the United Kingdom intelligence services to give him any evidence about development of atomic weapons. There has been an inference, I think either by yourself or the Prime Minister or both, that notwithstanding the fact that that Niger thing was totally falsified, we have been fooled here, not only that but there was some other intelligence which does support the fact that Saddam was seeking materials to develop nuclear weapons. My question is not coming to that, because we might go into that on Friday, but was El-Baradei given this information by the United Kingdom?
Mr Straw: The documents?

Q833 Andrew Mackinlay: Not the Niger stuff, which we now know is falsified, but what other information was he given? I understand that yourself and the Prime Minister, and it may well be right, think notwithstanding that we had some evidence that we cannot reveal.

24 June 2003   Rt Hon Jack Straw MP, Sir Michael Jay KCMG and Mr Peter Ricketts CMG

Mr Straw: First of all, just to repeat, and it is very important that we should repeat, the documents which turned out to be forged did not come from the United Kingdom and in any event they were not available to us in here, and neither did we supply those to the IAEA. That is point one. Point two: there was other evidence, which was available, which was the background to the claims made in this document of 24 September. As to sharing this information with Dr El-Baradei, I will give you a specific answer on Friday about that, having checked. What I should also say, Mr Mackinlay, is that we did share intelligence with both UNMOVIC and the IAEA. I think you will find that both heads were complimentary about the co-operation they received from us. I also make this point, which I think was underlined by Mr Taylor in his evidence, that we shared it as quickly as we could. We had to be satisfied about the security arrangements by IAEA and in particular by UNMOVIC and, as Mr Taylor explained, United Nations' agencies are not sovereign states and their ability to keep secure information is inherently more challenging, more difficult, than that of a sovereign state like the United Kingdom.

Q834 Andrew Mackinlay: Okay. Can I ask you about talking to the press, the security and intelligence services. I had a parliamentary reply from the Prime Minister. I asked him if he would make a statement on the system within the security services for maintaining contact with the press. He said: "In line with ministerial responsibilities, media inquiries about the secret and intelligence services are handled by the FCO press office, media inquiries about the security service are handled by the Home Office press office, GCHQ has its own dedicated press office which works closely with the Foreign and Commonwealth press office."
Mr Straw: True.

Q835 Andrew Mackinlay: A few moments ago you indicated, I thought, to the Committee that there were special, I think you used the word, "authorised" people who speak. These are different animals, are they not, from the press office? There are some blighters—There is some reluctance to concede that there are people who talk to journalists. There are journalists in this room who have told me that they speak to these people all the time. We had emphatic evidence from Gilligan that he has their phone numbers and they have his. Why do we have the secrecy that there is not a culture and a convention that people do talk?
Mr Straw: We do handle routine press inquiries for SIS, GCHQ has it its own, the Home Office has its own. We handled the security services. It is also correct, and I will go into more detail when I see the Committee in private session on Friday, as I said to Mr Illsley, that the agencies make arrangements for them to have somebody available who briefs particular journalists. That is something which is authorised. I do not see a problem about that at all.

Andrew Mackinlay: There is a problem, it is a constitutional point. These men and women can speak to journalists but they cannot speak to Members of Parliament. That is not a matter for secret session, it is fundamental.
Chairman: Final question, Mr Mackinlay.

Q836 Andrew Mackinlay: I want to hear the answer to that, it is important.
Mr Straw: These people, and neither do press officers, do not routinely come and give evidence to Select Committees because ministers are responsible for them, but the heads of the agencies who authorise this level of press briefing do give evidence to the intelligence and security community on a routine basis. Although, Mr Mackinlay, you prefer that to be a Select Committee, and as you know I have a great deal of sympathy with that opinion, it is nonetheless a committee of parliamentarians, senior parliamentarians, who are very independent minded and who do in practice report to Parliament.
Chairman: Foreign Secretary, we welcomed Mr Ottaway to this Committee for the first time just before the public session. I now call upon you to break his duck.

Q837 Richard Ottaway: Foreign Secretary, I act as sweeper on this occasion. With hindsight, listening to your evidence today and you describing the January dodgy dossier as an operation that was akin to "Horlicks", do you think on balance it would have been better not to have published it in the first place?
Mr Straw: Yes, given what happened—Certainly it would have been better not to have published it in that form or if it was going to be published to have ensured that it went through the same rigorous procedures as the dossier that was published in September.

Q838 Richard Ottaway: I agree. You said earlier on that it was to the "sexed up" but you did admit that there were some changes made. Have you any idea why the changes were made?
Mr Straw: No, we have been trying to find out how and why these changes were made. As I say, the key change that was made, which was changing "opposition groups" to "terrorist organisations" and I think as a statement it was entirely justified for reasons I have explained because it is a matter of public knowledge that the Saddam regime was actively supporting MEK, this very unpleasant terrorist organisation targeting Iran, and Hamas, Hezbollah and Islamic Jihad, paying the families of suicide bombers and so on. However, it should not have been changed in that context, which of course led to the difficulties it has led to. A better way of doing it would have been to quote directly from the PhD thesis and then say, "Our judgment is they are not only supporting opposition groups they are also supporting terrorist organisations", but made it a clear where we were quoting and where we were using our own judgment.

Q839 Richard Ottaway: Yet at the same time, if I can go back to Sir John Stanley's question on 3 February, when the Prime Minister said: "I hope that people have some sense of the integrity of our security services. They are not publishing this, or giving us this information and making it up. It is the intelligence that they are receiving and we are passing it on to people." Would you agree that that is now a shade inaccurate as a statement?

Mr Straw: I do not accept that because the first and third sections were the ones that were based on intelligence. I do not think there has been any challenge to those at all, apart from this slightly risible suggestion that there was an error between "Iraqi Security Service" and "General Security Service" which, as I say, is hardly a hanging offence. The middle part of it is a description of Saddam's security apparatus and when I read it through, bluntly, I thought, "Well, it is useful to know about this", but not suggesting that it was necessarily going to have this kind of architecture, it might be slightly different, but any regime like that was bound to have this kind of security apparatus.

Q840 Richard Ottaway: Would it be helpful if by Friday you were able to break down the January document to let us know who produced which part of it because it says at the top that it draws on a number of sources and I think it would be rather helpful to the Committee if we knew what bits were produced by whom.

Mr Straw: Of course I can do that in more detail, but the key point is that part two was drawn overwhelmingly from this PhD thesis, subject to these amendments which we have described and which we have identified. My understanding is that the first and third were drawn largely from intelligence but of course included some perfectly open information about the nature of the Ba'ath Party.

Q841 Richard Ottaway: So in truth when the Prime Minister says it is intelligence that the JIC is receiving, it is some of the intelligence that the JIC is receiving?

Mr Straw: It never claimed that it was simply from intelligence. The rubric at the top of page 1 says: "This report draws upon a number of sources, including intelligence material, and shows how the Iraqi regime is constructed to keep WMD . . . and is now engaged in a campaign of obstruction of the UN Weapons Inspectorate", which for certain it was.

Q842 Richard Ottaway: To go back to the point Mr Maples was making, as a backbencher who does not get the sort of intelligence you get, you have to make a decision on this and it was not unreasonable to believe, from what the Prime Minister was saying, that it was primarily intelligence based.

Mr Straw: As to burden, in terms of percentage it is more difficult to measure but I will try to give you an assessment. Mr Ottaway, I understand the point that Mr Maples was making and I dearly believe it would have been very helpful to the Government if the

provenance of this document had been made clear from the start, but I do also say in terms of should you believe the document or not, yes, actually this document was accurate and it makes it all the more aggravating that we have had to deal with the problems that we have about the inadequate sourcing and the changing of some words.

Q843 Richard Ottaway: Turning to the September 2002 document, you have sought today to play down the 45 minutes claim somewhat, and I wrote down the words you used, that "it has got a life of its own". I just draw your attention to the fact that it is referred to no less than four times in the September document and, indeed, on page 17 under "The current position: 1998–2002", it is described as one of nine main conclusions, along with uranium being sought from Africa. You then said that since then it had not been repeated. Of course, the President of the United States repeated it in his State of the Union address and you in your speech at Chatham House repeated it as well.

Mr Straw: I did not say it had not been repeated although, I must say, I had forgotten that. One of your other colleagues, I think, claimed that nobody in the United States ever mentioned 45 minutes, well it turns out, Sir John, that the President of the United States did in his State of the Union address.

Sir John Stanley: No, he did not.

Q844 Richard Ottaway: I stand corrected.

Mr Straw: It was part of this but plenty of other things in a document which has an Introduction, Executive Summary and a body. It was repeated four times. I think when people got this document subsequently they judged the 45 minute claim in context. It was not the revelation, the flash from the Gods, that led people to change their minds at all, it was simply one part of the evidence, the overwhelming evidence was about Iraq's use and capability of chemical weapons, its capability of biological weapons, its drawing up of a very extensive nuclear programme which it had, which was discovered in the mid-1990s, and all the other things that followed. This was further and better particulars. I just make this point: the 45 minutes issue was no more an issue in terms of the decision to go to war than a wide range of other matters until Mr Gilligan made his claim on the *Today* programme on 21 May.[7] Of course, I understand why people are now interested in this, but if you are looking at the decision to go to war, to claim with the benefit of hindsight since 21 May that this 45 minutes claim was somehow central to the consideration of that decision to go to war, that is simply not the case because people looked at the very much bigger picture. Here was Saddam, he was a threat to international peace and security, he had refused to comply with a Whole series of mandatory United Nations Security Council resolutions, we had gone back to the United Nations, he had been given a final opportunity to comply, he failed to take

---

[7] *Note by Witness:* The Foreign Secretary intended to refer to the claim made on 29 May.

it, and even then, let me say, was given an ultimatum by us, was offered, as both Donald Rumsfeld and I did in the middle of January, the opportunity to leave Iraq and be given safe haven and, as Donald Rumsfeld said on that occasion, a far better alternative than war, and I agreed with him, and he was given a 48 hour ultimatum once a decision was taken.

Q845 Richard Ottaway: Do you still stand by the 45 minutes claim?
Mr Straw: It was not my claim. I stand by the integrity of the JIC. This is a really important point—really important. I stand by the integrity of the people on the Joint Intelligence Committee—

Q846 Richard Ottaway: Do you still believe the claim?
Mr Straw:—who made the assessment. I believe that they made the assessment properly. Let us be absolutely clear about this. This was not my claim in the sense that I simply got together a pile of documents and thought "That is a nice idea". This was intelligence which came into the agencies in the normal way and was then subject to assessment in the normal way and was made by the JIC. I accept the claim but did not make it.

Q847 Richard Ottaway: So really you are just the advocate for the intelligence information that is put in front of you? On that point, do you agree with the Member for Livingston when he appeared in front of this Committee, your predecessor, he was talking about the way intelligence is put together and he said: "It is not perceived, it is not invention"—he was talking about the sincerity of yourself and the Prime Minister—"it is not coming up with intelligence that did not exist, but it is not presenting the whole picture. I fear the fundamental problem is instead of using intelligence as evidence on which to base the conclusion of a policy, we used intelligence as the basis on which we could justify a policy on which we had already settled". First of all, do you accept the cherry-picking argument that only certain bits of intelligence were being presented?
Mr Straw: No, I do not. I certainly accept what Robin says when he says intelligence necessarily gives an incomplete picture by definition. What you therefore have to do is have a very clear system of assessment in respect of that assessment and why we have a JIC process. It is why I quite often (not only in respect of Iraq) ask further questions about the provenance of particular sources and I will go into this in some more detail on Friday. But the case, Mr Ottaway, we made—and I just want to repeat this—did not depend on the 45-minute claim or any other individual claim, it depended on the overall assessment of the behaviour of Saddam and the threat that he posed, and most of that was in the public domain. I know that you and I think Mr Maples put to Robin what was said on his behaviour by Derek Fatchett and Doug Henderson in 1998 and I myself put to Robin what he wrote in the *Daily Telegraph* on 20 February 2001 in which he says: "We believe that Saddam is still hiding these weapons in a range of locations in Iraq and Iraq is taking advantage of the absence of weapons inspectors to rebuild weapons of mass destruction." What I readily accept is this: Robin on the basis of evidence judged that containment could work; I did not, and that was the difference.
Chairman: With brisk questions and brisk replies we can make progress. Mr Illsley, on this point.

Q848 Mr Illsley: In reference to the second dossier I think you said again a few moments ago that it was substantially correct. The Committee has received evidence from a Professor[8] which goes through that document page by page and indicates that pages 6 to 16 are all taken from internet sources, and pages 2 to 5 relate to the claims made by Hans Blix to the UN Security Council, which are then contrasted with other claims with the suggestion that those claims are wrong. The numbers of soldiers in the document have been substantially increased. To give you one quote from it, the original article referred to forces being recruited from regions loyal to Saddam and comprise 10,000 to 15,000 "bullies and country bumpkins". In the document that was published by the Government this then became "10,000 to 15,000 bullies", so words have been omitted, words have been added. The whole context of some parts of this document have simply been mistakenly put in there. The changing of names of organisations like General Intelligence to Military Intelligence suggest in a Government document that an organisation was founded in 1992 apparently before it had been created. There are a whole series of inaccuracies which have been put to us by Professor Rangwala.
Mr Straw: I have already accepted that there are sections from the internet, particularly in respect of the PhD thesis, should not have been changed. We have been over this before. If there are basic points made in that document which are themselves inaccurate I have yet to hear them, and I will go through his particular evidence, but the basic points made in the document about the nature of the regime and its failure to comply with the weapons inspectors and security structures were accurate. That does not excuse a separate issue which was about the provenance of the document but nor should you produce the defects about providing provenance for the document as a reason for saying therefore the document was inaccurate.

Q849 Chairman: Foreign Secretary, that document was sent to you. It would be helpful if you had a note with your observations on Mr Rangwala's submission.
Mr Straw: I will try and get that to you by Friday[9].

Q850 Sir John Stanley: Foreign Secretary, when you answered my previous series of questions you said towards the end that you believed in the total veracity of the September document, the September

---

[8] Ninth Report from the Foreign Affairs Committee, Session 2002–03, *The Decision to go to War in Iraq*, HC 813-II, Ev 30.

[9] Ninth Report from the Foreign Affairs Committee, Session 2002–03, *The Decision to go to War in Iraq*, HC 813-II, Ev 74.

JIC approved assessment of Iraq's weapons of mass destruction. I must put it to you that I can see no basis on which you can say that unless the weapons of mass destruction programme on the scale set out here is actually uncovered in Iraq, unless you believe that Saddam Hussein had a covert, secret massive destruction programme of his WMD. The Prime Minister, you will remember, looked at that possibility in his speech in the House on 18 March and he said: "We are asked now seriously to accept that in the last few years, contrary to all history, contrary to all intelligence, Saddam decided unilaterally to destroy those weapons. I say that such a claim is palpably absurd." I wholly agree with the Prime Minister, it is palpably absurd to suggest that the scale of this WMD programme has been secretary destroyed by Saddam Hussein. The issue is not whether he had some capability of some potential, so please do not ride off on that one, the issue is whether he had it on the scale set out to Parliament and to the British people and was used as a justification for war. I put it to you that there is no way you can say that this is correct until weapons of mass destruction on the scale set out in this document are uncovered.

Mr Straw: Let me say this in response to you, Sir John. Again, to repeat the point, what was in that dossier was corroborated by earlier evidence provided by UNSCOM and later evidence contained in UNMOVIC reports. If you want further corroboration, I did not refer in my speech on 18 March, nor in the much more extensive statement that I gave on 17 March, to this September dossier. I did refer to the 173 pages that Dr Blix had provided to the Security Council on 7 March of unresolved disarmament issues. Of course, it would be hugely helpful if further corroboration of the extent of these programmes was found, but the fact that evidence cannot be found does not mean that the programmes did not exist. Overwhelmingly, the rational explanation for Saddam's behaviour, all the evidence, has to be that programmes of the scale identified existed. What was in that dossier was also in here. It is in here that reference is made on 6 March 2003 to the fact that UNMOVIC believed in respect of 10,000 litres of anthrax—I am trying to dig out the exact statement—they said there was a substantial presumption that they still existed, and there were 29 separate clusters, a whole series of unresolved questions. My point is this: leave aside our dossier, look in here. It would have been utterly irresponsible for the international community in the face of this evidence here and Saddam's behaviour going back over 25 years to have simply sat on our hands and done nothing about his failure to comply with the United Nations. That was at the heart of the argument.

Q851 Mr Pope: Just a quick final question about the February dossier and Mr al-Marashi's evidence to us last week. Put in a nutshell, it appears that his thesis was downloaded off the Internet by someone—we will probably find out tomorrow by whom—that was not accredited to him, his permission was not sought, some of his work was

changed, as we have heard, and there were some inaccuracies in the final document. But worst of all—I just find this incredible—Mr al-Marashi is an Iraqi, his family are still in Iraq, and it seems to me that nobody at any point anywhere in the Government gave any thought to the effect that linking him intimately with the case for Britain going to war would have on his relatives in Iraq. Do you think that whoever compiled this document owes him an apology?

Mr Straw: He is owed an apology and I am very happy now to give an apology on behalf of the Government. Of course he should have been asked his permission and it is one of the many errors that were made.

Mr Pope: That is very helpful, thank you.

Q852 Andrew Mackinlay: One thing you might clarify for me about Hamill and Manning; one is FCO and one is Department of Defence.

Mr Straw: Sir David Manning is the Prime Minister's principal diplomatic adviser, very shortly to be Her Majesty's Ambassador in Washington and Mr Hamill, Sir Michael?

Sir Michael Jay: Mr Hamill was working at the time for the Communications Information Centre, the CIC.

Q853 Andrew Mackinlay: I am not being sarcastic, but his fingerprints are on this document we have focused on. Manning would not have seen this document, would he?

Mr Straw: I do not know.

Q854 Andrew Mackinlay: The final thing concerns Cabinet government. The Cabinet did not sit from the rise of Parliament at the end of July around to beyond the third week of October. I am wrong?

Mr Straw: Cabinet met in the very last week of July. I cannot give you the date but I am pretty certain about that. It definitely met on 23 September.

Chairman: Two final points, Foreign Secretary. Firstly, there are questions which we hope to address to Sir Michael at the beginning of this afternoon's session which will begin at 3.15, which have not been resolved this morning. Secondly, a final thought, you have said that the only rational explanation is that those weapons of mass destruction existed. Do you think it might be time now to think the unthinkable that in fact Saddam had destroyed those stockpiles or at least, as Sir John has said, a large part of those stockpiles from the time when UNSCOM made its report and that perhaps—

Sir John Stanley: I most certainly did not say that. I agreed with the Prime Minister that it was palpably absurd to suggest that Saddam Hussein had a secret WMD destruction programme.

Q855 Chairman: I am sorry, that the quantities were substantially less and that possibly there were valid reasons why Saddam Hussein deliberately kept up the pretence, namely to keep his enemies at home and abroad in fear and trembling and also perhaps for reasons of national prestige?

Mr Straw: I saw that that was one speculative explanation offered. No, I think for international peace and security it would have been irresponsible and rash, to pick up your phrase, to have thought the unthinkable here and completely inconsistent with the burden of the evidence and what we knew and know about Saddam, completely inconsistent with that. I must go, I am afraid. I am happy to see you again on Friday but I will just make this point: there were the most intensive inspections of the Saddam regime between 1991 and 1995 and it was not until a combination of the inspectors coming across some evidence and, above all, the defection of his son-in-law that anything was known of any significance about the scale of the biological weapons programme and the nuclear programme. I think Mr Taylor or Dr Samore made the point in respect of the Soviets, that the ability of totalitarian regimes to conceal programmes is really astonishing, but it is there. No-one has to speculate about the nature of this regime and what it had done, it is all here in perfectly open sources.

Q856 Chairman: Our debate will continue on Friday morning and with Sir Michael briefly at the start of this afternoon's session.

Mr Straw: We will make arrangements about what proportion of the session on Friday is in private and which public.

Tuesday 24 June 2003

Members present:

Donald Anderson, in the Chair

Mr David Chidgey
Mr Fabian Hamilton
Mr Eric Illsley
Andrew Mackinlay
Mr John Maples

Mr Bill Olner
Richard Ottaway
Mr Greg Pope
Sir John Stanley

Witnesses: **Sir Michael Jay KCMG,** Permanent Under-Secretary of State, and **Mr Peter Ricketts CMG,** Director, Political, Foreign and Commonwealth Office, examined.

Chairman: Sir Michael, may I welcome you and Mr Ricketts for the first part, which effectively is the spill-over of the proceedings from this morning, a matter which is particularly within your own sphere of knowledge and responsibility. I shall call a number of colleagues in respect of that. Then we will have a short break, when the proceedings there in respect of our Iraq inquiry will then be in abeyance until we meet the Foreign Secretary again on Friday morning, briefly, in public session, then in private session. We will move on then to the normal meeting with you and your colleagues in respect of the FCO administration, the Annual Report. So first then on to the Iraq inquiry. Mr Maples.

Q857 Mr Maples: Sir Michael, I wonder if you can help us with something that came up this morning, which I do not quite understand now. In answer to the different questions, the Foreign Secretary said that the Defence and Overseas Policy Committee last met on June 28, 2001, just after the election, and therefore it has not met since, in what is now two years, which included September 11, the Afghanistan war and the Iraq war, and the War Cabinet, which had a slightly different membership, met on 29 occasions, all apparently between 19 March and 28 April, in other words, when the war was actually on, which was what one would expect. So what I do not think I understand is, and, I think, several other members of the Committee, we used to understand the process by which foreign policy decisions were arrived at, through a Cabinet sub-committee meeting, with detailed papers, making a decision, reporting to the Cabinet and that being accountable to Parliament; how does that process work now, if OPD, or DOP, or whatever it is called now, effectively does not exist?
Sir Michael Jay: The main ministerial discussion which takes place on foreign policy issues is in Cabinet, and there is a Cabinet meeting, there are always foreign affairs on the agenda, and I think I am right in saying that Iraq was on the agenda of each Cabinet meeting, or virtually every Cabinet meeting, in the nine months, or so, up until the conflict broke out, in April. The main, formal ministerial forum for discussing foreign policy issues is in Cabinet.

Q858 Mr Maples: But those cannot be a meeting of 23 people, all with detailed papers, setting out military options and strategic options; presumably, there is some pre-meeting which brings to Cabinet, as OPD would have done, a policy suggestion?
Sir Michael Jay: There are informal meetings of ministers, which will be chaired either by the Prime Minister or by the Foreign Secretary, to discuss whatever the issues of the day might be, which will meet as necessary.

Q859 Mr Maples: So there is no formal structure, as there used to be with OPD, there is no formal channel by which matters reach the Cabinet, after having been considered in detail, as I say, with papers and options, and so on?
Sir Michael Jay: As the Foreign Secretary said this morning, OPD itself did not meet in that period.

Q860 Mr Maples: But there is no substitute for it, is what I am getting at?
Sir Michael Jay: There is no formal Cabinet committee substitute for it.

Q861 Mr Maples: So, if we take the fundamental decision about Iraq, which was, at some stage last year, the Government obviously took a decision basically to support the United States, maybe with some caveats and some exceptions, where would that decision have been taken and communicated to the Cabinet, because I do not imagine on each of these occasions the Cabinet discussed it and had the kinds of papers you would get at a Cabinet sub-committee?
Sir Michael Jay: I cannot myself go into the intricacies of what papers were or were not produced to Cabinet, but there would have been Cabinet discussion based on papers submitted to Cabinet and that would have followed meetings between the Prime Minister and other ministers meeting informally as necessary.

Q862 Mr Maples: Would the Foreign Secretary have been involved in all of those meetings, or would there have been meetings that took place in Number 10, in which, you know, for instance, that he was not involved?

Sir Michael Jay: I cannot imagine a serious meeting taking place on Iraq to which the Foreign Secretary would not have been invited had he been in the country.

Q863 Sir John Stanley: Sir Michael, you said this morning that Mr Campbell commissioned what has now become known colloquially as the "dodgy dossier"; when was it commissioned?
Sir Michael Jay: I think it was commissioned by the Iraq Communication Group meeting that he chairs, in, I think I am right in saying, earlyish January. I have not got the exact chronology, he will be able to give you the exact chronology, but early on in January there was a decision that it would be good to produce a briefing paper for use with the media which would describe the Iraqi regime's ability to hamper the weapons inspectors; that was the basis of the commission by the Iraq Communication Group.

Q864 Sir John Stanley: So it was commissioned, broadly, roughly two months in advance of it actually being published?
Sir Michael Jay: No, one month, it was commissioned in earlyish January and it was at the end of that month that it was published.

Q865 Sir John Stanley: Sorry, I apologise; so it was published around February 3, right. Could you tell us, within the Communication Information Centre, which was based in your Department, how many of your own officials were involved in the drafting of the document, what their positions were and to whom they reported?
Sir Michael Jay: I cannot, I have not got the details available of exactly what the membership of the CIC was. It was a Centre which originally was set up just after September 11, in order to bring together those concerned with the presentation of policy through the Afghan war, and then it went into abeyance, or became a sort of virtual unit, between the end of the Afghan war until the time when the Iraq issue clearly was going to become a crisis, and at that point it was thought sensible to revive it. And it had, I think, at its height, round about 25 members, who were drawn from a number of government departments, the Foreign Office, the Ministry of Defence, other departments too; those members would be allocated certain functions within it, as I understand, and some members of that group, and I do not know which members exactly, would have been involved in the preparation of the briefing note that we were concerned with. The head of the unit was from the Foreign Office, reporting to Alastair Campbell, in his capacity as the Director of Government Communications.

Q866 Sir John Stanley: So the head of the unit was a Foreign Office official, and if you could just briefly let us have a very quick note as to how many of your own officials were involved actually in the drafting of the document, if we could have that before tomorrow, I would be grateful?

Sir Michael Jay: I will try to do that, yes[1].

Q867 Sir John Stanley: Thank you. Can you tell us at what point your own officials first became aware that the material that was going to be incorporated into this document was going to be from open, public, printed sources?
Sir Michael Jay: I think what happened was that the CIC were asked, or tasked, by Alastair Campbell and the Iraq Communication Group to produce the briefing note; they then asked various government departments to produce for them background information which could go into the note. Some of that came from the Foreign Office, some of that came from other government departments, and some of that information was from Government sources and some of that information was from published sources, and that was then fed into the CIC. So I would expect that some members of the Foreign Office would have been aware, when they were passing information on, that some of it was published and some of it was not; which is what I would expect. If you are putting together a briefing note, you would expect that to be put together from a mixture of information which the Government had got, as it were, on its own authority and that the Government was getting from other sources; that would be the normal thing to do in producing a briefing note.

Q868 Sir John Stanley: At what point were your officials aware that other people's material was going to be used without attribution of sources?
Sir Michael Jay: As I understand it, the information was put in to the CIC; at that point, I think it was clear what the attribution was. At some stage during the compilation of the document itself within the CIC the attribution was lost; now exactly at what point in the preparation process, and how, I do not know, but the attribution was lost at that stage.

Q869 Sir John Stanley: Can we have a further note on that? Your officials inside the CIC must have been aware that the attribution, in your words, was lost, or was deliberately taken out, for whatever reason; could you tell us, please, in a further note, preferably before tomorrow's evidence session, at what point in January your officials became aware that public material was going to be used without attribution sources?
Sir Michael Jay: When you say my officials, Sir John, these were the officials working in the CIC, which is an interdepartmental unit, which was based in the Foreign Office.

Q870 Sir John Stanley: I am referring just to your own officials, your own FCO officials inside the CIC?
Sir Michael Jay: I think these are also questions which I imagine you may want to ask Alastair Campbell about tomorrow.

[1] Ninth Report from the Foreign Affairs Committee, Session 2002–03, *The Decision to go to War in Iraq*, HC 813-II, Ev 72.

---

24 June 2003   Sir Michael Jay KCMG and Mr Peter Ricketts CMG

Q871 Sir John Stanley: It would be very helpful to have your answers to these questions before we see him?
Sir Michael Jay: Yes[2].

Q872 Sir John Stanley: Thank you. Can you tell us also when your own officials inside the CIC first became aware that the material being used from Mr al-Marashi's work was based on the structure and practice of the Iraqi intelligence services 12 years previously, and the fact that that 12 years previously material was not going to be disclosed but it was 12 years prior to the time it was published?
Sir Michael Jay: I think, in a sense, that is the same question as the previous one, that the attribution I think was there when it went into the CIC but the attribution was lost when it was in the CIC, or at some point when the document was put together there was no longer an attribution.

Q873 Sir John Stanley: I understand that, but it is a slightly different point. There is an issue about attributing its source, but there is another issue when you are producing a document not to be putting it on the face of the document that the material you are referring to relates to 1990, 1991?
Sir Michael Jay: I had assumed that if you were putting the attribution on, it would also be putting the attribution and the date and the source, and it would say by whom and such and such a date.

Q874 Sir John Stanley: If you could cover that point; the thesis, of course, was much later, as you will appreciate, the thesis was published, I think, in 2000, something like that, relating to a situation ten years previously. So that is why I am asking that as a separate question, and would like to know when your officials became aware, and they must have been aware at the outset, it related to the Iraqi security services in 1991? They must also have been aware that that fact was going to be expurgated and expunged from the document?
Sir Michael Jay: I am not certain that it was a question of expurgating and expunging it, and they are not sure this was a conscious decision to do it. I suspect it was more that this got left out in the process of putting the thing together in the final stages. But I will try to answer your questions by tomorrow[3].

Q875 Sir John Stanley: Thank you. Another issue that your officials, particularly FCO officials, most particularly, I am sure will have been conscious of, or certainly should have been conscious of, was that there was a very, very high probability, in fact, a total certainty, that the publication of Mr al-Marashi's text was bound to be identified as to what the source was, even though the source may not have been stated in the document. And your officials also should have been aware that that was likely

potentially to endanger the lives of Mr al-Marashi's family in Iraq, and possibly himself, and he has given evidence to that effect to the Committee. Can I ask you, Sir Michael, whether at any point your officials flagged up to Mr Alastair Campbell that the publication of Mr al-Marashi's work and the racing certainty that it was going to be discovered where it came from and publicised was likely to endanger members of his family?
Sir Michael Jay: I am not aware that they did. But, there again, when you talk about my officials, you are referring to the officials within this interdepartmental unit, within the CIC, where, as I say, there were officials from a large number of government departments, there were some from the FCO. I do not know how far those ones from the FCO were involved in the preparation of the dossier. I do not know whether the particular point you mention was drawn to Alastair Campbell's attention or not, and, if so, whether it would have been by an FCO official or an official from another government department who was working within this interdepartmental unit.

Q876 Sir John Stanley: You have said that the head of the unit was an FCO official?
Sir Michael Jay: The head of the unit was an FCO person.

Q877 Sir John Stanley: And he, or she, must have been a person of some seniority, and one would have expected that that particular person would have been sensitive to this issue and should have made a warning to Mr Campbell. Perhaps you could respond to that when you give us the further answer?
Sir Michael Jay: Right.

Q878 Sir John Stanley: Can you tell us also whether there was a point prior to the publication of the so-called 'dodgy dossier', in the evidence we have it is not clear whether it was actually published on 30th, we have got two conflicting bits of paper, one that it was published on 3 February, the day of the Prime Minister's statement, and the other that it was published on January 30, but the dates do not matter very much, and I am going to come back to that in a moment. But, regardless of which date it was, can you tell us whether your officials, prior to the date when it was made public, became aware that the Government, and the Prime Minister, was going to present this document to the House as if it were a *bona fide* intelligence document, and, in the words of the Prime Minister, any questioning of it would call into question the integrity of the intelligence services?
Sir Michael Jay: As I understand it, as far as our officials were concerned, the document was intended to be a briefing document for the press, and it was in that capacity that it was taken and used as a briefing for the press and given to the press on, I think, 30 or 31 January, when the Prime Minister was visiting Washington. And the chronology after that was that, as I understand it, again, at a meeting on the morning of Monday, 3 February, which Alastair Campbell chaired, a decision was taken that the

---

[2] Ninth Report from the Foreign Affairs Committee, Session 2002–03, *The Decision to go to War in Iraq*, HC 813-II, Ev 72.

[3] Ninth Report from the Foreign Affairs Committee, Session 2002–03, *The Decision to go to War in Iraq*, HC 813-II, Ev 72.

paper should be put in the Library of the House, and, in that sense, it was published then. We were made aware of that by the Foreign Office Press Office official who was present at that meeting, who came and reported back to my Director of Information, who reported that to me at my morning meeting that day, at which the private secretaries of ministers were present too, and in that way we, in the Foreign Office at senior level and at ministerial level, became aware that the document was going to be put in the Library of the House.

Q879 Sir John Stanley: So when the Prime Minister came to say, later that afternoon, as we have quoted before, referring to this document, "It is intelligence that they are receiving," that is the intelligence services, "and we're passing it on to people," conveying the clear impression that this was *bona fide* intelligence material, when it was not, you are saying, as I understand it, to the Committee, that your officials were not aware at any point that this was the particular spin that was going to be put on this document, and I assume therefore you are saying that the responsibility for this spin lies solely somewhere in Number 10?
Sir Michael Jay: As I say, those were the circumstances in which we learned that the document was going to be given to the House. I think, as I understand it, the rationale was that, since the document had appeared in the newspapers the weekend before, and since the Prime Minister was going to be speaking in the House, it would be courteous to the House if the document were made available to them.

Q880 Sir John Stanley: Thank you. And you said that the document was released to the journalists on January 31?
Sir Michael Jay: Again, Alastair Campbell, I am sure, will be able to go into this in more detail, but, as I understand it, members of the party gave it to some journalists during the course of the visit to Washington.

Q881 Sir John Stanley: Sir Michael, when did this document first come to your knowledge?
Sir Michael Jay: I was first aware of it on the Monday morning when there was the report back to my ten o'clock morning meeting.

Q882 Sir John Stanley: And did you have any comments to make to your Secretary of State about a briefing note which had no attribution of public sources, and in certain key respects had the wording changed in material ways?
Sir Michael Jay: We discussed it, as you can imagine, and agreed, as the Foreign Secretary said this morning, as I said this morning, that this was not an ideal way to have handled it, and we agreed thereafter procedures to ensure that in the future there were different ways of handling such documents.

Q883 Sir John Stanley: Did you have anything to say to your officials as to why you had not been informed earlier?
Sir Michael Jay: I would not have expected to have been informed about a document which was being prepared as a briefing document of that kind; there were briefing documents of this sort being produced several times every day of the week by the CIC, that was its purpose, its purpose was to produce briefing documents, those were then used by ministers or by Number 10 to brief the press, this was happening daily. So the fact that such a document was being produced as a briefing document I would not have expected, myself, to have been aware of or to have seen; this is all part of the give and take of business. What was different was when it became a document put into Parliament.

Q884 Sir John Stanley: Can I say to you, I assume this is not what you are saying to the Committee, you are not suggesting it is an everyday occurrence that the Government's briefing documents are based on plagiarisation of printed work, without attributing sources and with materially changing, or some would say, twisting, the wording to suit the political purposes of the Government?
Sir Michael Jay: No; no, I am not. What I am saying is that I would not have expected to have been aware of a briefing document. The question of how that briefing document was put together was actually a question which only arose later on, when we learned from the newspapers about the allegations of plagiarism.

Q885 Sir John Stanley: So you were not informed, on the morning of February 3, that the briefing document was based on plagiarised material?
Sir Michael Jay: No.

Q886 Sir John Stanley: You were not?
Sir Michael Jay: No. We were unaware of that until we learned—

Q887 Sir John Stanley: Are you not somewhat shocked that your officials had not told you?
Sir Michael Jay: I do not know that they knew. I do not know, at that stage, who did know or had focused on the fact that the attribution had been removed, and, therefore, as it were, the information, as the Foreign Secretary said this morning, was accurate, the sourcing was missing.

Q888 Sir John Stanley: But your officials in the CIC, including the Head of the CIC, who was an official of the Foreign Office, must at that point have known without any doubt that the material was plagiarised and unsourced?
Sir Michael Jay: Not necessarily, because it depends on exactly how it was put together at the time. There may have been, and I have tried to verify that, people who were aware at that stage that the document was not attributed. I am not certain that the non-attribution of the material was seen at that stage as a significant fact. I think what was seen as a significant fact was, here was material which was, as

far as we were able to judge, useful and accurate material, which was germane to the case we were trying to make, or that CIC was trying to make. What became clear later on was that the attribution, which should have been on that document, was not on that document; that is the mistake that was made and that is the point that the Foreign Secretary was saying this morning should not have occurred, and that was the point that was made, certainly it should not have happened, it will not happen again. It is clearly necessary that any document of that kind, which draws on material from whatever source, public source, should have the attribution stated clearly on the document.

Q889 Sir John Stanley: But would you not agree that every bit as important as the attribution is the fact that not merely was the material lifted but the material was significantly and materially changed, as we heard from Mr al-Marashi, in his evidence to us, a reference to 'opposition groups' was turned into 'terrorist groups', which has a completely different meaning and a completely different association? Most people in the House, when they read that, would have said, "This is further, clear evidence of links between Saddam Hussein and al-Qaeda"?
Sir Michael Jay: Yes. As the Foreign Secretary said this morning, the preparation of the document was not satisfactory, although, as he also said, that change did not make the document inaccurate, because, in fact, it was correct, although it was not the language which it had inherited from the earlier document.

Q890 Sir John Stanley: So, finally, you are saying to us that the Foreign Secretary, like yourself, became aware both of the plagiarisation and also the changes of wording that had taken place only after February 3?
Sir Michael Jay: Yes. The Foreign Secretary and I were aware of the document's existence for the first time on the morning of February 3, and we were aware of the problems which had occurred in putting it together when those were the subject of press attention and interest a couple of days later.

Q891 Chairman: Thank you. The Head of the CIC was from the FCO and a number of members also were from the FCO?
Sir Michael Jay: There were some other members from the FCO.

Q892 Chairman: Were they, in fact, responsible to you, or were they responsible to Number 10?
Sir Michael Jay: The unit and the head of the unit, interdepartmental unit, were responsible to Alastair Campbell, in his capacity as Head of Government Communications. As far as their own line management, and so on, was concerned then they would report to my Director of Information.

Q893 Chairman: I did not understand one response. You said that when you and the Foreign Secretary were made aware, on 3 February, of this

change from a briefing document to a document for publication, you said this was not, and we agreed, I think, this was not an ideal way to handle it?
Sir Michael Jay: I think I misspoke slightly there, Mr Chairman. In a sense, I was answering what I thought was going to be Sir John Stanley's question, which was how we reacted to the knowledge that the document which had been put together had been put together without attribution. It was at that point that the Foreign Secretary and I accepted, or realised, that there needed then to be new methods, we needed to make certain that any further documents put together by the CIC were put together with greater care, that anything which came from intelligence sources should be cleared by the JIC, and that all information made available should be properly attributed to its source.

Q894 Chairman: But that recognition on both your parts did not come on 3 February but at a later stage?
Sir Michael Jay: No; it came afterwards, if I may just correct that.

Q895 Andrew Mackinlay: A thing which has occurred to me, listening to both this evidence you have given and the backdrop of the wider stuff, is, how are we going to avoid this happening again? Hopefully, mercifully, we will not have a comparable crisis and subsequent conflict for decades to come, if at all; but, nevertheless, it seems to me that is not this indicative of the shift of foreign policy from the Foreign Office to Number 10? You must have thought, as a manager, as the principal person at the top of the Foreign Office, "We must avoid this," or, "We must at least agree guidelines"? It is a Machinery of Government issue, and clearly it is a dog's breakfast. So, one, have you taken any initiatives to say, "Let's get lines of communication correct in the future;" two, what is your thinking?
Sir Michael Jay: I think, as I said, that the way in which this particular document was prepared was faulty, and I think we all accept that, and we have taken steps and done all we can to ensure that that does not happen again, and, in a sense, it is always useful to learn lessons from mistakes.

Q896 Andrew Mackinlay: But it might not be a document next time; a document is indicative, is it not, of who does what, who is in charge of pursuing foreign policy?
Sir Michael Jay: If I can just say that I think that the concept lying behind the CIC is a perfectly sound and rather good one; there are all sorts of ways now in which we have to join up government, because so many of the issues with which we deal cut across departmental boundaries. In Afghanistan and in Iraq there were issues which cut across the interests of the Foreign Office, the Ministry of Defence, agencies, other government departments and, of course, Number 10. Now rather than have each government department presenting things in its own way, separately, it made a lot of sense to try to combine that in one

unit, which then ensured that there was a coherent presentational strategy across government. So I think that the logic of the creation of the CIC is perfectly sound. So I think what we need to focus on is not so much should that sort of interdepartmental unit exist, it seems to me that, the way in which government is evolving, that sort of interdepartmental unit does need to exist, but that when it exists it handles itself in a proper fashion; that was what went wrong on this particular occasion, in this unit.

Chairman: Sir Michael, you have been extremely helpful. Mr Ricketts, I think that covers also your part of the operation. So perhaps we can have a five-minute break now before we move on to the examination of the Annual Report. Thank you.

Wednesday 25 June 2003

Members present:

Donald Anderson, in the Chair

Mr David Chidgey
Mr Fabian Hamilton
Mr Eric Illsley
Andrew Mackinlay
Mr John Maples

Richard Ottaway
Mr Greg Pope
Sir John Stanley
Ms Gisela Stuart

Memorandum submitted by Mr Alastair Campbell[1]

Witness: **Mr Alastair Campbell,** Director of Communications and Strategy, 10 Downing Street, examined.

Q897 Chairman: One preliminary announcement, which I hope will be to the benefit of everyone. We expect a division at around four o'clock and I then intend to adjourn for a period of some 15 minutes. Mr Campbell, welcome to what some will see as the lion's den, but which of the roles you play remains to be seen. I note that one newspaper talked of "Campbell in the soup", but we will wait to see. We would prefer to see your appearance before the Foreign Affairs Committee as one in which we are carrying out our task of a proper responsibility to Parliament and the public in a matter of very serious concern, namely the decision to go to war in Iraq. You know our remit is to test whether the information presented to Parliament was complete and accurate in the period leading up to military action in Iraq, particularly with regard to weapons of mass destruction. You know the charges which have been made against your role, effectively that in your zeal to make the case you embellished the evidence to the point of misleading Parliament and the public at a vital time relating to peace and war. There are four relevant documents. In 1998 the late Derek Fatchett and Doug Henderson presented to Parliament a three page paper. Again, we are told that in March of last year there was a Joint Intelligence Committee assessment which the *Independent* of 9 June claimed was suppressed after being put up by the JIC as not being sufficiently strong. The more relevant dossiers are those of 24 September of last year, based on a Joint Intelligence Committee assessment, and the dossier published in early February of this year where clearly alterations were made to enhance the effect, alterations to existing documents which had been plagiarised, for example "opposition" changed to "terrorist". Obviously my task is to provide the platform and I anticipate that my parliamentary colleagues on the Committee will be ready to question you on all the relevant matters, particularly on the document of 24 September of last year and that of 3 February of this year. First, some preliminary questions. Mr Campbell, looking back now, is there anything that you did which you regret?
Mr Campbell: In relation to the briefing paper that was issued in February 2003 I obviously regret the fact that a mistake was made within the drafting process whereby—

Q898 Chairman: A mistake?
Mr Campbell: It was a mistake, and I have set out the background to that in my memorandum to you. If you want I can go through and explain how I believe that mistake occurred, or I can answer more generally on whether you think there are more areas where I should regret. From the general perspective, I believe that we were involved in communicating on a very, very serious issue why the Prime Minister and the Government felt as strongly as they did about the issue of Iraq and Iraq's weapons of mass destruction. At various stages we were communicating the intense diplomatic activity that was going on as the Prime Minister and the Government sought to avoid military conflict. At a further stage we were communicating during what was a military conflict. Now, during all that time with a media that we are operating with around the clock, around the world, on an issue like that, we are involved in and responsible for a huge number of, if you like, pieces of communication. Within one of them, and I have explained the background in the memorandum, there was a mistake.

Q899 Chairman: You say "a mistake". Are you saying you are particularising a single mistake?
Mr Campbell: I am saying that, yes.

Q900 Chairman: What was that single particular mistake?
Mr Campbell: The mistake was as follows: in relation to the second paper, the paper that was issued in February 2003, the idea for that came from a group that I chair, continue to chair, and have chaired for some time now, called the Iraq Communications Group. That is comprised of people from the Foreign Office, from the MoD, from DFID, from the intelligence agencies, it is comprised of people from the unit that we can come on to discuss, the CIC. During January at one of those meetings the intelligence agencies gave information that had come to light, new information, which was releasable in the public domain, and they gave permission for that to be done, about the scale of the Iraqi apparatus that was working against the interests of the United Nations' weapons inspectors. In other words, the efforts that the Iraqis were

---

[1] Ninth Report from the Foreign Affairs Committee, Session 2002–03, *The Decision to go to War in Iraq*, HC 813-II, Ev 7.

making to prevent the weapons inspectors from doing their job. It was interesting. It was information, for example, about the fact that—

Q901 Chairman: You give more particulars, but there was new intelligence information provided?
Mr Campbell: That was, if you like, the catalyst for the idea for the paper that followed.

Q902 Chairman: What was the mistake?
Mr Campbell: This was discussed over a period of about three weeks at these weekly meetings that I chair. The mistake that was made was around about 20 January what had happened was this: I had asked the CIC to prepare a draft paper, at this stage we were not exactly clear about how we were going to deploy that paper, I can come on to how we did deploy it in the end,—

Q903 Chairman: Colleagues will no doubt come in on that.
Mr Campbell: What happened was I commissioned the CIC to begin drafting a paper which would incorporate the intelligence material, some of the intelligence material that had been authorised for use in the public domain, and other information about this theme, the whole theme of Iraq being configured as a state and its state apparatus designed to conceal weapons of mass destruction from the United Nations' weapons inspectors. The CIC then asked around the system if you like, the Foreign Office, MoD, other Government departments that may have an interest in this area, for any papers that they had on this, information that they might have on this in their research departments. People talk about this 12 year old PhD thesis, it was not a 12 year old PhD thesis,—

Q904 Chairman: What was the mistake?
Mr Campbell: I will come to the mistake but I think it is important that I explain the background because this is how the mistake happened. During that process the Foreign Office research department sent this journal from September 2002 by Mr al-Marashi, who you interviewed recently. That then went to the CIC. At that point within the CIC work from that paper was taken and absorbed into the draft that was being prepared within the CIC. That was the mistake, without attribution.

Q905 Chairman: So the mistake in the February document was to transpose that learned article without attribution?
Mr Campbell: It was to take parts of that article and put them into the draft that was being developed without attribution.

Q906 Chairman: Why did you then send a letter of apology to Sir Richard Dearlove, because he had nothing to do with that?
Mr Campbell: I did not send a letter of apology to Sir Richard Dearlove.

Q907 Chairman: Have you sent letters of apology to anyone?

Mr Campbell: I have not sent a letter of apology to Sir Richard Dearlove.

Q908 Chairman: Have you sent letters of apology to anyone?
Mr Campbell: Not in relation to this. I do not think we have actually got to the impact of that mistake.

Q909 Chairman: That will be pursued later. I am now on a separate question. Have you, as a result of that February dossier, sent letters of apology to anyone?
Mr Campbell: No. What I have done, and what I did immediately when the mistake subsequently came to light sometime after the February paper had been published—because at that stage I did not know this had happened, nor did anybody else outside the CIC know that this had happened—when that draft paper was circulated to us we assumed this was Government material, Government sourced material, so therefore some of the changes that you have been discussing in earlier hearings were made by experts within Government on a draft which they believed to be a Government draft. That was the mistake.

Q910 Chairman: Back to my question. Have you, as a result of that document, apologised to anyone?
Mr Campbell: On the day that the mistake was revealed, first on Channel 4 and then on BBC *Newsnight*, and Mr al-Marashi went on to the media, the following day—this indicates how seriously we took it—I spoke to the security intelligence co-ordinator, I spoke to the Permanent Secretary of the Foreign and Commonwealth Office, I spoke to the head of the Secret Intelligence Service, I spoke to the Chairman of the Joint Intelligence Committee to explain that something had gone wrong. Equally, the other thing that we did was the Prime Minister's spokesman on behalf of the Prime Minister at a briefing that day acknowledged that mistakes had been made and we said that this should not have happened, and obviously subsequent to that we sought to establish what had happened.

Q911 Chairman: What you did in those conversations could not be construed as an apology?
Mr Campbell: What it was, was saying to the intelligence services that the care that should have been taken in the production of a document which contained some of their material was not sufficient. I have a sufficiently good relationship with these intelligence officials not for them or me to present that as an apology but as a discussion about how this had happened and how we stop it happening again.

Q912 Chairman: You had that discussion. Have you thought of having a discussion with Mr al-Marashi who told this Committee last week, as you know, that certain of his relatives could have been put in danger as a result of the careless use of his material?

Mr Campbell: I have not had a discussion with Mr al-Marashi. I read what he said to the Committee and obviously that is something that you have to take seriously when somebody makes that sort of—

Q913 Chairman: How would you take it seriously?
Mr Campbell: I am happy to say to Mr al-Marashi that the mistake that occurred should not have occurred and apologise for that. I have to say in relation to what he said to the Committee, it does not really sit with the fact that this plagiarism was exposed by him on the BBC and, as he said to your Committee, he is the first person that you go to on the Internet if you look into these issues. It is not as if his expertise in this area and the fact that he has contributed material on this area was new. Having said all that,—

Q914 Chairman: It was not the fact of his expertise, it was the use made of his expertise in this document which could harm him.
Mr Campbell: I accept there is a palpable difference between somebody writing for a journal like the *Middle East Review* and somebody's material being used in a British Government paper. I should just emphasise on that, the criticism at the time was that we did not acknowledge him, not that we did. At the time of publication, with the exception of people within the CIC, nobody knew that that was where it came from.

Q915 Chairman: Do you accept that the effect of that 3 February dossier was to cast doubts on the credibility of the rather more important dossier of 24 September?
Mr Campbell: Only if Parliament and the public were to view them in exactly the same light. What I mean by that is that they were very, very different in their scale, in their breadth and in their intended impact.

Q916 Chairman: So it is less important as to whether one was well-founded?
Mr Campbell: No, I did not say that. The dossier in September 2002 was one of the most important pieces of work developed during the entire build-up to the conflict.

Q917 Chairman: And its impact could have been reduced by the rather slapdash negligent way of putting together the February document?
Mr Campbell: I do not accept that because I think the two have to be seen in isolation. The dossier of September 2002 was put together, as I say, over many months, it had the Chairman of the Joint Intelligence Committee in the lead on every aspect of its production, and it was a serious, thorough piece of work setting out why it was so vital to tackle Saddam and WMD. The second paper was not.

Q918 Chairman: It was not a serious piece of work?

Mr Campbell: No, the second paper was not vital to the case of why we had to deal with Saddam and WMD.

Q919 Chairman: Do you accept it was a "complete Horlicks"?
Mr Campbell: I accept that a mistake was made and I accept that it was right that we apologised for that mistake, and I think I have identified where the mistake was made.

Q920 Chairman: Do you feel now that you regret publishing it in the first place?
Mr Campbell: I think the idea of a paper setting out, as it sought to do, the scale of Saddam Hussein's apparatus of concealment and intimidation against the UN was a good thing to do. It should not have happened in the way that it did. I have explained as best as I can, having gone over it, why that happened. The reality is that had it not happened like that it would have been a perfectly good thing to do, but it did happen like that.

Q921 Chairman: And in the circumstances you were sorry it was done?
Mr Campbell: Yes, obviously I think it has been regrettable.

Q922 Sir John Stanley: Mr Campbell, I have to say I found some of the answers you gave to the Chairman less than credible. First of all, I must put to you your suggestion that the issue of concealment was some sort of peripheral issue as far as Members of Parliament were concerned in deciding whether or not to support the Government is wholly unfounded. The issue of concealment was absolutely central. The issue was why could the weapons inspectors not find the weapons of mass destruction and was it worthwhile going on pursuing that particular avenue of search. The Government's justification for the war was that we could not rely on further time being given to the weapons inspectors because of the programme of concealment. I have to put it to you that the judgment you have gained that the issue of concealment was peripheral, I think was profoundly mistaken.
Mr Campbell: I did not say the issue of concealment was peripheral, I said that paper was not remotely as significant as the dossier in September 2002. The dossier in 2002 attracted, I think I am right in saying, more interest around the world. Number 10, the Foreign Office and the BBC websites virtually collapsed on the day. It had a massive print run. It was the product of months and months of detailed work with the intelligence agencies. It was a huge break with precedent. It was a very important document. The briefing paper in February was given to six journalists on a plane to America. The reason that it was subsequently put into the House was to inform MPs on it because the Prime Minister, as you may recall, was in America at the time and was returning to make a statement on his talks with President Bush. I am

not saying the issue of concealment was not hugely important, I am saying that that briefing paper was not nearly as significant as the dossier.

Q923 Sir John Stanley: You have just touched on the second reason why I found your initial answer less than credible. You said that you were unaware, apparently, of this mistake, that you believed the so-called 'dodgy dossier', the one which in your memorandum you said you conceived, so it is your 'dodgy dossier', was a dossier which had the same intelligence veracity, the same level of intelligence approval as the original September document.
Mr Campbell: No, I did not say that.

Q924 Sir John Stanley: You said you assumed it was a document on all fours with the previous one. You said that in answer to the Chairman.
Mr Campbell: No. The procedures that the dossier of September 2002 went through were wholly different from those of February 2003, that is why as a result we have actually put in place new procedures about how intelligence material is handled in any documents put into the public domain.

Q925 Sir John Stanley: So you knew that the procedures that had been followed were wholly different from the ones that were followed for the September dossier?
Mr Campbell: Not until the mistake was exposed by the media.

Q926 Sir John Stanley: Mr Campbell, you are responsible as the Director of Government Communications not merely for what goes on inside Number 10 but also for the CIC unit inside the Foreign Office. You cannot seriously pretend to this Committee that you did not know the procedures that were being followed for the clearance or not of the second "dodgy dossier"?
Mr Campbell: I am well aware of what the procedures were. I am simply saying to you that the procedures were different. On the dossier of September 2002 the lead person was the Chairman of the Joint Intelligence Committee, it was produced by the Joint Intelligence Committee; the dossier in February was not. The point I am making, and that I have made in the memorandum I have given to you, is a mistake was made within the CIC. I was not aware that had been done until Channel 4 and then *Newsnight* revealed that. I had never heard of Mr al-Marashi, nor had the other people who had commented on the paper. The changes that the Chairman referred to on the text were made by people thinking they were making changes to make more accurate a Government draft.

Q927 Sir John Stanley: So you are saying to the Committee now, which is confirming what the Committee's evidence is, that you were aware of the different procedures and when the document came

to you for final putting to the Prime Minister, you were aware that it had not been through the normal intelligence clearance processes?
Mr Campbell: It had been through the procedures as they existed at that time. We put in place new procedures thereafter. The difference is that the Joint Intelligence Committee Chairman was responsible for the production of the WMD dossier in 2002, the second one I was responsible for as the Chairman of the group which commissioned it. The intelligence agency which provided intelligence for use in the public domain had authorised its use in the normal way as the procedures existed at that time. It was a result of the mistake in the way that it was made that subsequent to that we agreed new procedures so that anything with an intelligence input has to be cleared by the Chairman of the Joint Intelligence Committee.

Q928 Sir John Stanley: When you briefed the Prime Minister before he made his statement in the House on 3 February, did you tell the Prime Minister that the document which he as Prime Minister was placing in the Library of the House, the 'dodgy dossier' that day, had neither been seen in draft or in final form by the Chairman of the Joint Intelligence Committee?
Mr Campbell: There was no need for the Chairman of the Joint Intelligence Committee to see it under the procedures as they were then.

Q929 Sir John Stanley: That is not the question I put to you, Mr Campbell.
Mr Campbell: The answer is no, because it did not arise.

Q930 Sir John Stanley: The answer is no.
Mr Campbell: The answer is no, because it did not arise. There was no need for the Chairman of the Joint Intelligence Committee to see something which the issuing agency had already cleared for public use properly, according to the procedures as they were then, for public use in that document.

Q931 Sir John Stanley: We will see in a moment whether it was necessary for you to tell the Prime Minister that. I will come to that in a moment. Were you aware that the draft of the 'dodgy dossier' had neither been seen in draft or in final form by the Secretary of the Cabinet?
Mr Campbell: I was not aware or unaware of that. The Cabinet Secretary is not part of the group that I chair of senior people from various Government departments, including the Cabinet Office. I had not sent it to the Cabinet Secretary. The Cabinet Office is represented on that group.

Q932 Sir John Stanley: Do you think you should have sent it to the Cabinet Secretary, given the fact that it was going to be placed in the Library of the House of Commons?
Mr Campbell: It was not the sort of document that I felt should be sent as a matter of routine to the Cabinet Secretary.

Q933 Sir John Stanley: In your memorandum to us[1], Mr Campbell, you say in relation to the September dossier: "I emphasised at all times both in our discussions and in any written outcomes of our various meetings circulated within the system that nothing should be published unless the JIC and the Intelligence Agencies were 100% happy".
Mr Campbell: Correct.

Q934 Sir John Stanley: When you came to brief the Prime Minister on 3 February about the nature of the 'dodgy dossier', did you make clear to him that at no point had the intelligence agencies been consulted as to whether they were 100% happy with the document?
Mr Campbell: That there relates to the September 2002 dossier on WMD.

Q935 Sir John Stanley: It is equally applicable to this document.
Mr Campbell: It is not because, as I have explained, the procedures were different. I explained to the Prime Minister the purpose of the briefing paper, which was to give it to six Sunday newspaper journalists on a flight to Washington. I explained where there was new intelligence which had been cleared for public use and I explained that there was other material within the document about the nature of Saddam's infrastructure of concealment and intimidation. I certainly did not say to him, for example, that this was taken from a Middle East journal because I did not know that to be the case.

Q936 Sir John Stanley: But you must certainly have been aware that open sources were being used and the material had been culled off the Internet because the computer records show quite clearly that members of your own staff inside Number 10 were involved in the putting of this material on to the Internet and were involved in a major way in the drafting of it.
Mr Campbell: Well, if you read the memorandum that I gave to you, I think this story of the four people who allegedly authored the report says a huge amount more about the reporting of these issues than it does about the reality. If I may, Chairman, I would like to explain that in some detail.

Q937 Sir John Stanley: Can I just finish my line of questioning and perhaps we can come back to that.
Mr Campbell: Yes.

Q938 Sir John Stanley: As you know, Mr Campbell, the clear inadequacy of your briefing of the Prime Minister led the Prime Minister to—I am sure inadvertently—very seriously mislead the House of Commons on February 3. The Prime Minister said, and I will quote it in full: "We issued further intelligence over the weekend about the infrastructure of concealment. It is obviously difficult when we publish intelligence reports, but I hope that people have some sense of the integrity

of our security services. They are not publishing this or giving us this information, making it up, it is the intelligence that they are receiving and we are passing it on to people".
Mr Campbell: That is wholly accurate.

Q939 Sir John Stanley: Every Member of the House of Commons who heard that would have been in no doubt that this second dossier was taken through the full JIC process, had JIC approval, had full JIC status. In fact, as we know, it was very largely simply culled off the Internet and the House of Commons a few weeks later took a decision on whether or not to go to war on this country and this particular document was an element in that decision. That was a very, very grave failure of briefing of the Prime Minister by yourself, I suggest, Mr Campbell. Do you acknowledge that to be the case now?
Mr Campbell: I think that is a very, very grave charge and I think it is one that I reject. If you look at the front cover of the document: "The report draws upon a number of sources, including intelligence material, and shows how the Iraqi regime is constructed to have and to keep WMD and is now engaged in a campaign of obstruction of the UN weapons inspectors". That is accurate. In relation to the processes with the intelligence agencies, the SIS—the lead agency on this—volunteered the information for public use. They were content for it to be used in this paper. The reason I keep coming back to the difference between the two things is the JIC process that you describe in relation to the first and the most substantial report, that was a JIC document, it was produced by the Joint Intelligence Committee; this was a briefing paper produced by the team that I chair. The Prime Minister put it into the House; he did not present it in the same way. If you recall with the first report, Parliament was recalled for the Prime Minister to make a statement and a debate to be held upon it. The procedures for that were different. The procedures that have now been put in place have been strengthened so that the procedures that applied to the WMD dossier of September 2002 now apply to all documents with an intelligence input. That was a change that I was instrumental in putting in place after this mistake in the CIC was exposed.

Q940 Sir John Stanley: Mr Campbell, do you not recognise that a hugely greater area of mistake resulted than simply the indefensible plagiarisation of material off the Internet? The hugely greater mistake that resulted in parliamentary and constitutional terms was your total failure to brief the Prime Minister correctly as to the process that had been used, the fact that none of this material had come through with the Joint Intelligence Committee Chairman's approval, and the House of Commons was left under the illusion, as indeed was the Prime Minister, that in terms of the authenticity and reliability of this information it came with the JIC seal of approval on it when that was not the case?

[1] Ninth Report from the Foreign Affairs Committee, Session 2002–03, *The Decision to go to War in Iraq*, HC 813-II, Ev 7.

Mr Campbell: The Prime Minister did not say it was with the JIC seal of approval and as the Prime Minister made clear in the—

Q941 Sir John Stanley: ". . . issued further intelligence over the weekend"; did any Member of Parliament think that did not mean something with JIC approval?
Mr Campbell: I think any Member of Parliament would recognise the difference between a document such as that one, with the detail that is in it and the kind of production that it is and the way that it was put out at the time, as I say, as part of a massive, global communications exercise, and this paper that was given to a few Sunday journalists travelling with the Prime Minister. The Prime Minister, as he made clear again in the House today, was content with the paper as it was. What he is not content with, and nor am I, is the fact that in its production a mistake was made. We have acknowledged that mistake, we have apologised for that mistake and we have put forward these new procedures to make sure it does not happen again, and I do not honestly see there is much more that we can do than that.

Q942 Sir John Stanley: Mr Campbell, I have to put it to you the contrast between the covers makes it absolutely—
Mr Campbell:—I think the contrast is far greater than that.

Q943 Sir John Stanley: The contrast between the covers makes it absolutely clear that you should have alerted the Prime Minister unmistakably to the fact that the preparation of these two documents was quite different—
Mr Campbell: He knows that—

Q944 Sir John Stanley:—That the second document had no JIC approval and that he, I am quite certain, if he had known that and had been told that there is no way he would have said what he did to the House of Commons when he made his statement on 3 February. That statement suggested that this was intelligence of veracity coming from intelligence sources with intelligence approval; we now know that to be false.
Mr Campbell: Had the Prime Minister had those concerns he would have raised them directly with me; he has not. Equally, I have had many, many discussions with the intelligence agencies, and the intelligence material that was in that document was accurate. The reason I keep coming back to the difference in these documents is the fact that that first document of September 2002 was hugely important; it was a huge break of precedent for the intelligence agencies to be sharing so much information like that with Parliament and the public. The second document was a different sort of communication, and the Prime Minister has not said to me, "I should have been told that this had not gone through the JIC clearance", because he knew that where there was intelligence material in

that document it had been cleared for use by the issuing agency, and that was the procedure at the time.

Q945 Sir John Stanley: Yes, but I am sure the Prime Minister is sufficiently aware of the huge dangers of mixing intelligence material with material taken off the internet and I am sure the Prime Minister is also aware that if he had been properly briefed on those dangers the first thing he would have said to you is, "Mr Campbell, make certain this is cleared by the Chairman of the JIC before it is put in the Library."
Mr Campbell: All I can do is refer you to what the Prime Minister said in the House of Commons today where he makes clear—

Q946 Sir John Stanley: He made the statement today, absolutely rightly, that he was left completely in the dark at the time he made his statement on 3 February that the greater part of this document had been culled off the internet and there were these two significant inaccuracies in it.
Mr Campbell: Can I just say on that at that point, neither he nor I nor anybody in a senior position on my Iraq Communications Group was aware that that was the case. That is the point I keep coming back to. In relation to the changes, I have explained those changes were made by experts within the government commenting upon what they did not know to be Mr al-Marashi's work. It is only, for example, where "hostile groups" became "terrorist organisations", and it was because they said, "Hold on a minute, you are not talking about hostile groups, you are talking about terrorist organisations, you are talking about Islamic Jihad, you are talking about Hamas, you are talking about some of the groups that are trying to destabilise the Iranian regime."

Q947 Sir John Stanley: Is it not a fact that the Prime Minister has, rightly, instructed that all published material that contains intelligence material must in future be cleared by the Chairman of the Joint Intelligence Committee? Does that not of itself make it self-evident that the procedures you were following and the briefing of the Prime Minister were grossly inadequate?
Mr Campbell: No it does not because it was not initially the Prime Minister who got in place these new procedures, it was me with the Joint Intelligence Committee and the Security and Intelligence Co-ordinator, and the Prime Minister is content with the decisions that we came to.

Q948 Sir John Stanley: I am fascinated to know that in this matter apparently you seem to determine the Government's procedures.
Mr Campbell: I do not determine the Government's procedures and that totally misrepresents what I said. I entered into a discussion with the Head of the Secret Intelligence Service, the Chairman of the JIC and the Security and Intelligence Co-ordinator, Sir David Omand. The procedures were agreed in an exchange of correspondence between me and Sir

David, having been discussed with the agencies, and they were signed off by the Prime Minister. Those procedures are now in place.
Chairman: Thank you. Mr Mackinlay please?

Q949 Andrew Mackinlay: Mr Campbell, on page 4 of your statement you make it clear, as you have over the past few minutes, and you say: "When new SIS intelligence came to light, which was authorised for use in the public domain, which revealed the scale of the regime's programme of deception and concealment, it was my idea to base a briefing paper for the media upon it." You also went on a few moments ago to explain on 3 February and you said: "I explained"—that is to the Prime Minister—"where there was new intelligence." Would you be able this afternoon to take us through those paragraphs or sections of this document which were the new intelligence material?
Mr Campbell: The bulk of any new intelligence material was principally in sections one and three. It related to the activities of the Iraqi regime. It is the material about the bugging of hotels, about the monitoring of the movements of officials; it is the material about the organisation of car crashes and the like.

Q950 Andrew Mackinlay: Indeed, it is very precise, and therefore it would be possible for you overnight, would it not, with a highlighter to highlight precisely that which is above the line in terms of this intelligence material and that which is "other sources"?
Mr Campbell: It would be but I would also have to check if the agencies were happy for that to be done.

Q951 Andrew Mackinlay: You overlook the chasm you are falling into. You have said repeatedly that they have signed this information off.
Mr Campbell: There may be information within that paper which is intelligence information but not necessarily identified as such.

Q952 Andrew Mackinlay: You have confused me because the way I was following you, you said that new information came to light which was authorised for use in the public domain. That is all I am asking for, that category which was authorised for use in the public domain.
Mr Campbell: I have referred to some of that in the answer that I gave to you earlier.

Q953 Andrew Mackinlay: You understand the category I am asking about. Overnight would you highlight, or however way you want to indicate that which is in that category?
Mr Campbell: I think it would probably take longer than that.

Q954 Andrew Mackinlay: Why?
Mr Campbell: Because I would have to go through the kind of processes that Sir John has just been talking about.

Q955 Andrew Mackinlay: By Friday morning?
Mr Campbell: I would hope to be able to do that and the Foreign Secretary could perhaps bring it, but that is something that would have to be agreed by probably all of the intelligence agencies[2].

Q956 Andrew Mackinlay: If it was not, I think you would need to come up with an explanation as to why because I just cannot understand the logic of it. I do not want to labour the point. It was only when the "plagiarism" issue came to light that media attention grew, you say. When did you have that awful moment when you discovered now what has become known as the "Horlicks"? When was that moment, that sinking feeling (we have all had it) of "whoops"?
Mr Campbell: As I recall, that moment was on the way back from an interview the Prime Minister had done with Jeremy Paxman and I think—this is from memory, dredging my memory here—when we were going through what we described as our "masochism" strategy whereby the Prime Minister basically went out and was getting beaten up by the public in interviews. I think I am right in saying Channel 4 made a reference to this story on the 7 o'clock news and *Newsnight* did a very brief interview with Mr al-Marashi in the evening.

Q957 Andrew Mackinlay: Approximately, which day was that then?
Mr Campbell: That was the day—

Q958 Andrew Mackinlay: It is beyond 3 February, is it not?
Mr Campbell: I think it was the 7th. I think it may be in my note.

Q959 Andrew Mackinlay: Okay, can I assume that within an hour or two the Prime Minister was told?
Mr Campbell: It may have been the 6th. The Prime Minister was told pretty quickly, yes. He by then, I think from memory, had gone on to his constituency and I was on the way back to London.

Q960 Andrew Mackinlay: I have to say to you I have been reading this afternoon and I have listened carefully to Sir John Stanley reading out the precise words of the Prime Minister's statement of 3 February. You might think me stupid—
Mr Campbell:—no.

Q961 Andrew Mackinlay:—but I cannot conclude any other reason, reading those words again and again, than that this document was an intelligence document. It is not conditional. In fairness to you, it says the document draws upon a number of sources including intelligence sources, but did you and the Prime Minister discuss him making a formal statement or using a parliamentary occasion (taking the initiative rather than responding to questions) to clarify that point?

---

[2] Ninth Report from the Foreign Affairs Committee, Session 2002–03, *The Decision to go to War in Iraq*, HC 813-II, Ev 10.

Mr Campbell: The briefing paper that had been given to the Sunday papers on the trip to Washington was put in the Library in the House on the Monday in advance of the Prime Minister's statement on his talks with President Bush.

Q962 Andrew Mackinlay: I have told you on the receiving end of his statement what I interpreted it to be.
Mr Campbell: All I can say on that is if you look at the first dossier, the 2002 dossier, it actually makes a very big point of the fact that this is an unprecedented development. It explains what the JIC is, who is on it and how it works. I think if you do look at the other one, particularly, as I say, the way it was used, this is a huge communications exercise, I think all I can do is point to the front of the paper which says it draws upon a number of sources including intelligence.

Q963 Andrew Mackinlay: By the time it has gone beyond this awful moment, what I cannot understand is, bearing in mind it is not just Andrew Mackinlay who is confused, clearly it is a lot of other people, probably 650-odd MPs, why did the Prime Minister and/or yourself (you counsel him legitimately) not say we really ought to clarify this in a formal statement or even a written statement to the House?
Mr Campbell: The Prime Minister was asked about it, again from memory, in the House and has also had a number of written questions about the issue.

Q964 Andrew Mackinlay: But he was never proactive on it, was he?
Mr Campbell: On the day Channel 4 and the BBC exposed the fact that some of this material had come from Mr al-Marashi's article in September 2002, the Prime Minister's spokesman in the very next briefing said, "Something has gone wrong here, it should not have happened, mistakes have been made and we will have to look at it." It did not take us that long to establish what had happened. Those in the CIC responsible admitted what had happened and it was as a result of that we then discussed and put in place the new procedures.

Q965 Andrew Mackinlay: Who represents the Cabinet Office on the CIC? You said they are represented; who is he or she?
Mr Campbell: From time to time it is the Chairman of the Joint Intelligence Committee, it is sometimes his deputy, and that is who it usually is.

Q966 Andrew Mackinlay: So the Joint Intelligence Committee were privy to the document of 3 February?
Mr Campbell: They were part of the discussions about the deployment of the paper. Ultimately the decision finally to use the paper in the way that we did was made as part of our media strategy for the trip to the States. To go back to the point that I was discussing with Sir John, the issuing agency,

the Secret Intelligence Service, had already authorised us to use the intelligence material in the public domain.

Q967 Andrew Mackinlay: Yes, but presumably the Cabinet Office Secretary was represented at the critical moment when it was decided to go with this information, albeit it might have been delegated to you to sign it off?
Mr Campbell: There was a process that went on over a period of weeks. I think I am right in saying it was 7 January that the SIS said there was this new material which could be deployed in the public domain. Over the next three weeks there were three different meetings discussing all sorts of other—

Q968 Andrew Mackinlay:—Would the Cabinet Secretary be privy to the fact, to use the term, that there were other sources other than the intelligence material going to be drawn into this document?
Mr Campbell: I am not aware that the Cabinet Secretary himself was involved at all.

Q969 Andrew Mackinlay: No, but his representative.
Mr Campbell: Certainly because what my group did was commission—

Q970 Andrew Mackinlay: Who is that person?
Mr Campbell: I cannot remember who for sure was around the table at that time.

Q971 Andrew Mackinlay: It is minuted so you could let us know, please.
Mr Campbell: On 7 January?

Q972 Andrew Mackinlay: Or if you think there are a number of meetings you could say Joe Bloggs on that day and so-and-so on that day.
Mr Campbell: In relation to this particular document there were four meetings.

Q973 Andrew Mackinlay: Let's have whoever is privy to, present or the circulation, please?
Mr Campbell: Yes[3].

Q974 Andrew Mackinlay: On the September document, on page 2 of your statement you say discussions with the Chairman of the JIC on presentational issues, which is your job as a journalist.
Mr Campbell: Former!

Q975 Andrew Mackinlay: Very good. The point is presentational issues, drafting suggestions and PM's suggestions. Those were your words. Did he accept your suggestions?

[3] Ninth Report from the Foreign Affairs Committee, Session 2002–03, *The Decision to go to War in Iraq*, HC 813-II, Ev 10.

Mr Campbell: Some he did and some he did not.

Q976 Andrew Mackinlay: Okay, would you be able to tell us which ones (not now) were included in, even if you cannot tell us the ones which were excluded out?
Mr Campbell: I can probably say some of both.

Q977 Andrew Mackinlay: Overnight perhaps?
Mr Campbell: I think, for example, the first draft was put forward by the Chairman of the JIC and I looked at it. For example, there was a paragraph about Saddam Hussein's illicit earnings and it said about £3 billion of earnings, the bulk of which was illicit. I asked whether it is possible to quantify just how much of that was illicit and the answer came back from John Scarlett 100%, that kind of thing. In another area—and I know the accusation is I sexed it up, I think this is sexing it down—in the passage on human rights, for example, there were some very graphic descriptions of the nature of the regime which the draft described as "vivid and horrifying". I felt we should let it speak for itself. Do you need to say that? The Prime Minister also made suggestions.

Q978 Andrew Mackinlay: Do you know which they were?
Mr Campbell: He made suggestions about the structure of the document at quite a late stage in the drafting and the Chairman of the JIC, as it happened, said he did not think that was a better structure than his and stuck with his.

Q979 Andrew Mackinlay: Did you write the Executive Summary?
Mr Campbell: No.

Q980 Andrew Mackinlay: Who would have done that?
Mr Campbell: The Chairman of the JIC wrote the Executive Summary.

Q981 Andrew Mackinlay: Did subsequently any member of the SIS complain about the production or the conclusion, anything about the document or the manner of its presentation?
Mr Campbell: Not to me and not to the Prime Minister.
Andrew Mackinlay: You are not aware of that? Thank you very much.

Q982 Richard Ottaway: Mr Campbell, the Prime Minister today and you this afternoon have said that every word of both the dossiers is true. As you are well aware, the September 02 document has nine main conclusions of the current position, one of which is that uranium had been sought in Africa and had no civil nuclear application in Iraq. Are you still saying that is true?
Mr Campbell: I am saying that is the intelligence that the JIC put forward. I am not an intelligence expert and my position on this is if something

comes across my desk that is from John Scarlett and the JIC, if it is good enough for him, it is good enough for me.

Q983 Richard Ottaway: Given that the documents on which that claim was based have been passed to the International Atomic Energy Authority and found to be false, have the JIC notified you they had doubts about this?
Mr Campbell: I am aware of the issue. I am equally aware, and this is probably something best raised with the JIC than with myself, that the JIC say it does not necessarily negate the accuracy of the material they, the JIC, put forward.

Q984 Richard Ottaway: You are saying rather what the Foreign Secretary said yesterday and saying this is not my claim, we are just passing on intelligence here.
Mr Campbell: I am certainly not and the reason why I say if it is good enough for John Scarlett it is good enough for me is that I completely accept the integrity and professionalism of their process.

Q985 Richard Ottaway: As far as you are aware, he is still standing by that claim?
Mr Campbell: As far as I aware the claim he puts in this document, whilst I understand there is this issue to do with forgeries, my understanding (and again this is something that is not necessarily my expertise) is that that is not British intelligence material that is being talked about.

Q986 Richard Ottaway: The second main conclusion that is being queried is the 45-minute point, which you have dealt with quite extensively in your memorandum. The Foreign Secretary made a similar point yesterday about the 45 minutes. Are you saying the same today that this is what the intelligence people are telling you and it must be true?
Mr Campbell: When the first draft of the September 2002 dossier was presented to Number 10, I think I am right in saying that was the first time I had seen that and again, as I say, having seen the meticulousness and the care that the Chairman of the JIC and his colleagues were taking in the whole process, I really did not think it was my place, to be perfectly frank, to say, "Hold on a minute, what is this about?" What is completely and totally and 100% untrue—and this is the BBC allegation, which is ostensibly I think why the Chairman called me on this—what is completely and totally untrue is that I in any way overrode that judgment, sought to exaggerate that intelligence, or sought to use it in any way that the intelligence agencies were not 100% content with.

Q987 Richard Ottaway: You use some rather interesting wording in your memorandum that to suggest it was inserted against the wishes of the intelligence agencies was false. Was it put in at your suggestion?

Mr Campbell: No, otherwise—It existed in the very first draft and, as far as I am aware, that part the paper stayed like that.

Q988 Richard Ottaway: Have you gone back to the JIC on that point since publication?
Mr Campbell: I can assure you that I have had many, many discussions about this issue with the Chairman of the JIC, not least in preparation for this hearing.

Q989 Richard Ottaway: And they are still standing behind it?
Mr Campbell: Absolutely, absolutely. In relation to that particular story, which as Sir John Stanley said to the BBC correspondent last week, is about as serious an allegation as one can make, not just against me but against the Prime Minister and the intelligence agencies, they are basically saying that the Prime Minister took the country into military conflict and all that entails—loss of military and Iraqi civilian life—on the basis of a lie. Now that is a very, very serious allegation.

Q990 Richard Ottaway: Can I suggest it is Parliament that took the country into war.
Mr Campbell: The allegation against me is that we helped the Prime Minister persuade Parliament and the country to go into conflict on the basis of a lie. I think that is a pretty serious allegation. It has been denied by the Prime Minister, it has been denied by the Chairman of the Joint Intelligence Committee, it has been denied by the Security and Intelligence Co-ordinator and it has been denied by the heads of the intelligence agencies involved, and yet the BBC continue to stand by that story.

Q991 Richard Ottaway: You believe that time will prove you right on that one?
Mr Campbell: I know that we are right in relation to that 45-minute point. It is completely and totally untrue, and I do not use this word—

Q992 Richard Ottaway: I am talking about the substance.
Mr Campbell: It is actually a lie.

Q993 Richard Ottaway: You are being accused of being involved in its insertion in the document. I am quizzing you on its veracity.
Mr Campbell: I am saying in relation to that if it is good enough for the Joint Intelligence Committee, it is good enough for me. I am not qualified to question their judgement upon it but I have seen and been privy to the kind of processes and the meticulousness with which they approach that. When you have a situation when all of those people, from the Prime Minister down, the Foreign Secretary, the FCO Permanent Secretary, the heads of all the agencies deny a story and the BBC persist in saying it is true, persist in defending the correspondent whom you took evidence from last week, when I know and they know that it is not true, I think something has gone very wrong with the way that these issues are covered.

Q994 Richard Ottaway: One of you is wrong.
Mr Campbell: I know who is right and who is wrong. The BBC are wrong. We have apologised in relation to Mr al-Marashi and I think it is about time the BBC apologised to us in relation to the 45-minute point.

Q995 Richard Ottaway: I will leave that to the BBC, if you do not mind. Can I move on, in the preparation of the September 2002 document did the Government ever receive any information from the intelligence services that Iraq was not an immediate threat?
Mr Campbell: Sorry, can you just repeat that point?

Q996 Richard Ottaway: Did the Government ever receive any information from intelligence services that Iraq was not an immediate threat?
Mr Campbell: Not to my knowledge. I really do think that is a question for the intelligence agencies.

Q997 Richard Ottaway: You were looking at the intelligence there.
Mr Campbell: I do not see all the intelligence and I would not expect to see all the intelligence.

Q998 Richard Ottaway: But you were having meetings with the JIC.
Mr Campbell: I was but that is not a point of which I am aware. You asked whether the Prime Minister received any and I am saying it is not for me to know.

Q999 Richard Ottaway: You will be well aware of the source of this question because it was on the radio this morning; is it true that the intelligence agencies produced a six-page dossier March 2002 which stated there was no new evidence of a threat from Iraq?
Mr Campbell: Not that I have seen. The genesis of the September 2002 document, as again I set out in the memorandum, did start out as a broader document that was being prepared in the Foreign Office about the general issue of weapons of mass destruction, including other countries that it was looking at. It was as the Iraqi issue developed during the course of that year that a decision was taken by the Prime Minister and his colleagues to focus on Iraq and focus in the way that we duly did on the report on the intelligence assessment of Iraq's WMD.

Q1000 Richard Ottaway: So the answer to that is no, you did not see anything?
Mr Campbell: No.

Q1001 Richard Ottaway: Three weeks before the dossier was published Whitehall sources were quoted as telling the Defence Editor of *The Times* that they would not be revelationary. A few days later another Whitehall source tells the Security Editor of *The Guardian* that the dossier would no longer play a central role because there was very little new in it. Then comes a document which you have described as a very important document. How do you account for the difference in the comments and the dossier that emerged just a few weeks later?

Mr Campbell: I happen to think that the Defence Editor of *The Times* is an extremely good journalist. I have probably ruined his career by saying that! All I can say about that is that it is not true. There has been this vein of reporting for some time that the WMD dossier was transformed in the last few days prior to publication, and that was not the case. The very first substantial draft that was put forward by the Joint Intelligence Committee was very largely the basis of what was duly published and presented to Parliament.

Q1002 Richard Ottaway: Fine. Can I go to a question which the Chairman brought up at the beginning about whether you apologised to anyone and, frankly, I thought you slightly skirted round some of the direct questions. Did you apologise to the John Scarlett, the Head of the JIC, for what had happened?

Mr Campbell: Again it depends—I phoned up and said to John, who is a friend of mine and who I work with closely and regularly, "Something terrible has gone on with this. We have got to sort it out because I do not want anything that we do to reflect badly upon you and your reputation and we have got to sort that out." I have got no doubt in the various conversations during that period— and I spoke to him, I spoke to the head of the SIS, I spoke to Sir David Omand, I spoke to a number of people in the intelligence agencies—I will have said, "I am really sorry this has happened." I saw there was some story which appeared recently that I wrote this grovelling personal letter of apology to the Head of the SIS. I am not saying this because I do not believe in apologising, it is just as a matter of fact I did not send him a letter, but no doubt I have acknowledged many times our regret about the mistake made in the production of the February 2003 briefing paper.

Q1003 Richard Ottaway: So you did apologise verbally?

Mr Campbell: I certainly said, "I am really sorry for the mess this has caused and for the fact it is going to be said that this casts doubt upon you guys." The fact is my assessment of them within the government and large parts of the public at large is that their integrity is pretty much unchallenged.

Q1004 Richard Ottaway: Can I quickly ask you about the Coalition Information Centre; who appointed them?

Mr Campbell: The Coalition Information Centre started as an entity during the Kosovo conflict where it was made up of people from different government departments and also from people from other overseas governments, the United States, Spain, France I think at some point, Germany, a number of governments. In terms of how they are appointed, once we were setting up this cross-departmental team, which continues in a smaller form now, essentially what happens is we

trawl departments to try to find people who can be seconded, so on that, again from memory, I think there were discussions between myself, the head of personnel at the Foreign Office, Mike Granatt who is in charge of the GICS and trying to find people who could be seconded for three months, six months, what have you. The other personnel issues are resolved by me getting on to my opposite numbers in different parts of the world and saying, "Can you spare anybody good to come and work on this operation?"

Q1005 Richard Ottaway: What sort of data did they have access to?

Mr Campbell: It would depend on the level of clearance that they had within their home departments. For example, the person who was its last head until recently (who is now on secondment to the CPA in Baghdad) I would think had pretty high security clearance. Most of them I suspect would not.

Q1006 Richard Ottaway: And are they still in operation?

Mr Campbell: It is not operating in the same way that it did and, as I say, the people who were there during the height of the recent military conflict have actually gone to Baghdad.

Chairman: We have now come to the point where there is one minute before 4 o'clock. So I think it probably best rather than start with Greg Pope if we adjourned at this stage for a quarter of an hour and Greg Pope will begin immediately when we return at quarter past four.

The Committee suspended from 4.00 pm to 4.15 pm for a division in the House.

Chairman: The division is over. Mr Pope?

Q1007 Mr Pope: Thank you, Chairman. Mr Campbell, the charges against you really are of the gravest nature: that you exaggerated the evidence to persuade a reluctant Parliament to vote for a war which was not popular. We heard in evidence from Mr Gilligan of the BBC last week and he alleged that you transformed the original September dossier, and if I can just quote what he said in evidence, my "source's claim was that the dossier had been transformed in the week before it was published and I asked"—that is Gilligan—"'So how did this transformation happen?', and the answer was a single word, which was 'Campbell'". That is an incredibly damaging allegation. Could you comment on its veracity?

Mr Campbell: As I explained earlier, the story that I "sexed up" the dossier is untrue: the story that I "put pressure on the intelligence agencies" is untrue: the story that we somehow made more of the 45 minute command and control point than the intelligence agencies thought was suitable is untrue: and what is even more extraordinary about this whole episode is that, within an hour of the story first being broadcast, it was denied, emphatically: it then continued. We were in Kuwait at the time—

the Prime Minister was about to get a helicopter to Basra—it was denied: the story kept being repeated: the following day the BBC returned to it and it was denied—by now we were in Poland and I remember being called out of a breakfast with the Prime Minister and the Polish Prime Minister because I had asked to speak to John Scarlett, the Chairman of the Joint Intelligence Committee, just to absolutely double/triple check that there was nothing in this idea that the intelligence agencies were somehow unhappy with the way that we behaved during the thing and that there was no truth at all that anybody at the political level put pressure on the 45 minute point and John said, "Absolutely. It is complete and total nonsense and you can say that with my authority". Then the Prime Minister had to come out of the breakfast with the Polish Prime Minister; he was about to do a press conference about the Polish EU referendum campaign and, of course, the British media are all asking about this lie, which is what it was.

Q1008 Mr Pope: On the 45 minutes, what you have refuted up until now is the allegation that you inserted the 45 minute claim into the dossier and I am trying to make a different point which is that there is an allegation not that you inserted it but you gave it undue prominence; that this was a background piece of information; it was based on a single piece of uncorroborated intelligence advice and yet it was given undue prominence. It is mentioned in the foreword by the Prime Minister and it is mentioned three other times throughout the document and it is a chilling allegation—that our troops in Cyprus or our troops perhaps if they went into Iraq could face a 45 minute threat of the deployment of a chemical attack?

Mr Campbell: Well, it is true that when the BBC representative came to the Committee last week he claimed that all he had ever alleged was that we had "given it undue prominence". I am afraid that is not true. What he said last week was not true. It was a complete backtrack on what he had broadcast and written about in the *Mail on Sunday*, The *Spectator* and elsewhere. Now the reason why I feel so strongly that we, the government, from the Prime Minister down deserve an apology about this story is it has been made absolutely clear not just by me—you can put me to one side and I am well aware of the fact that I am defined in a certain way by large parts of the media, but when you put in the Prime Minister, the Foreign Secretary, the Chairman of the Joint Intelligence Committee, the Head of the Secret Intelligence Service, the Government Security and Intelligence Co-ordinator all saying emphatically "This story is not true" and the BBC defence correspondent on the basis of a single anonymous source continues to say that it is true, then I think something has gone very wrong with BBC journalism.

Q1009 Mr Pope: Are you saying that he lied not just to the Committee but on the radio? I have the transcript of the *Today* programme of 4 June. He said, "The reason why this story has run so as long"—and this is a direct quote—"is nobody has actually ever denied the central charge made by my source".

Mr Campbell: The denial was made within an hour of the lie being told on the radio. Now, I am not suggesting that he has not had somebody possibly say something to him but whatever he has been told is not true, and I think in relation to the briefing paper, when that mistake was discovered, we put our hands up and said "There is a mistake here" and we found out where it happened and we dealt with it, and I would compare and contrast with an organisation which has broadcast something—not just once but hundreds of times since—that is a lie.

Q1010 Mr Pope: And on the other charge that you pressurised the intelligence agencies to exaggerate the evidence, that is also a lie?

Mr Campbell: Totally untrue and what is more, again, the Chairman of the Joint Intelligence Committee, the Head of SIS, the Intelligence and Security Co-ordinator have all authorised me to say with their full support that is not true.

Q1011 Mr Pope: Can I move on to a different area about the machinery of government? Clare Short came before the Committee recently and she said that crucial decisions in the run-up to the conflict with Iraq were made by an entourage in No 10, that this entourage sucked the decision-making process out of the Foreign Office into No 10, that the people who make up the entourage are not elected, that the members of the entourage are yourself, Sally Morgan, David Manning, Jonathan Powell? Is that the case?

Mr Campbell: No, it is not. What is true is that I would say, if you were to say who in relation to Iraq were the officials in Downing Street who spent the most time with the Prime Minister in terms of the many foreign trips that he was doing, in terms of briefing, in terms of general meetings, it probably was the four, but in relation to that whole period he had meetings every single day with the Foreign Secretary and the Defence Secretary in particular, with the Deputy Prime Minister, with the group that comprised those three plus the Chancellor of the Exchequer, the Home Secretary, the Leader of the House—now the Health Secretary, with Margaret Beckett, and with Clare Short, and also with officials including some of the intelligence officials that we have been discussing.

Q1012 Mr Pope: What I am putting to you, though, is there is a lacuna here in that the Defence and Overseas Policy Committee of the Cabinet has not met since 28 June 2001; the War Cabinet, the ad hoc committee on Iraq; did not start meeting until mid-March, so we have this long period of time when there is no Cabinet Sub-committee meeting, the ad hoc committee, the sub-committee of the Cabinet on Iraq, had not started meeting and in that gap the decision-making process on a day-to-day basis about Iraq was essentially being made by an unelected coterie around the Prime Minister.

Mr Campbell: No. I really do not accept that because the decisions were being taken by the Prime Minister and by ministers and it has always been the case that Prime Ministers and ministers have advisers and I just do not accept the picture as it was portrayed by Clare Short when she came to the Committee. As I say, in the build-up to the conflict and during the conflict that group was meeting the whole time. Prior to that the Prime Minister was meeting with his ministerial colleagues all the time. As Robin Cook said to the Committee last week there was regular discussion in the whole Cabinet. I do not think a week went by where Iraq for some months was not the dominant issue.

Q1013 Mr Pope: A couple of brief questions about the second dossier, the February one. I notice that in your memorandum to the Committee on page 6 you said that during the third week of January the material, that is Dr Marashi's material, was simply absorbed into the briefing paper. Could you tell us who absorbed it into the briefing paper?
Mr Campbell: I think it would be wrong if I were to name the individual within the CIC who did that because I think it would look like, and I no doubt would stand accused of, seeking to evade responsibility. I take responsibility for that paper. It was done by an official to whom had been passed a number of different papers and, as I say, I do not think there was any malign intent, I do not think there was any attempt to mislead, and it is also worth pointing out, as the Prime Minister did again today, that nobody has seriously challenged the substance. Also a lot of the changes which were discussed earlier were changes, as I say, made by experts within government who possibly had more up-to-date information than Mr al-Marashi, which is not to undermine him or his work. I think that is probably as much as I really should say about the individual. It was simply within the CIC.

Q1014 Mr Pope: But you can see why the Committee is concerned and why Parliament is concerned, because what you have essentially got here is an academic thesis that has been down-loaded, it has been used without—
Mr Campbell: No. We keep going back to this myth about the twelve year old PhD thesis. It was an article from a Middle East journal.

Q1015 Mr Pope: But the article is used without Mr al-Marashi's permission, he is not credited with it, and worst of all, I think, is the possibility that his relatives back in Iraq may have been persecuted because of that.
Mr Campbell: Well, were that the case it would be very, very regrettable and I completely accept that, and I certainly hope that is not the case but, as I said earlier, the accusation that we faced when I was having the horrible moment coming down from the *Newsnight* studio in Gateshead was that we had not drawn attention to him and, as he said himself to the Committee, he is well known in this field, but I do accept there is a world of difference

between writing something in the *Middle East Review* and something being subsequently discovered to be part of the British government's briefing paper that we issued to the Sunday press.

Q1016 Mr Pope: Just finally, do you share the Foreign Secretary's assessment that the second dossier in hindsight was a mistake? In fact, a complete Horlicks?
Mr Campbell: I certainly accept it was a mistake. You and he both support Blackburn and maybe you drink Horlicks down there but I think down the road in the rather less effete Burnley they will probably say it is a storm in a teacup—or drink Bovril!

Q1017 Mr Chidgey: Mr Campbell, I would like to come back to an area that Mr Mackinlay was discussing with you earlier in this session in relation to the September dossier. You, I think, confirmed for the record then that you discussed with the Chairman of the JIC the presidential issues—I should not say that—the presentational issues regarding the dossier?
Mr Campbell: There probably were, "presidential" issues.

Q1018 Mr Chidgey: I bet there were. Anyway, let's come back to the issues. It is rather complicated but I think the Committee really does want to get to the bottom of this. Can you try to visualise for us how different the September dossier would have been if it had not been for your discussions on presentational issues?
Mr Campbell: The short answer is not very much. It was agreed fairly early on in the process that the Prime Minister would write a foreword. Other than literally drafting points I do not recall any substantial changes being made to the executive summary. As the draft evolved there were discussions about structure and the ordering material and the use of graphics and the use of pictures and such like and some of the titles of the different chapters, but the honest answer is not very much. This is the work of the Joint Intelligence Committee.

Q1019 Mr Chidgey: You appreciate how important this issue is. The accusation has been made that this document was adjusted, altered, sexed up—whatever—for a particular political purpose so one has to be somewhat pedantic and get exactly to the bottom of how the process worked. You said, and it is on the record elsewhere, that this process took many months to evolve. I think it would be very helpful if, perhaps not today but shortly afterwards, you could let the Committee have information on the suggestions that were made by you and your team as this document evolved. For example, it must be the case surely that in this process, as the drafts were continuing or continuously upgraded or amended, copies of earlier drafts would have been kept electronically within your Department, within your team. It would be very helpful if it was possible for us to have copies of those earlier drafts so that we could satisfy ourselves that there were no attempts to change the essence of the document in order to pursue a particular political point. Is that possible?

Mr Campbell: Can I say again on that the JIC would have to be content that they were willing to do that but that is certainly something I can take back and ask them if they are.

Q1020 Mr Chidgey: I accept that, of course, but this is at the heart of the issue—that this document was deliberately changed for political purposes.

Mr Campbell: I accept that.

Q1021 Mr Chidgey: And anything you can give us to demonstrate otherwise would, of course, be very helpful, by Friday.

Mr Campbell: As I say, I do not think I can make that judgment for the intelligence agencies who were producing the various drafts as they evolved, but in relation to the changes that I was suggesting on either changes that I was suggesting or that I was putting forward to the Chairman of the Joint Intelligence Committee on behalf of the Prime Minister, and I have gone and looked at all of them, I have no difficulty with you seeing any of them but, again, I just have to be sure that the Joint Intelligence Committee are happy that there is nothing in there that does reveal things they might not want revealed.

Q1022 Mr Chidgey: I understand that but can you also let us have them in calendar order so we can have them dated so we can see how the process evolved from the CIC?

Mr Campbell: I think I am right in saying that the CIC—this is where I think these things, I have to say, I think in large parts of the media deliberately have been completely conflated.

Q1023 Mr Chidgey: In your discussions with the Joint Intelligence Committee, put it that way.

Mr Campbell: Yes. I have no problem with that. As I say, I cannot sit here and say on behalf of the Chairman of the Joint Intelligence Committee that he would be happy with every single draft being put into the public domain. I just do not know.

Q1024 Mr Chidgey: Well, perhaps you can have that discussion and do what is necessary from that position. You mentioned also earlier in response to Mr Mackinlay that the executive summary of the dossier of September was written by the Chairman of the Joint Intelligence Committee. Did you in any way assist with the presentational issues in that foreword?

Mr Campbell: Given that on the presentational issue it says "Executive Summary" and then it is the text there is not much by way of presentation there. I accept that but, again, I would have to go back and look at all the different drafting suggestions that I made but, in terms of any substance, none at all.

Q1025 Mr Chidgey: That would be helpful. Also I think Mr Mackinlay asked you whether anyone in the SIS or any other security agencies was unhappy with the end result of the dossier. Can you confirm that nobody expressed any concern or reservation about the dossier as it was finally published from our security intelligence?

Mr Campbell: None of the people who were involved in its production that I was dealing with expressed any misgivings.

Q1026 Mr Chidgey: So you were unaware should there have been anyone who was so described?

Mr Campbell: I was not aware of anybody within intelligence agencies who was saying to us in relation to the production of this dossier they were unhappy with it.

Q1027 Mr Chidgey: You mentioned in your note to us, and I am paraphrasing to save time, that it was a major break with precedence for the intelligence community to allow information from them to be put into the public domain, which of course we understand, and that this break with precedent was not something taken lightly. Did any of the people involved in the intelligence and security agencies at any time question the wisdom of this procedure, this precedent in breaking with the traditional method of keeping their information close to the secret? Did anyone resist your decision to break with the established policy?

Mr Campbell: No. I have no doubt at all there would have been a debate within the intelligence community, because it was such a break with precedent, as to whether it was the right thing to do and all I can say is that the Joint Intelligence Committee, which as you know includes the heads of the agencies and obviously the Chairman, expressed no such reservations to Prime Minister or to me.

Q1028 Mr Chidgey: So as a result of the debate that was held with the Joint Intelligence Committee, at the end of that debate all those involved were content?

Mr Campbell: That is correct.

Q1029 Mr Chidgey: And there would be no reason for anyone therefore to pursue the route that we have discussed at length with the BBC?

Mr Campbell: No, and that is why I was so confident in issuing the denial that we did of the initial BBC story, and then, once the stories persisted, why I went back and said, "Look, this thing is still kicking around somewhere, is it true?", and they were emphatic, "It is not".

Q1030 Mr Chidgey: You say in your note that the intelligence judgments contained in the dossier were entirely those of the Joint Intelligence Committee. Can you tell us at all what in the dossier falls into the category of intelligence judgments, and what does not?

Mr Campbell: I think I would have to say it all does in that the document is, if you like, their assessment of the state of Saddam Hussein's weapons of mass destruction programme. Now, if you are saying which of it is, as it were, secret intelligence then that is really something for them to say, but this is the distillation of the Joint Intelligence Committee assessments that were being presented to the Prime Minister.

Q1031 Mr Chidgey: For example, we know from evidence we have taken from the Foreign Secretary that the Foreign and Commonwealth Office takes the credit for parts 2 and 3 of the dossier, so I presume—
Mr Campbell: In the drafting.

Q1032 Mr Chidgey: I see. There is a distinction.
Mr Campbell: But the document has the imprimatur of the Joint Intelligence Committee. It is their document and, as I said in my written statement to you, this process evolved at the start though the initial drafting was being done in the Foreign Office. Once the decision was taken for this to be primarily an intelligence-based document, the Chairman of the Joint Intelligence Committee took responsibility for it.

Q1033 Mr Chidgey: And so—
Mr Campbell: Not the Foreign Office.

Q1034 Mr Chidgey: So he, as the Chairman of the Joint Intelligence Committee, signed off the whole dossier. He was not just signing off that which involved a judgment on the intelligence?
Mr Campbell: The whole thing, and what is more I literally mean "signed off" because the foreword was agreed—the Joint Intelligence Committee had to be happy that the foreword was a fair reflection; it was obviously going to form part of the basis of what the Prime Minister was going to say to Parliament when he presented it when Parliament was recalled; when the document after all the various drafting processes was presented, it literally was presented. The Chairman of the Joint Intelligence Committee said. "Right, here you are, here it is", not "Here you are, have another go at rewriting it". That is not how it worked.

Q1035 Mr Chidgey: Can I just make some specific references to the documents, and I will try not to be too long on this but when you look in some detail and read very carefully I think it is chapter 3, page 19/20, where we talk about chemical agent production capabilities, that struck me as a particularly even-handed written explanation of Iraq's capabilities, or potential in terms of their ability to produce chemical weapons in relation to the basic infrastructure and processing equipment that would be necessary for an industrialised country to produce the chemicals that that economy would need. It seemed fairly even-handed. But when we go forward in the document to the foreword or to the very summary that occurs the language becomes much tougher and I am sure,

Mr Campbell, as an extremely experienced journalist you understand exactly how words can be used with a slightly different emphasis which together in a document create a much stronger emphasis. The impression I got reading this through was that, whilst in the foreword in the early parts of the document it would appear that there was absolutely no question at all that Iraq had not only the capabilities but the stocks, the intent, the delivery systems—the whole charabanc, if you like—to launch a very serious threat against its region and ourselves if our forces were in the theatre through chemical weapons, the actual detail within the document did not put that emphasis on at all. It pointed out capabilities, possibilities, maybe, could be—you understand where I am coming from?
Mr Campbell: I do.

Q1036 Mr Chidgey: I wonder if you could help us on how has that happened in the drafting of the report which you were so closely involved with, clearly?
Mr Campbell: On that specific I cannot. I think that it is not for me to speak for the Chairman of the Joint Intelligence Committee but I think if he were here he would point out that there are various ways in which intelligence can be assessed and judged. For example, I can recall, I think Mr Ottaway earlier asked for the sorts of changes that we might have discussed and you are absolutely right that words can say different things. I remember in relation to the uranium issue, and I think it says in the document, that they had "sought to secure" and I can remember saying, "Well, can that be explained? Have they actually secured anything?", and he said, "Well, intelligence, our best assessment of it, is not, therefore 'sought to secure' is the best way to express the reality of our current intelligence assessment". Now, I am happy to look at the two passages you have drawn attention to—

Q1037 Mr Chidgey: That would be very helpful.
Mr Campbell: I was very conscious when this process was being gone through of how assiduous the Chairman of the Joint Intelligence Committee in particular was at spotting potential inconsistencies, things being expressed in slightly different ways that might lead to cause for doubt or confusion, and my experience at the time was that they did an extraordinarily good job at addressing those and, as I say, I am happy to look at that one in particular.

Q1038 Mr Chidgey: Can I just take that slightly different aspect of this discussion? On page 16 the dossier sets out the quantities of various chemicals that were unaccounted for, and I am not going to record these figures of course—they were used by the Foreign Secretary and I think again by the Prime Minister at various times—but what to me is missing from this report is any indication of the implications of the degree of threat that those quantities could pose. For example, 8.5 thousand litres of anthrax sounds an awful lot but in fact it is less than a quarter of a petrol tanker load leaving the terminal in my constituency seventy times a day, so there is no indication here what degree of threat these quantities or other quantities that could be produced could cause. Was that ever discussed? Was there ever any discussion with the intelligence services that one should try to put some scale on this?

Mr Campbell: No. This is often described as a dossier that was used to "make the case for war". Now, it actually was not. It was a dossier that was produced to set out the reason why the British government were so concerned about the issue and the Joint Intelligence Committee put together its best assessment of that situation. What it did not do then was speculate as to how these might be used, the sort of damage that they might do, and I think if it had been that sort of document we would have fallen foul of the criticism that we were trying to exaggerate, alarm. If we were suddenly to say, "With this much of anthrax you could do this"—there were other pieces of communication around the system that were doing that kind of thing but this was not one of them.

Q1039 Mr Chidgey: But those assessments must have been made because you say the dossier is not making the case for what we were considering but we were clearly considering that as an option, so assessments must have been made of what the impact of the capability that it was claimed Iraq had or Saddam Hussein had on our troops or armed forces. That must all have been done.

Mr Campbell: Again, I cannot recall that there was a discussion about developing the document in the way that you are suggesting. It think it was always envisaged as this kind of document.

Q1040 Mr Chidgey: You are aware that in evidence yesterday the Foreign Secretary—I think his phrase was that the document did make "the best case"?

Mr Campbell: It made the best case, our best assessment of the state of Saddam Hussein's weapons of mass destruction—

Q1041 Mr Chidgey: Not the best case for going to war?

Mr Campbell: It is not that sort of document.

Mr Chidgey: Thank you.

Q1042 Ms Stuart: Mr Campbell, may I refer you to your own statement in submission to the Committee? You say in opening that the overall strategy for Iraq was laid down by the Prime Minister?

Mr Campbell: And other Cabinet members.

Q1043 Ms Stuart: And others, yes, "from where I sat". Can I go just a little bit further, and precisely where you did sit? Did you sit in on those meetings only wearing the hat of Director of Communication, or would you in that process have an input into policy and strategy?

Mr Campbell: No. In relation to policy, as I say in the note, policy decisions are taken by the Cabinet headed, as you know, by the Prime Minister. Now I was involved in a lot of the discussions about policy and strategy on Iraq and I am there as an adviser to the Prime Minister.

Q1044 Ms Stuart: In that context, if I follow up a submission made by Mr Pope and drawing reference to Clare Short's evidence, she drew the conclusion from the information she had been given and discussions within the Cabinet that it was quite clear that the decision was made by the international community or others that we would go to war in February and March, and that from about September onwards the rest of it was simply preparing the country for that fact. How would you assess that statement?

Mr Campbell: I reject it. I was with the Prime Minister, for example—I cannot remember exactly which weekend it was—when he seemed to spend literally into double figures of hours on the telephone to I think at the time the leaders of Mexico and Chile and others seeking to keep the whole issue of the United Nations' route as a way of avoiding conflict, and that was the strategy at that time. Equally, however, the Prime Minister made clear before that in his phrase the United Nations had to be the place where this was resolved, not avoided as an issue. I just do not recognise this characterisation of the Prime Minister as somebody who had taken a prior decision and that then we were all just—not just me but the intelligence agencies and everyone else— pawns in his game to take the country into a war with George Bush. I do not recognise that. On the contrary, I saw somebody who was working round the clock, flat out, trying to keep this thing on the United Nations' route as a means of avoiding conflict. Clare Short has to speak for herself in relation to what her impression was of what the Prime Minister was doing at the time but, as she said, I spent a lot of time with the Prime Minister and that is the Prime Minister I saw. Again, I just think that sometimes people make assumptions about not just this Prime Minister but any senior politician that they are acting out of some terrible motive, and it is nonsense. I have seen the Prime Minister now in relation to several conflict situations where he is very, very conscious of the responsibility of saying, "We are going to send British forces into military action and some of them may die". Now, the idea that you just do that glibly or that you try and "sex up" a dossier as a way of trying to persuade the public that you should do it actually—I know scepticism is fine but are we really so cynical that we think a Prime Minister, any Prime Minister—forget the fact it is Tony Blair, any Prime Minister—is going to make prior decisions to send British forces into conflict and would not rather avoid doing that?

Q1045 Ms Stuart: I think it would be useful to have your interpretation of this but can I come back to the second dossier and again your own evidence on this where you make reference to how you commissioned that dossier back in January, which was then subsequently used as a briefing for six journalists on the way to the United States? What were the instructions as to the purpose of this second dossier back in January? What did you tell them to prepare? For what?

Mr Campbell: As you say, I deliberately, both in giving evidence to you and in my paper—as far as I am concerned the dossier was the WMD dossier of 2002. The purpose of the briefing paper that we commissioned in January was to get our media to cover this issue of the extent to which Saddam Hussein was developing his programme of concealment and intimidation of the United Nations' inspectors because, if you remember, at the time there was a lot of discussion "Why is it so hard for the inspectors to get in and find these weapons?", and in a sense this was a part of that answer. It actually was not the full answer. As I have said in my paper to you, I never envisaged this as being a significant thing, and I can send to you the coverage at the time. It was minuscule. It got a few paragraphs in the Sunday papers, it got no broadcast coverage, it was only when this Mr al-Marashi issue came to light on my train journey from Gateshead that it started to get any coverage at all, so it was intended—it was a tactical decision, if you like, in relation to giving it to those journalists as opposed to any other group of journalists or putting it out on the website or whatever we might have done. This was just a decision taken at that time just as the Prime Minister was going to see George Bush, but it was never meant to be a huge deal. I always felt that the information within it that they would find interesting, which, indeed, was the case, related to the fact that there was this ratio of 200:1—200 Iraqi agents to every UN inspector—and also some of the things they were doing in relation to bugging and following and organising car crashes and all the rest of it was interesting but it was not making the case for war, and I think in relation to both of these documents all of these facts were well known when it came to the most important debate in Parliament about committing British forces; all these issues were well known by then. People knew by then that something had gone badly wrong in relation to the second document and as I recall it, in relation to the first, nobody in that debate raised the issue of the 45 minutes point. So this idea that we had pumped this out as the most significant piece, if we had we had done it pretty badly because it did not appear to resonate with members of Parliament at all.

Q1046 Ms Stuart: But what I am still not clear about is you must have given some indication of what you wanted this document prepared for. It then ends up being in the House of Commons and it is being referred to by Secretary of State Colin Powell. Are you suggesting that any MP would have been able to know the difference between the significant one—

Mr Campbell: No.

Q1047 Ms Stuart: Yet he quoted it so it was taken seriously?

Mr Campbell: Okay. To answer your question directly, what was it intended for, it was intended to generate some media discussion and debate about this issue. Why was it so hard for the UN weapons inspectors to do their job? That is what it was for, and I think I probably have to take some responsibility for Colin Powell raising it because when we were out in Washington I gave a copy to my opposite number, and I suspect that is possibly how it got into, as it were, the American system. I do not think there has been quite the fuss there that there has been here, I have to say.

Q1048 Ms Stuart: On the bottom of page 6 of your submission you say, again in relation to the second dossier: "The changes were made because the officials making them believed they rendered the account more accurate". Now my understanding of a process which would render something more accurate would indicate you go back to source. How else do you know the changes you are making would make it more accurate?

Mr Campbell: No. The point I am making on page 6 of my note is that those commenting upon it were not aware of who the source was and in any event, within that document, there was government-sourced material so, for example, in relation to some of the changes that were made, as I say, in some cases as has been pointed out there have been changes that you could argue make the situation more dramatic, for want of a better word. In others, Mr al-Marashi's paper has suggested there are more Iraqi agents involved in certain operations than our experts believed to be the case, so again this was, as it were, "sexed down" rather than up.

Q1049 Ms Stuart: But I think I still have a slight difference with your definition of how you render something more accurate because if I render it more accurate then I go back to check my sources and change my wording rather than—

Mr Campbell: No. The point I am making is that the CIC asks for these various pieces of work, all sorts, whether it is an article or a briefing paper or whatever, they go in and somebody puts together a draft; it absorbs part of this material without attribution and, as I said before, that was the mistake. The attribution was not put on to it as it should have been. Now, had those then looking at this known that was where part of this source material came from, you are quite right, you could have got on the phone and said to Mr al-Marashi, "Look, you say in your paper this. Would you mind if we use this?", and judging from his evidence he might well have said "No", in which case that would have been the end of the matter. Had he said "Yes", you might have said, "Well, it says this, we have information based on—whatever it might be, intelligence or whatever—that, in fact, it is this. Is that something you would think is right or wrong?" Or what you might do, and this I do not think would have detracted anything from the paper at all because, as I say, nobody seriously challenged most of the content, is say to him, "Could we use it simply with your name attached to it?"

Q1050 Mr Illsley: Just following on from that I am going to challenge some of the serious content of it. The one thing that we have received evidence on in this Committee which is worrying me from start to finish is the quality of the intelligence material which you have obviously worked with and which has gone into the document.
Mr Campbell: On the second dossier?

Q1051 Mr Illsley: Yes. I am just going to follow on from what my colleague, Gisela, was speaking about. There is a section at the beginning of the document, page 3, which relates to Hans Blix and the UNMOVIC team and the document says that, "Journeys are monitored by security officers stationed on the route if they have prior intelligence. Any changes of destination are notified ahead by telephone or radio so that arrival is anticipated. The welcoming party is a giveaway". That was in the second document published on 30 January. On 14 February, two weeks later, Hans Blix told the United Nations, "Since we arrived in Iraq we have conducted more than 400 inspections covering more than 300 sites. All inspections were performed without notice and access was almost always provided promptly. In no case have we seen convincing evidence that the Iraqi site knew in advance that the inspectors were coming". Now, granted that was two weeks after your document was published but it tends to suggest that some of the intelligence you were working with or which had been provided to you was either out of date or wrong.
Mr Campbell: Well, in relation to that, again, all I can say is that this, from my perspective doing the job I do, came to light through one of the chief intelligence agencies. It was their intelligence.

Q1052 Mr Illsley: I am not disputing that.
Mr Campbell: I know there was some co-operation between Hans Blix and the intelligence agency but I am not aware of what Hans Blix would or would not know about—what he said is not inconsistent with the idea that there was a significant campaign of intimidation and deception. That was the point the document was meant to make. In other words, when they get these welcoming parties, is that because they know where they are going and they have managed to clean up the place they are going to? I think that is partly the point that is being made. Now that has come, as I say, as intelligence, and the issuing agency was the SIS.

Q1053 Mr Illsley: As I say, I am challenging the content of the document because, in my opinion, I do not think it is a document that adds anything to the argument basically and I think the whole thing is a complete mess—but anyway. Coming back to the point about intelligence, did you see raw intelligence material that security services had or were you provided with assessments from the senior intelligence community?
Mr Campbell: In relation to this?

Q1054 Mr Illsley: In relation to the first dossier now. In general, the intelligence you were able to see up to September before and after, did you see raw intelligence or was this material provided to you as assessments from the intelligence services?
Mr Campbell: Again, I am not sure how much or how little of this I am supposed to divulge but I certainly saw the Joint Intelligence Committee assessments on which the September report was based.

Q1055 Mr Illsley: Did you ever have any discussions with the intelligence services as to the quality of the material that was coming your way? Were you happy with it? Did you ever pass any comment on it? I think you said to one of my colleagues earlier that if the head of intelligence service said this was a kosher piece of information, that was fine by you. Did you ever argue with them? Challenge them?
Mr Campbell: It was not a question of arguing. On that Iraq Communications Group that I chair, as I said in my note, there is a senior representative of the SIS—in fact, two—so you have discussions with them the whole time, and often if at a particular time as a communications strategy might be evolving there is a particular theme that you were seeking to pursue, there are people within the intelligence services who will just—and I am not saying these are full-time presentation people— think "Well, I know that No 10 has got an interest in this particular theme at the moment, might this be something they might be interested in? Should I discuss it?" They might come and see me and say "Look, this has come from this or that", but I think I probably have to leave it there in relation to what they showed me and how we discuss it.

Q1056 Mr Illsley: Does nothing occur that would have led anybody within the intelligence services to resent your involvement or your presence on these committees, and I am thinking now in terms of the Gilligan argument and the leaks from intelligence sources pointing the finger at you for everything?
Mr Campbell: The BBC's defence correspondent came here and talked about his weird and wonderful meetings with his source, and that may be the person he knows within the intelligence community. I do not know who that is, I do not know how serious a person it is or how senior. All I know is that the people that I deal with and have dealt with now over some years in several very difficult sets of circumstances like Kosovo, like Afghanistan, like Iraq, I find of the highest professionalism and, in many instances, the highest bravery. Now it is not a question of me just saying, "Well, if it is good enough for him it is good enough for me". You form judgments about people over time and, as I say, the people that I have dealt

with on this are the people in the leadership of the intelligence community who, I think, are people of very high standard.

Q1057 Mr Illsley: But you are adamant that you never throughout the whole of this went to the intelligence services and rejected a piece of evidence that they put forward, enhanced it, exaggerated it, doctored it?
Mr Campbell: Absolutely not and there are many reasons why I wanted to come to the Committee and I agree with some of the comments that have been made in recent weeks and I think it would have been very odd to have done this inquiry had I not—that is something we can discuss but I felt that from the start—but one of the reasons from my own perspective, because the truth is, if you are in my position or even more if you are in the Prime Minister's position, lots and lots of things get written about which are completely untrue, and to be perfectly honest 95% of them do not matter a damn and are forgotten the next day, but I think to say, not just in the *Daily Mail* or the *Daily Telegraph* but on the BBC, that I was involved conniving with the intelligence agencies to do this—I just cannot think of a more serious allegation than that, and to have a culture that says, "Well, it is just another story. Who cares? What are you bothered about?"—and, as I think I explained to you in my note, I have been trying to get an acknowledgement from the BBC that this story is wrong for weeks. I have a sheaf of correspondence with them about it. Now, what are you supposed to do?

Q1058 Mr Illsley: That is the point I am going to come on to in a second. I think we could place on record here as well that perhaps your presence would not have been required had this Committee's request for scientific intelligence material been agreed to by the Prime Minister and the Foreign Secretary. We could have satisfied ourselves had we seen that information.
Mr Campbell: Can I just say on that, in relation to the scrutiny of the intelligence services for which the Prime Minister has ministerial responsibility, there have been a lot of changes and developments on that but it is fair to say that that particular one, to go back to your point, is a bit above my pay grade.

Q1059 Mr Illsley: Just on the question of the evidence, we did hear in relation to journalists and intelligence sources, were we to believe what we were told the other day, that every major newspaper has two or three, perhaps even four, contacts within the intelligence agencies; that they have got each other's telephone numbers, and they have easy access to information. Do you believe that, given your background as a journalist and given your position over the last few years working with the intelligence agencies, or do you accept that there is that amount of leakage of material to journalists?

Mr Campbell: No. There are systems, and again it is probably not for me to explain them in detail but there are systems, that allow the press to make inquiries of the intelligence community but this picture that was painted by one of the witnesses last week of intelligence agencies wandering all round London meeting BBC correspondents—

Q1060 Mr Illsley: In their own offices.
Mr Campbell: I am sorry. Maybe I am terribly naive and maybe Chris Mullin's book was spot on about it but I have to say that is not my experience, fine book though it was.

Q1061 Mr Illsley: Are you just going to take it on the chin then as regards the BBC, or is there anything you can do as regards those allegations? Can you challenge them or do you think it is just not worth the candle?
Mr Campbell: No. As I say, a lot of the stories are not worth the candle; I think this one is. One of the reasons I raised that point with you in my memorandum was because I envisaged that one of the questions might be, "Well, if this story is so bad what have you done about it?", and the truth is privately we have been trying to seek acknowledgement about this for some weeks and it is absolutely hopeless, because when you are dealing with the BBC I am afraid they just will not admit that they can get things wrong.

Q1062 Richard Ottaway: Now you know how the Tory party feels!
Mr Campbell: I am really not here to make political points.

Q1063 Mr Maples: You used to encourage them!
Mr Campbell: Encourage them to—? The point is that I think there is a world of difference between political exchanges and the rest of it and a story broadcast on the BBC followed up by every single national newspaper, followed up in newspapers around the world, that says the Prime Minister, the Foreign Secretary, with the connivance of me and the intelligence agencies, persuaded Parliament and the country to go to war on a false basis I think is a pretty unbelievable allegation to make unless you can sustain it, and I have not seen a single thing that sustains it. I have seen the defence correspondent change his story time and time again, talking about one source, then there were four sources, then his sources were journalists on other newspapers—if that is BBC journalism, then God help them.

Q1064 Mr Maples: Can I take you back to what we affectionately now here call the "dodgy" dossier—
Mr Campbell: I have noticed the phrase being used repeatedly.

Q1065 Mr Maples: I just wanted to make sure we were talking about the same document. I am interested in the role of these four officials whose names were originally on the website and you have

gone some way to explaining their role in your note to us and let us just go through them. The one who you do not know who you say was a member of the CIC was, I believe, a Foreign Office official called Peter Hamill?
Mr Campbell: That is not the name, no. There was a—actually, I think his background is not Foreign Office, I think he may be MoD, but there was an official who was working in the CIC that is certainly one of the four names.

Q1066 Mr Maples: Well, the name that was on the website—?
Mr Campbell: Was Paul Hamill.

Q1067 Mr Maples: I am sorry. My mistake. What was his role in this? He was part of the CIC?
Mr Campbell: He was a full-time member of the CIC.

Q1068 Mr Maples: So he was an important person in the preparation of this assessment?
Mr Campbell: He was a member of the CIC team.

Q1069 Mr Maples: Did you know that in the Foreign Office register his job title is "Head of Story Development"?
Mr Campbell: I did not know that but—

Q1070 Mr Maples: Do you think that is an appropriate title for somebody involved in—
Mr Campbell: I can see why, if you are not involved full-time in communications issues, it might sound a bit odd but actually what that means is somebody who takes a brief, an issue—as I say, we are talking about different themes that we are trying to pursue, and then turns them into products that might be of interest to the media. That is what they do.

Q1071 Mr Maples: Mr Campbell, I put it to you that no government before this one has ever had an official with the job title "Head of Story Development"?
Mr Campbell: I do not know that was the job title that was given to him. I know what he did in the CIC and what he did in the CIC and what he continues to do on behalf of the government is perfectly legitimate and necessary work.

Q1072 Mr Maples: Where is he now?
Mr Campbell: I honestly think—I do not think it is right for me to talk about individual officials—

Q1073 Mr Maples: I put it to you that he is in Baghdad.
Mr Campbell: He still works for the Iraqi information operation.

Q1074 Mr Maples: In Baghdad, and I wonder whether he is there to keep him from us or whether that is where you put people who offend?

Mr Campbell: No, it is not.

Q1075 Mr Maples: Let us go through the other people in this. Alison Blackshaw is your PA and you say that her involvement was that she typed changes that you made, so you had an editorial input into this document. You actually made changes to it.
Mr Campbell: As I have explained in the memorandum.

Q1076 Mr Maples: Yes, but you made changes obviously at a fairly late stage.
Mr Campbell: I made changes at the very final stage. I changed the title and I stripped out what I considered to be repetitions.

Q1077 Mr Maples: And that is as far as it went?
Mr Campbell: That is as far as it went and in relation to my personal assistant—and forgive me if I feel quite strongly about this one as well—the journalists who have been writing these stories know her because her job on these trips overseas is to look after them and make sure they have visas and their bags are picked up and the rest of it, and the idea that she would write a paper like this is totally absurd.

Q1078 Mr Maples: I am not suggesting that for a moment; what I am simply saying—
Mr Campbell: Well, the newspapers have, and in questioning to witnesses it has been put by members that that is the case.

Q1079 Mr Maples: It has, but you have explained what her involvement was and I am simply saying that was to put in place amendments which you had made to the document. Now, one of these people was the Downing Street news editor on the website, and I accept your explanation of his involvement, but you dismissed John Pratt as, I think you say, a junior—
Mr Campbell: No. I do not say "junior"; I say he is an assistant.

Q1080 Mr Maples: I cannot find it now.
Mr Campbell: He is an administrative support assistant in my office.

Q1081 Mr Maples: You describe him as a "member of the support team in my department". Who does he work for?
Mr Campbell: He works obviously for me but the person he works for is Peter Hyman.

Q1082 Mr Maples: Did Peter Hyman have input into this document?
Mr Campbell: Absolutely not.

Q1083 Mr Maples: Nothing at all?
Mr Campbell: Nothing at all.

Q1084 Mr Maples: But he is a politically appointed specialist adviser in No 10?

Mr Campbell: Who? John Pratt?

Q1085 Mr Maples: No. Peter Hyman.
Mr Campbell: Peter Hyman is. He had nothing to do with this whatever.

Q1086 Mr Maples: Somebody who works for him does, but he had nothing to do with it?
Mr Campbell: Can I explain what John Pratt's role in this ridiculous story was? John Pratt—and I think when people hear this they will be stunned that this is how stories get into newspapers—this story appeared in *The Guardian* as I explained in my note and it said these four people worked on this report. I can explain to you what the people in my office did, and I think somebody has got hold of the record of this thing and it appears apparently in today's *Independent* newspaper. It was e-mailed from the CIC to one of my staff in No 10 because I wanted to take the latest draft on the plane to America. The person to whom it was sent sits next to John Pratt. She said, "John, have you got a spare disc that I can copy this on to?" John Pratt gave her a disc. It was copied on to the disc. The disc was then handed to my personal assistant. My personal assistant took it on the plane. I made some changes in manuscript, she typed them in. On bringing it back to No 10, she gave it to the website editor. On those prosaic realities is built the most absurd mountain of conspiracy and nonsense.

Q1087 Mr Maples: Well, you have gone some way to correcting that in your memo to us and I accept that, but when we find that somebody is a relatively junior official and all he did was lend somebody else a disc but he works for a politically appointed special adviser who works for you—there are more politically appointed specialist advisers in Downing Street under this administration than there have ever been in the past and their fingerprints are awfully close to all these documents, and I am just suggesting here is another link.
Mr Campbell: I am a special adviser and I have taken responsibility for the second paper. In relation to this, there would be no reason by the way, had I felt it appropriate for Peter Hyman to be involved in this, that he should not have been, but the fact is he was not and I do think—you were saying this was not a time for political discussion but I do think there is a political point.

Q1088 Mr Maples: Let me ask something in relation to the Foreign Secretary. In his note to us the Foreign Secretary said in relation to this document, "No FCO ministers or FCO specialist advisers were consulted in the document. No 10 officials including special advisers asked for some changes"[4].

[4] Ninth Report from the Foreign Affairs Committee, Session 2002–03, *The Decision to go to War in Iraq*, HC 813-II, Ev 61.

Mr Campbell: That is me.

Q1089 Mr Maples: That is only you?
Mr Campbell: That is me. I am a special adviser.

Q1090 Mr Maples: It says "including special advisers", in the plural. Is that just a grammatical thing?
Mr Campbell: All I know is that the special adviser who was involved in this is the special adviser who was the chair of the Iraq Communications Group and that is me. Peter Hyman had nothing to do with it whatever.

Q1091 Mr Maples: Could we move on to the dossier of the weapons of mass destruction because I want to put to you that we were told by two of our witnesses, Dame Pauline Neville-Jones who is a former Chairman of the Joint Intelligence Committee and a former Australian intelligent agent, that this document did not read like a Joint Intelligence Committee assessment. The language was not like a Joint Intelligence Committee assessment, and there may be perfectly acceptable explanations for that but the Joint Intelligence Committee assessments tended to be full of qualifications and ambiguities, and "maybe this" and "perhaps that" and equivalents, whereas the document, at least in its executive summary, is much more certain. I do not know if you are aware of the document that was published in 1998 before Desert Fox, and again this is published over the name of Derek Fatchett, the minister at the Foreign Office at the time and is an intelligent assessment, and I want to quote to you two short lines from it: "The Iraqi chemical industry could produce mustard gas almost immediately and limited amounts of nerve gas within months"—"could"— "Saddam almost certainly retains some BW production equipment, stocks of agents and weapons". But in the summary to this document, admittedly four years later, we have, "Iraq has continued to produce chemical and biological agents. Some of these weapons are deployable within 45 minutes". The language is much more definite. What Dame Pauline Neville-Jones said to us is to have been able to go from one to the other there would have to be some new piece of intelligence which really substantiated in a much harder form the second statement, because it is not fundamentally different but certainly different in quality to the first, and I wonder if you saw such intelligence which justified the making of a much stronger claim?
Mr Campbell: I am not intimately acquainted with the Derek Fatchett paper but if you go back to the whole background to the WMD dossier of September 2002 I think the Prime Minister said publicly that one of the reasons why he wanted to do this was because there was continuing new intelligence that he was seeing that made him feel there was a growing threat from Iraq's weapons of mass destruction programme. Now, again, it is not for me to talk about the intelligence or the assessments that are made by the Joint Intelligence

Committee but I can only assume that, if there was a change in position, it was as a result of new intelligence which, as the Prime Minister said, was crossing his desk the whole time.

Q1092 Mr Maples: But would you agree the language is different, it is more definite in this dossier? There is another point too, if you look at what is actually said in the dossier the Government published in September, it said, "The JIC concluded that Iraq had sufficient expertise, equipment and material to produce biological warfare agents within weeks using its legitimate bio-technology facilities", and that, "The JIC assessed that Iraq retained some chemical warfare agents, precursors, production equipment and weapons from before the Gulf War. These stocks would enable Iraq to produce significant quantities of mustard gas within weeks and of nerve agents within months." But in the summary that has become, "Iraq has continued to produce chemical and biological agents." I suggest to you that the summary is a much stronger statement than actually what the main body of the document says. Can I give you another example before you respond to that. On the 45 minutes piece on page 19 of the dossier it says, and this it seems to me is a much lower degree of certainty remark, "Intelligence indicates . . ."—not, "The JIC has concluded"—". . . that the Iraqi military are able to deploy chemical or biological weapons within 45 minutes." The summary says, "Some of these weapons are deployable within 45 minutes." I am putting to you that there are three respects in which the summary is, I would suggest, almost fundamentally different from what the body of the document suggests.

Mr Campbell: All I can say to you on that is that the executive summary—and this goes for the entire document—was the product of the pen of the Joint Intelligence Committee chairman. So if these are intelligence judgments that he is putting into the dossier, that is because they are the best assessment of the Joint Intelligence Committee. Again, I do not think it is for me to sit and do textual analysis on them. That document was the document which was presented to us. The changes we made in relation to it had nothing to do with the overriding intelligence assessments. I think the point you are trying to put to me is that the executive summary was harder than the body of the text. All I know is that the Joint Intelligence Committee chairman stands by every word of the document.

Q1093 Mr Maples: That may be, but it does not necessarily belie the point I am making. The Prime Minister in his introduction says, "The document published today is based, in large part, on the work of the Joint Intelligence Committee"—

Mr Campbell: A lot of it, for example, is UNSCOM reports. The JIC imprimatur is on this but it is not as if this issue just sort of started in September 2002.

Q1094 Mr Maples: We know how Government documents are prepared, somebody prepares a draft, it is circulated, points go in and I am perfectly prepared to accept what you say that the first draft came from the JIC and the final product was signed off by them, but I suggest that when you said, "I had several discussions with the chairman of the JIC on presentational issues and made drafting suggestions", you had some responsibility for the sort of things I was saying.

Mr Campbell: I can say that is not the case. As I pointed to in earlier exchanges, there were points that I raised, on some of them the Joint Intelligence Committee chairman would say, "That is absolutely fine, I have no trouble with that at all", on others he would say, "We cannot say that because it would not be our best assessment" or "In fact I think the way we have done it is better." It was that kind of discussion. It was, as presented as a first draft, a very good and thorough piece of work. So I do not accept the premise, I am afraid.

Q1095 Mr Maples: The problem with this is that when this document was produced everybody, even your political opponents like me, believed it because here is the Government publishing something which is the product of the Joint Intelligence Committee and we believed it. Then along comes the dodgy dossier and it turns out to be certainly not what it said but an amateurish, irresponsible and misleading piece of work, and it was presented by the Prime Minister to Parliament as the product of the intelligence services, and we all find out then what it was. Then we start to think, "Hang on, it casts this in doubt". That, I suggest, is the problem you have got. That incredibly amateurish, irresponsible, dodgy dossier is what has created your problem. I do not think people would give much time to the allegations that you and the people who work with you improved—to use a neutral word—this document if it had not been for the whole story of the dodgy dossier.

Mr Campbell: People can make whatever allegations they like, the serious allegation against me is that I abused intelligence, and that is a pretty serious allegation which we should take seriously and I hope I have made clear that with the authority of the intelligence community leadership I can say that is completely untrue. I made the point earlier that the second briefing paper got next to no coverage. It has had hundreds of thousands, possibly millions, of words written about it since that one mistake within the CIC was made. As I said to you in my memorandum, I simply do not think that should be allowed to define the totality of a huge amount of communications which went on between the Prime Minister and the Government, Parliament and the public. I have given you one example, how many times have you heard on the television or the radio, "This report which was authored by four people working in my office". I have explained to you, that is simply not true. We have said to the media time and again it is not true, but they still run it.

Q1096 Mr Maples: I am not responsible for them.
Mr Campbell: I know you are not, but a lot of the questions you are putting to me are based upon false stories whose authors somehow feel that if they say them often enough people will believe them.

Q1097 Mr Maples: The basis of the questions on the dodgy dossier is us discovering the extent to which you used Mr al-Marashi's paper—
Mr Campbell: And I have explained how that happened.

Q1098 Mr Maples: I know.—and that that work was altered in what is obviously an incredibly amateurish way in which this—
Mr Campbell: No, if I may. It was not altering Mr al-Marashi's work, because the people who were suggesting changes had no idea who Mr al-Marashi was. You can accept that or not. That is where the mistake was made.

Q1099 Mr Maples: Precise sentences—
Mr Campbell: How many times do we have to acknowledge it was a mistake, apologies were given, new procedures put in place. I can say it hundreds of times if it helps but that is the fact, there was one mistake in this.

Q1100 Mr Maples: What I am pointing out to you is when the public, media and Parliament—
Mr Campbell: I accept that.

Q1101 Mr Maples:—they suspect everything else. What I put to you is that what will probably happen is that it is perfectly possible you, and Andrew Gilligan, actually told the truth and what happened here was that everybody slightly exaggerated their position.
Mr Campbell: I did not. I did not have a position. This is the Joint Intelligence Committee. Andrew Gilligan's allegations were about the Joint Intelligence Committee paper, not the other one.

Q1102 Mr Maples: He said that you sought to change it—
Mr Campbell: No, he said, I sexed it up and I made changes against the wishes of the agencies. That is a lie.

Q1103 Mr Maples: I am suggesting to you it is possible that you sought changes to this document which did not involve countermanding intelligence. After all, your craft is presentation, that is what you are extremely good at, and it would be almost unbelievable if you did not have some input into how this document was presented.
Mr Campbell: As I have said many times before, there is a legitimate place in the political process for dealing with issues of presentation and communication now we have a 24-hour media, round the world, round the clock. He did not say that. He said that I abused British Intelligence. He went further and said it was done against the wishes

of the intelligence agencies; not true. I think that is a pretty serious allegation which is why I am very, very grateful for the opportunity to rebut it.

Q1104 Mr Maples: The same allegation has apparently been made—I do not know whether you have seen it—in yesterday's *New York Times*. It says, "'A top State Department expert on chemical and biological weapons told Congressional Committees in closed oral hearings last week that he had been pressed to tailor his analysis on Iraq and other matters to conform with the Bush Administration's views', several Congressional officials said today." You may say, "Here is some rogue agent in the State Department saying this to a rogue journalist", but it is interesting, is it not, how this allegation crops up here and now it has cropped up in Washington as well.
Mr Campbell: Can I explain why I think the allegation crops up. Again, I think this goes to the heart of the way some of these issues are covered by the media. I do not think we should make any bones about this. There are large parts of the media which have an agenda on the issue of Iraq. For most of those parts of the media their agenda is open, it is avowed. If you bought the *Daily Mirror* in the run-up to the conflict, you knew that paper was against our position. If you bought *The Sun*, you knew that paper was passionately supportive of our position on dealing with Saddam. I would identify three stages in this. In the run-up to conflict there was an agenda in large parts of the BBC—and I think the BBC is different from the rest of the media and should be viewed as different from the rest of the media because it is a different organisation in terms of its reputation, in terms of its global reach and all the rest of it—and there was a disproportionate focus upon, if you like, the dissent, the opposition, to our position. I think that in the conflict itself the prism that many were creating within the BBC was, one, it is all going wrong, and I can give you an example—

Q1105 Mr Maples: Well, I think probably many of us would agree with that.
Mr Campbell: And now what is happening now, the third, the conflict not having led to the Middle East going up in flames, not having led to us getting bogged down for months and months and months, these same people now have to find a different rationale. Their rationale is that the Prime Minister led the country into war on a false basis, that is what this is about.

Q1106 Mr Maples: It is terribly important for all of us that that allegation is laid to rest. I agree it is incredibly serious. I suggest to you the problem we have got now is that it is your word against Mr Gilligan's.
Mr Campbell: No, I do not accept that. It is my word—

Q1107 Mr Maples: Can I make a suggestion about how it might be possible for us to resolve this. I am not quite sure whether you answered this question

before. If we as a Committee were able to see the JIC assessment on which this document was based—because I do not think this in itself was a JIC assessment—and if it takes out the references to bits of sensitive intelligence—
Mr Campbell: That is a matter for the Prime Minister, not for me.

Q1108 Mr Maples: But you have some input into these decisions. If that were available to us and, as is your view, that is substantially the same as what the JIC assessment says, it would resolve the issue. Can I move for a couple of minutes to these issues of the machinery of government. It is worrying to some of us who understand, or thought we understood, how the Government works, that the DOP has not met virtually since the election, through Afghanistan, the war on terrorism and the run-up to the Iraqi war. The procedure as I understood it always used to be that the relevant Cabinet Committee would meet, with papers setting out options, really considered Civil Service assessments of what the position was, they would discuss it, make decisions which would be reported to the Cabinet. It says there have been a lot of discussions in Cabinet but those are 23 people, they get $1\frac{1}{2}$ minutes each or whatever, they never get into the issues. To find that committee does not meet and has been substituted by informal *ad hoc* meetings—
Mr Campbell: They were not informal *ad hoc* meetings.

Q1109 Mr Maples: Minutes were taken of them?
Mr Campbell: Ministerial meetings, certainly.

Q1110 Mr Maples: But you said that those people who met—David Manning is an official of the Foreign Office but the other three of you are political appointments in Downing Street—Sally Morgan, yourself and Jonathan Powell—you said you were at meetings with the Prime Minister, was the Foreign Secretary always at those meetings?
Mr Campbell: No is the answer to that because the Foreign Secretary does not work in Downing Street. I sit in an office and my phone goes regularly during the day, "Can you pop round and see the Prime Minister". He does not say, "Can you bring Jack Straw every time you come."

Q1111 Mr Maples: So there were meetings which the Prime Minister called at which his special advisers were present and his foreign policy adviser but no other minister?
Mr Campbell: Absolutely, of course there were.

Q1112 Mr Maples: Quite a lot?
Mr Campbell: For example, ministers do not come to meetings with the Prime Minister when he is preparing for Prime Minister's Questions, unless he—

Q1113 Mr Maples: No, I do not mean that.
Mr Campbell: Those are the sort of meetings I am talking about.

Q1114 Mr Maples: I mean meetings at which decisions were made about advancing—
Mr Campbell: I did not make decisions.

Q1115 Mr Maples: No, but were you at the meetings?
Mr Campbell: I was at a huge number of meetings with the Prime Minister during the Iraq conflict, and before and since.

Q1116 Mr Maples: No, the meetings at which decisions were taken at which no other minister was present.
Mr Campbell: It depends what sort of decisions you mean. If I were having a meeting with the Prime Minister about whether he should do *Newsnight* with Jeremy Paxman or ITV with Trevor McDonald—

Q1117 Mr Maples: No, no.
Mr Campbell: That is a meeting, that is a decision. If you are saying that there is a decision about whether the Prime Minister might go to see President Bush on a Tuesday or a Thursday, that is the sort of decision we might take in that group. If you are talking about a decision about whether the Prime Minister was going to commit British forces into action, the idea something like that is going to be taken without full consultation of his ministerial colleagues in the Cabinet is nonsense. Likewise in relation to something like the production of the WMD dossier. The decision to have such a dossier would have been taken with ministers. I just think it is absurd if you think that the Prime Minister, who is one of the busiest, most high profile, most written-about, most talked-about, scrutinised person in the world, does not have a support team around him, whether they happen to be special advisers—and I am well aware the aim of the Conservative Party is somehow to contaminate the concept of special advisers. I work for the Prime Minister, I work very hard for the Prime Minister, I work very hard for the Government, and I do so because I believe in what the Government is doing and I do so not because I am a special adviser but because I work for the Government.

Q1118 Mr Maples: I do not think people would find it extraordinary to find that the Prime Minister had meetings that ministers did not attend, but I think they would find it very surprising that there were meetings at which neither ministers nor officials attended.
Mr Campbell: Sorry, I am an official.

Q1119 Mr Maples: Well, you are a special adviser.
Mr Campbell: Jonathan Powell is the Chief of Staff in Downing Street.

Q1120 Mr Maples: You are both political appointments.

25 June 2003   Mr Alastair Campbell

Mr Campbell: Does that mean when Jonathan Powell leaves a meeting with the Prime Minister he somehow is less able or less qualified to write up a note of the meeting and circulate it round the departments which need to be informed?

Q1121 Mr Maples: It does not mean that, but it means you both have great positions of power not having either been elected or gone through the Civil Service selection and reporting and career procedure, and that is a novelty, and it is a novelty to have people in such senior positions. You know this, an Order in Counsel had to be passed—
Mr Campbell: No, the Order in Counsel is the novelty.

Q1122 Mr Maples: The position which you and Mr Powell hold are what is the novelty. We all know what the facts of this are. What I am suggesting to you—
Mr Campbell: I think the facts are sometimes hugely exaggerated.

Q1123 Mr Maples: I think people will find it extraordinary that meetings were being held by the Prime Minister at which neither Foreign Office officials nor ministers were present but he held those with politically appointed—
Mr Campbell: What sort of meetings are you concerned about?

Q1124 Mr Maples: I am concerned about meetings that advance probably the most important foreign policy decision this Government has taken.
Mr Campbell: There was no such meeting about advancing foreign policy positions without ministers if it was a question of formulating policy. Most days during the conflict Jonathan Powell and I would go and see the Prime Minister very early in the morning to discuss what he was going to be doing during the day, what his diary looked like, what phone calls he might be making, what meetings he might be having. The idea that because I am a special adviser somehow there is something terrible about that—I am sorry, I think it is absurd.

Q1125 Mr Maples: All I would put to you, Mr Campbell, is—
Mr Campbell: Or the idea that I am doing it for political reasons.

Q1126 Mr Maples: You and Jonathan Powell are the first people who have been politically appointed to hold the jobs of the Government's Chief Information Officer and the—
Mr Campbell: I am not the Government's Chief Information Officer, I am the Prime Minister's Director of Communications. The person in charge of the Government's Information Services is Mike Granatt.

Q1127 Mr Hamilton: Mr Campbell, can I come back very briefly to the Andrew Gilligan accusations against you. You have forthrightly and robustly corrected what you called the lies told by the BBC. I wonder whether you can speculate as to why so-called rogue elements in the Intelligence Services or intelligence community should feed lies to the BBC's defence correspondent, Andrew Gilligan? I am sorry if that sounds like a line out of Chris Mullin's novel but I wonder if you could speculate.
Mr Campbell: I do not think it is sensible to speculate. I do not know who this person is, whether they are what Mr Gilligan says they are, I just do not know. Honestly, I do not worry about what Mr Gilligan does, says, other than where, as I say, he makes a fundamental attack on the integrity of the Prime Minister and the integrity of the Government.

Q1128 Mr Hamilton: Why, when you have very convincingly and persuasively shown that Mr Gilligan has told lies about you and the Prime Minister as far as the 45 minute claim is concerned, were they not corrected?
Mr Campbell: I have no idea. I have, as I say, a stack of correspondence, of exchanges, with the Director of News at the BBC about trying to get some sort of redress for this story which, as I say, is a complete lie. I think his very first reply said to me something like, "I do not think we are going to agree on this" and ever since the posture has been, "We have to defend this story", even though I know there are people within the BBC who have huge concern about it, huge concern about what it does for the reputation of the BBC. That is a matter for them but all I know is that I am going to keep going until we get an apology.

Q1129 Mr Hamilton: Could it not be laid to rest by using the JIC assessment or using the Intelligence data and information, the basis on which you wrote the document? Could it not be for once and for all sorted out by that intelligence assessment being shown to certain individuals within the BBC?
Mr Campbell: I think that would be a pretty extraordinary step, and I would be very surprised if the intelligence agencies supported that.

Q1130 Mr Hamilton: But they are being damaged at the moment, are they not?
Mr Campbell: I think the public are a bit cannier about this than people think. I think they will spot an agenda a mile off. As I say, most agendas in the media are open, people avow them. When I was a journalist I went to the *Daily Mirror*, I was avowedly pro-Labour, anti-Conservative Government and never hid it. I used to see it as part of my job to go on the television and say, "Vote Labour". I was up-front about it. The *Daily Mail* loathes the Prime Minister, loathes me, loathes the Government, does not hide it. That is an agenda. People are aware of that. The BBC is different. The BBC has got a deserved reputation around the world. I think some of the best journalism during the conflict was on the BBC, I think they have adapted to this whole 24 hour media thing better than a lot of news organisations,

but when they have bad journalism amid the good then I think they have a responsibility to admit that. We admit when things go wrong, we have done that in relation to one of the issues we have been discussing today, but they have broadcast it not just once but now hundreds of times.

Q1131 Mr Hamilton: Surely the canny public must conclude they have very good evidence from very good sources?

Mr Campbell: They may do. My experience of the public, whatever YouGov polls say, which usually say whatever they have been asked to say by the paper which has commissioned them, my experience going round the country with the Prime Minister is that actually when it comes to the big issues—and this was a huge issue, taking the country into war in Iraq—they listen to senior politicians, they listen to them with a certain amount of respect because they understand the gravity of the decision they have to take, and I think they believe, contrary to the way the media portray politicians and politics, not just the Prime Minister, not just ministers, but the vast bulk of politicians are in politics for good reasons, trying to do their best by their constituents and by the country. If I say that now, I can hear journalists sitting there in vans outside, waiting and saying, "Shall we say he did well or did badly?" rather than actually give any sense of what was discussed, I can hear them say, "Oh, God, blah, blah, blah", but that is the reality. I think if we carry on with this constant denigration of politics, the political process, we are going down a very bad route. People can say to me, as they do and as I have admitted, "You were pretty heavy when you were a journalist" but I never did not have respect for the political process, Parliament, the politicians and the work that they did, and that included politicians with whom I fundamentally disagreed. I find it incredible and I mean incredible that people can report based on one single anonymous uncorroborated source—and let's get to the heart of what the allegation is—that the Prime Minister, the Cabinet, the intelligence agencies, people liker myself connived to persuade Parliament to send British forces into action on a lie. That is the allegation. I tell you, until the BBC acknowledge that is a lie, I will keep banging on, that correspondence file will get thicker and they had better issue an apology pretty quickly.

Mr Hamilton: That is very clear. I am going to move on to a slightly different subject now.

Chairman: Let's hope the BBC covers that.

Q1132 Mr Hamilton: I hope the BBC does cover that. I want to take up the point John Maples made about the quality of intelligence. I want to draw your attention to something in the September dossier which reported, and I quote, "There is intelligence that Iraq has sought the supply of significant quantities of uranium from Africa." The claim was repeated by President Bush in his State of the Union address in January 2003 when he said, "The British Government has learnt that Saddam Hussein recently sought significant quantities of uranium from Africa. The documents relating to the alleged agreement for the sale of uranium between 1999 and 2001 were passed to the IAEA for investigation. The Agency concluded fairly rapidly that the documents were in fact not authentic and the specific allegations were unfounded. Subsequent reports suggested the documents have been proved forgeries, one bearing the name of a Niger minister who had been out of office for years." My question is, when did you first become aware of the uranium from Africa claim?

Mr Campbell: The claim as it was put into the dossier?

Q1133 Mr Hamilton: Yes. The claim as it was put into the dossier. When did that become available to you, that information?

Mr Campbell: From memory, when it was in the first draft, but I would have to go back and check that.

Q1134 Mr Hamilton: Is that something you could confirm to us during the course of this week, if possible?

Mr Campbell: Yes[5].

Q1135 Mr Hamilton: Thank you very much. Did you or anybody at No 10—you because you are the person responsible for the production of the document—seek—

Mr Campbell: No, I was not responsible for the production of the document.

Q1136 Mr Hamilton: Sorry, responsible for the presentation of the document as Communications Director.

Mr Campbell: Yes, okay.

Q1137 Mr Hamilton: Did you specifically seek to put the claim about Iraq's attempts to get uranium from Niger, or anywhere in Africa, into that document? Was that a very important part of the document?

Mr Campbell: I do not know whether it was an important part but in answer to the question whether it was I who tried to put it into there, no is the answer.

Q1138 Mr Hamilton: Was any attempt made to highlight the fact that Iraq was trying to buy uranium from Africa? The point is, we are being told on weapons of mass destruction we have evidence of pre-cursor chemicals, or anthrax, of growth media, but we have no evidence of any nuclear production at all, and this was obviously a crucial bit of evidence which was subsequently discredited. Was any attempt made to draw attention to the fact that at the time that claim was being made through intelligence sources?

---

[5] Ninth Report from the Foreign Affairs Committee, Session 2002–03, *The Decision to go to War in Iraq*, HC 813-II, Ev 10.

Mr Campbell: I think there is documentary evidence of Iraq's nuclear weapons programme ambitions but in relation to this, I suppose what you are saying is, were the discussions about how prominently to deploy that piece of information. To be honest with you, I cannot remember the nature of those discussions. I think it was an important point. As I have alluded to earlier, it was one of the points I discussed with the chairman of the JIC. When it says they have sought it, I asked what has been the result of that seeking, has it actually resulted in them acquiring any of those, to which the answer was, "To the best of our assessment, no."

Q1139 Mr Hamilton: When it was clear from the IAEA that the documents were forgeries—

Mr Campbell: I think there is a dispute about this. I am not as qualified to speak on this as the Intelligence people are. As I understand it, there is a dispute as to whether the documents which are being described as forgeries are the documents on which the claim in the dossier is based. Again, I think that is something where I might be able to go back and speak to the JIC chairman about and see if there is any more he can add to that but I do not think that is for me to—

Q1140 Mr Hamilton: I accept it is not for you to do that but I think for this Committee that information would be quite important because if the claims that different parts of different documents were based on dodgy intelligence are disproved, that greatly strengthens the case that we, Parliament and the public and the media, were being told some pretty correct bits of information about Iraq's weapons of mass destruction and their threat to the region and to the rest of the world. It would back up the Government very strongly, I would have thought.

Mr Campbell: I am aware of the public dispute there has been about that. I think it is probably better that I go back and ask the JIC whether there is any more they can or should say about that.

Q1141 Mr Hamilton: That would be very helpful. Thank you very much. Can I briefly move on to a few questions about your role in Intelligence and foreign policy making. I know you have been through this quite a lot and you have had a fairly long session with us today, and I am grateful for that, but I want to clarify one or two points in my own mind. Are you responsible as Communications Manager for the terms on which members of the intelligence agencies talk to the press?

Mr Campbell: No.

Q1142 Mr Hamilton: Who has that responsibility?

Mr Campbell: I presume the agencies themselves.

Q1143 Mr Hamilton: You do not have any input into that at all?

Mr Campbell: I know the people who do that but how they operate is entirely a matter for them.

Q1144 Mr Hamilton: I appreciate you may not be able to answer this but why is it that certain members of the intelligence agencies are authorised to talk to the press but not to Members of Parliament, apart from those on the Intelligence and Security Committee?

Mr Campbell: It is very rare for officials like me to talk to Members of Parliament. Ministers are accountable to Parliament. The fact is—and I do not know how long this has gone on—the intelligence agencies are more in the open than they were in the past and they do have, if you like, a media profile. What they do is try to have people who journalists with an interest in some of the areas that the intelligence agencies are involved with can at least have a dialogue with, but I do not think it is as it were any stronger than that.

Q1145 Mr Hamilton: Do you see all JIC papers that come to Downing Street?

Mr Campbell: Not necessarily because a lot of the time they will be assessing things which will not necessarily be of interest, of relevance to the kind of issues I might be involved in at any given time. I can go days and weeks without seeing intelligence if my focus professionally is something to do with public services for a few weeks. Obviously during something like the Iraq conflict or post-11 September there was a lot of intelligence relevant to what I was doing. I think one of the interesting developments there has been in relation to the intelligence agencies is actually their very sophisticated understanding of how within all these conflict situations in particular—and this is something which evolved through Kosovo, Afghanistan and then Iraq—how the realities of the modern media have changed the terms of conflict. We may not like that but it is a fact. So, for example, part of our strategy in those three conflicts was actually to deal with the communications strategies of a dictatorship, under Milosevic, of the Taliban and of Saddam, and therefore it was helpful to have as much information as possible about what their communications plans were. I have to say they relied in very, very heavy part upon the free speech of the United Kingdom and they exploited it pretty ruthlessly.

Chairman: Some colleagues have further questions.

Q1146 Sir John Stanley: Mr Campbell, as you have made very clear to the Committee, you have been the subject of extremely serious personal allegations which have been made against you, most particularly the charge that you were responsible for sexing up the JIC-approved dossier of September 2002. The Committee will want to reach a conclusion on that based on the maximum evidential basis it can obtain and I would like to repeat what my colleagues, Mr Mackinlay and Mr Chidgey, said: I think it would be most helpful if you could put in writing to this Committee a list of the drafting amendments you proposed as that document evolved and those that were accepted by the chairman of the JIC and those that were not. If we can have that as fast as possible, that would be very helpful to us.

Mr Campbell: I hope somebody has been taking note of the various requests you have made. On several of them I have no doubt there will have to be discussions in the intelligence community as to what can and cannot be divulged.

Chairman: I can assure you that the Clerk has been taking a list of the requests being made by this Committee. Of course, we understand if some are oral discussions during the course of the meetings you mentioned. It would help this Committee enormously, one, if we could have any written alterations which you have made. We are under a time constraint in that we hope to produce our report by 7 July so ideally we would like them by Friday morning when we meet the Foreign Secretary.

Q1147 Andrew Mackinlay: Just as a point of order, Chairman, that is not quite what I asked for. The narrow issue I asked for was if you would ring-fence that which was the intelligence information which was in the so-called dodgy dossier, bearing in mind it had been signed off and, yes, I want to see what Sir John has asked for. I cannot see there would be any difficulty because the guy said, "Here, Campbell, you can have this, this is in the public domain." All I want is a ring-fence.

Mr Campbell: Yes, but he might have said, "By the way, Campbell, there are bits in here which we do not necessarily want to be identified as intelligence."

Andrew Mackinlay: Okay, I hear what you say.

Q1148 Chairman: We can provide you with a list this evening of those further discussions and questions we would like to be clarified by you.

Mr Campbell: Okay. Some of them will have to go through the Joint Intelligence Committee and that may not be able to be done very quickly.

Chairman: As speedily as you can.

Q1149 Sir John Stanley: Mr Campbell, I phrased my request specifically in terms of the drafting amendments which you had proposed to what was a non-classified document which is going to be made public. I did it in those terms because I believe that cannot raise any intelligence issues. In terms of those amendments which were rejected, we are not looking for reasons why they were rejected, which might raise some intelligence issues, but what you proposed and the list of what was accepted and rejected. I do not believe it can raise any intelligence issues and I hope we can have that.

Mr Campbell: It might if within the responses there were intelligence issues giving explanations as to why something was or was not possible.

Q1150 Sir John Stanley: I am not looking for that at all. I am looking entirely at your requests and whether they were met or not, full-stop.

Mr Campbell: Fine.

Q1151 Sir John Stanley: Mr Campbell, you have made a very strong pitch on a personal basis for why you require an apology to yourself from the BBC.

Mr Campbell: It went beyond myself.

Q1152 Sir John Stanley: I would like to turn to another apology which I think is very seriously outstanding and on which you may wish to correct your evidence. If I heard you correctly you suggested the Government had made an apology to Mr al-Marashi. Mr al-Marashi's work was lifted off the internet without attribution; it was used in a highly political context to help make the Government's policy case for going to war against Iraq which was a matter which concerned him very greatly. His thesis or his article in the *Middle East Review* in certainly one crucial respect was substantially changed to suggest terrorist linkage between the Saddam Hussein intelligence agency and al-Qaeda which was not what he said in his *Review* article, and members of his family were endangered. I questioned him on the issue as to whether he had had an apology, "Has the Government made any expression of regret or apology to you for the plagiarisation of your thesis? Mr al-Marashi: I have never been contacted directly, either by phone call nor in writing, since February 2003 up to the present. Me: Do you think you might be owed an apology. Mr al-Marashi: I think the least they can do is owe me an apology." I do not believe he has received an apology, I think Mr Campbell you said earlier he had, I hope he will receive a personal apology from you.

Mr Campbell: As I say, I take responsibility for that paper. I have explained why the mistake was made. I am happy to send an apology to Mr al-Marashi on behalf of the entire communications team at No 10 and the CIC, I am happy to do that. As I said earlier, the moment this mistake was exposed by Channel 4 and subsequently by Mr al-Marashi himself on *Newsnight*, that next morning the Prime Minister's spokesman has never attempted to avoid it, hands up, it should not have happened, we are going to look at how it happened, we are going to put procedures in place and that has been done. I have no desire here at all to do anything other than deliver that apology and do that sincerely. If it would help to do that in writing to Mr al-Marashi, I am perfectly happy to do that.

Q1153 Sir John Stanley: I am sure he would appreciate that.

Mr Campbell: Fine. I noticed, when I read Mr al-Marashi's evidence, that one of the Committee members—I think it was Mr Pope—said he would be recommending that we did apologise, that the Committee would be seeking to recommend that we did apologise to Mr al-Marashi. I am happy to do that. If I can pray you in similar aid in relation to Mr Gilligan's story in the BBC, I would be very grateful.

Q1154 Sir John Stanley: Can I turn to what I think is a fundamental aspect of your evidence and your position. Do you recognise that the launching by you of the so-called dodgy dossier has done very, very serious damage to the wider perception of the veracity of the Government's case for prosecuting the war against Iraq?

Mr Campbell: I accept that is stated and I accept there may well be people who believe that. That is why I think it is important, as I have tried to do, to separate out the two documents, underline the significance of the first one, underline the responsibleness and thoroughness with which we in the intelligence agencies approached that, explain the difference in relation to the second one and its intended purposes and intended use. As I say again, we are involved in an awful lot of pieces of communication, as I have said several times, and when we make a mistake we hear about it for quite a long time. I actually do not think we have made that many mistakes. This was a mistake, this one we have acknowledged many, many times, it is one which the person responsible for making that mistake feels wretched about, and I know that because I work with the guy. Mistakes do get made. I just ask the Committee, as I have said in my note, to understand the wider context of the amount of communications work we are involved in trying to deal on a really difficult complicated issue like this with different audiences around the world. We had strategies for the UK, for the Moslem community in the UK, for Europe, for Asia, for the United States, for the Middle East. I know people talk about, and John Maples has alluded to, the whole issue of this so-called explosion of special advisers in Downing Street, I have a pretty small team and, yes, I can call in some circumstances on resources across government, but in Downing Street I have a pretty small team. We do a lot of work and occasionally mistakes get made.

Q1155 Sir John Stanley: Can we continue on my particular line of questioning. It is a matter of concern to me that you still do not appreciate the fundamental issue which is—

Mr Campbell: I do.

Q1156 Sir John Stanley: I am sorry, I do not believe you do, which is the relationship between the communications part of Government and intelligence. As you know, I was a ministerial recipient of intelligence for many years and there is one particular sentence I read in your memorandum which filled me with very considerable concern and it is the sentence which reads, in relation to the September 2002 dossier, "I had several discussions with the Chairman of the JIC on presentational issues arising from the dossier and, in common with other officials, made drafting suggestions as the document evolved." The most crucial aspect of the interface between intelligence and policy—and you, Mr Campbell, sit right down in the middle—is that intelligence helps to formulate policy and that policy never, never helps to formulate intelligence. The position which

you have now made clear to the Committee, and I believe this is the first time this has come into the public domain, that you are in the business of making and drafting suggestions to the chairman of the Joint Intelligence Committee, that in my judgment, unfair as this may be to you, is seriously going to compromise the integrity of such documents in the future, as indeed they have been compromised in the case of the two Iraq dossiers. You are a very, very skilled communicator, you are known universally as the Government's spin doctor, your business is to put the best possible presentation on the Government's policy, a perfectly *bona fide* role, everybody understands that, but I have to put it to you—and I do not put this to you in an offensive or personal way but in all seriousness because I share one thing in common with you, you said you were concerned to safeguard the integrity of the intelligence services and that is absolutely my position as well—as long as that policy in your paper is known, that you are in the business of making drafting suggestions to the chairman of the JIC, that Alastair Campbell's fingerprints are going to be on JIC source documents, I have to say I do not believe that is conducive to the integrity of the intelligence services.

Mr Campbell: I suspect that is because you may be not persuaded by my integrity in relation to the work that I do. That, if true, is obviously from my perspective regrettable. All I can say is that the memorandum that I submitted to you was seen by and cleared by the chairman of the JIC who had discussed it with the agencies. Like you, I think the intelligence agencies do an extraordinary job for the country, and the reason why I felt that the briefing paper mistake was so serious was because it did obviously lead to the controversy about which we are still talking. The reason why I moved so quickly to speak to the leadership of the intelligence community and to agree the new procedures now in place was because I do value that hugely. Provided the intelligence services and the leadership are satisfied with the role I play on behalf of the Prime Minister at his instruction, I think that is a perfectly proper thing to do.

Q1157 Sir John Stanley: My colleague, Mr Ottaway, yesterday asked the Foreign Secretary, "Do you think on balance it would be better not to have published it in the first place . . .", referring to the dodgy dossier, and the Foreign Secretary replied, "Yes, given what happened—Certainly it would have been better not to have published it in that form or if it was going to be published to have ensured that it went through the same rigorous procedures as the dossier that was published in September." Do you agree with the Foreign Secretary it would have been far better in hindsight for the Government if the second dossier, the dodgy dossier, had not been published?

Mr Campbell: Clearly.

Sir John Stanley: Thank you.

Chairman: Mr Ottaway, if you could be brief.

Q1158 Richard Ottaway: I will. During the interval I have been musing that a question I put to you may only have been partially answered. I would just like to put exactly the same question to you again. Did the Government ever receive any information from intelligence services that Iraq was not an immediate threat?
Mr Campbell: Not that I saw.

Q1159 Richard Ottaway: That was not the question I asked though.
Mr Campbell: I cannot answer for what the Government may have received if I was not aware of it.

Q1160 Richard Ottaway: You were chairing a cross-departmental—
Mr Campbell: I was not sitting there looking at raw intelligence the whole time.

Q1161 Richard Ottaway: I am not saying raw intelligence. Did you get any assessment from the intelligence services that Iraq was not an immediate threat?
Mr Campbell: In relation to this point about the immediate imminent threat, the Prime Minister is on the record, I think either in the House or to the Liaison Committee, saying nobody is saying Saddam Hussein is about to launch weapons on the UK next week, the week after, this year, next year, so I am not clear.

Q1162 Richard Ottaway: Did you get any intelligence reports that Iraq was not an immediate threat?
Mr Campbell: None that I can recall that I saw. I do not go around looking for every piece of intelligence.

Q1163 Richard Ottaway: You were chairing a group which covered a heck of a lot of departments.
Mr Campbell: It covered the communication issues on Iraq. Very few of those meetings would have discussed intelligence at all. The discussions that we were involved in there were issues like, for example, when we were trying to get the second resolution. They would have been about which countries we should be speaking to their media. This was not a group that sat with a sheaf of intelligence on the table; in fact it never did that. As I have explained in my memorandum to you, the idea for this second briefing paper arose when one of the SIS representatives at that meeting said there was some new intelligence which could be used publicly on this theme. We did not then sit around saying "Well, let us have a look at this", that was not how it worked.

Q1164 Richard Ottaway: Everyone knew that you were putting together an intelligence case to argue that Iraq was an immediate threat and no-one involved in that at any time picked up any

intelligence that this was not the case coming from a different assessment or different approach or different line?
Mr Campbell: I am sorry if I am being thick but I do not understand the point given that the position of the Government was throughout the entire thing that nobody was ever saying that Iraq was going to whack off a missile at Peterborough.

Q1165 Richard Ottaway: Did you get a report saying "It is improbable that they are going to whack off a missile anywhere"?
Mr Campbell: Not that I have seen.

Q1166 Richard Ottaway: Has anyone seen?
Mr Campbell: How can I answer that if I have not seen things that other people have seen?

Q1167 Richard Ottaway: It is possible that someone might have?
Mr Campbell: I really do not know. As I say, forgive me if I am thick but I do not really get the point.

Q1168 Richard Ottaway: The point is it is quite possible that such an assessment was made.
Mr Campbell: But I am not aware of it, therefore how can I comment upon its existence or non existence.

Q1169 Mr Hamilton: Just a very minor point, Mr Campbell. When it was discovered that the February dossier included plagiarised material, would you have expected the Permanent Under Secretary of the Foreign Office, Sir Michael Jay, to have been informed straight away?
Mr Campbell: Well, he was.

Q1170 Mr Hamilton: He says he was not informed straight away on the morning of 3 February.
Mr Campbell: No, no, we did not know until 6 February. 3 February was when the document was put in the Library of the House of Commons.

Q1171 Mr Hamilton: Right.
Mr Campbell: At which point none of us knew.

Q1172 Mr Hamilton: Okay. So he was informed immediately on 6 February when it was discovered, as far as you know?
Mr Campbell: He probably had exactly the same sinking feeling as I had when I saw the news. He and I had discussions, not on the intelligence side of things but about procedures for the CIC, and there was an exchange between me and him. What was agreed there was any material kept within the CIC, used by the CIC, had to be properly sourced, which is the system which operates in Number 10 anyway.

Q1173 Andrew Mackinlay: Just 15 seconds. You understand the thing I have asked, and I understand your point saying you have to clear it in case there was intelligence which was in the so-called 'dodgy dossier' but there might be—might

be—a reluctance to identify precisely what it is. Just for the purposes of this conversation, if that is what is told to you, and you relay it back to us, that would rather infer they might have said "Do a document but bring in some other material in order to disguise what is intelligence".
Mr Campbell: No.

Q1174 Andrew Mackinlay: I have misunderstood then. I cannot for the life of me understand why, in a sense, you have got to go back to these fellows because if they said "Here, Alastair Campbell, is intelligence. Sign it off. It can be in the public domain".
Mr Campbell: Yes.

Q1175 Andrew Mackinlay: Then we know the history of the production of this document and also things which were brought in. I cannot see, therefore, how it is impossible to identify with clarity precisely what was handed over?
Mr Campbell: As I say, I did not work on the editorial of this until it was time to sign it off. In the process that went over four weeks there were discussions as the thing was evolving between the people in the CIC working on it and the SIS. Now I am simply saying I do not personally know the judgments which were applied as to what could be identified as intelligence and what might be intelligence that was not thus identified.

Q1176 Chairman: Mr Campbell, one final observation from you. It has been put that the choice before the Committee is whether we believe Gilligan or you, what are your observations on that?

Mr Campbell: All I can say—
Andrew Mackinlay: I am not sure that is so.

Q1177 Chairman: Let me ask the question.
Mr Campbell: I work in a pretty exposed position. I work for a Prime Minister who is answerable to Parliament. The media can bandy all sorts of allegations about what I do and they can say things about the Prime Minister but the one thing you cannot do, as everybody in this room knows, if you are an elected politician is lie to the House of Commons. Now, the allegation that has been made by the BBC's defence correspondent, repeated in large parts of the media, as I say, here and around the world, is that the Prime Minister did exactly that, he put to the country and to Parliament a false basis for putting at risk the lives of British servicemen. That is an accusation against the Prime Minister, against the Foreign Secretary, against the Cabinet, against the intelligence agencies, against me and against the people who work with me. Now that is why I take it so seriously, not because of me because, as I say, I am absolutely used to being described in all sorts of ways by journalists who, frankly, I would match a politician's integrity against theirs any day of the week. I simply say in relation to the BBC story: it is a lie, it was a lie, it is a lie that is continually repeated and until we get an apology for it I will keep making sure that Parliament, people like yourselves and the public know that it was a lie.
Chairman: Mr Campbell, this is the Committee's first meeting with you; I hope it will not be the last. Thank you very much.

Friday 27 June 2003

Members present:

Donald Anderson, in the Chair

Mr David Chidgey	Mr John Maples
Mr Fabian Hamilton	Richard Ottaway
Mr Eric Illsley	Mr Greg Pope
Andrew Mackinlay	Sir John Stanley

Witnesses: **Rt Hon Jack Straw,** a Member of the House, Secretary of State for Foreign and Commonwealth Affairs, **Mr Peter Ricketts, CMG,** Director General, Political and **Mr William Ehrman, CMG,** Director General, Defence/Intelligence, Foreign and Commonwealth Office, examined.

Q1178 Chairman: Secretary of State, we welcome you today, again, together with Mr Peter Ricketts, the Director General, Political and Mr William Ehrman, who is the Director General, Defence/ Intelligence. Today, Secretary of State, we are reaching the very last lap of our planned sessions, with a public session with you initially and then at an appropriate stage we shall move into private session. Clearly our aim throughout has been to examine whether the information presented to Parliament and the public in respect of the decision to go to war was accurate and complete. This was sparked by a BBC report. Perhaps it would be helpful to begin by seeing where we are now. There is some agreement, I think we all agreed when we last met, that the February 3 document was a "Horlicks", and you did not resile from that.
Mr Straw: Carry on and I will offer you my view in a moment.

Q1179 Chairman: Do you accept that the unfortunate consequences of the preparation of that document is that the Prime Minister inadvertently gave to Parliament not the full information in respect of the intelligence services?
Mr Straw: The February dossier, no.

Q1180 Chairman: When he reported to Parliament immediately afterwards?
Mr Straw: The point of my remarks, this was also made clear by Mr Campbell, is that we accept that the process is unsatisfactory and the result of that, so far as the 3 February document was concerned, is that there was not a proper provenance for some of the material in the document, and that includes now, as everyone knows, the fact that a large part of part two was taken from this PhD thesis and was not properly attributed. That is accepted. However, I hope that you in return will accept that in every material particular the February 3 document was and is accurate. Even where there were changes made in the text from the PhD thesis to the text that was issued those changes accurately reflected the reality. For example there was a change made from "opposition groups", from "Saddam Hussein was supporting opposition groups" to "Saddam Hussein was supporting terrorist organisations". Saddam Hussein was supporting terrorist organisations, every member of this Committee knows that and all but one member of this Committee voted to proscribe the terrorist organisations, MEK, Islamic Jihad, Hamas and Hezbollah, whom Saddam Hussein was supporting.

Q1181 Chairman: The effect of that change was to dramatise the words used and that it part of the charge that it was "sexed-up".
Mr Straw: There has never been any claim that I have been aware of that the document issued on February 3 was on "sexed-up". The only reference to "sexed-up" was made by Mr Gilligan on the *Today* programme on 29 May in respect of the first document and the 45 minutes, so it is very important that we do not conflate these two. For reasons that have now been explained at very great length the attribution of part two of February 3 document was dropped out as it went through processes, literally through word-processing. When others came to go through the document they thought, and maybe quite correctly, that saying that Saddam Hussein was supporting opposition groups was not actually giving the full picture. He was indeed supporting the opposition groups but the serious charge against him was that he was supporting terrorist organisations. I say again, with respect, everybody knows that. There was no "sexing-up" of that document. What happened to that document was that the process by which it came to be produced was not satisfactory and therefore we have faced, what I have said to everybody and accept it is an embarrassment of having to explain that part of it came from a PhD thesis and from a *Jane* document and that was not properly attributed. It does not affect the veracity of the document. My last point on February 3 document is this, in the hearing on Tuesday I asked your colleagues if they could name or point to any part of the February 3 document which was inaccurate and as I recall the only inaccuracy that could be pointed to, substantive inaccuracy, was that at one point military security services was confused for general security services. Whatever else was the reason for making a decision to go to war it was not that.
Chairman: I am going to continue with the point of where we are. Mr Illsley on this.

Q1182 Mr Illsley: I have to challenge that because I challenged it with Alastair Campbell as well when he said that the accuracy of the document has never been challenged. Almost every page has been challenged in evidence given to the Committee, and whether it is inaccurate or out of date or whatever we can debate but some of the intelligence material contained within the document, and I think it is on page three where there are two references to the weapons inspectors having been prevented from visiting sites, having their movements known, their whereabouts monitored, having been interrupted by arguments with officials to prevent them getting to sites that was released in the document on 30 January and on 14 February, granted it is two weeks later, Hans Blix contradicted that in his evidence to the United Nations. He said: "We have not had any problems visiting sites". Either that evidence is out of date or it is wrong?

Mr Straw: With great respect, first of all, Mr Illsley, if the basis of you claiming that this was out of date was evidence which arose after date of publication it could not conceivably be out of date. Secondly, I am familiar with what Dr Blix said in a whole series of reports on 27 January, again on 14 February I was in the Security Council when he issued that report and again on 28 February and 7 March, and subsequently. What Dr Blix said, and I can look up what he said here and come back to it in a moment, first of all on 27 January, which was after all the most current report that we had when this was put together, Dr Blix was critical of the co-operation which he had received from the Iraqis. I will see if I can turn it up. He talked about a degree of co-operation on process but he then criticised the co-operation on substance. He said notably, this is paragraph 69 of the Command Paper I put before Parliament. He said: "Paragraph 9, the Resolution 1441, 2002 states that this co-operation shall be active; it is not enough to open doors. Inspection is not a game of catch as catch can". Let me also make it clear that our assessment backed up by repeated evidence put before the Security Council by the inspectors was, yes, the tactics of the Iraqis was to appear to co-operate on process but still to interfere on substance. Until quite late into the inspection process they are insisting that five Iraqi minders should accompany any Iraqi scientist who was interviewed. They refused at every stage to allow any Iraqi scientist to be interviewed outside Iraq and told those scientists if they co-operated in that way their families would be at risk. We were as certain as we could be that the premises in which the scientists were to be interviewed were bugged. There was also significant evidence of the Iraqis seeking to bug UNMOVIC's headquarters to gain advance information about sites to be visited, and of course they were always followed. There is nothing here, certainly nothing to which you have drawn my attention, which would suggest what was said here is inaccurate.

Q1183 Mr Illsley: We are talking about the document being inaccurate. On page three of the document the quote is: "Journeys are monitored by security officers stationed on the route if they have prior intelligence. Any changes of destination are notified ahead by telephone or radio so that arrival is anticipated. The welcoming party is a give away".

Mr Straw: That was absolutely true all of the way through the inspection process.

Q1184 Mr Illsley: That was published on 13 January. On 14 February Hans Blix said: "Since we arrived in Iraq we have conducted more than 400 inspections covering more than 300 sites, all inspections were performed without notice and access was almost always provided promptly. In no case have we seen convincing evidence that the Iraq side knew in advance that the inspectors were coming". The two do not stand together there, do they? There is a two week gap between the publication of the dossier on 30 January and Blix's statement on 14 February. What I am saying is I am challenging the assertion that nothing in the second document is untrue or misleading?

Mr Straw: What Dr Blix said, and I will go through other aspects of what Dr Blix said on 14 February. What he said here is entirely consistent. I also have to say to you, Mr Illsley, if the only inaccuracy you are pointing to is something which was known and was never challenged in the Security Council by any partner, that the Iraqis had an immense security apparatus monitoring UNMOVIC then again I am confident in saying there is no material fact in 3 February document that is challengeable, and it has not been.

Chairman: On those material facts the Committee will draw its own conclusions. I am just aware that there is a danger in this public session of going round and covering the same ground as last time. I hope we can all discipline ourselves to that extent to try and answer questions which have arisen from Alastair Campbell. Sir John, I think you have a point of order.

Q1185 Sir John Stanley: I do have a point of order; my point of order is that the Foreign Secretary is here to answer questions as a witness to this Committee. The Foreign Secretary is not here to pose questions himself to the Committee. Most certainly the Foreign Secretary is not entitled to deduce from the fact that the Committee choose not to answer his particular question agreement with his statement. On the specific change to which we referred, the change from "opposition groups" to "terrorist organisations" I just want to place on the record that as far as Members of Parliament are concerned the significance that was attached to the reference to support by Saddam Hussein's regime of terrorist organisations did not relate to organisations such as Hamas it related to the Government signing up to linkage between the Saddam Hussein regime and al-Qaeda. That was a materially significant change in the document. I just want to put that on the record.

Mr Straw: I may be wrong but I do not recall that 3 February document mentions al-Qaeda.

Sir John Stanley: It referred to "terrorist organisations" and was taken by most people in the House to suggest linkage between Saddam Hussein and al-Qaeda.

Q1186 Chairman: We will draw our own conclusions.

Mr Straw: Just allow me to make this point, I never claimed, neither did the Prime Minister that there was any direct linkage between al-Qaeda and the Iraqi regime. Indeed we were both extremely careful when such claims and charges were put. It was never part of the decision to go to war, full stop. I am very happy to supply the Committee with extracts of the statements that both the Prime Minister and I made when we were repeatedly asked about whether there was any connection. I said in November 2002: "I have seen no direct evidence of the Iraqi regimes involvement in the al-Qaeda operation before September 11". The Prime Minister gave a more detailed but similar response to the Liaison Committee, you will recall this Mr Anderson, in January 2003. Mike O'Brien gave a number of such replies. We do not have to speculate about al-Qaeda, what is incontrovertible is that this statement on page nine that the Iraqi regime's external activities include, "supporting terrorist organisations and hostile regimes" is true. The hostile regimes were one, Iran, where Iraq continued to support MEK, an extremely unpleasant terrorist organisation. Ask the Iranian Government about MEK. Secondly, the Iraqi regime was supporting three terrorist organisations operating under the territory of Israel and the occupied territories, and ask the Palestinian authorities or the Government of Israel if you do not believe me really that the Iraqis were actively supporting those organisations.

Q1187 Chairman: I am now moving to the charge in respect of the accuracy of information. This is from Mr Gilligan who met, apparently, at least he claims, a man from the services in an office and claims that the document published on 24 September was transformed in the last few weeks. We have heard evidence from Mr Campbell to the effect that the document was that of the Chairman of the Joint Intelligence Committee and remained his throughout. Do you agree that the best evidence to help this Committee in trying to ascertain whether that document was changed now we have the document itself is for us to see the original document and to see the extent to which it was changed?

Mr Straw: Chairman, we are going into private session and I am happy to share with you the details of what was in the key JIC assessment when we go into private session. You will also be aware that the Parliamentary Intelligence and Security Committee has a complete remit on behalf of Parliament to go in and analyse all of the background intelligence documents. We have discussed that. We have been extremely forthcoming with this Committee, as is quite right, and in the private session that we are going to go into I intend to be more forthcoming. I am confident that I will be able to satisfy any questions that you have. Could I just also make this point about this claim, what Mr Gilligan claimed on 29 May was, and I quote directly from the transcript, "The Government probably knew that the 45 minute figure was wrong even before it decided to put it in [the dossier]". He then went on to say, "our source

says that Downing Street a week before publication ordered the dossier to be 'sexed-up', to be made more exciting and ordered more facts to be discovered". None of those claims is true. They are all simple and straightforward falsehoods. The September dossier was written by the Chairman of the JIC and his staff. At no time did anyone wish to seek nor sought to override his judgments. There was no ordering by Downing Street or by myself or anybody in the Foreign Office for more facts to be discovered. The claim that the Government probably knew that the 45 minute figure was wrong is totally incorrect. The idea that uncorroborated evidence of a 45 minute threat was given undue prominence in the dossier at the behest of the Prime Minister.

Q1188 Chairman: That is a case which we have to examine. Would you agree that again the best evidence in terms of whether that was at the beginning the property of Chairman of the Joint Intelligence Committee and remained his throughout is to see the Chairman of the Joint Intelligence Committee?

Mr Straw: We have been through that and as I have said to you in private sessions, and I thought you and your colleagues had accepted this, what is unfair—

Q1189 Chairman: We had not accepted it.

Mr Straw: This Committee is looking at the decision to go to war. I am going to make one other comment about the 45 minute claim.

Q1190 Chairman: Briefly, because we want to make progress.

Mr Straw: The simple fact of the matter is apart from anything else the 45 minute claim was a supporting fact in the decision to go to war but it was not remotely a central fact in the decision to go to war, and that is shown very, very clearly by any analysis of all the discussions and debates on whether we went to war. Yes, of course, there was some attention paid to this claim and others in September when the document was published but as the process evolved that fell way.

Q1191 Chairman: We have heard you on that. I just want to centre on this point, on the key charge of that document being transformed within the past weeks we are not going to see the various amendments to the document?

Mr Straw: Mr Campbell is also seeking to put together a very detailed letter to you. He promised you a detailed letter of the exchanges between him and the JIC. It is a very substantial piece of work, it is still being prepared. The combination of that and what I say in private session should satisfy you.

Q1192 Chairman: We are not going see the various amendments to the document. You do not think Mr Campbell's letter will answer that.

Mr Straw: What you will see is what I am able to help you with in the private session. We can get on to that in a moment. As you know, Chairman, time and again where further information is sought I have been happy to provide that. I just wanted to say about this point in the public session, about the 45 minute claim—

Q1193 Chairman: We can come on to that and our colleagues may want to visit that. I am centring on a different point, if it be the case, and this would be very powerful argument, that the Chairman of the JIC produced the document, kept control of the document, was wholly satisfied with the end product why cannot the Committee see the Chairman of the Joint Intelligence Committee to hear that?

Mr Straw: Because, Chairman, what you are seeking to do is embroil me in a turf war between the Foreign Affairs Committee and the Intelligence and Security Committee. You know as well as I do the appropriate body to deal with the details of intelligence is the ISC, they are set up by Parliament, they are colleagues of people in this room from all parties. I say to Mr Mackinlay that Mr Mackinlay also knows that the process by which members of the ISC are chosen is a very similar process in practice.

Andrew Mackinlay: It is not, it is not, it is not.

Q1194 Chairman: What you are saying in effect is you are using this jurisdictional point to stop the Committee having what can be absolutely decisive evidence?

Mr Straw: No. I will be producing decisive evidence to you in any event, Mr Anderson. Unless you are saying that I have come here not to tell the truth but to tell other than the truth it ought to be believed.

Q1195 Chairman: I am making the simple point that the best evidence which could be before this Committee in respect of that simple point on the role of the JIC and the views of the Chairman of the JIC would be to allow us to see the Chairman. You are saying that you are not going to allow that.

Mr Straw: The key evidence, which I shall be reading to the Committee, is to compare what was said in the JIC assessment with what was in the final document.

Andrew Mackinlay: Presumably we reserve our right, sometime during these proceedings it open to us, notwithstanding what the Foreign Secretary has said, you would if motioned for us to request, or summons—I am sure of the terminology—the ball would be lobbed back into his court or the foreign secretary to either deny Parliament that opportunity or to acquiesce. I do not want to prejudge it. Am I correct in saying that is an option open to us?

Q1196 Chairman: Nothing is prejudged I just wanted to ascertain that on the face of it the Committee is being denied the best evidence because of your insistence on this jurisdictional point.

Mr Straw: Mr Anderson, it is not just a jurisdictional point, it is about which is the appropriate body to examine the Chairman of the JIC and also the heads of the agencies. I have discussed this perfectly amicably with you and your colleagues in the past.

Q1197 Chairman: We have never accepted your position.

Mr Straw: I thought we had reached a common understanding about this. We have been more open with the FAC on this inquiry than any other.

Andrew Mackinlay: You have been more open. That is an entirely different issue. Mr Straw is right; to his credit he has been more open with this Committee than any other committee. I have to say we had to have two requests to see Mr Campbell, do not forget, but nevertheless those who repent at the gates of heaven. . . What we never conceded, and I never shall, is that the Security Intelligence Committee is an alternative to this Committee, it is a Parliamentary committee, it is created by statute, it is not a Parliamentary committee, its selection is fundamentally different to how I got on this Committee and I shall never concede that, ever.

Q1198 Mr Pope: I cannot be alone in feeling really frustrated about this, the charge that is being made by Mr Gilligan is essentially uncorroborated, we are having to take his word he has a credible source who has alleged firstly that Alastair Campbell "sexed-up" the document and it was transformed in the week prior to publication. You are saying that it is not. Are you saying in the private session we will be allowed to see the last JIC assessments prior to the publication of the documents so that we can compare and contrast the two?

Mr Straw: I will read out to you the relevant sections of that. In addition to that what Mr Campbell is preparing, and he was working very late on this last night and again very early this morning, and hopes to try and have this with you before the session is through today, is a detailed summary of the exchanges between him and the JIC, saying: Can I suggest this? What about that? And the response from the JIC, which will give you, as it were, the most complete and accurate running commentary on that process. I wonder if I can just say this, I think in making judgments about the credibility of this source of Mr Gilligan's, I have no idea who it is, I think it is worth bearing in mind how far the senior people in the BBC are now palpably shifting from Mr Gilligan in an apparent defence of Mr Gilligan.

Richard Ottaway: You are using the Committee for propaganda.

Chairman: I end on this point, as far as I am concerned we have never yielded in respect of the fact that we should be entitled to have intelligence material which is germane to our inquiries. When the Intelligence and Security Committee was established it was said in terms by the then minister that it would not cut across the work of existing select committees.

Q1199 Mr Pope: In some sense this is a political fiasco at the moment and it is all over today's papers. There is a serious point here , which is not a party political point at all, the source Mr Gilligan quoted to us, I wanted to get to the bottom of this about Mr Gilligan's source, it seems to me that his source must be somebody fairly senior, either somebody in an intelligence agency or in another department. I just put it to you, Secretary of State, as the minister responsible for some of these agencies, it must be in the public interest to find out who the source is and get the source to either put up or shut up. At the moment there is no evidence before the Committee that is corroborated about the "sexing-up" of the evidence. I think this is right at the root of the charges that the Government have to face. I want to get to the bottom of this, it is not about scoring party political points I want to know what the truth is: Was the evidence "sexed-up"? How credible is that source?

Mr Straw: We do not believe the source is credible. I will say this, what I note is that I think Mr Richard Sambrook also now has doubts about the credibility of the source because when he did an interview yesterday on the *Today* programme—

Q1200 Mr Maples: That is not answering the question.

Mr Straw: With great respect, Chairman, it may be that Mr Maples thinks I should not be allowed to answer it, but I will answer it.

Q1201 Chairman: I am allowing you to answer, but briefly.

Mr Straw: What I noted was that Mr Sambrook did not repeat the charges made by Mr Gilligan, which were very specific, all he said was: "There was disquiet within the intelligence service about one piece of evidence, that one 45 minute claim". Mr Gilligan did not say there was "disquiet", he made very specific charges, which are wrong, and that is one reason why the BBC does need to apologise.

Q1202 Richard Ottaway: On this point about when the 45 minute claim first appeared Mr Campbell told us not once but twice on Wednesday that it appeared in the first draft of the report, do you agree with that?

Mr Straw: The first draft of? The one produced in September, yes I think so, because we had the JIC report in early September. Mr Ottaway, the crucial point about the 45 minute claim is that it came from intelligence through the JIC, which was assessed to be credible.

Q1203 Richard Ottaway: That is not the question, there are two points here: When did it go in? Was it credible?

Mr Straw: We will deal with the narrative in the private session.

Chairman: The question put by Mr Ottaway was rather different, Mr Ottaway would you repeat it?

Q1204 Richard Ottaway: I am asking when it appeared in the draft of the September document.

Mr Straw: I can give you the date.

Q1205 Richard Ottaway: Was it in the first draft?

Mr Ricketts: It was as soon as it was received and assessed.

Q1206 Richard Ottaway: Was it in the first draft?

Mr Straw: As we will explain in the private session the drafts of information to be made publicly available of some kind about Iraq went back to the

early side of the summer, we have already made this clear. Then drafts of the document that was being published were being prepared. This information came to the attention of the JIC, as I recall, in early September and from that date and the assessment by the JIC that intelligence was accurately reflected in the dossier.

Q1207 Richard Ottaway: It was added later.

Mr Straw: That is what I am trying to tell you.

Q1208 Richard Ottaway: The answer is that it was added later and it was not in the first draft.

Mr Straw: Again we can go into detail.

Q1209 Richard Ottaway: This is a very important.

Mr Straw: Mr Ottaway, it is a completely trivial point, with great respect to you.

Q1210 Richard Ottaway: It is one you have spent the last 30 minutes refuting.

Mr Straw: It is not remotely material. The allegation was not that it appeared in the first draft rather than the second draft, let us be clear about that, the allegation was that the 45 minute claims was not properly sourced or corroborated and was then "sexed-up" in the final document.

Q1211 Richard Ottaway: We will come to that. I am asking a totally different line of questioning here; did it appear in the first draft?

Mr Straw: What I am saying to you is—

Q1212 Richard Ottaway: You can cut right through this by saying yes or no?

Mr Straw: It appeared in the first draft after the intelligence was received.

Q1213 Richard Ottaway: It was not in the first draft it was in a subsequent draft, so it was added later.

Mr Straw: That is a ludicrous way of describing it, Mr Ottaway.

Q1214 Richard Ottaway: It seems pretty reasonable; people of basic intelligence can understand it.

Mr Straw: We did not get the intelligence and it was not assessed until early September, palpably it could not have been included in earlier drafts if we did not know about it.

Q1215 Richard Ottaway: It was not in the first draft?

Mr Straw: I have answered the question, Mr Ottaway. I have given you a perfectly satisfactory answer to the question.

Q1216 Richard Ottaway: I will repeat it, was it in the first draft?

Mr Straw: I answered you; it was in the first draft after the intelligence was received, by definition it could not have been in any earlier draft.

Q1217 Richard Ottaway: Was it in one of the subsequent drafts?

Mr Straw: I have given you an answer.

Q1218 Chairman: Mr Ottaway was talking about the first draft, when was that first draft prepared by the Chairman of the JIC?

Mr Ricketts: If we go back to the beginning there were drafts discussed in March and obviously by definition there was no reference to the 45 minute in the first draft because it had not been received or assessed. The Prime Minister announced on 3 September an intention to produce a more detailed dossier drawing more fully on intelligence. The Joint Intelligence Committee then discussed drafts twice in the course of September. As far as I am aware that material was already included in those drafts because it had figured in a Joint Intelligence Committee report of 9 September.

Q1219 Richard Ottaway: Mr Campbell told us it was in the first draft, you just seem to be contradicting that?

Mr Ricketts: It does depend on your definition of first draft. If you mean March then clearly no.

Q1220 Richard Ottaway: It was decided not to publish the March draft, so there was a several months delay. The Prime Minister then said on 3 September, "I think we ought to publish this" and a first draft was produced. Mr Campbell was implying that no one tried to get that in, it was in the first draft.

Mr Straw: No one did try to get it in.

Q1221 Richard Ottaway: I do not want a diversion on that. Mr Ricketts, was it in that first draft?

Mr Ricketts: If you mean in the first draft after the Prime Minister's announcement on 3 September my belief is that it was.

Q1222 Richard Ottaway: Was that the first draft of the September document? This is not complicated, it is not rocket science.

Mr Straw: I agree, it is not complicated, which is why I am slightly surprised you are asking a series of questions. We have already explained there was information that was coming in about Iraq over a 20 year period and that is iteratively added to. By definition the information was not in draft before we received the information, it was in draft afterwards and after it was properly assessed.

Q1223 Richard Ottaway: I do not think we can take this any further. My understanding, if I can take your joint evidence together, is a first draft was produced, but it was in the first draft after the information became available.

Mr Straw: Mr Ricketts and I have just given you the answer. Mr Ottaway, you ask your questions and allow me to give my answer in my own way, I have already provided you with a summary.

Q1224 Andrew Mackinlay: Just a quickie, the Chairman of the JIC, is he on or is he represented on the CIC?

Mr Ricketts: No.
Mr Straw: He is not directly represented on the CIC.

Q1225 Andrew Mackinlay: Indirectly?

Mr Straw: The easiest thing for us to do is to give you details about the background of who has been on the CIC.

Q1226 Andrew Mackinlay: We did that quickly. In the *Independent* newspaper, I think it was the *Independent* newspaper, they actually indicate the number of sites which are to inspected and numbers which have been inspected post-war. There were some Parliamentary replies to my colleague Harry Cohen—which I do not have in front of me—rather indicating that a lot of this work had been done. There seems to be a gulf between, if you like, the task perceived or seen and what has been reported to Parliament. Is there anything you can tell us in this public session with regard to what has been done and what is yet to be achieved?

Mr Straw: Again the numbers are obviously changing. I have a note here that as of 21 June 159 sites have been examined out of the US master list of 578 but with no confirmed results. The note goes on: "This is misleading because each known site tends when investigated to throw up several more previously unknown ones and so far 83 of these *ad hoc* sites have been visited. Most, if not all, of the known sites were also known to the United Nation, as the Iraqis were aware, so we should not expect to find much evidence there. The Iraq Survey Group will shift to a more intelligence-led approach to counter this".

Q1227 Andrew Mackinlay: Indeed. For the purpose of this morning what you said, in fairness, was the process was just beginning in terms of the search. I woke up this morning to Mr Robin Cook on the radio. I think I faithfully summarise him by saying the issue is not the dodgy dossier, the issue is they have not found chemical plants, the nuclear thing was found to be a forgery and just generally they have not found any weapons of mass destruction. I would not normally be a conduit for Mr Robin Cook, and also I do not see why you should have a second bite of the cherry but it would be a great pity if we concluded our proceedings by not putting to you once more that which he uttered on Radio Four. What say you to that? I do not want anybody, whatever side of this they fall, to be able to repeat that without you being able to rebut it?

Mr Straw: You are very generous, I am grateful to you. The first thing I would say is I agreed with Mr Cook in his statement—I paraphrase but I do not think inaccurately—that the issue of the 45 minutes and still more about the provenance of the February dossier is a huge diversion. These were not remotely central to the decision to go to the war, which was the nature of your inquiry. I say that to you with respect, Chairman, historians I think would not give you an alpha marking if you suggested that Mr Gilligan's claim on the 45 minutes was the basis on which we went to war, because it was not. It is important but it is important we pin down the untruth.

Q1228 Chairman: Mr Mackinlay that has given you the opportunity to respond to your predecessor?
Mr Straw: Robin has a different view from us, his view was very honourable and he acted entirely honourably throughout. He resigned on 17 March and he voted against the Government on 18 March. His view was that containment was working and for that reason he disagreed with the Government. I disagree with him and his judgment. I do not have any complaint, none whatever about the way he behaved, he behaved honourably and correctly throughout. My disagreement with him is, and I have said this publically and I have said it to him, the judgments I made between June 2001 and the day we went to war were based on very similar evidence and remarkably similar terms to the judgments he made when he was Secretary of State explaining the decision to go for Desert Fox in the time that it did and for a later bombing operation in 2001. I am glad to have this opportunity to say that the decision to go to war on 18 March was justified on the day it was made on the evidence that was before the House, the country and the international community on that day. Nobody in the international community disputed that Saddam Hussein had the capability for chemical and biological weapons programmes nor that he was seeking to build up a nuclear programme. No one disputed in the Security Council that Saddam Hussein posed a threat to international peace and security, because that was the phrasing used in SCR 1441. Nobody disputed that at all, not withstanding that he had 130 days in which to co-operate actively, completely and immediately with the weapons inspectors he failed to do so. The only question was, what do we then do in the face of that threat and that defiance?" We came to the view, and I am quite clear it was justified, that the only thing to do was to, first of all, issue an ultimatum to him and if he failed to take that to take military action. I very much hope that, of course, we find further corroborative evidence about Saddam's chemical and biological capabilities and his nuclear plans, but whether or not we do the decision to take military action was justified on the date, 18 March, on the basis of perfectly public information, for example these two command papers which I published which laid out the full facts of Saddam's defiance.

Q1229 Andrew Mackinlay: I asked Alastair Campbell the other day, and I want to ask you whether you know if it is in train, basically in relation to the dodgy dossier he said that the security intelligence folk said, here is a parcel of intelligence you can put in the public domain, and it then emerged in the February dossier. I then asked him, if that is so can you highlight that for us and he was somewhat anxious about that. Can I say for the record the reason why I thought about this was because when we had Mr al-Marashi's evidence he gave evidence which he said in his estimate, and he

had gone through this pretty thoroughly, he thought something up to 90% of that dossier was drawn either from his work or *Jane's* or these other publications. It does seem to me quantum is going to be important, if it is only 10% intelligence, if it is only 15% intelligence it does alter the nature of that document. In a sense I want to put that to you in open session, is it substantial intelligence? Do you reiterate it is substantial intelligence, is it half or is it—?
Mr Straw: Mr Mackinlay, what can I tell you is as we speak this analysis is being done to highlight which parts of part one and part three were drawn from intelligence. That will be with the Committee as quickly as possible. The process of this was unsatisfactory, we have all accepted that. The differences should have been made clear. However, I would also say, and I hope the Committee are able to conclude this, that in every material particular, this document, the February 3 one, was and remains accurate.

Q1230 Mr Maples: I wonder if I can go back to the weapons of mass destruction dossier?
Mr Straw: The September one.

Q1231 Mr Maples: I want to find out the process by which the document came into being. These are not trick questions, presumably in the period between March and the decision to publish a dossier there were lots of JIC reports coming out on the state of Iraq and its weapons of mass destruction. By the time the decision was taken, just before the decision was taken to publish a document, which you told us was taken late summer, late August/early September, at that point would all of the JIC assessments about Iraq and its weapons of mass destruction have been in one JIC paper or in a lot of different papers?
Mr Ricketts: They would have been in a series of papers. The September dossier pulled together work from a number of different JIC assessments.

Q1232 Mr Maples: This was a culminative process. Each edition of the JIC paper, not the draft of this document, but the JIC assessments that were being circulated to ministers like yourselves, they did not simply build on the one before, there was a new one.
Mr Ehrman: No. The implication of that is we just regurgitated what was in earlier drafts, that is not true. Each time a JIC assessment is done you look at the intelligence, you analyse it, you see what is new, you do not just accept that what was in the previous one is taken as read.

Q1233 Mr Maples: Just before the decision was made to produce a document for publication there was in existence a JIC assessment, presumably the latest one at that point, which would have included everything that JIC thought was relevant about Iraq and its weapons of mass destruction for ministers to see.
Mr Ehrman: There was a series of JIC assessments which covered different aspects of the programmes.

Q1234 Mr Maples: I am confused now, I thought what you said to me is that each edition updated the previous one and made the previous one irrelevant.
Mr Ehrman: These were done over the years, not everyone covered every aspect.

Q1235 Mr Maples: At this point there would have been several JIC papers in existence which were relevant to this document. The Prime Minister in his introduction said this is based in large part on the work of the Joint Intelligence Committee, what other organs of Government were feeding in information at this point other than JIC?
Mr Ricketts: Parts two and three cover other issues where the Foreign Office took the lead in drafting them, the history of the UN weapons inspections and Iraq under Saddam Hussein.

Q1236 Mr Maples: Would it be far to say that part one was based entirely on the JIC assessment?
Mr Ehrman: There is a lot of open source material, like UNSCOM reports.

Q1237 Mr Maples: No secret material available to you that did not come through JIC, it was either from JIC or it was open source material or available from UNSCOM?
Mr Ricketts: Can I make one point on the JIC process, the JIC process does not only draw on secret intelligence, the JIC papers put together secret intelligence but also publically available information, diplomatic reporting, material from a whole series of places. It gives a complete assessment, so in any JIC assessment there will be secret material but also material from other sources.

Q1238 Mr Maples: When the decision was taken in late August or early September to produce a document for publication somebody took these various JIC assessments and produced a first draft of what became this publication. What I am interested in is, who produced that first draft? Was that produced from within JIC?
Mr Ehrman: The JIC Chairman was in charge throughout September.

Q1239 Mr Maples: Presumably there was a first draft of this paper?
Mr Ehrman: If you go right the way back to March the process was that a paper was commissioned and the assessment staff even then put together a draft, that was with help from other departments.

Q1240 Mr Maples: After the decision was taken to produce something for publication presumably then a draft was produced, which then became the working document?
Mr Ehrman: Yes.

Q1241 Mr Maples: Who produced that document?
Mr Ehrman: The Chairman of the JIC was in charge throughout.

Q1242 Mr Maples: It would not just have been the JIC?

Mr Ehrman: The chairman of JIC working with the assessment staff but also there were people from other departments who came to a mass of meetings throughout that month producing that document.

Q1243 Mr Maples: I am trying to get to the first draft of it and before people started to comment on it and suggest amendments. That first draft was produced under the auspices of the Chairman of the JIC, which seems to imply it was not just JIC and its assessment staff that worked on it but that people from the Foreign Office or Ministry of Defence or Number 10 staff were involved in the preparation of the first draft?
Mr Ehrman: It then came to the JIC who saw it on a couple of occasions.

Q1244 Mr Maples: I understand that. I drew your attention the last time you appeared before us to what I perceive to be a difference in emphasis in what it says in the body of the document and what it says in the executive summary and you did not concur with me there was a substantive difference in the evidence. At what point did the executive summary start to get produced, presumably when the document was almost finalised?
Mr Ehrman: The executive summary was also produced by the chairman of the JIC and the assessment staff, so it was exactly the same process.

Q1245 Mr Maples: It was presumably produced when the main body of the document was almost finalised.
Mr Straw: I made this point in one of the many answers I provided to your Committee, there was also a conclusion but it was decided to drop that because it was just repetitive of the body of the report and the executive summary introduction.

Q1246 Mr Maples: The executive summary was also prepared in exactly the same way, it was not a bolt-on, done by somebody else afterwards, it was prepared in the same way with the JIC Chairman in charge of that process. My final question on this is were there several meetings or was most of the input of suggested amendments and changes done in writing?
Mr Ehrman: There was certainly a good many meetings but there were people from their own departments looking at drafts and sending comments in.

Q1247 Mr Maples: Did you represent the Foreign Office there?
Mr Ehrman: No, I did not represent the Foreign Office in the drafting of that document, other members of the Foreign Office were closely involved in the drafting.

Q1248 Mr Maples: In those meetings at which it was discussed were you the Foreign Office's representative at those?

Mr Ehrman: No, I was not. I became a member of the JIC in October but I was responsible for that general area before I came a member of the JIC. Many members of the Foreign Office were involved in the drafting.

Q1249 Mr Maples: Can I ask the Foreign Secretary, was he present at meetings?
Mr Straw: No, no, no. What happened so far as my offering comments on the draft was that the draft would appear in a box. I think we have given you some details about this, I will give you some more. There were a number of drafts that had been floating round from back in March, just information summarising, as it were, the case again Saddam, some drawing on intelligence, some from wholly public sources, one which I published to the Parliamentary Party, it has now been widely circulated, which was drawn almost entirely from open sources. The process of this one was it came in my box, I cannot remember on how many occasion, I offered some comments on the layout, for example I favoured the inclusion of more graphics and diagrams, and a suggestion to include in the foreword a reference to Saddam's defiance of the United Nations and his unprecedented use of WMD. For the sake of completeness you may like to know Mr O'Brien commented on setting out the context better by greater use of the UNSCOM report.

Q1250 Mr Maples: Who else was at the meetings, neither of you ever went to a meeting?
Mr Straw: I never went to a formal meeting, that would have been completely inappropriate and an interference with their process.
Mr Ehrman: It was done at the working level, chaired by the Chairman of the JIC and then came to the full JIC, as I mentioned a couple of times.
Mr Maples: That is enough for the time being.

Q1251 Mr Chidgey: Foreign Secretary, in response to a question raised by Mr Mackinlay earlier about the fact that the whole international community accepted the case as set out on the basis of the assessments of going to war on 18 March you say that you very much hope, or words to that effect, that further evidence of Iraq's weapons of mass destruction would be found in due course. What evidence has been found in Iraq of weapons of mass destruction since the end of the conflict?
Mr Straw: We can give you some details. As you know we have explained, and so did Mr Taylor in some detail, about the reasons for the delay in the Iraq Survey Group getting going. In terms of the statements made in here, how many of these—

Q1252 Mr Chidgey: On assessment what evidence has been found of weapons of mass destruction?
Mr Straw: Illegal programmes to extend the range of al-Samoud missiles borne out by UNMOVIC findings of instructions from al Samoud. The concealment of documents associated with WMD programmes. You may have seen, we have not had a chance ourselves to fully assess it, a report

yesterday by a senior scientist involved in the Iraqi nuclear programme about documentation that he had hidden in his own garden and how the Saddam regime indeed maintained a policy of trying to improve and develop their nuclear programme.

Q1253 Mr Chidgey: Can I stop you there, you are talking so far about plans, proposals and programmes. You just said they were talking about plans to develop, has there been any hard evidence found in Iraq post-conflict of the existence of weapons of mass destruction?
Mr Straw: Mr Chidgey, whether there has been a physical find of a chemical or a biological compound ready for use in some delivery system the answer to that, as you know, is no.

Q1254 Mr Chidgey: Weaponisation.
Mr Straw: Has there been significant evidence of the existence of the these programmes, including the things we have discovered and including the suspect mobile traders which are the still the subject of analysis? Yes is the answer to that. I hope that nobody here is suggesting that what the United Nations concluded, what UNSCOM and the UNMOVIC concluded was that without any peradventure at all Saddam had these programmes over many years and had failed to answer for them, but that is not true. I just say this: it would have been utterly irresponsible in the face of all the evidence, which we knew for certain, about Saddam's programme, chemical and biological programmes, and having had a nuclear programme, his wish to re-establish that, and his abject failure to provide any credible explanations about what had happened to those programmes, for us just to have sat on our hands.

Q1255 Mr Chidgey: Thank you, Foreign Secretary, but can I just say this. As I understand it, the last evidence of the programmes of Saddam Hussein were available up until the time that UNSCOM left the country in 1998.
Mr Straw: Sorry, say that again?

Q1256 Mr Chidgey: Up until the time when UNSCOM left the country in 1998—I think you say as much in your report—"since the UN weapons were withdrawn in 1998 there has been little overt information on Iraq's chemical, biological, nuclear and ballistic missile programmes", and from that point, and I will paraphrase, we have had to rely on intelligence and intelligence very rarely offers a complete account of activities. That is perfectly acceptable, I am not challenging that. The point I am making is it is absolutely vital to make a distinction between evidence and assessment and much of what we have discussed over these last few weeks and months is the action that we have taken n the basis of assessments rather than evidence. I put it to you, Foreign Secretary, that we have been dealing at great length with the work of the JIC and the best intelligence available which was sufficient to convince the international community of the case to go to war, but it would appear that after the event there is something lacking between the veracity of the assessments and the evidence that we are finding on the ground. I asked you earlier in the week whether any inspections have been undertaken of the sites that were mentioned in this document as being the main concerns in terms of the chemical and biological weapons potential in terms of production and you were not able to tell me then whether they had been inspected. You did mention that there were decontamination programmes possible, but we had very little on that. I would have thought that would have been the very first priority, to prove the case on the basis of evidence rather than assessment, and it has not been forthcoming.

Mr Ehrman: If I could try to answer that. Every single site in the dossier has been visited by UNMOVIC.

Q1257 Mr Chidgey: Post-war, pre-war or both?

Mr Ehrman: Pre-war. Every site that was in the dossier. I would just like to describe some of the findings that they got. All of the sites listed in the dossier were visited by UNMOVIC inspectors, and most revealed—to a greater or lesser extent—an intent to develop prohibited programmes. The dossier said that Fallujah was a facility of concern which had been rebuilt since *Desert Fox*, though we did not claim there was specific evidence of CW precursor or agent production. Its production of chlorine and phenol could support CW agent and precursor production. UNMOVIC declared that three pieces of equipment found at Fallujah—destroyed by UNSCOM and subsequently refurbished—should be destroyed. UNMOVIC also established that the castor oil production plant at Fallujah, which could have been used to produce ricin, had been rebuilt and expanded. UNMOVIC confirmed that equipment had been rebuilt at al-Mamoun: two rocket motor casting chambers, destroyed by UNSCOM as being part of a prohibited missile programme, had been refurbished by Iraq. Those chambers were subsequently destroyed by UNMOVIC. UNMOVIC also confirmed that a large missile test stand had been constructed at al-Rafah, far larger than required for Iraq's declared missile programme. Five items of refurbished equipment, proscribed by UNSCOM as being part of prohibited CW programmes, were also found at al-Qa'qa. This was slated for destruction by UNMOVIC but they did not have time to carry that out. Iraq declared that it had restarted research and development of UDMH[1], which is a powerful and prohibited missile fuel, at the chemical research facility at Tarmiyah. UNMOVIC suggested that this could have been intended as part of a programme to develop a missile with a range far in excess of 150kms. That was what happened at the particular sites mentioned in the dossier.

Q1258 Mr Chidgey: The particular point I was making was about weaponising of chemical and biological weapons. You mentioned, if I remember correctly, that the capability in the phenol and

---

[1] Unsymmetrical DiMethyl Hydrazine.

chlorine plants had been re-established or existed, but you also said which could be used for chemical weapons.

Mr Ehrman: This was what UNMOVIC said.

Q1259 Mr Chidgey: That is right. I am quoting what you said. The point is that is exactly what it says here, that it could be used for chemical weapons. I am looking for hard evidence that the weaponisation had taken place and that does not seem to have been found.

Mr Ehrman: That was what UNMOVIC found from going through the sites.

Q1260 Sir John Stanley: Foreign Secretary, there are three issues I wish to pursue with you and your colleagues. The first relates to the whole issue of the uranium from Africa. That is a central issue and was a central element in the Government's September 2002 dossier and the Government on page 27 of the dossier said, for example: "We therefore judge that if Iraq obtained fissile material and other essential components from foreign sources the timeline for production of a nuclear weapon would be shortened and Iraq could produce a nuclear weapon in between one and two years." Can you confirm what has appeared extensively, and this may be one for your officials, in both the British and the American press that in February 2002—I stress 2002—the American administration sent a retired US ambassador who had had experience of serving in Africa to Niger to investigate allegations, documents, that Niger was involved in the supply of uranium to Iraq?

Mr Straw: I am sorry, I have got no knowledge of that claim one way or the other.

Q1261 Chairman: Would one of your officials?

Mr Ehrman: I am not aware of that.

Q1262 Sir John Stanley: I find that a very, very surprising answer and it suggests to me that we do not have the appropriate officials. This is important information that has been shown extensively in the American press and also in the British press. Only as recently as June 12 in the *Washington Post*, this public source, it is stated: "Armed with information reportedly showing that Iraqi officials had been seeking to buy uranium in Niger one or two years earlier, the CIA in early February 2002 despatched a retired US ambassador to the country to investigate the claims". Indeed, that was further confirmed by Dr Glen Rangwala in the *Independent* on 22 June who said that he himself had met the particular former US ambassador a few days ago, and I myself have spoken to Dr Rangwala about the conversation he had. The ambassador returned to the United States in a matter of three weeks, as was reported in the *Washington Post*, and the article says: "After returning to the United States, the envoy reported to the CIA that the uranium purchase story was false." Can you, or your officials, tell this Committee at what point, given the closeness of the intelligence relationship between Britain and the United States, the British intelligence community, presumably in the United States, was informed that the CIA had made this investigation and had reported that the conclusion of the former US ambassador was that the documentation and the allegations were false? At what point was that reported to the British intelligence community?

Mr Ricketts: I cannot answer that, Sir John. I would recall that the fact that uranium—yellow cake—had been supplied from Niger to Iraq in the 1980s is a confirmed fact, so reports of continued Iraqi interest in sourcing uranium from Niger did not seem to us to be implausible.

Q1263 Sir John Stanley: That is not the point I am putting to you at all. The point I am putting to you is a very simple factual point. The former US ambassador made the visit to Africa, returned in early March after three weeks and reported to the CIA that the uranium purchase story was false. I would find it inexplicable if that particular result of the envoy's visit was not reported to British defence liaison staff in Washington. As you are not able to give me the answer to this question, which is a very material question for reasons I shall come on to, Foreign Secretary, please could you very, very quickly tell us the answer to my question, when did the CIA report to the British intelligence community the result of the former US ambassador's visit to Niger?

Mr Straw: I will seek to get you an answer as quickly as possible, Sir John, as I always do. I would like to say this: number one, I have learned that the IAEA—

Q1264 Sir John Stanley: I am sorry.

Mr Straw: Allow me to say this because it is rather important. I learned that they had judged that the documentation relating to Iraq having bought yellow cake were forgeries at the Security Council when the IAEA published them.

Q1265 Sir John Stanley: I am coming on to these issues, Foreign Secretary, and please at that point give me the answers to those questions. I just want to take this issue through chronologically in my own order, if I may. That was a report made by the former US ambassador and I would find it wholly inexplicable if that was not shared very promptly with the British defence liaison staff in Washington. The question I now want to come to is what was said in the September 2002 dossier. On that particular issue, as we know, in the foreword under the name of the Prime Minister there is a reference to the fact that Saddam Hussein is continuing in his efforts to develop nuclear weapons, and in the bullet points: "Saddam Hussein sought significant quantities of uranium from Africa, despite having no active civil nuclear power programme that could require it". Given the fact that the Niger documents were certainly at that time known to the Americans, and I believe also to British intelligence, to be forgeries, it is clear that the statement made in the September 2002 dossier was clearly based on separate intelligence in which the British Government had confidence. The point I want to put to you is that when the Prime Minister came to the House on

September 24 at the time when the September 2002 dossier was published, he said: "In addition, we know that Saddam has been trying to buy significant quantities of uranium from Africa, although we do not know whether he has been successful". The question I have in my mind is why did the Government, either in the document or in what the Prime Minister said in the House, at least not put some degree of health warning over the statements that appeared in the September 2002 dossier to the effect that alongside intelligence in which the British Government clearly had confidence there were already, and had been known for some six months previously, forged documents in circulation? I have to say I am somewhat surprised that no reference was made to those forged documents in the very self-same area in which the Prime Minister was saying without qualification, without ambiguity, "we know that Saddam has been trying to buy significant quantities of uranium from Africa, although we do not know whether he has been successful or not". Why was there not any sort of health warning?

Mr Straw: Sir John, we will find out what the state of knowledge was about the story that you gave in your previous question. What I can say, however, as far as I am concerned is that I had absolutely no knowledge of any documents relating to this area being forged until the IAEA said that in one of their reports in February or March 2003. I am confident in saying that that I also speak for the Prime Minister.

Q1266 Sir John Stanley: I am not suggesting, Foreign Secretary, that you did have any knowledge but I think you will be quite interested, therefore, in the answer to the earlier question which I put to you. I am quite interested to know what was the date on which the British intelligence community were informed by the CIA that this forged documentation existed.

Mr Straw: We will find out.

Q1267 Sir John Stanley: And why, perhaps, so very, very many months elapsed even after the publication of the September 2002 dossier with these very emphatic statements when neither the Prime Minister nor yourself were informed as to the existence of the forgeries. Can I go on now beyond the September 2002 document. This issue is one which Mr Mackinlay did raise in the last session and I would like to carry it on. As you well know, the British Government was under direct United Nations obligations on Security Council resolutions to provide information that was going to be of value to the IAEA in investigating the compliance or non-compliance by Saddam Hussein with the issue of the procurement of fissile materials and materials that would be relevant to the Iraqi regime's nuclear production. I would like to point out to you, and I have the detailed texts of the various resolutions, that not merely was the British Government under an obligation to provide that information under Security Council Resolution 1441, which of course was only passed on 8 November 2002, but the British Government was under an even stronger obligation, an even more mandatory obligation, under Security Council Resolution 1051 of 27 March 1996 in paragraph 12. The British Government clearly had strong intelligence, in its view, supporting the Prime Minister's statement that Saddam Hussein was in the market for procuring uranium from Africa. What was the date, Foreign Secretary, on which the British Government complied with its obligations under the two Security Council resolutions and passed the firm intelligence that it had, which underpinned what was in the September 2002 document, to the IAEA?

Mr Straw: I will ask Mr Ricketts and Mr Ehrman to give more detail, but—

Q1268 Sir John Stanley: I just want the date, I do not want a long response. I am just asking a very simple question. I am asking your officials if you cannot give the answer. I want to know, please, the date, that is all I am asking for. What was the date on which the British Government complied with its Security Council obligations to pass information on to the IAEA?

Mr Straw: I am going to give an answer and, if I may, I will give the answer in my own way. Resolution 1051, to which you referred, was passed before we came into office in March 1996, so I cannot give you the exact date. I assume, that as with every other kind of obligation, the previous government, of which I was not a member but you were, was co-operating fully with the United Nations in this particular as in others. What I also know—

Q1269 Sir John Stanley: I am sorry, Security Council Resolution 1051 was ongoing at the time we are talking about. We are talking about fresh intelligence which came to your Government and which underpinned putting into the September 2002 dossier the detailed statements that were made in emphatic terms about uranium supplies to Africa. That intelligence was under the obligation of your Government to pass on to the IAEA. When was it done?

Mr Ehrman: The intelligence came from a foreign service and we understand that it was briefed to the IAEA in 2003.

Q1270 Sir John Stanley: What date in 2003?
Mr Ehrman: I would have to check.
Mr Straw: We will have to give it to you later.

Q1271 Sir John Stanley: That is a very, very important date, extremely important, because the dossier became available in September 2002, so how long did it take the British Government to comply with their UN obligations?

Mr Straw: We were complying with those obligations and co-operating to a very high degree, as both the IAEA, UNMOVIC and its predecessor, UNSCOM, always accepted.

Q1272 Sir John Stanley: Can I come back to you, Mr Ehrman. You said in 2003. If you know the year, surely you must know the month, Mr Ehrman.

Mr Ehrman: I would have to check the exact month.

Q1273 Sir John Stanley: If you would let us know the exact month very precisely and very quickly. This brings me to the last point I want to make on this which is that if the British Government were complying with their obligations under the United Nations Security Council resolutions then I have to say I am exceedingly surprised by the wording of Dr Mohammed El-Baradei's statement to the United Nations Security Council on 7 March 2003. I am very surprised by the final sentence. These are the three sentences, but the final one is the significant one: "Based on thorough analysis the IAEA has concluded with the concurrence of outside experts that these documents which form the basis for the reports of recent uranium transactions between Iraq and Niger are in fact not authentic. We have therefore concluded that these specific allegations are unfounded." This is the key sentence which puzzles me hugely: "However, we will continue to follow up any additional evidence, if it emerges, relevant to efforts by Iraq to illicitly import nuclear materials." It would appear to me, therefore, that at the time when Dr El-Baradei made that statement to the UN Security Council on 7 March the British Government at that point had still not provided the intelligence which it had, which underpinned what appeared in the September 2002 document, to the IAEA. Why not?

Mr Ehrman: I was saying that my understanding was that the intelligence was passed to the IAEA in 2003, I did not say by the British Government. My understanding is that it was by the country which had that intelligence.

Mr Straw: I make clear, Sir John, as far as—

Q1274 Sir John Stanley: I am sorry, Mr Ehrman, if we are at cross-purposes let us just sort it out. The British Government's statement—I quoted what the Prime Minister said in the House—"We know that Saddam has been trying to buy significant quantities of uranium from Africa, although we do not know whether he has been successful", and repeated in the dossier, in the bullet points, "sought significant quantities of uranium from Africa, despite having no active civil nuclear power programme that could require it. . .", that was clearly British information based on British intelligence. Anyway, it is information for which the British Government is responsible.

Mr Straw: But, Sir John,—

Q1275 Sir John Stanley: I am just asking why was that information apparently not passed on straight away to the IAEA?

Mr Straw: We will have to get you a detailed answer but may I say that my understanding throughout this, and it is something that the IAEA and UNMOVIC themselves acknowledged, was that we were indeed co-operating actively with both agencies of the United Nations. You understand the distinction, but I think people may be forgiven for thinking there has been a conflation here of the intelligence relating to yellow cake, which was the subject of the forgeries, which as I said in the session on Tuesday did not come from British intelligence. There was some inadvertent reporting that it did, but it did not. That is just a fact. We can go into more detail in private session.

Q1276 Sir John Stanley: If I may say so, that is a red herring.
Mr Straw: That is not a red herring at all.

Q1277 Sir John Stanley: I am not talking about the forged documents. The Minister has already stated that that particular documentation, that particular source material, did not come from the UK. It has been widely reported in the press that it came from Italy, I have no means of knowing whether that is the case or not. I am talking about the intelligence which underpinned the statement in the September 2002 dossier and which obviously underpinned the statement made by the British Prime Minister. Foreign Secretary, you say in your public document to us in relation to the statement on page 25 of the dossier that "There is intelligence that Iraq has sought the supply of significant quantities of uranium from Africa" and you go on to say: "This reference drew on intelligence reporting from more than one source". Fine. I am simply asking why that intelligence reporting drawing from more than one source, for which the British Government took responsibility, which the British Government used, which when the President of the United States referred to it in his State of the Union address referred specifically to the fact that it came from Britain, did not claim it came from America, that intelligence reporting was not forthwith passed to the IAEA because if it had Dr El-Baradei in his statement on 7 March could not have been referring to "continuing to follow up any additional evidence, if it emerges, relevant to efforts by Iraq to illicitly import nuclear materials". Foreign Secretary, we want to know when was this substantial intelligence information that underpinning the document passed on and why was there such a delay?
Mr Straw: We will get you an answer and you will then be able to assess whether there was a delay, Sir John.
Sir John Stanley: Can I now come to—

Q1278 Richard Ottaway: Can I ask one quick question. Are you still standing by the uranium claim?
Mr Straw: What was in the document, yes.

Q1279 Richard Ottaway: What is the source of that?
Mr Straw: We will come to that in private session, Mr Ottaway.

Q1280 Richard Ottaway: Are you verifying the claim? Are you continuing to verify it?
Mr Straw: We will talk about sources in the private session.
Chairman: Sir John will continue. I want to move on to the private session very soon.

Q1281 Sir John Stanley: I have got just two more issues. The next issue I want to come to is a very crucial dimension to the 45 minute claim and it emerged in the evidence we took previously from Mr Andrew Gilligan and in answer to a question which Mr Pope posed. Mr Gilligan revealed to us that his source had said that the Iraqi intelligence source in turn from which he got his information, which was the single uncorroborated source which the Government has acknowledged underpinned the 45 minute claim rested the 45 minute claim on the use of missiles to launch WMD at a 45 minute state of readiness. Foreign Secretary, as you have clearly read the transcript, and as my colleagues will know, I came in very shortly afterwards and said if the 45 minuted claim rested on the capability of Iraq, from what I knew about this particular business that would almost certainly invalidate the 45 minute claim if it was based on delivery and 45 minute activation of missiles with a WMD capability. Foreign Secretary, when you came before us you picked up that point and you said in one of the answers you gave to me: "No reference to missiles, by the way, as some of your evidence givers have suggested, none whatever". In the dossier there is no reference to missiles in conjunction with the 45 minute claim, it is all in relation to weapons. That is something that could be credible if the intelligence is there. It refers, by implication, to artillery pieces and if chemical weapons are held forward that makes a 45 minute claim credible. The question I want to put to you is, therefore, there is a very, very significant word change that may or may not have taken place. The word change from "missiles" as alleged was the intelligence information that came in from Mr Gilligan's source, which makes the 45 minute claim non-credible, to "weapons", as used by the Government, which providing the intelligence is there makes the 45 minute claim credible. The question I want to put to you is, and again it may be one for your officials who may know the background in more detail, when the intelligence came in, and we have just heard in response to Mr Ottaway's questioning that it came in in September 2002 shortly before this document was published, allegedly from an Iraqi general, as Mr Gilligan's source said, was the wording that came in in relation to "missiles" or not?
Mr Straw: As far as I am aware no, the intelligence related to other delivery systems.

Q1282 Sir John Stanley: I am afraid it cannot be "as far as I am aware . . ."
Mr Straw: Not missiles.
Mr Ehrman: The intelligence related to "weapons".

Q1283 Sir John Stanley: It did. From the very beginning it related to "weapons"?
Mr Straw: Yes.

Q1284 Sir John Stanley: So you are saying that on this particular point Mr Gilligan's source is wrong in saying that the intelligence that came in related to "missiles"?

Mr Ehrman: The intelligence related to "weapons".

Q1285 Sir John Stanley: Thank you very much, that is a very important point that I wanted to establish. So there was no word changing that went on between when the intelligence first came in and when the dossier was published. Thank you. The final point I want to raise, Foreign Secretary, is this very important policy point. You will remember that in our earlier evidence session this week I said that "one of the central issues is whether the degree of immediacy of the threat from Saddam Hussein's regime that was conveyed to Parliament and to the wider public was justified on the basis of the intelligence information that was available to the Government" and you somewhat rode off with an answer to a question that I did not put to you. I never suggested at any point that the Government had used the word "immediate". If I can just put it in your own words. You said in your answer: "I wonder if I may be allowed to make this point in response to Sir John, so far as we can ascertain by word searches and so on, neither the Prime Minister nor I or anybody acting on our behalf has ever used the words 'immediate or imminent' threat, never used those words, in relation to the threat posed by Saddam Hussein. What we talked about in the dossier was a current and serious threat, which is very different." We can debate whether it is very different or not, but that was what you said. Then you went on to say: "The Prime Minister said on 24 September, the day the dossier was published in the House: 'I cannot say that this month or next, even this year or next, Saddam will use his weapons'." The point I want to put to you, Foreign Secretary, is that it is true to say that the Government used the words "current threat", sometimes the Government used the words "present threat", but that was coupled on a number of occasions, including by you at one of the speeches you made outside the House and by the Prime Minister in the House and in the dossier itself, with a reference to the 45 minutes. A current threat but coupled with a 45 minutes timescale for the activation of weapons of mass destruction. If I can just quote what the Prime Minister did say, also on 24 September, in relation to the document: "It concludes that Iraq has chemical and biological weapons; that Saddam has continued to produce them; that he has existing and active military plans for the use of chemical and biological weapons which could be activated within 45 minutes". I think all of us who were in the House hearing the Prime Minister saying that, hearing the references to "serious and current threat" were certainly charged with the view that this was a threat of some considerable near-term risk, even though the Prime Minister made it clear that he was not predicting when such use might be made. What I want to ask you, Foreign Secretary, is in the reply you gave to me earlier this week, I was not clear whether you were trying to row back from what the Government had said previously about the degree of immediacy of the threat following the publication of the dossier and up to the start of the war or whether your position, and therefore the Government's

position, is that you stand by exactly the terms which you expressed to the House and in the dossier as to the degree of immediacy of threat prior to the war taking place?
Mr Straw: The latter, Sir John. I would say this: of course I stand by it and I also stand by it in the context in which this was made. It is only, and the Chairman acknowledged this in his opening statement, since Mr Gilligan made these claims on May 29, which are false, that the 45 minutes has assumed any great significance at all. Of course it was part of the argument. Far from resiling from it, it was part of the argument, but it was not absolutely central in the way Mr Gilligan has claimed. The reason I did make the point I made about imminence was because the claim made, which this Committee subsequently responded to, from Mr Gilligan was that the 45 minutes was not just a detail, it went to the heart of the Government's case that Saddam was "an imminent threat". There is a difference, everybody understands that, and I am grateful to you for acknowledging this, between an "imminent and immediate threat" and the kind of threat which we described in a balanced and accurate way.

Q1286 Sir John Stanley: I did not acknowledge any substantial difference between a current threat coupled with a statement by the Prime Minister of 45 minutes away from activation of weapons of mass destruction. I just put this final point to you, Foreign Secretary. You are downplaying the significance of the 45 minutes. I put it to you as a question that it was actually very significant, not least for every Member of the British Parliament when they came to vote on March 18. I can tell you that it was a significant issue for me for this reason: every Member of the British Parliament knew when they came to vote to decide whether or not to support the Government on March 18 that if they did not support the Government and Saddam Hussein used those weapons of mass destruction held at 45 minutes readiness of activation then they would have to face their constituents as people who had not supported the Government when the Government was trying to remove those weapons of mass destruction which at that time could have caused massive casualties. I believe that was a very, very significant influence on a lot of Members of Parliament, the 45 minutes, when they came to vote.
Mr Straw: Sir John, I respect what you say. I was not downplaying it, I am just anxious that it should be put in context. I do say that it is of some interest—it will be to historians—that in the debate on 18 March and also in the 80 or 90 minute statement which I handled on 17 March I do not believe that 45 minutes claim was referred to on one occasion.

Q1287 Sir John Stanley: Can I just say why it was not referred to, Foreign Secretary. It was not referred to for the very simple reason that Members of Parliament of all sides accepted that this came from a reliable intelligence source and regarded it as not being an issue for debate. They took the Government's word for it.

Mr Straw: By that stage, Sir John, speaking for myself, and as you will recall I made the statement on 17 March and wound up on 18 March and made a number of Speeches in the Security Council, the argument for me was based on profound concern about Saddam Hussein's intent and capability, not least on his record of defiance following 1441. Chairman, can I just crave your indulgence now that Mr Ottaway is back in the room to give you some clarification on something he asked.

Chairman: Finish with Sir John and then you can clarify it.

Q1288 Sir John Stanley: I want to return to one question I put to you earlier this week. Can you produce any reason, other than American doubts about the credibility of the 45 minutes, why the Americans at no point ever used the 45 minutes?

Mr Straw: I do not know why they did not happen to use it. We do not have any doubt about the credibility of the assessment made by the JIC in September reflected in the dossier.

Q1289 Chairman: Can we have your response to Mr Ottaway?

Mr Straw: I have been passed a note. This is about whether the drafts were first, second or third. I have been passed a note to this effect, "I understand Mr Campbell will make it clear in the written material that he is going to provide to the Committee that the 45 minutes point was included in the first draft of the dossier which was presented to him by the Joint Intelligence Committee." I hope that is helpful.

Q1290 Richard Ottaway: This draft presented to him was not necessarily the first draft?

Mr Straw: That was why I was having to be conditional, because as I was seeking to explain, to be as accurate as possible, there was a whole series of draft, but it was the first draft presented to him.

Q1291 Mr Pope: I have got two really quick questions. The first one is did anybody in the SIS or the JIC object to the 45 minute claim?

Mr Straw: No.

Q1292 Mr Pope: The second question is Alastair Campbell, when he came before us earlier in the week, said that the head of SIS, the intelligence and security co-ordinator and the Chairman of JIC all authorised him—Campbell—to say that it is not true that he exaggerated or "sexed-up" that September dossier. As the Minister responsible for those services, do you stand by that?

Mr Straw: Absolutely, 100%. Let me make clear, nobody "sexed-up" or exaggerated that September dossier, no-one at all, and that includes Alastair Campbell.

Q1293 Chairman: One point of clarification. The point was made about the delays in passing the possible information to UNMOVIC and to IAEA. I recall in the evidence of Mr Taylor he expressed certain doubts about the security procedures and leakability of those organisations. Did you share any of those doubts?

Mr Straw: For sure. Mr Taylor, I thought, was very compelling in the evidence that he gave explaining that there is an inherent problem with United Nations agencies. They are not run by a single nation state, they are run by an international organisation, so the security problems are much greater. That is acknowledged by the UN. The senior people take a great deal of care to try and ensure that the information that is passed is kept secure but there are inherently greater problems and that was recognised both by UNSCOM when it was operating up to the end of 1998 and by UNMOVIC and the IAEA. That said, Chairman, I repeat the point because it is very important, I think you will find if you ask the IAEA and UNMOVIC whether they had good intelligence co-operation from the United Kingdom, they would say yes and would compliment both the quality and the range of the material they received.

Chairman: Foreign Secretary, we have covered substantial ground. I think it is now appropriate for us to move into private session and I would propose that we have a five minute break.

[The following evidence was taken in private. Material not published at the request of the witness is indicated by the notation ***]

Q1294 Chairman: Foreign Secretary, we are now on the transcript in private session and anything which is said will be negotiated between the two sides as to what can and cannot be disclosed. Foreign Secretary, you are a very busy person and we have also all got things to do, let us try and come straight to the point. You know the allegation which is made: the "sexed-up" dossier of 24 September, making the case from the first draft of the publication. What are you prepared to show us?

Mr Straw: Sorry?

Q1295 Chairman: What are you prepared to show us in private which can help to assist us in reaching a conclusion?

Mr Straw: What I am prepared to read to you, and I will do so as soon as we have recovered from our coffee break and find the relevant document, is the section of the JIC report that refers to this.

Q1296 Chairman: Could you produce the section, read it to us and tell us from where and when it comes so it can help to make up our minds.

Mr Straw: This is the JIC assessment of 9 September.

Q1297 Chairman: Was this the first assessment subsequent to the PM's decision?

Mr Straw: Yes.

Mr Ricketts: This was the formal JIC assessment, not a draft of the dossier. This was the formal JIC assessment which was then the basis for the dossier.

Q1298 Chairman: So could we read that?
Mr Straw: Sure. ***

Q1299 Sir John Stanley: This is very important. Could you just read that again slowly?
Mr Straw: The opening of the sentence is: ***

Q1300 Chairman: Let me just confer with colleagues and openly with you on this. It is a question now of whether we stop at each point. You have got a whole series of matters of that nature that you are going to put to the Committee, have you?
Mr Straw: That is really the whole basis on which the dossier was prepared as far as that point is concerned. I would also say to you, Chairman, and I know that you do not like me saying this and I do not want to start an argument here, the ISC is there and we have to respect that. *** we have dealt with all this and it is not—apart from the fact that I tell the truth unembroidered and so, of course, do officials, your insurance here is if for some mad reason I am not telling the truth, the ISC will have full access to your transcript, I hope, and to all the documents we are going to go through and will be saying, "Hang on a second, what Straw said is wrong" and they will be able to look through a lot of the background.

Q1301 Chairman: That is the key point that you want to make to us at this stage?
Mr Straw: By the way, I think we have also got most of the answer to Sir John's question.

Q1302 Chairman: On the munitions or the missiles?
Mr Straw: About yellow cake and Niger.
Chairman: Shall we deal with that first?

Q1303 Mr Maples: In quoting that point you said "munitions", so very specifically I take munitions to mean weapons other than missiles, things that are fired from artillery. Was that the sense in which it was used or was it more general than that?
Mr Ehrman: It could be from a variety of ways. It could be artillery. It could be bombs.

Q1304 Mr Maples: Could it be short-range missiles?
Mr Ehrman: It could be short-range missiles. It includes the lot.

Q1305 Mr Maples: So you see it as meaning the same as "weapons"?
Mr Ehrman: It is a generic word, "munitions".

Q1306 Mr Maples: You do not draw a distinction between "munitions" and "weapons"?
Mr Straw: I was going to ask Mr Ricketts and Mr Ehrman to give you some more detail about the source as well.
Mr Pope: That is what I wanted to ask. I wanted to ask about the source and which agency received the material.
Mr Maples: Let us go on with that because I think that is important. I would rather hear you than my question.

Chairman: John, I think you have asked your question.
Mr Maples: I had something else I wanted to ask but if Mr Ricketts is prepared to tell us about the source of the 45 minutes, let us go straight to that.
Chairman: Greg, that was your point as well.
Mr Pope: Which agency got the information?

Q1307 Chairman: Can we clear this point first.
Mr Ehrman: It is quite simple. ***

Q1308 Mr Maples: In Iraq?
Mr Ehrman: Yes.
Mr Straw: Can I just say this: our colleague, the Minister of State for Defence, Adam Ingram, said on the radio, quite correctly, that it was a single source. *** This man was judged to be very reliable.

Q1309 Mr Maples: *** ?
Mr Straw: ***

Q1310 Mr Illsley: How old was that piece of information by the time British intelligence received it? Are we talking about in the last few weeks or months before September or could it be a year or two years?
Mr Ehrman: The information on the 45 minutes came shortly before the JIC assessment on 9 September. It was British intelligence.

Q1311 Mr Illsley: It is just to gauge the age.
Mr Straw: There is a flow of reporting from Iraq and as these reports come in they are assessed, first of all digested by the relevant agency concerned and then they come forward, sometimes as freestanding reports for ministers and senior officials, sometimes it may not be appropriate to put it that way in a formal report. It was fed pretty quickly into the JIC process, was it not?
Mr Ehrman: It did come forward in a formal report. It is also perhaps worth emphasising that the reports themselves assess in almost all cases the reliability of the source and put comments on the source and how reliable it is thought to be.
Mr Straw: Caveats and things like that. I made this point the other day, but it is really a very important point, that the JIC system was set up to ensure that people who, quite naturally, were committed to their sources, the people in the front line, were not people also providing the assessment on them. Quite a lot of assessment is done within the relevant agency but even at that point it is passed on to the JIC for assessment.
Mr Ricketts: The agencies make an assessment of the reliability and credibility of their sources and then the JIC puts it together with other information. This 45 minute point, although it is a striking figure, was not at all out of the flow of our assessment of how Iraqi armed forces were deployed and their modus operandi, so it fitted into a broader pattern of what we knew about Iraqi armed forces.

Q1312 Mr Maples: I want to come back, if I may, to these points that I drew your attention to as to what I saw as the difference between the text and the

Executive Summary. In relation to the JIC assessment of 9 September you say on page 18 of the actual document at the end of paragraph one: "The JIC concluded that Iraq had sufficient expertise, equipment and material to produce biological warfare agents within weeks . . ." Are those the words that are used in the JIC assessment? I have got three of them, so would it help for you to find the lot?
Mr Ehrman: Yes.

Q1313 Mr Maples: The next one is at the beginning of the next paragraph where it says: ". . . Iraq retained some chemical warfare agents, precursors . . . These stocks would enable Iraq to produce significant quantities of mustard gas within weeks and of nerve agent within months." That is page 18, paragraph two. Finally, in paragraph four: "In the last six months the JIC has confirmed its earlier judgments on Iraqi chemical and biological warfare capabilities and assessed that Iraq has the means to deliver chemical and biological weapons." It is those three points.
Mr Ehrman: All of those points accurately reflect the 9 September JIC assessment.

Q1314 Mr Maples: Are those words pretty much used in that?
Mr Ehrman: Yes.

Q1315 Mr Maples: What I am getting at is in the Summary I think it is tougher.
Mr Straw: Mr Maples, you will have seen, and you picked up, "munitions" and "weapons".

Q1316 Mr Maples: You draw no distinction between them.
Mr Straw: I can understand the point you are making.
Mr Maples: I do draw a distinction, for instance, if we go back to the 45 minutes. At the end of the second paragraph on page 19 it says: "Intelligence indicates . . ." *** In paragraph six of the Executive Summary it says: ". . . we judge that . . . some of these weapons are deployable within 45 minutes . . ." I would argue that is stronger. Coming back to the other points, I am interested if the precise wording in the body of the document on pages 18 and 19, the words that I have quoted, is the wording that was used in that 9 September JIC document, or was it stronger?

Q1317 Chairman: That is a key question in terms of—
Mr Straw: However, the heading to the sentence in paragraph six on page five of the Executive Summary is: "As a result of the intelligence we judge . . ." ***

Q1318 Mr Maples: Okay. If I can make my other point. It says "continued to produce chemical and biological agents . . ." There is a slight ambiguity there.
Mr Straw: I do not mind telling you this, that what this says is: ***

Q1319 Mr Maples: That is in the JIC assessment?
Mr Straw: Yes.

Q1320 Mr Maples: Can you say that again?
Mr Straw: ***

Q1321 Mr Maples: *** ?
Mr Straw: ***

Q1322 Chairman: John asked three questions relating to the wording on pages 18 and 19. He asked whether those exact words had been transposed from the JIC assessment and I heard William Ehrman say "Yes". Was my hearing correct?
Mr Ehrman: I would have to actually sit down and look at the precise words but it is wholly consistent and, as the Foreign Secretary has read out, those were the words that were in the report.
Mr Straw: In some respects this document—***—is actually more cautious than the assessment.

Q1323 Mr Maples: If I can just complete this. I am interested, as you can imagine, in where the Executive Summary comes from. At what stage of the evolution of this document from 9 September until the end of the month, when this was ready for publication, did the Executive Summary come into existence?
Mr Ehrman: I cannot tell you was it this day or that day, but what I can tell you is when JIC assessments are being done they themselves essentially have an Executive Summary. So they put the key points at the front of an assessment, so this was—

Q1324 Mr Maples: So what was in them?
Mr Ehrman: The team who drafted the body of the report also drafted the Executive Summary.

Q1325 Mr Maples: So did that 9 September document you have quoted from have an Executive Summary appended to it?
Mr Ehrman: Yes, it did.
Chairman: Can we get an answer to that? It was a simple question from John.

Q1326 Mr Maples: He said, yes, it did have an Executive Summary appended to it or on the front of it. Is there some reason why we cannot see that?
Mr Straw: I will read it out to you: ***
Mr Maples: What I am—

Q1327 Chairman: Complete that and then we will continue.
Mr Straw: I am trying to be helpful.

Q1328 Mr Maples: You are not going to read the whole thing out, are you?
Mr Straw: No, I am going to read the whole of the Summary out.

Q1329 Mr Maples: I was going to ask if we can have it.

Mr Straw: *** That is almost word for word.

Q1330 Chairman: Is that the totality of the Executive Summary?
Mr Straw: No, sorry, that bit was from the body of the report.

Q1331 Mr Maples: I thought you were quoting from the Executive Summary.
Mr Straw: The Executive Summary had the *** points I read out.

Q1332 Chairman: The *** points you read out is the totality of the Executive Summary?
Mr Straw: Yes.

Q1333 Mr Chidgey: Foreign Secretary, you will obviously remember that I have been questioning you at some length about the—Can you hear me all right?
Mr Straw: Can I just say that Mr Ricketts has said that people are really worried about sharing this information. I have been doing my best, as I said I would. Mr Ricketts has pointed out that this is very highly classified and it is extremely important that it remains so—we will have to deal with what is there—because of the sourcing. People are still highly vulnerable. ***
Sir John Stanley: I do not want to say anything even now except to say I agree with everything you have said, Foreign Secretary.

Q1334 Mr Chidgey: Back to the more mundane after that, Foreign Secretary. You will recall over the course of these sessions I have been questioning you in more detail about the capability of Iraq to use their multi-use chemical and petro-chem industries to convert over to production of chemical and biological weapons. We have had a lot of evidence that points out the difficulties of making a distinction between the particular plant and what it is being used for and the ability to switch from one line of production to another at very short notice. The whole thrust of my questions to you, and you said you would respond to me on this,—
Mr Straw: I have sent you the answers. Have you not seen them?

Q1335 Mr Chidgey: I have not seen them yet, no. No matter, we can probably go a bit further.
Mr Straw: I signed them off last night.
Mr Illsley: Iraq 32.
Andrew Mackinlay: Chidgey's name is all over it.

Q1336 Mr Chidgey: I do apologise, Foreign Secretary. Clearly much of evidence that was being used by JIC was based on intelligence sources on the ground because that is the way it was. I really would have thought that you personally and your team would have been very, very keen to verify post-war the accuracy of the intelligence information you were getting, which obviously helped form the judgment that we should go to war in term of the capacity and the extent to which Iraq was able to launch a defence through using chemical and biological weapons. Can I say finally on this one before you answer me, it seems to me, generally speaking, when we have these meetings with our American friends about the "Axis of Evil" and whatever else, they are very good about telling us about the capability of other countries but they are very bad about telling us about the intent, and they leave it to politicians. It seems in this case we are very clear about the intent but not too sure about the ability, just as a throw-away remark.
Mr Straw: To pick up the point that you were making to me in the public session, we have as much interest as anybody else, and to a degree much greater, in finding as much corroborative evidence of the judgments that were being made in advance of military action. Aside from anything else. there is an obvious political dimension to this which is the more firm evidence we can get post war the more reassurance we can provide to people who have got questions about the decision to go to war. That goes without saying, I am really repeating myself. I am still very clear about the nature of the threat from Saddam, which was a combination of both our assessment about his capability, based on this remarkable evidence, most of which is public, and our judgment about his intent, again based on good evidence about his past behaviour. Also just in terms of the intelligence, not only am I concerned, as we all are, to get as much corroborative evidence now but, as I indicated to the Committee when I was giving evidence on Tuesday, aside from the JIC assessments, if I am presented with a piece of intelligence and I have got questions about it I will ask. It does not often happen because most of the time the stuff is clear, with the caveat what it is saying is clear, but sometimes I will send back a note on a piece of intelligence I have received saying "Get me more detail". In addition to that, *** on a number of occasions I discussed with heads of the agencies and other people, this is in very private conversation, the nature of the sources, whether the head of the agency really felt that they were reliable and accurate and so on, because I wanted to satisfy myself that they in turn really were being very careful about the sourcing and the reliability of the evidence we were getting through, and I was satisfied. I just want you to know that the assessments are made by the JIC, of course, but I start with all these things from a position of scepticism, as any good officer in the agencies will do, because of the nature of both human intelligence and others.

Q1337 Mr Chidgey: Can I just continue, I have had a chance to read your note quickly when you were talking, thank you very much for that, and it still does not provide us with anything further than was in the original September document, particularly in regard to the dual use of the plants at the Ibn Sina Research Centre. It still tells us that it has the capacity to deliver or to produce phenol and chlorine. It does not tell us there is any evidence that weaponised chemical weapons were produced?
Mr Straw: We have done our best to answer it. By the way, there is a typo on your question which was: "Was there any assessment made of surplus

production or devotion of production?", it should be "diversion" of production in the typed version you have got there.

Q1338 Mr Chidgey: I am sorry, can I just hear that answer again, I was not able to hear it because the Chairman was talking in my ear, I do apologise.

Mr Straw: I draw attention to the fact that in your question 2 we mis-typed it and I apologise. It says: "Was there any assessment made of surplus production or devotion . . .", it should be "diversion". That is the first point. The second point, and we have done our best to answer your questions here and answer them quickly, is a large part of the Iraqi's capability was based on dual-use facilities and that is inherent in the nature of chemical and biological weapons. It is to a degree with respect to nuclear weapons too. If you had had the pleasure of going through the endless pages of the Green List under 1284, the dual uses you will have seen that the United Nations got down to the description of the chemical compounds that could be used in a dual use way, this was hundreds and hundreds of pages that they, with the help the UNSCOM and UNMOVIC and others, had identified as dual-use compounds and engineering, so it is an immensely complicated area.

Q1339 Mr Chidgey: Very quickly, it has not been possible to confirm through analysis at those sites that there were production lines for chemical weapons rather than industrial use at this time?

Mr Ehrman: At this time, no. I mentioned to you what UNMOVIC had done in terms of going over some of those sites. The Foreign Secretary mentioned the sites that had been gone through since the war, the 159 as of 21 June, but we have nothing confirmed, as he said—

Q1340 Mr Chidgey: No trace elements whatever?

Mr Ehrman: There is nothing confirmed.

Q1341 Mr Pope: This is a brief point that follows on about chemical weapons. In the 45-minute claim what we are talking about here is artillery, for example, which can be deployed fairly quickly, but we did hear evidence before that it is not safe to keep the chemical elements of a missile in the missile, they have to be assembled forward as it were. It struck me as being quite surprising. I am sure we have come across the delivery systems, you can find the rocket launchers and mortars and so on, but we have not found any of the chemicals and I wanted a confirmation of whether or not we have found the chemicals or is it the case that the Iraq Survey Group is keeping it to themselves to disclose it all in one go, or is it just the case they have not found anything yet?

Mr Straw: I will ask Mr Ricketts to answer.

Mr Ricketts: No, the Iraq Survey Group are not keeping back a mountain of material to produce all at one time. I have no doubt that if they were to find some physical chemical weapons munitions that would become public pretty quickly.

Mr Illsley: I would have thought so as well

Q1342 Mr Pope: That is not necessarily the case. I can see why you would say that but there is also a case for not providing a running commentary on each small discovery that you make.

Mr Straw: Can I just say this: the most likely evidence would come from interviews and information provided by scientists. In their case it is highly probable that the Survey Group will decide to hold back on any kind of running commentary because if you do an interview with one person you will want to measure that against what others are saying. Let me say there is no decision of which I am aware that everything is going to be held back to the last minute.

Mr Pope: I have got other questions, I will come back to them.

Q1343 Richard Ottaway: It a question you said you would rather deal with in private. Are you still standing by the uranium statement, and what is the source?

Mr Ehrman: Yes, we certainly do not have a problem in standing by the uranium statement. If I can find the relevant page—We stand by the fact that the intelligence referred to in the dossier drew on information from more than one source and we remain confident in it. It is different from the information which the IAEA said later on was a forgery.

Mr Ricketts: Could we follow that up, just to go a little further in response to Sir John Stanley's questions about the reporting.

Mr Straw: We used the coffee break to try and find the answer.

Mr Ricketts: ***

Q1344 Andrew Mackinlay: *** ?

Mr Straw: ***

Mr Ehrman: ***

Q1345 Sir John Stanley: *** ?

Mr Ehrman: ***

Q1346 Richard Ottaway: I am happy for them to wrap up uranium because I have got one more question.

Mr Straw: Can I say this to Sir John, and it is on this, ***

Q1347 Richard Ottaway: This is an unrelated question. Did at any time the Government receive reports from intelligence agencies that Iraq was not an immediate threat?

Mr Ricketts: No, I do not recognise that as anything we have ever seen from the intelligence agencies.

Mr Straw: We have been over the ground about was the test an immediate threat and we have dealt with that pretty thoroughly and the adjective "imminent" has even been used. No one has ever suggested that there was a threat from Iraq that they were about to start a war the next day or the next week necessarily. That was a point made in the House of Commons by the Prime Minister on 24 September. We tried to present as balanced and comprehensive picture of the level of the threat as we could and, to repeat

27 June 2003   Rt Hon Jack Straw, Mr Peter Ricketts CMG and Mr William Ehrman CMG

myself, that was also shared by the Security Council. In fact, I was, and so was Mr Ricketts, completely immersed in negotiations on 1441 and the idea that the other 13 countries were somehow patsies is a total reversal of the truth. ***

Q1348 Richard Ottaway: The suggestion is that in March 2002 a report was received that Iraq was not an immediate threat.
Mr Ehrman: No.

Q1349 Richard Ottaway: That question was on the radio the other day.
Mr Straw: Let me just say, do not forget *The Guardian*—

Q1350 Richard Ottaway: There was a report on the radio.
Mr Straw: I know there was a report on the radio, but we have had to put up with all sorts of complete nonsense. *The Guardian* ran a lead story saying there were transcripts of a private and secret meeting that I had with Colin Powell on 4 March. We have to be aware of the fact that disinformation round here has been huge. They ran that story, we told them it was untrue. We told them I was not with Colin Powell on 4 February in New York, I was with Dominique de Villepin in Le Touquet on 4 February.

Q1351 Richard Ottaway: We have heard you on that.
Mr Straw: The fact it is on the radio or in the newspapers does not make it true.
Mr Ehrman: I think that what may be happening is a whole of lot of stories are getting conflated. There was a story that there was a report suppressed in March 2002 and some of the press reported it as a JIC assessment suppress; it was not. There was a JIC assessment on the Iraqi programmes that month and it was not suppressed, it was put up in the normal way. There was work that was being done on a public document which was not proceeded with and then I suppose that could got conflated so that this showed that Iraq was not a threat, but that is not the case.

Q1352 Mr Pope: In the September dossier there is a reference to the al-Hussein missile which has a range of 650 kilometres and could clearly reach our sovereign bases in Cyprus. I am sure I was not alone in thinking that was quite a shocking revelation, that our sovereign bases could be attacked, possibly with a chemical weapon. Was that assessment in the original JIC assessment? By the original JIC assessment I think I mean the one at the end of August.
Mr Ehrman: There was not one at the end of August, there was one on 9 September and one back in March.

Q1353 Mr Pope: September.
Mr Ehrman: Yes, that has been in all the JIC assessments.

Q1354 Mr Pope: Okay. At any stage did officials complain about pressure being put on them by special advisers or ministers or Number 10 in the drafting of these documents? One thing we have heard is that there was widespread concern in the intelligence community about the pressure that was put on the people doing the drafting.
Mr Ehrman: I have spoken to John Scarlett and he is absolutely clear that he was put in charge and he was put in charge on the basis that nothing was going to be published that he and the JIC were not happy with, and he is not aware, I think he said publicly he is not aware—

Q1355 Mr Pope: People have not complained verbally about pressure being put on them?
Mr Ehrman: No.
Mr Straw: It was a proper process. I have received no complaints whatever. Let me say that I have a direct relationship with the head of SIS and the head of GCHQ. I see them regularly. I see the head of SIS much more often than I see the head of GCHQ because it is a different operation, but they both report to me. As far as the head of SIS is concerned, I have seen him very regularly indeed in a variety of settings and he is not somebody who hides his light under a bushel. He does tell you things and what he feels about things and if there had been any suggestion there had been pressure on his staff that would have come to my notice through him and ditto with the JIC people who again we were seeing, and William and Peter would be very quickly through my door if they had felt that there was unacceptable pressure being put on X or Y?

Q1356 Chairman: What was the response of John Scarlett and his colleagues about the allegations that have been made about political interference?
Mr Ricketts: He does not accept them.

Q1357 Chairman: The printable response is that these allegations are untrue and, of course, they not only imply misconduct by politicians and special advisers but they also imply a dereliction of duty by him and by his colleagues, and neither are true.
Mr Ricketts: I entirely agree with that, but as a supplementary point I believe that the dossier was considered twice, on 11 and 18 September, in the full JIC, and from my open personal knowledge of the JIC it is not a body that would accept political interference in its judgments and assessments.
Mr Ehrman: John Scarlett is quite clear when he signed off that draft on 20 September it went to the printers then and he remained in charge of it through the printing process and he was quite happy with it.
Mr Straw: Can I make this point about the role of this Committee and the ISC, and this is a difference between now and 50 years ago, the level of accountability of ministers has increased phenomenally over this kind of detail. 50 years ago the only chamber was the House. Now we have to be conscious all the time, and absolutely rightly (I believe in this system) that if you do things for the wrong reasons or with inadequate information this will come out and come out quite quickly. The idea

that we would have had in mind publishing something that was not supportable by the best available evidence and assessment is mad because this would be have been us entering voluntarily into a suicide pact at a political level.

Chairman: Eric did not have any chance in the first part of the session.

Q1358 Mr Illsley: I want to follow on firstly to what you have just been saying. Do you completely dismiss Gilligan's accusations? Do you think there is no intelligence source or do you think—

Mr Straw: No, I think he has a source. I do not know this, I am offering you my belief, not evidence, he is somebody who obviously has *** contacts particularly with the MoD. I think he has a source and I think he spoke to somebody, I think that much is evident, but I do not know the nature of the conversation. I do know that some journalists sometimes slightly embroider what they are told.

Q1359 Mr Chidgey: A bit like politicians!

Mr Straw: I am talking about journalists.

Q1360 Mr Illsley: At a very senior level.

Mr Straw: But my best judgment again, Mr Illsley, not on the basis of evidence but trying to put two and two together, reading through his transcripts and so on, is that the person concerned is unlikely to have been centrally involved in the preparation of the dossier in any event, but I cannot be certain about that. What I can be certain about is that the key allegations which he made are simply wrong, they are literally and palpably untrue. I made that point in open session, to some interest from the left. The other point I keep making from the point of view of the history that you are writing is (because it would be very serious if it were wrong) is, as I have said, that the 45 minutes was part of the argument but it was not the totality of it.

Mr Ricketts: It was very striking reading the transcript of Mr Gilligan appearing before you in answering Sir John his insistence that the underlying intelligence referred to missiles, where it does not. There is a material point there, he was very insistent and he was wrong.

Q1361 Mr Illsley: Has the intelligence continued to come out of Iraq? Do we still continue to get intelligence assessments from Iraq and do they indicate that the weapons are still there or the chemicals are still there? Is there any information coming out of Iraq now to say, "We have got it wrong, chaps, we cannot find it."

Mr Ehrman: *** What needs to be borne in mind is that in the immediate aftermath of the war the priority task for the forces was security and starting reconstruction. So there were these exploitation teams that went to these sensitive sites and we have mentioned the number of sites that they have gone to, but I think that the Iraq Survey Group, that was deployed inter-country, are now going to put more emphasis on intelligence-led investigations and not simply going round the sites when those sites were on

a list with UNMOVIC so of course the Iraqis knew about them. So, yes, a great deal of evidence is being put into getting intelligence after the war as before it.

Mr Straw: If the point of your question has been have we had any clear proof that claims made in this document were wrong then no. I think I gave you a list in one of the earlier sessions. Some of the claims/ assessments in here have been proved to be correct and there are others that have not been disproved. There is quite an issue about the missile engines because what we are facing not in this Committee but often outside is people pocketing the things that prove this. On the missile engines it is quite an interesting story. Iraq declared—and do not forget one of the things we know *** is that the Iraqi government took rather an interest in this dossier—

Q1362 Mr Pope: I bet they did.

Mr Straw: We made claims about missiles in here, not in relation to 45 minutes but others. They claimed they had 151 Volga missile engines in their December 2002. An UNMOVIC inspection in January 2003 *** discovered 231 engines. The Iraqis then admitted, having been found red-handed—to have illegally imported a further 149 and an Iraqi engineer told UNMOVIC they had imported 567. A little vignette of how information had to be dragged out of the Iraqis. Since they had these hundreds of missile engines, which could, I gather, have a wide range of uses, and given everything else we knew, I think we were quite right to be worried. Evidence as it emerged was corroborating what was in here, not the reverse.

Q1363 Mr Illsley: You have absolutely no doubt in your mind that the evidence that this country received in relation to Iraq's weapons was good evidence?

Mr Straw: No, I have not.

Q1364 Mr Illsley: It was good intelligence?

Mr Straw: If you want my own personal experience of this, this is self-evidently the most serious matter I have ever had to deal with, and deciding to embark on the strategy as we did and then follow it through, conscious from an early stage that if we judged in the circumstances it was necessary, we would recommend to the Commons that military action was taken, was a very heavy responsibility so we had to think about these things very, very carefully. Moreover, I had to go into all of this in immense detail, first of all because of the intense discussions that were taking place with other members of the Security Council. Some days you get down to arguing about a certain passage. I remember one day I must have made 15 or 20 phone calls and I spoke to Powell seven times and twice to Ivanoff all on the same day. This is one illustration. Then of course post-441 we had these very, very intensive discussions inside the Security Council and I had discussions with Blix as well. I became more and more convinced about the case against Iraq, not less. ***

Q1365 Chairman: Before I call John, one quick question, has there been intelligence of destruction or concealment of WMD on the part of the Iraqis that has come to light since as a reason why we cannot find any?
Mr Ehrman: ***

Q1366 Chairman: Is there any intelligence on that?
Mr Ehrman: Perhaps I could say most of the sites known to have been associated with the programmes and the ones that have been visited have been looted to some extent, and some looting and destruction has been very specific, which might indicate an effort to conceal proscribed activity. Most ministry buildings in Baghdad were extensively looted and some evidence may have disappeared, as President Bush suggested.

Q1367 Chairman: Is there evidence from our own contacts that the Iraqi regime deliberately sought to destroy evidence of WMD prior to the conflict?
Mr Ehrman: ***

Q1368 Sir John Stanley: Could I have written answers, non-classified, to the questions which I put to you on uranium? The questions are on the public record. I would like to have written answers. I just want a written response on the timing of the forged documents, getting knowledge of those going to the British intelligence community, and whatever your response is on a non-classified basis about the question I put to you as to whether Britain had fulfilled its UN obligations to put the substantive material. Answer it in whatever terms you can but I would like a written response.
Mr Straw: I will provide as much as I can unclassified, some of it will have to be classified.

Q1369 Sir John Stanley: I would be grateful for whatever you can do on a classified or non-classified basis.
Mr Straw: We always do.

Q1370 Sir John Stanley: Thank you. There are a number of points I would like to put to you. You very helpfully read out the summary of the JIC assessment *** Does that raise any questions in your mind about the other areas of assessment?
Mr Straw: ***

Q1371 Sir John Stanley: It would be very helpful if you could read out again the wording in the Executive Summary.
Mr Straw: ***

Q1372 Sir John Stanley: ***
Mr Straw: ***

Q1373 Sir John Stanley: I know. All you can do is on the best you have got, I understand that. I am not making a criticism but it is an important fact.

Mr Straw: ***

Q1374 Sir John Stanley: That is a different point. What the military do is a different point. I am talking about the intelligence assessment.
Mr Ehrman: Can I just say one thing. *** I think it is true to say we do not know yet the reason why they did not use it on the battlefield. We hope we may find out but at the moment I think it is fair to say we do not know the reason. For the longer range missiles, post this assessment, post the dossier, there was information that they might have been seeking to conceal some of their long-range missiles from UNMOVIC, and may have even disassembled them into parts and hidden them, and then between UNMOVIC leaving and the war there was very little time so there may have been a physical constraint on getting those missiles into shape to fire, but for the battlefield munitions we do not know why.

Q1375 Sir John Stanley: There would be no such constraints, and I am coming to the battlefield munitions in a moment, but I just register that fact—
Mr Ricketts: ***

Q1376 Sir John Stanley: Yes, but with respect, the 45 minutes is not just an assessment of capability, it is also an assessment of the command and control systems relating to those weapons of mass destruction, and certainly in terms of the presentation which the Government made publicly there is a very real degree of suggestion of intention.
Mr Straw: Sure, we can speculate as to why Saddam did not use it.

Q1377 Sir John Stanley: I have covered that point. The next point I want to cover is that the assessment suggested—and you repeated it in public and it is also in the JIC assessment—that production of BW and CW is taking place. Now there is a lot of reference to capability but in the public statement made by the Prime Minister he said on 24 September: "Saddam has continued to produce them"—that is chemical and biological weapons—and you have confirmed to us today that the JIC assessment absolutely underpinned what the Prime Minister said to the House. The question on that is here we are, we have been all over Iraq, I know all about that it is quite easy to conceal BW production, but it is not so easy to conceal any significant scale of CW production. The assessment was that CW and BW were in production and it raises quite serious questions in my mind why so far not a stitch of those on-going production facilities have been uncovered.
Mr Straw: Of course we want to get the best evidence we can. Where we are at the moment is the point where we have reached. Mr Taylor explained in some detail the explanations for the delay in getting the Survey Group going. One of them to which I think he referred is that there had been an assumption in terms of military planning, based on best intelligence assessment, that the Iraqis would indeed use some of their chemical and biological capability and therefore we would not need to have a Survey Group afterwards because it would have

been obvious they had used them. In the event they decided not to. To come back to the point there is nothing in here which has been disproved and there is a good deal already which has been effectively corroborated.

Q1378 Sir John Stanley: I do not think on this particular issue, Foreign Secretary, you can rest on not disproving. The case was made in very specific, positive terms in terms of capabilities, possession of weapons systems and the scale of possession and so on. There is a very, very real wish and expectation that positive expectations were raised in terms of what Saddam Hussein had would be somehow fired. I have to put it to you if a year from now, let alone two years from now, nothing has turned up I do not think the Government is going to find it at all easy to rest on nothing has been disproved on the basis nothing was found.
Mr Straw: I note what you say. Can I also say with respect that the judgment that you will be wanting to make in producing your report on the decision to go to war is not a judgment based on 20/20 vision. It is a judgment based on whether what we were saying to the House and to the country between September and March was based on the best available evidence, the most objective analysis and the best and most rational judgment that we could bring to bear, and I believe that in all of those we satisfied the tests.

Q1379 Sir John Stanley: Yes, but there will be issues as to whether the intelligence supporting it justified the public position that the Government took.
Mr Straw: So long as we have not been able to find 10,000 litres of anthrax people who were in any case opposed to the war are going to say, "There you are." What they fail to take into account is the threat that was shared across the international community. ***
Sir John Stanley: There is the non-use and the CW and BW production and the third area which at the moment appears to have been basically disproved by events is the wording which you have now very helpfully shared with us that your source of the 45 minutes said that CBW munitions could be moved into place within 45 minutes. I am assuming the definition of "in place" is to weapons system or to artillery positions. Mr Ehrman is nodding. We do now know as a matter of fact, as I understand it, that no CW or BW storage sites have been found anywhere near the forward positions that the Iraqis had.

Q1380 Chairman: Is that correct?
Mr Ehrman: I am not aware, no, since the war we have not found any CW sites.

Q1381 Sir John Stanley: There has been a huge search of things within a 45 minute radius?
Mr Ehrman: Not a huge search, no, there has not. As I have mentioned, some of the sites have been gone through, a proportion of the sites, but the ISG, which is the sizable body, is only now deploying—

Q1382 Andrew Mackinlay: New sites have been found.
Mr Straw: I want to underline the point Mr Ehrman made a little while ago. We have a serious problem in terms of the work of the Survey Group because of the looting and disruption of sites.

Q1383 Sir John Stanley: I want to ask you to clarify, and this is a very important point that was not clear to me when you got on to discussing the source of the 45 minutes. As I understood you in what you said, we are talking about ***
Mr Ehrman: Yes.

Q1384 Sir John Stanley: *** ?
Mr Ehrman: ***

Q1385 Sir John Stanley: *** ?
Mr Ehrman: ***

Q1386 Sir John Stanley: All sorts of people have all sorts of motivation. In terms of testing this it is quite evident that your *** source out there has a very high degree of reliability but the question certainly in my mind is whether the *** source might have been wanting to create a favourable position for himself if the worst happened or whether he was in a trade. There are all sorts of questions in my mind. Let's remember the whole of this 45 minutes hangs on this one source. Just before everybody jumps in, I am not going to give any credence to the manipulation accusation that Mr Gilligan has made but Mr Gilligan's source has proven to be spot on in two respects, spot on in saying to Mr Gilligan there was one single source, confirmed by the Government. He has also proved to be spot on in your evidence today Foreign Secretary, that the 45 minute intelligence came at the last moment shortly before the publication of the document. Again he said that.
Mr Ricketts: He has also been proved to be dead wrong in saying relating to missiles.

Q1387 Sir John Stanley: I am not giving any credence to that, but everything we have now heard suggests that he was a well-placed source.
Mr Straw: How well-placed I do not know. I would make this point about the reliability of sources.

Q1388 Sir John Stanley: Is there anything specific you can tell us. This is a very key point on the *** person who provided the information.
Mr Straw: Sir John, allow me to make this point. ***
Mr Ricketts: Could I add two points in amplification of the Foreign Secretary. This did fit with our assessment of the *modus operandi* of Iraqi sources and our knowledge of them in the past so it is not arriving in a vacuum. Secondly, as the Foreign Secretary says, the Secret Intelligence Service are professionals and are having to deal with these questions all the time as to whether sources or sub-sources are exaggerating or have a personal agenda, and in the judgment of the professionals this was a credible source *** So the advice of the professionals to us is that they checked and they checked down the line rigorously about this report.

Q1389 Sir John Stanley: In the key word you used Mr Rickets, ultimately it came down a judgment.

Mr Ricketts: Everything does in this business, I think Sir John.

Sir John Stanley: Judgment, single source, and a lot of profile (and in my view more than profile) hung on the decision to put this into the document. But anyway, I fully accept that the JIC community—and I have got the highest possible respect and I was, as you know, trenchant in the session with Andrew Gilligan about the implications that his accusations were having for the integrity of the security services, which I thought were totally unjustified, and that is still very much my position.

Mr Pope: Chairman, what time are you intending to end this session?

Chairman: We did say midday and I am aware Fabian has not yet had any input.

Andrew Mackinlay: I have not had an input at all in this private session and I have been waving at you.

Chairman: A number of colleagues want get in. Fabian?

Mr Hamilton: I think colleagues who have been here the whole time should pick up first and I will step in.

Q1390 Andrew Mackinlay: Our colleagues on the Hill, Carl Levin, the senior Democrat in the Senate Armed Services Committee and another guy, criticised and probed in comparable sessions to here whether the CIA had been as forthcoming with intelligence to UNMOVIC as they should have been. I know you do not answer for the CIA but because we are in private session, do you think the United States were as up-front as they could or should have been or did the United Kingdom have to prompt them, what is your read of the candour from that side?

Mr Straw: Honestly, Mr Mackinlay, you would have to ask the CIA and UNMOVIC that. I genuinely cannot answer for the CIA.

Q1391 Andrew Mackinlay: You are happy, in other words?

Mr Straw: They were co-operating at the time and we co-operated a great deal. I know the CIA were co-operating. ***

Q1392 Andrew Mackinlay: ***

Mr Straw: We co-operated fully. ***

Q1393 Andrew Mackinlay: I would have thought that could be woven into the public domain, this lack of discussion between—

Mr Straw: ***

Q1394 Andrew Mackinlay: We were right in history at the time as well. The third and final point I want to go to is going back to this business not so much of Gilligan and the BBC and your colleagues in government, but I am concerned about the constitutional point. It is a matter of fact if you go back to Chapman Pincher and the guys like the academic whom you authorised (or your predecessor did) the Mitrokhin papers, but the point—

Mr Straw: ***

Q1395 Andrew Mackinlay: What I am trying to say is demonstrably there are people at high level who either by convention or specific authorisation do talk to journalists/academics and it has struck me throughout these hearings that it needs to be re-visited because it does seem to me there is an absence of ground rules, that while there is this tremendous culture of secrecy, quite prudently, quite correctly, you cautioned about this today, absolutely, there is one glaring area where there is a licence. Really all I want to ask you is do you not think now in the light of what has happened and the representations we have made there is a need right across the security intelligence services to re-visit the ground rules? I am not saying you do not have an intercourse with these folk but it is a bit anarchical.

Mr Straw: I do not think it is anarchical. I understand the point you are making, it was an authorised publication.

Q1396 Andrew Mackinlay: I do not want to go down that road.

Mr Straw: I said what I said in open session on Tuesday about the integrity of the staff in the agencies. I also spelt out these arrangements for there to be some press briefing of journalists, (who have to be trusted to a degree because otherwise the relationship would not be there) by people acting on behalf of the heads of agencies. I do not find that a problem because the consequence of much greater public parliamentary scrutiny of what the agencies are doing is they have to be able to explain in broad terms what they are doing to a degree they did not have to 50 years ago. 50 years ago the existence of SIS, the Security Service and GCHQ was denied and none of those were statutory bodies either. What can I say except to say that I understand the point that you are making. ***

Q1397 Andrew Mackinlay: ***

Mr Straw: ***

Chairman: Time is short and four colleagues want to make, hopefully, brief questions, Fabian, John Maples, David and Greg. Not David? Thank you, David.

Q1398 Mr Hamilton: Apologies I was late, Network Rail, I am afraid. I will try and be very brief. On the question of the rocket engine I thought this was a very good illustration of the way that the Iraqi regime was constantly trying to lie and pull the wool over the eyes of UNMOVIC inspectors. You mentioned there was evidence, I think I am right, from one of the *** people that they had imported 500 of them. My question is do we know how powerful those engines might have been? I do not understand rocket technology but great play has been made of the fact that ballistic missiles were being developed that could have reached Cyprus and Israel.

Mr Straw: They have a variety of applications but they were using them, I am reliably informed, in the Al-Samoud 2 missiles which had a range of up to 200 kilometres.

Mr Ehrman: And which were declared by UNMOVIC to be illegal.

Q1399 Mr Hamilton: Can these rocket engines be adapted to go further? Can you put three engines in a rocket to make it go three times as far?

Mr Straw: They tried I am told. We will send you a note.

Q1400 Mr Hamilton: I am sorry to go back to this wretched BBC/Andrew Gilligan business, the reason we are all going on about it, well certainly my concern is it is hugely damaging.

Mr Straw: Of course.

Q1401 Mr Hamilton: One of the things I put to Alastair Campbell, and he was not qualified to make a judgment on this, is if we are absolutely sure, the Government is absolutely certain, JIC is absolutely certain that its assessment of intelligence is right, from what you are saying, can there not be a break with precedent, can you not show one of the senior executives at the BBC under oath the assessments that you have got to lay the whole matter to rest?

Mr Straw: It is an interesting idea. Let me just say that. I think they will probably wait for your inquiry amongst other things and the ISC, but there is a prior issue here which is that ministers and officials are not in the business of telling lies and one of the problems we have got with modern journalistic culture is that in the BBC, and for example just before you came I mentioned *The Guardian,* you can say to these people this is simply wrong and they will go ahead and print it. As parliamentary accountability of ministers has increased and I believe the standards which were high anyway have gone up because of the increase in that accountability and other things, so the standard of journalistic culture in this country has gone down, and we all suffer from it.

Q1402 Mr Hamilton: The problem is that the public believes that journalists are telling the truth and politicians are lying?

Mr Straw: I know. It is damaging for everybody, not just the party.

Q1403 Mr Hamilton: Of course it is.

Mr Straw: I take note of the point you make, Mr Hamilton.

Q1404 Mr Hamilton: Thank you very much. One final very brief point. Obviously the other big concern is that the public believe that the intelligence was dodgy, the 45 minutes thing we have heard about, the uranium question—

Mr Straw: We did deal with that.

Mr Hamilton: All right. I will not deal with that then.

Q1405 Mr Maples: Foreign Secretary, in paragraph four of the confidential document which you have made available to us, in relation to this dossier it says: "4. Representatives from the Number 10 and FCO press offices were present on at least one occasion". Were they present on the same occasion?

Mr Straw: I do not know, sorry. I assume so. Yes, they were.

Q1406 Mr Maples: Who were those people?

Mr Straw: ***

Q1407 Mr Maples: Do you know whether or not Alastair Campbell was present at any of those meetings?

Mr Straw: He was not at that meeting, I am told. I am told by the other side he was at neither meeting.

Q1408 Mr Maples: He was at neither meeting that either of you two were present at?

Mr Straw: No.

Q1409 Andrew Mackinlay: That gentlemen is whom?

Mr Straw: ***

Q1410 Mr Maples: In the document which you circulated to us describing how this thing came into being, answers to our very original questions, we asked you "Did ministers or special advisers ask for amendments to the document before it was published". You said "As noted, ministers and special advisers offered comments during the drafting process in the normal way". In this document, in the red folder, you refer to yourself and Mr O'Brien offering comments but you do not refer to special advisers offering comments. I wonder, presumably special advisers did offer comments or you would not have said it, and who was the special adviser who offered comments?

Mr Straw: I have two special advisers, both are here. Dr Williams did not offer any comments and Mr Owen offered some drafting ones.

Q1411 Mr Maples: Do your special advisers normally see checked reports?

Mr Straw: They see ones as relevant.

Mr Ricketts: Provided they are cleared to do so.

Q1412 Mr Maples: I was going to ask about their level of clearance.

Mr Ehrman: Providing they are appropriately cleared.

Mr Straw: They are highly reliable, my special advisers.

Q1413 Mr Maples: We were told by Dame Pauline Neville Jones that when she was Chairman of JIC no special adviser would ever have seen a JIC report.

Mr Ricketts: With respect, the world has moved on a bit since Dame Pauline was Chairman of the JIC.

Q1414 Mr Maples: It has moved on because the whole place is stuffed full of politically appointed special advisers.

Mr Straw: Hang on a second, that is not true. When I worked as one of the first political advisers in the 1974 Government there were two. I have two. It has actually not changed that much.

Mr Maples: Your press secretary is a political appointment too.

Q1415 Chairman: Move on, Mr Maples

Mr Straw: I have got to go, that is what has changed.

Q1416 Mr Maples: Paragraph eight says the Executive Summary was drafted by the same people as the co-ordinated document. The foreword to the dossier was drafted in Number 10. Do you know who drafted it?

Mr Straw: I do not, no. It went back to the JIC.

Q1417 Mr Maples: Can I ask you one really final question. You said in reading out bits of the Executive Summary to us that they really were substantially the same as what was eventually published in the document. Would it be fair to say that the Executive Summary to the 9 September document is, in all material respects, the same as the Executive Summary?

Mr Straw: I think the JIC report is in all material respects the same. The Executive Summary of the JIC report is much shorter than that. Bear in mind, that drew also from open sources as well, the history of that.

Q1418 Mr Maples: What I am going to ask you—

Mr Straw: Sorry, Mr Anderson, I am afraid I am really going to have to go.

Q1419 Mr Maples: Can I ask you, could we read, in confidential conditions, the Executive Summary to the 9 September report and compare it with—

Mr Straw:—I gave it to you completely. I dictated it.

Q1420 Mr Maples: It is on the record.

Mr Straw: Yes.

Q1421 Mr Maples: The whole thing?

Mr Straw: Yes.

Mr Maples: Okay.

Q1422 Mr Pope: My final question is Gilligan has four sources and one of them, he said, had sight of a GIS document that he said was classified "Top Secret". I am not an expert on the Official Secrets Act, that would seem to me, at least, *prima facie*, a breach of the Officials Secret Act. Will there be an inquiry to find out who those sources are?

Mr Straw: *** It is a matter for senior people in the MoD, I think. I am sure they will be pursuing the matter.

Chairman: Jack, you are busy and you have given us the time. Can I thank you and your advisers and close the meeting.

Written evidence

APPENDIX 3

ANALYSIS OF THE FEBRUARY 2003 DOSSIER BY ANDREW MACKINLAY MP

This copy of the February dossier entitled "Iraq 'Its Infrastructure of Concealment, Deception and Intimidation" has been analysed with the help of Dr Rangwala's evidence.

The following styles will be used to emphasize;

| Material copied from Mr Al-Marashi's article in Middle East Review of International Affairs.

|| Material copied from Mr Boyne's or Mr Gause's articles in Jane's Inteligence Review.

||| Comments which are in contradiction to Dr Blix's evidence (See Dr Rangwala's evidence to the Committee[1].

IRAQ—ITS INFRASTRUCTURE OF CONCEALMENT, DECEPTION AND INTIMIDATION

This report draws upon a number of sources, including intelligence material, and shows how the Iraqi regime is constructed to have, and to keep, WMD, and is now engaged in a campaign of obstruction of the United Nations Weapons Inspectors.

Part One focusses on how Iraq's security organisations operate to conceal Weapons of Mass Destruction from UN Inspectors. It reveals that the inspectors are outnumbered by Iraqi intelligence by a ratio of 200 to 1.

Part Two gives up to date details of Iraq's network of intelligence and security organisations whose job it is to keep Saddam and his regime in power, and to prevent the international community from disarming Iraq.

Part Three goes on to show the effects of the security apparatus on the ordinary people of Iraq.

While the reach of this network outside Iraq may be less apparent since the Gulf War of 1990–91, inside Iraq, its grip is formidable over all levels of society. Saddam and his inner circle control the State infrastructure of fear.

Part One: The Effect on UNMOVIC

The role of the Inspectors is to monitor and verify the disarmament of Iraq as demanded by the international community at the end of the Gulf War, 12 years ago. Inspectors are not a detective agency: They can only work effectively if the Iraqi Regime co-operates pro-actively with the Inspectors. We know this can be done successfully: South Africa did it.

But Iraq has singularly failed to do this.

Iraq has deliberately hampered the work of the Weapons Inspectors. There are presently around 108 UN Weapons Inspectors in Iraq–a country the size of France. They are vastly outnumbered by over 20,000 Iraqi Intelligence officers, who are engaged in disrupting their inspections and concealing Weapons of Mass Destruction. This is a ratio of 200 to 1. Even with the obstruction, concealment and intimidation, the inspectors have made a number of significant and disturbing findings.

But as Hans Blix reported to the UN Security Council on 27 January,: "It is not enough to open doors. Inspection is not a game of catch as catch can".

Documents

The Iraqi security organisations work together to conceal documents, equipment, and materials.

The Regime has intensified efforts to hide documents in places where they are unlikely to be found, such as private homes of low-level officials and universities. There are prohibited materials and documents being relocated to agricultural areas and private homes or hidden beneath hospitals and even mosques.

This material is being moved constantly, making it difficult to trace or find without absolutely fresh intelligence.

And those in whose homes this material is concealed have been warned of serious consequences to them and their families if it is discovered.

---

[1] Ninth Report from the Foreign Affairs Committee, Session 2002–03, *The Decision to go to War in Iraq,* HC 813-II, Ev 30.

Surveillance

The Iraqis have installed surveillance equipment all over hotels and offices that UN personnel are using. All their meetings are monitored, their relationships observed, their conversations listened to.

Telephone call are monitored. Al-Mukhabarat, the main intelligence agency, listen round the clock. Al-Mukhabarat made telephone calls to inspectors at all hours of the night during the days of UNSCOM. Intelligence indicates they have plans to do so again to UNMOVIC.

Inspectors meet to co-ordinate activities–the meeting rooms are arranged for the inspectors by the Iraqis and contain eavesdropping devices. Hidden video cameras monitor the progress of meetings, to check the faces of the inspectors and to identify the key personalities.

Monitoring

From the moment the UNMOVIC personnel enter Iraq, their every movement is monitored.

They are escorted by seemingly helpful security guards and almost all of them are members of the Al-Mukhabarat. If the driver is an Iraqi, he is Al-Mukhabarat too.

Journeys are monitored by security officers stationed on the route if they have prior intelligence. Any changes of destination are notified ahead by telephone or radio so that arrival is anticipated. The welcoming party is a give away.

Escorts are trained, for example, to start long arguments with other Iraqi officials "on behalf of UNMOVIC" while any incriminating evidence is hastily being hidden behind the scenes.

Al Mukhabarat have teams whose role is to organise car crashes to cause traffic jams if the Inspectors suddenly change course towards a target the Iraqi wish to conceal. Crashing into inspectors' cars was a ploy often used on UNSCOM.

Interviews

Venues for any possible interviews between inspectors and scientists or key workers are arranged by Iraqis. They are then monitored by listening devices and sometimes video. Most of the staff in the building where interviews take place are Al-Mukhabarat officers, there to observe any covert behaviour such as whispered conversations, the passing of notes or conversations away from microphones.

The interviewees will know that they are being overheard by Iraqi intelligence or security.

The inspectors want to interview some key people outside Iraq, without minders. All scientists and key workers have been made to draw up a list of their relatives by Al Mukhabarat. The interviewees know only too well what will happen to them, or their relatives still in Iraq, if it is even suspected that they have said too much or given anything away.

None have agreed to be interviewed outside Iraq.

Inspection Technology

The inspectors use sophisticated technology to detect hidden Iraqi programmes. Many of these are safety systems from the nuclear and chemical industries which are also available to the Iraqis.

When a detectable chemical or substance is hidden, the Iraqis do not just hide it and hope the Inspectors will not find it. They check that the technologies which they know the Inspectors have and use will not detect what they have hidden.

For example when an illicit piece of equipment (say a missile warhead) or substance is buried by the Iraqis, they make sure it stays hidden by using Ground Penetrating Radar to determine whether the inspectors will be able to detect the cache.

Psychological Pressure

Before UNMOVIC personnel arrive in Iraq, their names are sought by at least one and probably several of the Iraqi intelligence and security services. They will find out as much as possible. Do they have family, do they have any weaknesses that can be exploited? Are they young, nervous, vulnerable in some way?

The inspectors' personal security and peace of mind is a concern both to the individal inspectors and to UN management. So the Iraqis disrupt their work and daily lives by staging demonstrations wherever they go and having stooges making threatening approaches to Inspectors–such as the Iraqis who recently tried to enter the Inspectors' compound armed with knives or climbed into UN vehicles which were going out on an inspection. The whole effect is one of intimidation and psychological pressure.

Part Two: The Security Apparatus

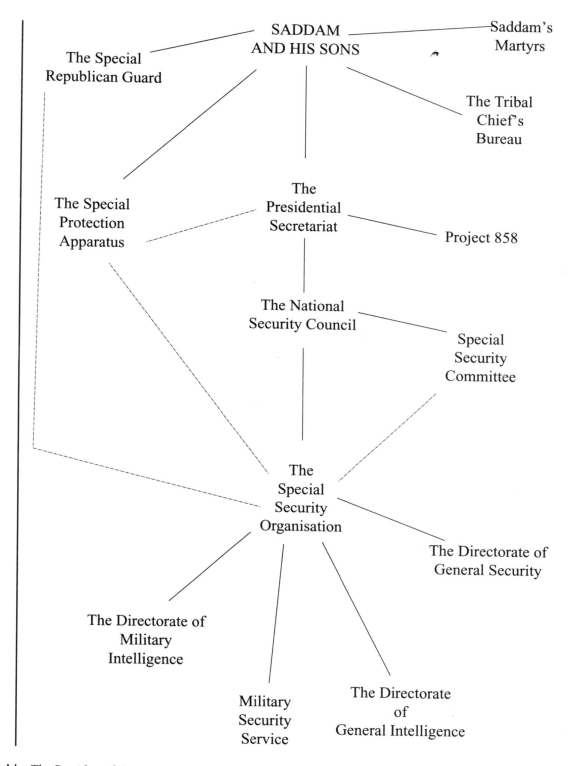

The Presidential Secretariat

The Presidential Secretariat has around 100 staff, who are drawn from the security agencies. The Secretariat is responsible for Saddam's personal security, as well as defence, security and intelligence issues.

It is overseen by Saddam's personal secretary, Lieutenant General Abid Hamid Mahmud. Mahmud is Saddam's distant cousin and is the sheikh of both the Al-Bu-Nasir and Al-Khattab tribes.

Mahmud is regarded by some as the real number two figure in the Iraqi leadership. He controls all access to Saddam–possibly with the exception of Qusay and Uday Hussein–and has the ability to override government decisions.

Al-Majlis Al-Amn Al-Qawni
The National Security Council

Headed by Saddam Hussein but usually chaired by his son Qusay Hussein, it oversees the work of all other security agencies.

Membership in Majlis Al-Amn Al-Qawni includes chosen people from;

— Iraqi Army.
— Special Security Service.
— General Intelligence Directorate.
— Military Intelligence.
— General Security Service.
— Office of the Presidential Palace.
— Majlis Al-Amn Al-Qawni, headquartered at the Presidential Palace in Baghdad, meets on a weekly basis.

Special Security Committee

Qusay Hussein is the deputy chairman of the Special Security Committee of the Iraqi National Security Council that was created in 1996 as part of the President's office.

The Committee membership includes:

— Tahir Jalil Habbush al-Tikriti, the director of the Public Security Directorate.
— Dahham al-Tikriti, Director of the Iraqi Intelligence Service–Al Mukhabarat.
— Abid Hamid Mahmud, the president's personal secretary.
— Faris 'Abd-al-Hamid al-'Ani, the director general of the Presidential office

This special body also includes representatives of the Republican Guard.
The Committee is supported by over 2,000 staff. The staff is drawn from the Republican Guard, or the Special Guard, and the intelligence services.
Their main task is preventing the United Nations inspectors from uncovering information, documents, and equipment connected with weapons of mass destruction.

They are recruited for this specific mission and chosen from the most efficient and loyal units.

The work is divided between two sections, each of which has a staff of about 1,000.

The first section focuses on the daily work of the UN monitoring commission, including sites to be visited and inspected, escorting UN inspectors, preventing them from carrying out their mission effectively.

The second section conceals documents, equipment, and materials and moves them about from one location to another. Several facilities have been especially built for collecting and hiding such selected material. This section is responsible for material that is imported through "special channels" as part of the programme of rebuilding the strategic military arsenal, including chemical and biological weapons as well as missiles and associated technology.

Al-Mukhabarat The Directorate of General Intelligence

4,000 people.

Created out of the Ba'ath party.

Al-Mukhabarat is roughly divided into a department responsible for internal operations, co-ordinated through provincial offices, and another responsible for international operations, conducted from various Iraqi embassies.

Its internal activities include:

— spying within the Ba'th Party, as well as other political parties;
— suppressing Shi'a, Kurdish and other opposition;
— counter-espionage;
— targeting threatening individuals and groups inside Iraq;
— spying on foreign embassies in Iraq and foreigners in Iraq;
— maintaining an internal network of informants.

Its external activities include:

— spying on Iraqi diplomats abroad;
— collecting overseas intelligence;
— supporting terrorist organisations in hostile regimes;

— conducting sabotage, subversion, and terrorist operations against neighbouring countries such as Syria and Iran;

— murder of opposition elements outside of Iraq;

— infiltrating Iraqi opposition groups abroad;

— providing dis-information and exploitation of Arab and other media; and

— maintaining an international network of informants, using popular organisations as well such as the Union of Iraqi Students.

It has long been known that Al-Mukhabarat uses intelligence to target Iraqis. It forces Iraqis living abroad to work for Saddam by threatening dire consequences for relatives still inside Iraq.

It is reported that an Iraqi cannot work for a foreign firm inside Iraq without also working for Al-Mukhabarat directly or as an informant. This includes those allowed to work with foreign media organisations.

All Iraqis working with foreigners have to have a special permit which is not granted unless they work for Al-Mukhabarat.

They carry out tests which include approaches to Iraqi officials with false information to see whether they report it to Baghdad or foreigners.

Al-Amn al-Aam The Directorate of General Security

8,000 people.

The oldest security agency in the country.

The Al-Amn Al-Aam supports the domestic counter-intelligence work of other agencies.

As a policy, Saddam staffs key positions in Al-Amn Al-Aam with his relatives or other close members of his regime.

In 1980, Saddam appointed 'Ali Hassan al-Majid, who would later be the architect of the regime's anti-Kurdish campaign, as its director to instill the ideology of the Ba'ath Party into the agency.

Al-Amn Al-Aam was given more political intelligence responsibilities during the Iran-Iraq War. When Majid was put in charge of repressing the Kurdish insurrection of 1987, General 'Abdul Rahman al-Duri replaced him until 1991 when Saddam Hussein's half-brother, Sabawi Ibrahim al-Tikriti (who had served as its deputy director prior to 1991), then became head of this agency.

In 1991, Saddam Hussein provided it with a paramilitary wing, Quwat al-Tawari, to reinforce law and order, although these units are ultimately under Al Amn al-Khas control.

After the 1991 Gulf War, Quwat al-Tawari units were believed to be responsible for hiding Iraqi ballistic missile components. It also operates the notorious Abu Ghuraib prison outside of Baghdad, where many of Iraq's political prisoners are held.

Each neighbourhood, every office and school, every hotel and coffee shop has an officer assigned to cover it and one or more agents in it who report what is said and what is seen.

Al-Amn Al-Aam runs a programmes of provocation where their agent in a coffee house or work place will voice dissident views and report on anyone who agrees with those views.

An Al-Amn Al-Aam agent or officer will sometimes approach an Iraqi official pretending to recuit him for some opposition or espionage purpose and then arrest him if he does not report it.

They also look for foreigners who might be breaking Iraqi law or seeking to stir up anti-regime feelings among native Iraqis.

Technically, it is illegal for an Iraqi official or military officer to talk to a foreigner without permission from a security officer.

Al Amn al-Khas.
The Special Security Organisation

2,000 people.

The most powerful and most feared agency, headed by Qusay Hussein.

It is responsible for

— the security of the President and of presidential facilities;

— supervising and checking the loyalty of other security services;

— monitoring government ministries;

— supervising operations against Iraqi Kurds and Shias; and

— securing Iraq's most important military industries, including WMD.

The Al-Amn al-Khas is nebulous and highly secretive and operates on a functional, rather than a geographical, basis.

Qusay Hussein supervises the Special Bureau, the Political Bureau and the Administration Bureau, the agency's own military brigade, and the Special Republican Guard.

Its own military brigade serves as a rapid response unit independent of the military establishment or Special Republican Guard. In the event of a coup attempt from within the regular military or Republican Guard, Special Security can call up the Special Republican Guard for reinforcements as this unit is also under its control.

— The Security Bureau: The Security Bureau is divided into a Special Office, which monitors the Special Security agency itself to assure loyalty among its members. If necessary, it conducts operations against suspect members. The Office of Presidential Facilities, another unit of the Security Bureau, guards these places through Jihaz al-Hamaya al-Khas (The Special Protection Appartaus). It is charged with protecting the Presidential Offices, Council of Minsters, National Council, and the Regional National Command of the Ba'ath Party, and is the only unit responsible for providing bodyguards to leaders.

— The Political Bureau: The Political Bureau collects and analyses intelligence and prepares operations against "enemies of the state". This unit keep an extensive file on all Iraqi dissidents or subversives. Under the Political Bureau, the Operations Office implements operations against these "enemies", including arrests, interrogations and executions. Another division is the Public Opinion Office, responsible for collecting and disseminating rumours on behalf of the state.

The operations of Special Security are numerous, particularly in suppressing domestic opposition to the regime. After its creation in 1984, Special Security thwarted a plot of disgruntled army offices, who objected to Saddam's management of the Iran-Iraq War. It pre-empted other coups such as the January 1990 attempt by members of the Jubur tribe to assassinate him.

It played an active role in crushing the March 1991 Shi'a rebellion in the south of Iraq. Along with General Intelligence, Special Security agents infiltrated the Kurdish enclave in the north of Iraq in August 1996, to hunt down operatives of the Iraqi opposition.

It serves as the central co-ordinating body between Military-Industrial Commission, Military Intelligence, General Intelligence, and the military in the covert procurement of the necessary components for Iraq's weapons of mass destruction.

During the 1991 Gulf War, it was put in charge of concealing SCUD missles and afterwards in moving and hiding documents from UNSCOM inspections, relating to Iraq's weapons programmes.

It is also thought that Special Security is responsible for commerical trade conducted covertly in violation of UN sanctions.

The members of Al-Amn al-Khas are primarily drawn from Saddam's own tribe, the Abu Nasr, or from his home district of Tikrit.

Jihaz al-Hamaya al-Khas.
The Special Protection Apparatus

Charged with protecting Presidential Offices, the Council of Ministers and the Regional and National Commands of the Ba'ath Party.

It is the only organisation responsible for providing boydguards to the very top of the regime.

Approximately 40 personal bodyguards are responsible for Saddam's immediate security.

Al-Istikhbarat al-Askariyya.
The Directorate of Military Intelligence

6,000 people.

Its main functions are ensuring the loyalty of the army's officer corps and gathering military intelligence from abroad. But it is also involved in foreign operations, including assassinations.

Unusually the heads of Al-Istikhbarat al-Askariyya have not been immediate relatives of Saddam.

Saddam appointed Sabir'Abd al-'Aziz al-Duri as head during the 1991 Gulf War. After the Gulf War he was replaced by Wafiq Jasim al-Samarrai.

After Samarrai, Muhammad Nimah al-Tikriti headed Al-Istikhbarat al-Askariyya in early 1992 then in late 1992 Fanar Zibin Hassan al-Tikriti was appointed to this post.

These shifting appointments are part of Saddam's policy of balancing security positions. By constantly shifting the directors of these agencies, no one can establish a base in a security organisation for a substantial period of time. No one becomes powerful enough to challenge the President.

Al-Amn al-Askari.
Military Security Service

6,000 people.

Established as an independent entity in 1992, its function is to detect disturbances in the military.

The Amn was initially headquartered in the Batawen district of Baghdad. In 1990 Amn moved to a new headquarters in the Al Baladiat area of the city, with the Bataween building becoming the agency's main prison.

The Secret Police also has a number of additional facilities and office buildings. Amn maintains a presence in every town and village, with personnel stationed in civilian police stations across Iraq—normally the "ordinary" police are on the ground floor and the Secret Police on the second floor.

The Security branch is responsible for monitoring and countering dissent within Amn, and the Military Brigade provides rapid intervention para-military capabilities—the Brigade commander was executed in August 1996 for alleged involvement in a coup attempt.

Amn is currently headed by Staff Major General Taha al Ahbabi, who previously headed the Military Security Service and served as the head of the secret service section of the Mukhabarat. As with many other senior Iraqi leaders, he is a native of Saddam's home town of Tikrit.

Al-Haris al-Jamhuri al-Khas.
The Special Republican Guard

15,000 people.
Headed by Qusay Hussein, it serves as a praetorian guard, protecting Presidential sites and escorting Saddam Hussein on travels within Iraq.

The Al-Haris al-Jamhuri al-Khas are the only troops normally stationed in Baghdad.

It consists of four brigades, three infantry and one armoured.

Al-Haris al-Jamhuri al-Khas also has its own artillery battalions, air defence and aviation assets. Units consist mainly of individuals from tribes loyal to Saddam Hussein.

Al-Haris al-Jamhuri al-Khas has played a role in securing WMD warheads and maintains control of a few launchers.

Al Hadi project.
Project 858

Al Hadi is estimated to have staff of about 800.

The Al Hadi Project is the organisations responsible for collecting, processing, exploiting and disseminating signals, communications and electronic intelligence.

Though it reports directly to the Office of the Presidential Palace, Al Hadi is not represented on the National Security Council, and the intelligence it collects is passed on to other agencies for their use.

Fedayeen Saddam.
Saddam's Martyrs

30,000 to 40,000 young people.

It is composed of young militia press ganged from regions known to be loyal to Saddam.

The unit reports directly to the Presidential Palace, rather than through the army command, and is responsible for patrol of borders and controlling or facilitating smuggling.

The paramilitary Fedayeen Saddam (Saddam's "Men of Sacrifice") was founded by Saddam's son Uday in 1995. In September 1996 Uday was removed from command of the Fedayee. Uday's removal may have stemmed from an incident in March 1996 when Uday transferred sophisticated weapons from Republican Guards to the Saddam Fedayeen without Saddam's knowledge.

Control passed to Qusay, further consolidating his repsonsibility for the Iraqi security apparatus. The deputy commander is Staff Lieutenant General Mezahem Saab All Hassan Al-Tikriti. According to reports, control of Saddam Hussein's personal militia was later passed back to his eldest son, Uday.

It started out as a rag-tag force of some 10,000–15,000 bullies. They are supposed to help protect the President and Uday, and carry out much of the police's dirty work.

The Fedayeen Saddam include a special unit known as the death squadron, whose masked members perform certain executions, including in victims' homes. The Fedayeen operate completely outside the law, above and outside political and legal structures.

Maktab al-Shuyukh.
The Tribal Chief's Bureau

This was created after the Gulf war as a vehicle for paying tribal leaders to control their people, spy on possible dissidents and provide arms to loyal tribesmen to suppress opposition.

Part Three: The effect on the people of Iraq

The Iraqi on the Street

Close monitoring is a feature of everyday life in Iraq. Saddam's organisations all run elaborate surveillance systems including mobile teams that follow a target, fixed observation points overlooking key intersections and choke points on routes through Baghdad and other major cities, networks of agents in most streets—the watchmen on buildings, the guards on checkpoints, the staff in newspaper kiosks—all linked by modern real time communications.

The effect is to make is extemely difficult and dangerous to try to hide activity from the State.

Saddam's Favourites

Iraqis who are members of Saddam's favourite tribe find it easier to join the Ba'ath Party. Some have even been members since childhood.

If they aspire to be part of the inner circles of the regime, they can work their way up the party ladder—and work towards the Presidential palace.

But they must not show dissent from Party line or appear too influential.

They must always remember that anyone who is a threat to Saddam or his sons will not be tolerated. And if they become a threat, someone will know—they will be reported. Imprisonment or execution may follow.

Other Iraqis

Iraqis who are not members of the favourite tribe must join the Ba'ath Party to progress in Iraq.

They then could join one of the security or intelligence services—but they must avoid being seen as a threat.

If an Iraqi wants to work for a foreign firm, Al-Mukhabarat would soon know of their application. Whether they get the job depends on their willingness to spy on the firm from inside.

If they have an opportunity to travel, Al-Mukhabarat will know and give them instructions about reporting in.

If Iraqi's do not want to participate, Al-Mukhabarat will know where their family lives inside Iraq. And if they think that living abroad will protect them—they must remember that Al-Mukhabarat has a long arm.

In September 2001, a report on human rights in Iraq by the UN Special Rapporteur noted that membership of certain political parties is punishable by death, that there is a pervasive fear of death for any act or expression of dissent, and that there are current reports of the use of the death penalty for such offences as "insulting" the President or the Ba'ath Party.

The mere suggestion that someone is not a supporter of the President carries the prospect of the death penalty.

Iraq Ba'ath Party

The Ba'ath Party is central to the Iraqi infrastructure of fear.

Everyone's name and address is known to district Ba'ath Party representatives. It is they who will know if there are signs of people deviating from unswerving support from Saddam.

When the Royal Marines occupied the Ba'ath Party offices in Sirsank in Northern Iraq in 1991, they found records detailing every inhabitant of the town, their political views, habits and associates. This included a map showing every household, colour-coded to show those who had lost sons in the war against Iran and those who had family members detained or killed by the security apparatus or Ba'ath Party.

The Media

The Iraqi Regime exerts total control over the media. When the domestic or foreign media interview a seemingly ordinary person on the street in Iraq, they will often be members of one of the security agencies, mouthing platitudes about Saddam and his regime. If the media do manage to find "an ordinary voice" those people are well aware they are being watched by the Regime. They know they have to say they love Saddam, and that the West is evil. They know if they don't keep to the script, they risk serious consequences including death.

Even off-camera, only a few are prepared to run the enormous risk of revealing their true feelings.

The overall effect of the systems of control and intimidation is that every Iraqi is suspicious of all except closest family.

Andrew Mackinlay MP

July 2003

Printed in the United Kingdom by The Stationery Office Limited
9/2003   877037   19585

ISBN 0-215-01309-3

9 780215 013095